A Journey Through Ruins

By the same author
On Living in an Old Country

PATRICK WRIGHT

A Journey Through Ruins

The Last Days of London

RADIUS

London Sydney Auckland Johannesburg

© Patrick Wright 1991

The right of Patrick Wright to be identified
as Author of this work has been asserted by Patrick Wright
in accordance with Copyright, Designs and Patents Act, 1988

All rights reserved

This edition first published in 1991 by
Radius

Random Century Group Ltd
20 Vauxhall Bridge Road, London SW1V 2SA

Random Century Australia (Pty) Ltd
20 Alfred Street, Milsons Point, Sydney, NSW 2061, Australia

Random Century New Zealand Ltd
PO Box 40–086, Glenfield, Auckland 10, New Zealand

Random Century South Africa (Pty) Ltd
PO Box 337, Bergvlei, 2012, South Africa

British Library Cataloguing-in-Publication Data
Wright, Patrick
A journey through ruins: The way we live now.
– (Radius)
I. Title   II. Series
307.7609421

ISBN 0–09–173190–9

Photoset by Speedset Ltd, Ellesmere Port
Printed and bound in Great Britain by
Mackays of Chatham PLC, Chatham, Kent

This book is dedicated
to Lady Margaret Thatcher

A folly is glass and bones and a hank of weeds.
Barbara Jones, 1953

Contents

At long last (it seemed to be only through the lapse of ages) it was judged that my condition improved. Some garments were brought, which I recognized with surprise as my own, wondering how they could have survived the destruction of the rest of the normal world.

Thomas Hennell.
(*The Witnesses*, 1938)

Part One

The Undemolished World of Dalston Lane

1

Street-Corner Vision

Among the under-estimated attractions of Dalston Junction is a street corner full of forgotten municipal services. The public lavatories are of the attended Victorian variety with wrought-iron railings, descending steps and lunettes in the pavement; and, on good days at least, they still function as originally intended – unlike many of their equivalents in more right-thinking and fortunately placed London boroughs that have been sold into private use as wine bars, pool halls, and design consultancies. There's a distinctly village-like Public Notice Board provided by the council but now only used by the fly-posting militants of the Revolutionary Communist Party and the exiled Turkish Communist Party. Proudest of all, however, is the 'Hackney Town Guide', which offers to orientate the enquirer with an apparently unambiguous message: 'You are here'. Displayed inside a glass-fronted 'Town Guide Cabinet', the map is perforated with little holes harbouring tiny light bulbs: the visitor is instructed to identify his intended destination by the 'appropriate title' and then press the button below it to 'illuminate place/s selected'.

Made by the Paramount Publicity Service of Manchester, the 'Town Guide Cabinet' is an example of the kind of street furniture that might more normally be expected to grace seaside resorts and historical towns, but the one at Dalston Junction has been confidently adjusted to its inner-city setting. Light bulbs peep out beside such municipal 'places of interest' as the labour exchange, the cemetery and the sewage works, and the twenty-four available buttons have been labelled according to appropriate themes, such as Tennis, Cricket Grounds, Public Utilities, Football Grounds, Cinemas, Town Halls, Fire Stations, Libraries, Railway Stations, Hospitals, Police Stations, and Courts. Nowadays, however, this careful differentiation comes to nothing: the buttons slide in and out with well-exercised ease, but the London Borough of Hackney refuses to light up.

A stray tourist (and they do sometimes end up here after falling asleep on the bus) may not realise it immediately, but Dalston Junction's vaguely streamlined 'Town Guide Cabinet' is a rare period piece left over from a bygone age. The 'G.P.O.' still has a tenuous hold on reality, but the button labelled 'LCC & HBC Flats' has been out of date since 1965 when the London County Council was replaced by the Greater London Council and Hackney Borough Council was merged with Shoreditch and Stoke Newington to produce the London

Borough of Hackney. The town guide shows the Hackney that Nikolaus Pevsner surveyed shortly after World War Two (remarking that 'a general leafiness' was still 'pleasantly noticeable over large areas'), but it is plainly deficient in its attention to more recent detail.[1] The southern part of the borough, the area that used to be Shoreditch, is simply missing. Many of the stations and hospitals (the German, the Metropolitan, the Eastern, the Mothers, the French) have been closed and replaced. Swimming pools have come and gone. The sponsoring businesses that were granted lights and a place on the map (activated by the button designated 'Advertiser's Highlights') have long since given up the ghost. As for the street plan, this looks plausible enough, but a person who tried to follow it through Hackney as it is today would keep bumping into vast and unexpected council estates. Those modest 'LCC & HBC Flats' notwithstanding (and for Pevsner they had already 'altered the appearance of Hackney decisively'), the real monuments to post-war comprehensive re-development – high-rise estates like Nightingale, Holly Street, Trowbridge, and Clapton Park – were all built after this time-warped town guide was completed.

In most places a town guide like this would long since have been adjusted or disposed of as a broken relic, but at Dalston Junction it can stand unnoticed for forty years and then find new life as the map of a world on which the lights have gone down. I must have fallen into a reverie as I stood there musing on this curious fact, for suddenly a dark-blue Bentley, which was flying two pennants (one marked with the letters 'CPS' and the other with the word 'Bovis'), pulled up and deposited two gentleman of advanced years on the pavement. One of them was carrying an old soap-box in his hand, while his comrade struggled awkwardly with an ungainly roll of canvas the chauffeur had fetched out of the boot and dumped rather ungraciously into his arms. I recognised this phantasmagorical pair as they approached. The man in front was Sir Alfred Sherman, former resident of Hackney, former Marxist and volunteer with the International Brigade, former adviser to Margaret Thatcher. His assistant was instantly recognisable by the distracted look in his eye as none other than Lord Keith Joseph of Portsoken, former intellectual and moral force behind Margaret Thatcher's government, former Secretary of State for Education, former Minister of Housing and Local Government, former Chairman of Bovis Ltd, former Chairman and co-founder with Margaret Thatcher of the Centre for Policy Studies – the influential right-wing think-tank with which Sir Alfred has also been associated.

After glancing round uneasily at the nearby council estates, Lord Joseph unrolled a banner on which were printed the words 'How Hackney Went to Hell', shook it out, and then hung it up, with a little help from Sir Alfred, on the ornate iron railings of the Gentlemen's Lavatory. He then handed Sir Alfred an extended lecturer's baton –

the sort preferred by true think-tankers that folds like a telescopic car aerial and can be fitted into a Savile Row breast-pocket – and stood back to survey the unmarried mothers while his companion mounted his soap-box just next to the Town Guide Cabinet and launched into the speech that would inaugurate this unsuspecting visual aid into its new function as a guide to the abyss.

Sir Alfred whacked the glass of the Town Guide Cabinet and told the gathering crowd that, while it certainly provided some valuable clues, the map inside wasn't really old enough to teach them more than part of the story. As he had known it before World War Two, Hackney had been a 'socially mixed area, attractive in many parts, with good solid residences built for City gents and smaller houses for artisans and clerks'.[2] It had been a place where local-government officials were happy to live themselves, and though there was hardship – Sir Alfred paused to stress that he himself had suffered from rickets as a child – the immigrant communities of that time recognised that British values were worth emulating, and got on with assimilating themselves as quickly as possible. Elementary school-teachers were paid far more than skilled manual workers, and 'enjoyed correspondingly higher prestige', and the borough had been blessed with a rich cultural and social life. Unsatisfied by the paltry collection of cinemas and sports amenities indicated on the broken town guide, Sherman went on to itemise the superior facilities of his own day; he remembered 'a whole range of lectures, concerts, charities, well-attended churches, chapels, synagogues, masonic lodges, the British Legion and Territorial Army, Salvation Army, Scouts, youth clubs, and Jewish Lads Brigade'. There were, it had to be admitted, some rough streets and a relatively small 'underclass' in the borough, but for the vast majority 'Respectability was the watchword' and, as Sir Alfred stressed to a vigorous nod of agreement from His Lordship, the community was, by and large, 'self-policing'. The streets and parks were safe for women and children, and in the few cases of illegitimacy, there were 'communal pressures' that generally 'brought about marriage, and kept it going'.

While the map in Dalston Junction's Town Guide Cabinet helped Sir Alfred to demonstrate the decency, even the modest nobility, of old Hackney, it also offered him a chance to expatiate on the no less romantic theme of 'What Went Wrong'. Lord Joseph's eyes widened in anticipation as the man who had pulled himself up by his boot-straps prepared to treat those who hadn't to a description of their own miserable plight. Lesser orators might have backed off at the challenge of putting such an awful reality into words but, as a seasoned think-tanker, Sir Alfred was well equipped with the rhetorical devices that would help him to get a grip on the situation. He was adept with the anti-communist stereotypes that would enable him to identify the Town Hall with Stalin's Kremlin. He was also well versed in the demonic Victorian imagery of London's East End, and it was from this source that he drew such stock devices as the Road to Ruin and the quasi-medical theory of the slum dweller whose degeneracy had been symbolised for the Victorians by the monstrous deformities of the Elephant Man.[3]

Sir Alfred was in no doubt that the first steps down the Slippery Slope had been taken during the mid-Twenties when rent controls, introduced during the Great War to relieve the hardship of soldiers' families, started to yield the inevitable fruit of 'blight and housing shortage'. This issue was quickly dwarfed by the council housing that was built in a misguided attempt to solve the problem. The new council estates only became 'costly slums': indeed, some were so bad (and by this time Sir Alfred had the confident look of a speaker who knows that the imaginative truth will always override the odd detail that may be wrong) that 'desperate people would not live in them rent free'. Meanwhile, as Sir Alfred knew for sure, every acre of council estate meant ten blighted acres all around it. By the mid-Thirties, the Jewish migrants who had come to Hackney from Whitechapel and Bethnal Green – 'Hackney was a step up' in those days, as Sir Alfred reminded his audience – had moved on to such places as Hampstead, St John's Wood and Golders Green. Things went from bad to worse after World War Two; there was more council housing, and the 'more intelligent working-class families' were 'decanted', at considerable cost, into the new towns, thus depriving East London of still more of its 'social leaven'.

By this time, Sir Alfred had warmed to his theme. He cast an unforgiving eye over the crowd – so mixed, so unassimilated, so alien – and thrashed once more at the forgotten Town Guide Cabinet. The next disaster came in the Fifties when, 'on the pretext of a fictional labour shortage . . . our masters' – and Lord Joseph of Portsoken, who had been among the masters at that time, looked a bit sheepish as Sir Alfred charged into this well-rehearsed part of his exposition – brought in the Afro-Caribbeans and 'speeded up the exodus of the leaven, downgrading the social composition' still further.

The audience was beginning to look a bit restive at this point. The slur on the Afro-Caribbeans hadn't gone down quite as well as it would have done elsewhere (better to keep that for the rural voyeurs of *The Sunday Telegraph*) and the metaphoric loaf of unleavened bread didn't look as if it was going to make the distance either. Undeterred, Sir Alfred switched clichés, bringing his theme of 'further down-grading' into the more recent past of the 'permissive society' and 'the Welfare State', which had, as he explained, combined to produce a 'dependent single-parent subculture' in which 'fatherless children provide a source of income for their welfare mothers'. As for the future prospects of the lucrative brats who were the offspring of this subculture, our sloganeering knight didn't need a sociologist or a magistrate to know that 'by the time they are ten these children have graduated from vandalism to street crime and burglary' or that they are all 'thrown out on to the streets' when they reach the age of sixteen and their child allowance and other benefits terminate. These children are a worry to us all, but Sir Alfred is quite sure that they are 'not just wild': in many cases, as he pointed out, they are both 'mentally disturbed' and 'neurologically impaired' as well. Such is the hideous legacy of child-benefit allowances. They have filled the borough with mental defectives, and the schoolteachers probably wouldn't stand a chance even if they weren't all Marxists devoted, like their trade union, to 'demi-literate fads like anti-racism, anti-heterosexism, black consciousness, class consciousness, Third-Worldism – anything, that is, but reading, writing, and arithmetic'.

To begin with, Sir Alfred Sherman's audience appeared to relish this account of their plight. Many of Hackney's schools are in a shocking state. Basic services don't work. Appalling crimes take place. Some of the inhabitants of the borough are as idle and resourceless as any think-tanker could wish. But though Sir Alfred must have felt he was standing on safe ground declaring Hackney to be 'a picture of a blind alley', his litany was too blithely delivered, and some faces in the gathered crowd were crossed with growing irritation. People round here are familiar with visiting artists of the inferno, but they are not always happy to be used opportunistically, whether it is to confirm the Tory prejudices of *The Sunday Telegraph* or the more liberal ones of *The Guardian*. Indeed, as Sir Alfred wobbled rather hesitantly on his soap-box, I was reminded of an occasion in the early Eighties (well remembered in local lore) when the radical film-maker Mike Leigh encountered the wrath of the people on exactly this basis. A packed public meeting held at the Rio Cinema, just up the road from Dalston Junction, watched one of Leigh's television films from that time (if local memory is correct, it traced the activities of a drunken and zombified youth who spent his days vandalising the lifts on his high-rise council estate), and then launched into a bitter attack on the man who presumed to show Hackney in this way. The same audience also rounded on their other visiting speaker. Paul Harrison was there as author of *Inside the Inner City*, a book that started off with a view of Hackney's tower blocks as seen from Parliament Hill in Hampstead, and then used the borough to show that, thanks not least to monetarism, conditions to rival those in the Third World could be found at home. People had read his book and were insulted to find their home – which, as everyone admits, is far from perfect – being presented to the wider world as a leading contender for the title of 'The Most Awful Place in Britain'.[4]

There comes a point where a person should put up or shut up but Sir Alfred, when pressed to suggest some practical solutions to the problems on which he had expounded at such length, merely started to falter. After muttering, in apparent praise of his own performance, that 'an essential ingredient of any cure must be frankness', this notoriously outspoken man suddenly looked lost for words. He glanced in his companion's direction, but even though he had once written an influential tract called *Reversing the Trend*, Lord Joseph would now only stare fixedly at his own feet. So our speaker tried again by suggesting, in a roundabout sort of way, that further cuts in public funding would probably help: 'We must demand that the "caring society" cares more about the ravages it has already caused instead of using these very deformities in order to mulct yet more taxpayers' money for swollen budgets which go on to perpetuate these ills while feeding the "caring professions".' This didn't go down too well either, and Sir Alfred turned once again, waving his baton at the mute figure of Lord Joseph and shouting that the 'plea to preach morality instead of socialism', which had cost poor Lord Joseph his chance of the Conservative leadership in 1974, must once more become a political demand: 'organised state dependence' must give way to a new system of public administration that would 'embody the parable of the talents'. But Sir Alfred was floundering. He had run out of rhetorical tricks and had no choice but to resort to the think-tankers' last wheeze: the idea of Britain's *perestroika*. We must, as he yelled into the crowd, take on the 'Welfare State *nomenklatura*' or else Hackney will 'continue to slide' while 'the post-socialist states of Eastern Europe move forward into the sunlight'.

By this time the audience was taking over: somebody was reciting a list of senior officers from the council who actually lived in the borough: Chief Executive, Director of Finance, Head of Legal Services, Head of Works, Director of Education. . . . An unwashed character was even tugging at Lord Joseph's sleeve, demanding that he explain how, if Hackney was really so bad, the Town Guide Cabinet had survived forty years without being vandalised: was this just another example of the borough's idleness? Some social-worker type – perhaps a radical vicar's wife – broke in to correct Sir Alfred in one of his many areas of ignorance, remarking with undisguised contempt that the Welfare State had been a Christian State in inspiration, or a 'social-service State' as it had been called by Lord Beveridge, and that it had never had anything at all to do with communism. Others were just standing back and roaring with mocking laughter at the whole sorry performance.

For a while the situation looked dangerous, but suddenly a man broke in with the news that, after eleven years as Prime Minister, Margaret Thatcher had finally been deposed. Rude cheers went up from the crowd; then Lord Joseph started to mutter into the silence that followed: 'I came into politics thirty-five years ago to improve life for the majority of the British people, particularly the poor and downtrodden. I shared these aims with Margaret Thatcher'.[5] The poor, the downtrodden, and the not-so-badly-off-at-all of Dalston Junction stared back in amazement, but the stricken Lord Joseph was in a world of his own. As he continued: 'We all share some of the blame there. We knew what we rejected in the post-war economy and society, but we never worked out clearly enough our disengagement strategy . . .'. There would have been more in this remarkable vein, but the Bentley had pulled up again (the chauffeur at least was a master of timely disengagement) and, in a second, our two adventurous think-tankers had sunk back into seats of English hide and were speeding away towards the more easily adjustable futurity of the City and the Fortress of Portsoken, the towers of which loom up only a couple of miles to the south. In the words of a neglected expatriate poet, the thing to remember about the kind of 'upland vision' favoured by Lady Thatcher's think-tankers, is that its 'clarity depends on distance'.[6]

2
Around the World
in Three Hundred Yards

What is to be done about Dalston Junction? Successive governments have pondered this question. Their advisers take one look and quickly propose a road-widening scheme or, better still, a really ambitious new motorway that will obliterate the whole area. Ministers pretend to be surprised when carping residents come out against these generously offered 'improvements', and the blight settles a little deeper. In the most recent case it was Peter Bottomley, then Conservative Minister for Roads, who provided local campaigners with their best quotation. When questioned in the House of Commons on 10 February 1989 about the environmental damage that would be caused if the roads suggested in Ove Arup & Partners' East London Assessment Study were built, he replied for the government by saying: 'we want to improve the environment. If we look at the main spine road through the assessment study, it goes through the most run-down part of the area'.

Dalston Junction was under that spine, and a carefully placed rib also reached out to obliterate the short stretch of road that runs through the heart of this book. Dalston Lane extends east from Dalston Junction, and we need only follow it a few hundred yards up to the traffic lights at the next busy junction – a tangle of dishonoured roads still sometimes called Lebon's Corner in memory of a trader who has long since disappeared. This miraculously surviving fragment of old England consists of a constant and often choked stream of traffic edged by stretches of pavement that would not be out of place in the Lake District. The stones jut up like small cliffs, and then crash down as soon as the intrepid inner-city fell-walker mounts them, sometimes issuing a great gush of filthy water as they land.

The south side of Dalston Lane starts with an elegant stretch of ornamented Victorian brickwork, which is all that remains of the recently demolished Dalston Junction railway station. It then passes a tawdry amusement arcade, a few shops, and the New Four Aces Club (the site of occasional shootings and subject of intense Press speculation about the fabled West Indian Yardies). After a derelict site and an ailing public library, the street consists of two continuous blocks of run-down Victorian shops, some in use, others boarded up and abandoned. The first block is owned by Hackney Council, bought up in preparation for the demolition that appears to have been imminent for at least half a century; the second belonged to the now-abolished Greater London Council.

The north side of this unusually dishevelled street is slightly more varied. There are some shops with offices above them and an old pub, once known as the Railway Tavern but now a dingy betting shop with a satellite dish at the back. There is the notorious Dalston police station, a large red-brick building with an ominously windowless and fortress-like annexe that has stood boarded up and empty since early in 1990 when the police withdrew to their new 'supernick' up in Stoke Newington, where Chief Superintendent Twist offers visitors guided tours of his new 'cell-suites', stressing the ameliorating effects of a modern architecture that brings light into recesses where horrible acts of brutality might once have taken place. Then comes a terrace of stuccoed Victorian houses, set back a few yards and shielded from the road by a little strip of corralled dirt where heroic shrubs struggle up through the litter and four plane trees rise up to lend an unexpected touch of nobility to the area. Beyond this residential terrace, there's a nondescript factory, a large and surprising Georgian house used as workshop space by the Freeform Arts Trust, and, finally, a second Victorian ruin to match the shattered railway station with which this atmospheric stretch of English street opens. The old vicarage of St Bartholomew's may be derelict, but it can still be said to command the north side of Lebon's Corner. It stands like a hollow-eyed skull just across the road from the Unity Club where local Labour MP, Brian Sedgemore, goes to try his luck as a stand-up comic.[1] Saplings sprout from the vicarage's brickwork, and so too do the shattered marbled columns and ornately sculpted capitals left over from the church that was once adjoined to it. New settlers in the area often mistake the ruin for a bomb-site left over from the Forties, but it is actually the much more recent work of the Church Commissioners who, finding themselves lumbered with too many churches in this apparently God-forsaken place, called in the demolition men and never bothered to tidy up after them. The vicarage was listed, but due to the 'ecclesiastical exemption' that removes churches from the protection of the law, nothing could be done to protect the church from its fate. So this Gothic hulk stands there: a huge pigeon roost, a poster stand, a terrible warning of the destiny that awaits listed buildings in Hackney.

I've come to know this stretch of Dalston Lane well in recent years. I walk along it most days of the week and I'm familiar with its vicious side: I've seen the squalor and the many signs of grinding poverty; and like many other people round here, I've studied the psychotic antics of the man who spends a lot of his time on the traffic island at Lebon's Corner, reading the cracks in the asphalt and cleaning them out with a stick. I've walked into the aftermath of a mugging that could have been scripted by Sir Alfred Sherman: an elderly and blind white man had come out of the sub-post office at Lebon's Corner, having just collected his pension. Seeing his opportunity, a black youth had leapt off a passing bus, hit the man at full tilt, leaving him in a battered and terrified heap on the pavement, and made off with his pension. By the time I arrived on the scene the victim was lying in the stationary bus, surrounded by a great efflorescence of helpless concern: a shop-keeper had produced a cup of tea, the ambulance was coming, a white stick had been retrieved from the middle of the road, and a collection was under way to ensure that the victim was compensated for at least some of his losses. A few weeks earlier, I had caught the end of another desperate episode. This one was featured in the *Hackney Gazette* under the heading 'Devil dog mauls police woman'; it concerned a ravenous pit bull terrier ('Hackney has become London's centre for pit bulls'), which emerged snarling from under a boarded-up shop front, chased a twenty-year-old police-woman into a nearby bakery, and 'ripped her heel off'.[2] As a Cypriot witness told me in mitigation, the already exterminated beast had given the terrified WPC fair warning but, not being of local provenance, she hadn't been able to read the signs.

Blight has its hideous aspect but, as I try to convince unbelieving visitors, it can also resemble a condition of grace. Dalston Lane is a jumble of residential, commercial, and industrial activities, but zoning is not the only kind of development on which this street, if not its surrounding area, has missed out. In the Fifties it escaped the kind of standardisation Ian Nairn described as subtopia ('Subtopia is the annihilation of the site, the steamrollering of all individuality of place to one uniform and mediocre pattern').[3] While it has certainly suffered daily agonies through the Eighties, it was at least spared the kind of theming that has turned genuinely historical streets in more prosperous parts of the country into simulacra, gutting them in the name of taste. No 'lifestyle designer' has ever come to divide the 'targeted' denizens of Dalston Lane from the non-targeted, or to kill off the old street, with its confusion of nationalities, classes, and styles, and redefine it in marketing terms.[4] We may be sure that Sir Rodney Fitch, design mogul of the Eighties, has never worked here.

On Dalston Lane time itself seems to lie around in broken fragments: you can drop in on previous decades with no more effort than it takes to open a shop door. Pizzey's High Class Florist is still trading out of the Fifties, and the Star Bakery (a little further down the road) offers immediate access to the decade before that. Until a year or so ago there was even a time-warped estate agency, advertising houses at twenty-year-old prices. People would pause there and marvel at the opportunities they had missed.

This has a human aspect, to be sure. The people of Dalston Lane have their own ways of being in the world. They walk about in a distinctly unsuburban manner, and without necessarily following what planners would recognise as a proper 'line of pedestrian desire'.

They saunter and dawdle and fail to wait for the green light before crossing the road. They hang about without apparent purpose. They do things remarkably slowly, if at all. They indulge in habits that are being extirpated from the national culture. Anthropologists will soon be coming here to study the vanishing culture and society of the cigarette. It's not just that people still smoke on Dalston Lane. They stand around in huddles and offer each other cigarettes with a reckless generosity that is no longer to be found in more stable society. Some of this behaviour comes to Dalston Lane direct from the West Indies or the hills of Kurdistan, but there are more indigenous people round here who still find the health warning provided by HM Government less convincing than the caution that emerged from the trenches of the Great War, and stressed the dangers of the third light.

A broad-minded art historian could wander down this street and find residual traces of the 'unsophisticated arts' that Barbara Jones cherished against the industrial and technocratic bias of the Festival of Britain in 1951.[5] As she wrote, 'popular arts have certain constant characteristics. They are complex, unsubtle, often impermanent; they lean to disquiet, the baroque and sometimes terror'. Dalston Lane has its unnecessary and slightly excessive touches of ornamentation – exemplified, perhaps, by the fake and, like everything else round here, unexpectedly permanent ornamental urns that stand over some of the shop fronts on the south side of Lebon's Corner: most of them are full of weeds, but their teasing tribute to the superior versions that embellish grand Georgian buildings elsewhere is unmistakable. The best example, however, is provided by the undertaking firm of E. M. Kendall ('We are renowned throughout London for our complete inexpensive funeral service...') that, despite half-hearted attempts at modernisation, fits Jones's description perfectly. The ancient glass sign over the door still promises 'Funeral Feathermen and Carriage Masters', and the ornate promise of 'Courtesy' and 'Reverence' creeps round the side in gilded copper-plate letters. At night, the two main windows are deep-black squares with the words 'Funerals' and 'Cremations' lit up in dull purple and suspended, like souls in the void, at the centre of each. The pall-bearers may look like ghoulish extras left over from the comparatively recent days of Hammer horror films, but they too are the un-refurbished inheritors of the Victorian tradition that Jones celebrated as 'a nice rich debased baroque'. Dalston Lane still bears out Barbara Jones's assertion that 'the colours of death' in England are 'black and grey and purple'.

The whole area is alive with commercial and industrial activity. Just north of Dalston Lane there are Victorian factories, which resound with the hissing, snipping, and clacking of the textile trade, and the small workshops, some of them in a converted mews, of antique restorers, violin makers, and furniture makers. Dalston Lane itself has its shops and small businesses as well as its boarded-up voids: indigenous north-east London enterprise mixed up with a whole array of brave multicultural endeavour. Most of these traders are unsung heroes who fight on against unbelievable odds: their situation is epitomised by the lady in the Chinese takeaway who treats her customers with the care appropriate to an endangered species, asking repeatedly if they've been away on holiday.

Further down the road from Kendall's the undertaker is the shop of Nichols of London, declared by his own pocket label to be 'London's finest bespoke tailor'. The real name is Nicholas Economou, a Cypriot who knows better than to sell himself short. He makes high-quality clothes for one of the larger outfitters in the City, but he also maintains his own clients on Dalston Lane. The window shows Mr Economou with one of his more famous customers, Frank Bruno, the boxer who was a regular here until the sponsorship deals took over. But there are other stylish figures who have a regard for Mr Economou's needle. Use him for a bit, and the special offers will start coming through at knock-down prices: a richly patterned jacket made of a sumptuous blend of mink, chinchilla, cashmere, and lambswool; trousers in Prince of Wales check or the best white Irish linen; a sparkling suit made of grey silk with a prominent diamond pattern. One of Mr Economou's more ostentatious customers, a gentleman from Canning Town to be precise, had ordered a load of clothes in preparation for a prolonged sojourn in Spain, but he was arrested on charges of armed robbery a few days before departure and 'he'll be an old man' before he can come back to collect them.

A few doors up at No. 58, there's a restaurant called Pamela's. Not long ago, this was just another derelict poster site, but remarkable things started to happen early one recent winter. New hoardings went up, and an unmistakable designer logo appeared shortly afterwards: it showed a waiter in tails holding up a tray with a saxophone suspended above it. Serious money was being spent: a gallery went in, along with a lot of very stylish ironwork and an elegant parquet floor. By Christmas, a rather Utopian-looking establishment called Pamela's had opened for business. Squeezed in between Jon's scooters and a boarded-up shop front, it tempted the apprehensive denizens of Dalston Lane with new pleasures: 'a taste of the Caribbean, a hint of French cuisine' and, may Sir Alfred Sherman take note, the first 'business lunches' to be offered on Dalston Lane. Pamela Hurley is a fastidious young Anglo-Barbadian who trained as a chef in New York, and the success of her establishment will depend partly on her ability to create a new cultural settlement on Dalston Lane. On one side, as she explains, she has to convince Afro-Caribbean customers that her food is actually worth coming out for, and not just more of what mother does so well at home. On the other side, she is going to have to persuade some of the more affluent whites in the neighbourhood to get over some curious reservations of their own. These people live in the area in quite large numbers, but while they are not necessarily averse to signing away a small fortune at a restaurant table in Islington or Soho, they are less inclined to be seen indulging in conspicuous consumption right on their own doorsteps. Pamela is in a risky business, especially during a gathering recession, but the vision is grand. Come the spring, she wants to throw open her folding doors, and see her customers all mixed up together on the pavement: Montmartre will meet Montserrat on dingy Dalston Lane; the plane trees will burgeon and the traffic will thunder by regardless.

One trader on Dalston Lane has recently found a novel way of achieving corporate growth. If he was in a 'managed workspace', of the sort that sprung up in refurbished factories throughout London during the Eighties, he would be able to expand by pushing out the partitions a little, but he would also have to pay more rent for the privilege. On Dalston Lane those extra square feet can be had for free. The gentleman in question simply broke through the walls with a pickaxe and moved into the boarded-up shops on either side: his thriving emporium is now one-third legitimate, two-thirds squat. But while occasional success stories emerge from the strivings of Dalston Lane's entrepreneurs, the idea that a wider social redemption might be achieved through enterprise has never really made its way down this street. Most of the traders on Dalston Lane are too busy making ends meet to consider raising up the whole area as well, and they have sharp things to say about the Thatcher government, which banged on about supporting private enterprise and then turned round and hit them all with punishing interest rates and, with poll tax, the unified business rate. A more dynamic economy would doubtless pull this dishevelled street together in no time, but it would also wipe out most of its traders at a stroke.

Other hints of improvement can be traced along this undemolished stretch of Dalston Lane. The public library is named after Trinidad's revolutionary historian C. L. R. James, and its windows are plastered with yellowing obituaries to C. L. R. and a whole host of signs blazing with promised emancipation over three continents. The rhetoric is ambitious but the activity on the ground is sadly restricted: indeed, the library is closed most of the time due, as another notice explains, to funding and staff shortages.

The public sector flounders, but many of the derelict shops have been taken over and turned into the offices of voluntary organisations, which try to do rather better. The same pattern of refurbishment recurs from one organisation to the next: the windows are boarded up from the inside so one can't see in from the street, and then covered with messages announcing events or asserting this cause or that. Each one is, after its own manner, a wayside pulpit lost among the advertising hoardings. There is a whole archaeology of voluntary endeavour on Dalston Lane. To begin with, the British Red Cross Society has its Hackney Centre up at Lebon's Corner – a large

Victorian house with a flag-pole over the porch and a prominent red cross superimposed on a white circle painted on the side wall. This institution dates back to 1917, but its spirit belongs to the Forties. Indeed, it goes back to the 'improvised staffing' Richard Titmuss saw emerge in the early weeks of the blitz before the offical relief effort was organised: the British Red Cross Society was there with its volunteer ambulances, first aid, and 'light relief', and other more anonymous figures also stepped out of the crowd – people like 'Mrs B', the Islington beetroot seller who, as the raids started, 'left the first aid post where she was a part-time volunteer, walked into Ritchie Street rest centre and took charge'.[6]

That red cross on the corner of Dalston Lane speaks of the blitz, but it is also a more general memorial to the spirit of 'Voluntary Action', as Lord Beveridge conceived it during the founding years of the Welfare State: Voluntary Action as a trail-blazer for the emerging State ('It is needed to pioneer ahead of the State and make experiments') but also – and Beveridge didn't need a latter-day think-tanker to tell him this – as the self-willed and self-managed activity that defines the proper limits of the State and serves as the 'distinguishing mark' of a free society.[7] I sometimes look up at that recently repainted red cross and think of the remarkable, if now sadly disappointed, vision with which Beveridge signed off after the war against Hitler: 'So at last human society may become a friendly society – an Affiliated Order of branches, some large and many small, each with its own life in freedom, each linked to all the rest by common purpose and by bonds to serve that purpose. So the night's insane dream of power over other men without limit and without mercy shall fade'.[8] That was long before any alley cat dreamt up the idea of Britain's *perestroika*.

Like so much else, the dwindling spirit of 'Voluntary Action' has to struggle for life on Dalston Lane (following the example of the C. L. R. James library, the British Red Cross Society's charity shop is frequently closed due to a shortage of volunteers), and there is little sign of relief from Douglas Hurd's more recently enlisted 'active citizen' – that implausible hero of the think-tanks who, far from blazing trails for the expanding State as Beveridge imagined, sets out, wearing an inner-city Barbour jacket and a grin as wide as Richard Branson's, to compensate for a few of the more visible failings of a contracting and mismanaged one.

What comes after Voluntary Action on Dalston Lane is really still Ken Livingstone's GLC, and the efflorescence of community organisations that thrived under its wing – even when not directly supported by it. Hackney Cooperative Developments is based here, proudly advertising the alternative shopping centre it has made of a battered Victorian row of shops in nearby Bradbury Street ('A stone's throw from the High Street but miles ahead in style'). Then, in sharp contrast to the unachieved and often corrupted universality of conventional State provision, come the differentiated organisations of the rainbow coalition: the Asian Centre; Africa House with its special Advice and Community Centre and, Sir Alfred please take note, a Supplementary School; Hackney Women's Centre; Hackney Heat-savers; Hackney Pensioners. . . .

A passing think-tanker would be inclined to dismiss this collection of organisations as so many 'QUALGOs' ('Quasi-Autonomous Local Government Organisations'), political fronts accountable to no one and serving only to gouge the salaries of their well-connected and far-from-voluntary workers out of left-wing local councils.[9] There were certainly problems with the way the GLC and other Labour councils funded voluntary organizations in the early Eighties. Money went into agencies that simply couldn't cope with it, and staff numbers were built up in a way that could hardly have been better designed if it was intended to kill off the old spirit of 'Voluntary Action'. Voluntary committee members found themselves faced with an ever-increasing complexity of work and, in some cases, with a highly articulate and educated staff who were full of talk about their own collective rights as employed workers. Some organisations disappeared into themselves spending years fighting out the problems of the world internally, while others proved incapable of achieving in practice anything like what they promised in words.[10] When these organisations failed there was just another body of articulate professionals widening the gap between the State and the citizenry it was meant to serve; but when they worked, groups that had been stuck at the margins without effective representation within the Welfare State were suddenly enfranchised and a whole agenda of new concerns, whether cultural, political, or ecological, was brought into focus. The rowdy exuberance that followed was quite something.

Some of this energy continues to produce results in Dalston. The Women's Design Service has recently issued a well-received critical handbook on the design of public lavatories for women. The authors insist that 'women do not conform to standard sizes or requirements', comment on the 'implications of the loss of the GLC for the state of London's public toilets', and disclose that 'the building of women's public toilets was linked to the growth of feminism in the late nineteenth century, since it was largely the increased visibility of women working in the capital that persuaded the authorities to make provision for them'. This admirable manual found quite a lot to praise in the underground lavatories left over from the Victorian era (although, as they point out, working conditions for the attendants could certainly have been better). It also provided a key date for future historians of the monetarist experiment: it was on 5 May 1982 that the first coin-operated automatic public convenience to be fitted in Britain was installed by Westminster Council in Leicester Square.[11]

Nor should we overlook the Freeform Arts Trust, one of the organisations that founded the 'Community Arts' movement in the

Sixties and has been based on Dalston Lane since 1973, when it gained a short-life lease on a building ear-marked for demolition. The Freeform Arts Trust helped to pioneer the ideas taken up later by the big community-architecture practices. They offer design and 'technical aid' services to schools, community groups, and developers, always seeking to work with people in a 'participative' manner. The founder, Martin Goodrich, has watched the political framework shift around his practice: in the late Sixties his ideas and activities were considered radical to the left, but in the Eighties they seemed to find favour with the radical right. The Freeform Arts Trust has survived schisms, break-away movements, and the criticisms of those who want to be 'storming the citadels' rather than decorating the hoardings around capitalist building sites or joining 'the kindly folk who do good without ever causing trouble'.[12] Martin Goodrich is full of enterprising ideas for 'projects' and, in his time, he has had plenty for the miraculously enduring street he calls 'Dusty Dalston Lane'. There was a brave attempt to form a Dalston Traders Group: Goodrich remembers putting up Christmas lights at Dalston Junction while people passing below cursed and moaned at the folly of it all. There was a project that aimed to turn the derelict vicarage of St Bartholomew's into a workspace for community organisations, and another that hoped to landscape and put a few seats on the derelict site behind the bus stop up by Dalston Junction. But though Dalston Lane has proved intransigent, Freeform has been more successful up in North Shields at the mouth of the Tyne, a near-derelict fishing port, where a vestigial regatta has been transformed into an amazingly successful Fish Quay Festival, now attended by over a million people each year, which is being used to 'catalyse change and community development'. That's not 'storming the citadels' either, but it's one of Dalston Lane's better stories nevertheless.

3

All Cats are Grey at Night

In June 1990 Roy Kerridge wandered through Dalston for the benefit of readers of his 'In the City' column in *The Independent*. After relishing the vivacity of the 'buxom Nigerian shoewives' (whose 'elaborate head-ties' have a picturesque way of 'nodding' in the sweatshops) and declaring 'fascinating Kingsland Road' to be 'the best place for shoes outside Lagos', this beady-eyed social observer went on to describe his 'happiest discovery' in the area. Passing through 'a secret entrance' that runs below 'a narrow iron railway bridge', he found himself in Albion Square: a gracious and unexpected place that, with its 'church, inn, trees and opulent terraces', looked 'like a transplanted corner of fashionable Canonbury or Highgate'.[1]

It's not for me to begrudge Mr Kerridge the journalistic conventions that enable him to make his famously uncertain living, but Albion Square is really not a place that remains to be discovered – even by the Stanley of darkest London. Had Kerridge visited it a few weeks later, he would have ventured under that 'secret' bridge to find himself in an altogether more conventional film set. The BBC was producing David Hare's *Heading Home* – a film, as the production manager explained in a letter circulated to all residents, that was actually set in Notting Hill in 1947. That famously Bohemian part of west London no longer looks as romantically unimproved as it did in the Forties, but with a few minor adjustments Albion Square would do fine. Residents were asked to remove their cars, dustbins, and window boxes ('unfortunately they, too, are not in period'), and their cooperation was certainly forthcoming. Indeed, the Albion Square Residents Association was so impressed by the look of the concrete lamp-posts after the BBC had blacked them over, that it asked the council to consider introducing this improvement permanently throughout the square.

The whole borough of Hackney is like that: a bizarre confusion of fact and fiction, a place where one person's grim reality serves as everybody else's exotic film set. 'Locations' have been turning up all over the place. The empty German Hospital, just off Dalston Lane, is a favourite with film companies wanting looming Gothic elevations and spooky post-institutional interiors. The graffiti may insist that the unimaginably blighted Broadway Market is 'not a sinking ship but a submarine', but the people who make television crime shows recognise it as one of the choicest derelict streets in London. After filming the first two episodes of the BBC's *Paradise Club* here, the producer from Zenith Productions declared Broadway Market to be 'one of the last remaining sites in London with character'.[2] As for Fasset Square, just beyond Lebon's Corner and behind the German Hospital, this has been measured up and cloned as the Albert Square of the BBC soap *EastEnders*.

This promiscuous exchange between idea and reality takes a different form on Dalston Lane, where images are brought in by advertisers rather than sought out by television producers. The police may have retreated, but the briefest glance at the walls of their abandoned bunker reveals that the area is not entirely without rules. The law governing the appearance of Dalston Lane stipulates that the more blighted and derelict an area becomes, the fuller it will be with vivid, if not always fashionably designed, imagery. Every derelict site is quickly surrounded by hoardings and the blaze of colour begins.[3] Every abandoned office, shop front, or, for that matter, police station is an immediate poster site as, indeed, is every poster within easy reach. It is impossible to walk down the pavement without being struck by the discrepancies, the paradoxes, the little ironies that form the stock devices of second-rate inner-city art. The whole place becomes a two-way street between fact and fiction. Some of this imagery is offered as a stand-in for life, but Dalston Lane is a place where reality still strikes back, cutting every inflated idea, every improving illusion, every carefully styled huckster's lie down to size.

The law of Dalston Lane doesn't just apply to advertising. Sir Alfred Sherman uses Hackney to make 'a picture of a blind alley' that serves to show how far he himself has risen in the world, but he is not the only one who has tried to paint the borough over with political rhetoric. Down in the City the abolished GLC is remembered by the incomprehensible maps that only add to the confusion of pedestrians trying to negotiate their way through labyrinthine underpasses, but in Dalston Lane the monuments are brighter and more inspiring. A great mural showing the Hackney Peace Carnival of 1983 rises out of the buddleia on a derelict site opposite the demolished railway station. Opened, as a sign records, by Tony Banks, Chairman of the GLC, in October 1985, it shows a bustling multi-racial procession, complete with new-left mariachi band, CND banners, Uncle Sam on stilts, death masks, and great cruising sharks with Soviet bombs, gold coins, and capitalist cigars clenched in their jaws. Just the other side of Dalston Junction, a notice informs all-comers that they are entering the London Borough of Hackney's declared 'Nuclear-Free Zone'. Such loose talk billows overhead, left over from the early Eighties when Labour councillors were more interested in passing grandiose resolutions than in getting the basic administrative systems to work or, for that matter, even drawing up a budget for their revolutionary proposals. So the unemployment figures were strung up on red banners on municipal buildings – a gesture that made the borough look like a small Slovak town during the last days of communist rule. At about the same time, the signs went up declaring Hackney 'a Borough that Cares for its People' and the word 'men' was taken out of the phrase 'men at work' on the council's dustcarts and replaced with the more equally alienated designation 'operatives'. Hackney is all the better for never having been 'interpreted' by the Tourism authorities, but it has its own windbaggery to set against that of the brown 'heritage' roadsigns that now adorn trunk roads and motorways in more scenic or significant parts of the nation. (The most fatuous of all is surely the one on the M4 that announces 'WINDSOR CASTLE/ROYALTY AND EMPIRE/SAFARI PARK'.)

The nuclear-free zone sign should be transferred to Hackney Museum as a monument to the detached coinage that flourished briefly before rate-capping and the poll tax came along. More recently, it has been such organisations as the Turkish Communist Party (Marxist–Leninist), the Kurdistan Workers Party, the Liberation Organisation of Turkey and North Kurdistan, and the Union of Patriotic Revolutionary Youth of Kurdistan, who have produced the most striking political imagery along Dalston Lane. Their posters show young spring flowers being hoisted on the gallows, the braided and peaked caps of military dictatorship stuffed with dollars and ornamented with nooses, insurrectionary youths fighting it out on the streets. They show marching figures with Kalashnikovs and red banners held high. This imagery emerges from a direct experience of political violence and oppression that has taken place in Turkey since the military coup of 1980 and the confidently asserted hammers and sickels are apparently quite untouched by *perestroika*. Indeed, Gorbachev's troubled reforms and the gathering disintegration of the Soviet Empire seem only to have prompted a new alliance. The Union of Turkish Progressives in Britain recently held a festival of solidarity with Cuba and the pictures that inspired so many future televison producers and advertising executives in the Sixties were suddenly to be seen again: the red star on a dark beret, the right arm raised high, the resolute gaze – so handsome, so firm, so correct. For a fleeting moment, Che Guevara was back on Dalston Lane.

The text of these Turkish and Kurdish communications is only occasionally accompanied by a summary English translation (some of the gulfs on this street are apparently too wide to bridge), but this doesn't seem to worry those somewhat more indigenous passers-by who comment on the neo-Constructivist style of these otherwise incomprehensible posters and find the graphics to be interestingly reminiscent of the fashionable typography of Neville Brody. On Dalston Lane, Marxism is a life-and-death struggle or a designer T-shirt, depending on your orientation. Those posters must speak directly enough in their own world, but they had a special poignancy as they went up all along Dalston Lane in 1990. That was the year, after all, when Tariq Ali, the entrepreneurial figurehead of British

Trotskyism and self-appointed scourge of the liberal conscience, chose to write a satirical novel based on his own revolutionary past, leaving Britain's wealthiest man, the Duke of Westminster, to fight a High Court action against Westminster City Council in order to prove that the working class still existed.[4]

As for the rhetoric that emerges from the Church of England's most prominent establishment round here, this too is enhanced by blight. Revd Donald Pateman has been blasting away from the pulpit of St Mark's, Dalston, since 1956. He specialises in a kind of Gothic Revivalism that is only partly inspired by the architecture of Chester Cheston's vast church. As vicar of this remarkable pile, traditionally known as 'the Cathedral of the East End', Revd Pateman works hard to live up to his chosen church motto of 'Victorian in Architecture and Victorian in Outlook'. A notice at the door reveals him to be sticking to the Book of Common Prayer and King James's Bible with a determination that John Betjeman, as a long-standing enemy of 'With-Itry', would surely have admired. The bi-monthly parish magazine rails against the ways of the modern Church: synodical government, the use of mitres (or 'fish-hats' that are denounced as decadent and of pagan origin), the irreverent clapping that 'goes on far too much in Stepney churches', and the 'faceless' bureaucrats of the Church Urban Fund who wouldn't finance a minibus for St Mark's. But Revd Pateman saves his most resounding onslaughts for the degeneracy and Godlessness of the wider world. 'I believe', he writes, 'that this selfish and self-centred country lies under the judgement of Almighty God'. Hackney may be the dustbin of Europe ('the filth and degradation of Hackney is quite, quite appalling'), but the whole country is going to the dogs too: we have become 'a nation of gawpers', so glued to the television set that we have lost the art of conversation, and 'a nation of moaners' who fail to realise that we are 'living in the most wonderful country in the world, Kinnock or no Kinnock'. The good vicar continues to call out for the gallows for convicted murderers and the reintroduction of 'the cat and the birch' for violent offenders. He also deplores the 'slovenly' ways of the State school, and the lumpen manner in which both children and teachers 'comport themselves in public'; indeed, he is reputed to have offered to give a good thrashing to wayward children whose parents can't or won't do it for themselves. 'At St Mark's', the vicar writes, 'we are unashamedly old-fashioned.' He treats parishioners to extracts from his library, filling the St Mark's magazine with quotes from Shelley, Rudyard Kipling, Conan Doyle, and such mid-century ruralist books as A. L. Morton's *In Search of England*. In the first issue of 1990, he reproduced a Victorian print of a country cottage, bidding his inner-city reader to 'Study this charming picture carefully. No television aerial (thank God!), still less one of those hideous "dishes" (thrice may his Name be praised!). Just a simple family scene, and when the youngsters have finished sawing the wood, they'll come back home, and spend the evening quietly by the fire! "Turn back, O Time!" '

The Revd Pateman's church journal is produced for a moderate-sized but enthusiastic congregation that, for many years, had consisted largely of West Indian parishioners. Copies are also picked up regularly by unbelieving *Guardian* journalists who, while they care not at all for the cultural particularity of Revd Pateman's ministry, recognise St Mark's as an easy source of sniggers for their 'Diary' column. This hints at another modern truth about this part of London. While it may still serve onlooking polemicists as darkest London or 'a picture of a blind alley', Hackney is actually a mixed borough with an unmistakable proportion of young professionals who have brought their own outlook to the area. This population can be hard to please, as the John Lewis Partnership recently found out when they pressed ahead with the closure of Jones Brothers, an old-fashioned outlet on the Holloway Road, which was also one of the few department stores in north or north-east London. There were pickets and petitions, but in the argument it also emerged that the store's customers were famous among the staff for their awkwardness, their complaints, and their constant insistence on consumer rights. A representative story concerned an awkward customer who complained that the shop was 'really appalling': the exasperated assistant replied, 'Well, you'll be glad to hear that it's closing', only to have the customer burst into tears, demanding to know where the hell she was expected to do her shopping after that.[5]

A considerable number of Hackney's middle class are image makers of one sort or another. Indeed, the borough is stiff with journalists, poets, artists, people who work in advertising and television, freelance (or just plain unemployed) commentators who pass as 'cultural critics', and travel writers who haven't yet raised the necessary air fare. Alert observers will know that a Channel 4 commissioning editor has not yet moved out of the area: he can be seen pruning the tree in front of his home with a pair of pliers, or strolling down Dalston Lane, mid-morning, to take a bus for what the rest of us can only presume to be the first working lunch in a busy day. They may also be able to trace the flat by the bus stop in Graham Road, just east of Dalston Lane, where the late Peter Fuller lived in the late Seventies, feeling himself to be 'part of a garret-in-Grub-Street way of literary life which is withering away', and venturing out to join other residents in campaigning for a play area in nearby London Fields or to obstruct the road as part of a protest against the constant and periodically fatal stream of heavy lorries tearing along this noisy Victorian street.[6] The conversion of Hackney into art continues. A whole school of painters and sculptors are working on the theme of the council tower block. A modest community garden is no sooner established down in Haggerston than it features in a novel by Sara Maitland, the Christian feminist who writes about life as a 'vicar's wife' in an *Evening Standard* article entitled 'Why I live in

Haggerston' and who makes televison documentaries that could hardly be better calculated to confirm Revd Pateman's suspicions about the liberal progressives in nearby parishes.[7]

This incoming population might be thought to represent exactly the kind of leavening influence that commentators such as Sir Alfred Sherman and Richard North have declared Hackney to need, but the advocates of the Hackney-as-hell scenario have not greeted them as such. Sir Alfred Sherman can only fit them into his picture of the borough as members of the Marxist mafia. Paul Harrison also had little time for the 'radical professionals' and 'middle-class owner-occupiers' who live in this 'Slough of Despond' by 'choice, not by compulsion'.[8] Other observers have elaborated a scornful new coinage for the incomers, one that reduces a long tradition of sociological description to a succession of insults. For Julie Burchill this is the land of 'Mockneys', people who have affected to drag themselves down by their bootstraps in spurious solidarity with a working class that only wants to move the other way. The same population was described as 'drabbies' by Richard North – the increasingly anti-environmentalist journalist who, after many years, seems finally to have given up on the 'whingeing' and 'left-leaning' Borough of Hackney: the last time I read him, he was investigating the possibilities of moving his long-suffering family to a distant, unprettified city in the West Midlands. As for the more general term 'yuppies', this has circulated among the incoming middle class of Hackney like the parcel in a children's game – never quite seeming to belong where it is found when the music stops.

The truth behind this sneering coinage is that Hackney is where the idea of 'gentrification' (one of post-war Marxism's more successful concepts), has come to fall apart. There was a time in the Eighties when the property market was soaring and owner-occupiers could hardly meet without talking about the 'unreal' or 'insane' value of the modest properties they had bought for so much less only a few years previously; but all that is over now. Since the property market went into reverse we have been more inclined to declare the idea of gentrification too 'economistic' to grasp what has really been going on in places like Hackney over recent years. The incoming population may certainly have displaced some working-class people, but 'gentrification has also brought new skills, expectations, and markets into the area, along with lifestyles that don't simply conform to those of the conventional family household. Be this as it may, the economic arguments persist, albeit in new forms. Indeed, I recently heard a usage that is bound to interest Paul Harrison. A resident of one of the grandest houses in Hackney described how she herself was caught in 'the new poverty trap': mortgaged up to the eyeballs, punished by high interest rates, and unable any longer to anticipate moving to the next, more fortunately situated, rung of the property ladder. Sherman McCoy, the rug-pulled Manhattan yuppie in Tom Wolfe's *Bonfire of the Vanities*, found himself going broke on a million dollars a year. In Hackney some households are really struggling to make ends meet on a tenth of that. We've all got our problems.

For myself, I started to appreciate Dalston Lane as more than just a road to the bus stop when I recognised how well it served as the objective correlative of my own career in the Eighties. That decade was not always easy for independent-minded people. Roger Scruton has complained that the 'left establishment' delayed his appointment to a professorship,[9] and even the historian, Jonathan Clark, is reported to have felt bitter at the circumstances that forced him to spend a year or so working in the City before he was appointed to All Souls at Oxford. I too have had a chance to view the left establishment in higher education over the last decade, but I simply can't persuade myself that the threat is so great. As the decade opened, I was hanging on to some marginal teaching at a polytechnic in the Midlands. The situation was bizarre but, as I now believe, not untypical: an art history department had sensed the approaching chill, and launched a degree in 'Communication Studies' in an endeavour to bring in more students. This ruse certainly paid off, but it also meant that somebody had to come to teach the new course. A couple of full-time appointments were made, but this still left an unallocated residue of teaching to be carried out. Few of the art historians were interested or up to it, so a whole succession of part-timers were pulled in, myself among them. There was a bit of film studies, but I also gave lectures on a first-year course called 'Aspects of Visual Communication', which was designed to whisk students through classical aesthetics and then land them up in the (introductory) confusions of semiology. The art historians appeared to amble through the polytechnic day, teaching a few students, talking about the monograph they might one day write on Monet, and pinning xeroxed articles by Roger Scruton on the door of the lecture theatre to demonstrate their contempt for the obscure 'Media Studies' scam on which their own security seemed to depend. The head of department sat in the back seat through all the lectures taking copious notes. To begin with I was surprised that he found the endeavours of a temporary part-timer worth such thorough-going appraisal, but I soon realised what was really going on. At that time Lord Joseph of Portsoken was wielding his axe as Secretary of State for Education, and the cuts were under way. Indeed, the poor head of department had every reason to believe that the part-time budget would have collapsed by next year and that he himself would have to teach the course. . . .

Taking my cue from Sir Alfred Sherman who, as I understand, has a private practice as a 'public affairs adviser', I decided to refurbish myself as quickly as possible. So after a brief shopping trip (a couple of twice-bespoken suits from Nichols of London, a portable flipchart, and even a lightly used think-tanker's baton from Hewison's junk yard) I too joined the new age as a management consultant. After all those years in higher education, I knew how to write a sentence: a modest start, to be sure, but people have prospered on far less. I found my first job with the Industrial Society, a charitable management-training organisation that, although I didn't know it at the time, had played a leading role in the 'I'm backing Britain' campaign of the Sixties. At that time the director was an evangelising charismatic who ran the place with the fervour of a lay preacher. He would talk about the month's figures and then break into a hymn of praise to the crocuses, the blue sky, and the matching colour of his grandchildren's eyes. Staff who got up to testify at the monthly meetings would be commended for the 'courage' and 'bravery' with which they ventured to ask even the inanest of questions: as one of the director's favourite sayings went, 'One "How?" is worth all the research papers in the world'. Enthusiasm was everything, and learning was all about staggering ('Feet on the ground; eyes on the hills') from one 'blinding glimpse of the obvious' to the next. I joined the 'advisers' who toured the country, staying at modest expense-account hotels and delivering short courses on which even the jokes were prepackaged – two days here, two days there; letter writing with secretaries at BUPA at one end of the week; public speaking with mining engineers in Wigan at the other. I even gave an unbelieving sheikh and OPEC minister a one-man course in rapid reading: a formidable challenge, since the man was no fool and rapid reading is one of those con-tricks that only works when you've got people in a group and can whip up the competitive spirit between them.

The Industrial Society must have its strengths, but I certainly wasn't one of them. Nevertheless, I remain grateful to the organisation that allowed me to convert myself into a more viable proposition while occupying a modest position on its payroll. I moved on after a year and, as Sir Alfred will understand, it's been a little bit of this, and a little bit of that, ever since. Like other people round here, I have had a number of fleeting encounters with the disreputable world of 'quality' journalism. I've put a performance appraisal system into a merchant bank in Dublin but, to the uncertain extent that I have thrived, it has only been by becoming something of a specialist in the management of voluntary organisations, a field in which I still employ myself. Unlike Lord Annan, who recently published his memoirs of 'Our Age', I am not sure that my experience offers much for anyone else to go on; nevertheless, I can testify that the best way for a writer to get money out of the Arts Council in the late Eighties was by running short courses on business planning or the development of marketing strategies. A fair exchange, to be sure.

At the end of the decade I had another brief encounter with the polytechnic world, and it really was just like staggering from the demolished station at Dalston Junction to the derelict hulk of St Bartholomew's up at Lebon's Corner. This time it was a polytechnic much closer to home that asked me to become a 'visiting fellow' for a year in a newly established 'Centre for Applied Historical Research'. The aim of this centre, funded as it was through the Training Agency, was to engage in 'applied' activities that would open new sources of income for the polytechnic's beleaguered and demoralised historians. Knowing better than to look even a modest gift horse in the mouth, I accepted the offer, agreeing to give a number of visiting lectures and seminars on the subject of 'heritage' – its meaning and administration. The experience was accompanied by an abiding feeling of unreality throughout. Indeed, the whole polytechnic seemed to consist of meetings that somehow contrived to go ahead even though people no longer had the energy to turn up and participate in them. One evening I went to present a paper to a seminar and found that nearly all the students had backed off on account of the fog (there was the slightest twist of mist in the air). Of the four who did turn up one sat there reading a book on an entirely unrelated subject. Eventually I confronted the fellow and he explained, with a certain amount of indignation in his voice, that he wasn't even enrolled on the course: indeed, I should get on with it, since he was just waiting to go for a drink with his friend as soon as the seminar was over. I also spoke at a day-long conference, finding that most of the delegates (assorted antiquarians and museum administrators from within the polytechnic's catchment area) had been begged to attend without charge and, in a good number of cases, with the promise of a free lunch thrown in. It was at this event that a long-serving lecturer, whose confusions were doubtless aggravated by the fact that he had recently been converted into an 'enterprise officer', told me that 'everything is discourse' and then moved on to suggest that I spoke with the voice of an 'ideological State apparatus'. I believe this was meant critically, but it still turned on a light in my mind. I had been wondering, since the very beginning of my engagement as a 'visiting fellow', why I was repeatedly offered an office of my own, even though no one expected me to turn up more than once or twice a term. I was now able to reply that, far from being the voice of an 'ideological State apparatus', as this time-warped fellow suggested, I was just completing my run as 'visiting fellow' at a Centre for Applied Historical Research that didn't appear to exist. I billed them anyway; eventually they even coughed up the VAT. There were some gifted and devoted people in there, but the semi-privatised and derelict framework in which they have to operate is a scandal. If that is what's left of Professor Scruton's 'left establishment', then it's surely time to call in E. M. Kendall the undertaker, and I'm not too sure about the 'Courtesy' and 'Reverence' either.

Yet Dalston Lane is not just an alternative to proper institutional employment. It is also an open archaeological site in which the story of the nation's post-war history can be traced out in unexpected detail, and it is from here that I have read the signs of the times. I've watched symptomatic developments in the literary world. From Dalston Lane it has been impossible to observe, say, the success of those travel writers who have spent the last fifteen years ensuring that the old narrative conventions of colonialist observation (once connected to a whole machinery of administration) find their last efflorescence in a purely literary expression of personal style, without wondering why these intrepid and heroic authors, who have pursued what Jonathan Raban calls 'imaginative truth' to exotic places all over the world, don't just walk round the corner and address themselves to the richness of the inner city.[10] Similarly, it has been impossible to hear Malcolm Bradbury (imagine a whole row of him flickering from lack of vertical hold on the invalid sets of 'Mirror TV') claiming that the campus novel shows the university becoming a microcosm of the world, without knowing with old-fashioned certainty that the books he writes and champions are actually part of a mannerist retreat from what used to be called reality. As for those curiously paired themes of the late Eighties, 'Heritage' and entrepreneurial 'Excellence', from Dalston Lane there was never any doubt that both have arisen in reaction to the dishevelment and dereliction of the Welfare State. This failure is the central reality around here, and everything else seems connected to it. Dalston Lane has been a perfect place from which to observe the ongoing decline – the signs of which are sometimes quite unregarded elsewhere – of the professional and intellectual culture of the Welfare State. The death of *New Society* was disguised as a merger with the *New Statesman*, but the Pelican book-list closed a little more recently, without anyone appearing to notice at all.

Strange mutations occur in the void left by the decline of the Welfare State and its disciplines, and here again Dalston Lane has provided an admirable viewing point. I've observed the decline of modernism and the revival in its wake of so-called 'real' culture, represented by a whole company of neglected heroes brought forward and honoured, often posthumously, as the few who stayed true to traditions during the abstracted post-war age that is now coming to a close: classical revivalists like Erith and Terry in architecture; John Piper and other members of the retrospectively assembled 'neo-romantic' tendency in mid-century British painting. The reputation of human-scale poets like Betjeman and Larkin has risen on a similar wave in literature, and there has been no shortage of popular narratives in which displaced and ridiculed old men – from John le Carré's George Smiley to John Mortimer's *Rumpole of the Bailey* – returned to triumph over the lesser figures who have usurped them. The ideologically motivated think-tanker (a mere hit-man) stands in for the discredited figure of the impartial social scientist, and trivialising journalists thrive on a new kind of cynicism: the callow smirks of the *Guardian*'s Andrew Rawnsley being quite upstaged by the more knowing endeavour of Auberon Waugh, who has built a whole style out of finding cracks in the so-called post-war settlement, and then widened them by saying the very things common decency once held to be unsayable. I've watched and wondered as a whole succession of ideas have migrated from left to right across the disintegrating centre of political life. The deinstitutionalising vision of Laingian anti-psychiatry has turned up in league with right-wing ideas about the restructuring of the National Health Service. Left-wing arguments about 'media bias', or the iniquity of using public funding to subsidise élitist metropolitan culture like opera, have been enthusiastically adopted by such figures as Norman Tebbit and put into practice by Tory governments. The language has undergone some striking transformations as well. It really wasn't very long ago that the term 'opting out' implied deluded irresponsibility: people who proposed it were derided as 'drop-outs' and subjected to firm lectures in the quality papers, which quoted John Donne's line about no man being an island and stressed the virtues of social responsibility and the public good. Nowadays, of course, 'opting out' is government policy and public expectations of the State have been so reduced that, to quote an unexceptional example from this morning's paper, a government education minister provokes no reaction when, with the schools already in politically induced chaos, he describes breaking 'the monopoly of the teacher training colleges' as the 'key to change'.[11]

I have taken Dalston Lane as a vantage point for looking out at the wider world, but the government has turned out to have a use for this street as well. Indeed, in the last couple of years, it has become abundantly clear that dusty Dalston Lane has actually been a pilot project all along. The new roads proposed in the East London Assessment Study have been rejected, but by the time the reprieve finally came and the blight was lifted, the signs were unmistakable. Far from being demolished, Dalston Lane has been taken as a model for the rest of the metropolis. London has become Dalston Lane writ large. The congested traffic and the crammed and inadequate public transport are already everywhere. The litter gusts over the whole city, unimpressed either by the resolve with which Margaret Thatcher stepped out with a spiked stick for the sake of a photo-opportunity, or by the energy that Richard Branson put into travelling the country and standing next to litter-bins in order to smile at the cameras as the figurehead of the government's famously unsuccessful UK 2000 initiative. The conspicuous discrepancy between dingy reality and the manipulated imagery of the advertising agency is plain to see all over London, the recent trials of Saatchi and Saatchi notwithstanding. The dossers and derelicts are not just to be found on every street. They have found themselves at the centre of a new cult as noble examples of Unbadgered Man. Indeed, award-winning journalists have hailed them as true heroes of our time: rugged individualists who thrive on neglect and, in carefully accentuated contrast to the young beggar/profiteers of so-called 'street homelessness', would never dream of asking for a handout from the State.[12] The mugger, meanwhile, has found a job in one of those think-tanks: he travels round the country hitting up the public sector and then scurrying off before anyone can make him answerable for his actions. Even Dalston Lane's approach to listed buildings has been applied more widely throughout London. Indeed, St Bartholomew's vicarage turns out to have been an early trial in an experiment that has been producing more spectacular results elsewhere. Since the abolition of the GLC, County Hall has stood empty and undisposable despite the London Residuary Body's best endeavours to find an appropriate developer. The ruins of Battersea Power Station are to be found upriver, gutted in preparation for transformation into a leisure complex and then abandoned as the true costs emerged, the market turned, and the finance fell in. Doubtless the shrubs will be sprouting from those great sheer walls before long. In recent years, the thought that has always come to mind so easily on Dalston Lane has been muttered all over the city: what we need around here is some really effective State intervention.

4
Down in the Dirt

Anthropologists have produced elegant theories about dirt. Mary Douglas has described dirt as an idea that defines the outside of a culture, a conceptual domain in which all differences disappear and only the threat of defilement remains: as dirt, so the argument goes, everything is the same.[1]

We know about defilement on Dalston Lane too, but here the filth in the streets is far from undifferentiated. Indeed, it calls for discrimination of the closest kind. Children know better than to play in the autumn leaves without at first poking about in them with a stick to see what exotic content they might mask. The freakish winds that have, in recent years, torn up so many ancient trees in the shires and filled our leading novelists with a sense of impending doom, are recognised round here as Nature's way of cleaning the streets. One gust and the sky is filled with a marvellous diversity of things. A million plastic bags drift aloft. Tons of newsprint, hamburger wrappers, and umbrella silk from the City flutter overhead. The 'Great Wind' of 1989 even managed to pick up thousands of brand-new, black plastic rubbish bags from a council depot and distribute them evenly over this borough and the next. Here was the solution once again becoming part of the problem, but not quite in the manner Sir Alfred Sherman envisaged.

If dirt is where all differentiation finally stops, then litter must be the domain of its last feverish efflorescence. East London has long been full of scavengers and rag-pickers who eke out a living by sorting through the rubbish. A few totters still work the streets with horse, cart, and bell, and the street markets are going strong. Down in Whitechapel, Hogarthian characters sit on the wintry pavements offering up fragments of salvaged rubbish for a pittance: glass, bones, and a hank of weeds. Dalston Lane is also defined by this circulation. The street is really a clogged river of junk flowing through the city, eddying here, forming deep and stagnant pools there. There's an unexpected wealth of charity shops in the area: the British Red Cross Society's modest establishment has been joined more recently by Age Concern, the Family Welfare Association, and, just round the corner, a true hypermarket run by Oxfam. It's not quite clear whether these agencies are competing here for the sake of opportunity or from a sense of mission.

A whole collection of junk merchants work the same street, some of them as specialised as anyone's idea of niche marketing could demand. 'Mirror TV' revives exhausted television sets, while Ossie turns over already much-recycled kitchen equipment for canteens and restaurants. Further along stands the more generalist outfit of Collins & McCabe ('DHSS welcome – Enquire within'). You would have to be pretty desperate to find much of value among the exhausted household furniture on display here, and there's not a great deal to be said for the old technical manuals either: *Halsbury's Statutes of England, Accounting in the Foreign Exchange Market, Property Tax in Singapore.* . . . Indeed, the whole operation seems to be held together by the hard currency of a smelter behind the scenes. As the sign says, 'Spot cash for scrap metals'.

Collins & McCabe operate out of a battered old corner shop, but Mr Hewison across the road gets by without even this modest concession to the idea of permanent structure. He has learnt that, with the help of a ferocious dog or two, it is possible to run a demolition and salvage business without wasting time on bricks and mortar of your own. All that is necessary is to rent a derelict bomb-site, and then fence it off with huge advertising hoardings, which have the advantage of providing a handy little income while also bringing constant variation to the area. One week it's Moroccan holidays and rats courtesy of NALGO ('One family that's better off with the poll tax'); the next it's the new Volvo ('Where the Pursuit of Excellence Inevitably Leads You'), and an apparently stark-naked girl draped, like a bleached shrimp, over purple velvet to demonstrate 'the ultimate leg experience' of 'Voilance de Le Bourget'.

Inside this kaleidoscopic compound is a hastily improvised shanty of temporary structures, each one filled with different categories of upwardly mobile debris. Mr Hewison knows how to pull a likely proposition from its original setting, but he's no master when it comes to reassembly. So his collection mounts up like a great pile of quotations that won't resolve into a coherent statement, and customers are left to make whatever connections they can. He's got an old, red telephone box, an Ardizzone-style petrol pump, pub signs from some distant hostelry called the Chigwell Arms, a couple of red ticket kiosks for anyone who wants to open their home to the public, a huge chimney pot from a house on Piccadilly, garden seats, wagon wheels that still have the tinsel of some forgotten Christmas hanging from them, sash windows, wrought iron, a couple of fake Doric columns retrieved from a redundant theatre or restaurant design, and, of course, lots of stripped pine. I went by recently to find a lady from Islington trying to buy the collapsing wooden shed in which the caustic-soda bath is kept. Old Mr Hewison was having trouble containing his laughter, but he was certainly entertaining the offer.

This incessant scavenging has also achieved a cultural dimension. The used-book dealers are here, picking over the flow and finding new areas of sale in a dwindling market. Even the British Red Cross

Society is advertising for books. Driffield confines his notices to *The Daily Telegraph*. He specialises in finding back-titles for aged authors who have forgotten what they have written or, in some cases, for their widows. Iain Sinclair, who knows exactly which upmarket dealer was involved in levering up the reputation of which Faber or Chatto poet, runs his own experiments to see how far a literary reputation can be made from a heap of valueless old books. As the literary culture disintegrates into mutual backscratching in the Sunday reviews, jobs teaching 'theory' in North America, and the whimsical tipsterism of the literary prize, a mutant canon of English literature – quite distinct from the official one now under the management of American academics – emerges along the edges of Dalston Lane. John Lodwick, a novelist of the Forties and Fifties, is the latest addition. A few months ago, his books could hardly be given away, but a few carefully sown references have already cracked him up to £30 for a fine copy with dust-wrapper. Lodwick has been picked up by a pivotal mid-level dealer in Cambridge, and the critical profiles are bound to follow.

In the Sixties, members of the Exploding Galaxy (hailed and reviled as 'London's love-anarchist dance group') lived communally in a house a few hundred yards west of Dalston Junction. These performers, whose repertoire included such works as the 'Kineta-pocalypsoidal Bumping Bodies Ballet' ('Never have so many been so nude so early and for such good reasons', as an appreciative reviewer wrote in *International Times*), had a kinetic relationship with clutter, but they also had their own domestic problems with household filth. Indeed, in the autumn of 1967, their house at No. 99 Balls Pond Road was so infested with lice and the excretions of five or six untrained cats that a couple of residents became worried about the possible outbreak of disease, and decided that something must be done. After pondering the situation, they came up with a ploy designed to raise their fellow communards's consciousness of this hygiene problem without imposing anything so crude as a hierarchical decision on them. The answer, they decided, lay in cannabis resin. The 'increased awareness' brought by the drug would make the 'ugly aspects' of the house more noticeable. Some people might find such a revelation 'absolutely unbearable' and respond by getting 'withdrawn and cut off from the environment', but the members of the Exploding Galaxy were creative and artistic types who, so the advocates of the hashish solution calculated, would push through this initial sense of abjection to 'create works which act as a sort of "social antidote"'. The cannabis was given to the 'Exploders' as they woke up one morning, and it seems to have worked admirably: in fact, 'the entire house was cleaned, disinfected, and actions taken to ensure the restoration of hygienic conditions'.[2]

Through 1990 another marginal collective was finding a different kind of art in the rubbish, this time in a squat rather closer to Dalston

Junction at No. 147 Balls Pond Road, which happens to be another of Hackney's derelict listed buildings. The Maberly Chapel was taken over as a 'carcass' in 1825 by a certain Mr Ashley from Charles Square in Hoxton, who fitted it out with galleries and created a chapel capable of accommodating 'a congregation of Independents' of up to 800 souls. When I first noticed it a few years ago, this building had returned to its original state as a carcass. Still bearing the signs of discontinued industrial endeavour (the 'Regolux Venetian Blind Company', etc.), it was in use as a junk shop and crammed to the ceiling with knackered furniture. There were signs of a sporadic sifting process, for the objects that were finally deemed to have become unsaleable were hurled out of the door onto the few yards of ground (once a small graveyard) between the chapel and the street, where they lay rotting in an undifferentiated heap. 'Quite a mess', I once remarked to an elderly woman at the bus stop. She was in no doubt that there were better ways of keeping the rubbish off the streets: further, she told me that when she had been young, just before the war, the Maberly Chapel had been headquarters for Oswald Mosley and the blackshirted 'biff boys' of his British Union of Fascists. The young men who came here used to be given 'a free shirt and a pair of boots' – an offer that, as my interlocutor snarled before boarding her bus, was 'not to be scoffed at in those days'.

Since that fleeting encounter, the junk dealers have moved on too, and the Maberly Chapel, which is owned by the Sikh Society and, like too many other listed buildings in Hackney, well on the way to eventual demolition as a 'dangerous structure', has been squatted by a group of artists going (at least on the day I asked them) by the name of Dene Cholmeley. The corrugated iron along the street front has been turned into a collage, with cut-out fragments of bodies, holiday images, men in camouflage, and highlighted snatches of text ('He ended up making history', 'London Calling', 'How far will you be able to push the boat out?'). Behind this weirdly ornamented barricade, the forgotten graveyard has been turned into an installation. The junk that got left behind as worthless has been picked over yet again, differentiated and displayed according to the precepts of a renegade art. A straw man, made out of woven palm leaves, is leaping out of the window, and selected fragments have been stuck up all over the outside of the building: hub caps, dried flowers over the door, a typewriter, old romantic novels opened at gnomic places and nailed to the wall, paint pots, bits of a smashed-up cash register. As for the cavernous interior of this scorched and disintegrating edifice, it is filled by a huge ship made up from the ruined chapel's own timbers with translucent oiled paper stretched out between them and ornamented with diverse insignia and strange found objects. In 1840 this was the Maberly Sabbath School, an institution run for the children of the 'very poor' where, thanks to a recent alteration in Rule 27, corporal punishment was forbidden.[3] One hundred and fifty years later, the biblical apocalypse is back: Noah's Ark sailing out on a rising tide of filth, a fervid if not strictly dissenting cult of the Last Days of London.

This tacky sense of an ending has come to hang over the whole city in recent years. An interest in debris and human fallout is part of the New Baroque sensibility, shared by young Apocalyptics and played-out Marxists alike. The range runs from *Absolute Beginners* (the film) to a commentator like Elizabeth Wilson who, quick to adjust her dogmatic heart to the fashions of post-modernism, eulogises the spastic movements of the dancer in Covent Garden who has turned himself into a broken object or 'living doll'.[4] All over London young photographers have been reviving the black-and-white imagery of the rat-catcher, the old paraffin heater, the disused and cluttered-up church interior, the peeling walls of the unimproved slum tenement, the fragmentary but exotic combinations of the restaged bomb-site.[5]

London has been through something like this before: picking over the debris, finding surprising new meaning in the ruins. But the first blitz came with a greater sense of reality. Neo-romantic artists, such as John Minton and Graham Sutherland, found strange figures in the debris. The engraver, John Farleigh, wandered through the blitzed streets in 1941, recording that there was 'a loveliness about the whole atmosphere', and that bombing had cleansed Tottenham Court Road of its vulgarity and enabled it to achieve 'beauty and humility'.[6] He celebrated the fact that the signposts had gone, saying that they had really only been 'symbols of our suburbanity', and preferring to wander wide-eyed into the deeper meanings of a city reduced to rubble. He even found a consoling lesson in the fact that the fake Corinthian columns of an Oxford Street department store had outlasted the rest of the building: evidently, it was important not to cast tawdry design in such permanent form. But for many people, at least, the desperate aesthetics of the blitz were based on a commitment to something greater than the momentary and startling effect. In a commentary written to accompany a series of watercolours by the Polish artist, Wanda Ostrowska, Viola Garvin described the ruins of the city as 'pediments of solidity' on which the newly steeled spirit of the nation could rest.[7]

Fifty years later, the revived styles of the blitz find no such 'pediments of solidity' on which to base themselves. People who lived through the bombing talk of the palpable silence that came between the raids. The new cult of the blitz comes wrapped in the different silence, more like the one that follows an arrested bulldozer than an exploded bomb, that is to be found to the end of planning, the end of reform, the end of State responsibility. It is in this less palpable silence that the debris has started to glow again. The first blitz produced a spirit of solidarity and common interest that was built into the foundations of the Welfare State; the second is an aesthetic effect found in the ruins of that reforming endeavour.

Hackney Council doesn't need to trouble itself with the morbid aesthetics of the second blitz, but there's a lot at stake in its ongoing battle to keep the streets clean. On 9 February 1990, 67-year-old pensioner, Stephen McGrath, fell over and drowned at the Junction of Dalston Lane and Pembury Road. His misfortune was to have landed in 'a grassy hollow', which had been flooded for a week.[8] In a subsequent hearing the council admitted that the drains had been blocked with rubbish, claiming that the fault lay with an 'untrained' street sweeper who had apparently not understood that rubbish should be swept from the pavement out into the road. A week or two after Mr McGrath's accident, the body of a younger man named Mr Pat O'Reilly was found in the pond on nearby Clapton Common. He was estimated to have been floating there for a good three weeks. How does a body float unnoticed for so long in a large but much-visited ornamental pond? The police explained their own failure to find it by pointing out that 'the pond is so dirty, even though it is five feet deep you can't see down more than five inches'. As for the old-age pensioners who came to feed the geese and the children who fished there, they had been aware of something bulky in the water, but they hadn't bothered to distinguish it from all the other debris. As one local said: 'I'd seen it, but I thought it was a bag of rubbish. That was at least three weeks ago'. The police explained further: 'The man's clothes had filled with air . . . making the body look like a plastic dustbin bag of rubbish'. This gruesome story shocked many hard-bitten people into silence, but some were rightly moved to speak out. As leading members of the Hackney Irish Association, Councillors Lawless and Eustace (themselves subject to unjust ridicule as 'legless and useless' in some of Hackney's remaining public bars) issued an uncompromising statement claiming that the man had not been found sooner because he was Irish. They were reported to have slammed police suggestions that Mr O'Reilly had probably 'turned to the life of a vagrant'. This was 'a classic case of stereotyping' in which 'a perfectly respectable man was linked with vagrants simply because he was Irish, liked a drink and was missing'.[9] They were almost certainly right about the police; but so, apparently, was Mary Douglas with her idea of dirt as the domain in which all such differences are lost.

5

Dalston Lane Becomes
a Downland Track

The local government reorganisation of 1974 is still hotly contested in rural Lincolnshire. Two of the county's Conservative MPs, Mr Edward Leigh of Gainsborough & Horncastle, and Sir Peter Tapsell of East Lindsey, have recently joined forces to demand that the south bank of the Humber be brought back into Lincolnshire where it has always belonged. As Mr Leigh remarked in the House of Commons, 'In a balanced scale of history, tradition and local sentiment far outweigh the convenience of leaving in place the recent bureaucratic structure that is Humberside – ugly in name and cumbersome by nature'. Mr Leigh was in no doubt: 'the Humber is a divide between two different cultures' and the people should be allowed 'to do what they most want – return to their roots'. Those who live south of the Humber were proud to be 'yellow-bellies', and the new boundary was a monstrous and alien imposition that ran, 'like the Berlin wall in the minds of administrators', between villages that have been one for a thousand years. Despite relentless propaganda from its leaders, Humberside County Council had failed to 'inspire loyalty'; indeed, 60 per cent of the inhabitants wanted a return to the old boundaries. It was time to 'trust the people and abolish this bastard county and create one Lincolnshire again'.

I found this story under the headline 'Tradition and Sentiment Outweigh Convenience' on the front page of the *Market Rasen Mail* for 14 July 1990. I had bought the paper from a West Indian newsagent as I walked up to the bus stop at Dalston Junction. The *Market Rasen Mail* lay next to the *Louth Leader* on a multi-cultural rack that also held copies of *The Voice, Carribbean News, Asian Times, Irish World*, and other specialist sheets. The Lincolnshire papers had been delivered by mistake but the newsagent wasn't unduly perturbed. This being Dalston, he had put them on display nevertheless and for a while Deep England lay there, as if it were just one more distant homeland among others.

Dalston Lane is thick with homelands. There are places to come from, places to go back to, places to visit, fear, dream, and agitate about. But it would be deluded nonsense to suggest that England has the same kind of presence on this street as Trinidad, Poland, Nigeria, Hong Kong, Turkey, or Cyprus. Market Rasen evidently has a great deal going for it, but it is because England is not merely one root among others in a multi-cultural democracy of nations that I have placed my English homeland in Dorset, and not the Dorset of customary definition either. As I view it from Dalston Lane, rural England settles into an only moderately picturesque configuration at the centre of which stands a 725-acre stretch of nondescript agricultural land at Crichel Down near Tarrant Rushton in the east of that much loved county. This land is nothing much to look at, but some forty years ago it stood at the centre of a controversy that every resident of the inner city would do well to remember. In 1938 it was bought by the Air Ministry, after some argument but without the use of compulsory powers, from three different owners. At that time Crichel Down was a stretch of poor grazing land, a rabbit-run of minimal agricultural value, but after using it as a practice bombing range for a number of years the Air Ministry transferred it in 1950 to the Ministry of Agriculture, which, following the imperatives of the Labour government's Agriculture Act 1947, set about turning it into a model farm on which new industrialised agricultural techniques could be demonstrated. With the help of artificial fertilisers and a 'prairie buster' imported from North America the land at Crichel Down was quickly converted into what *Farmer's Weekly* described as a stretch of 'American wheatbelt' and the 'largest wheat field in England'.[1]

It was during this transformation that Commander Marten, the new owner of the Crichel Estate, launched the campaign that would make the name of Crichel Down nationally famous. He wanted to buy back his wife's much improved ancestral acres, and he had the support not just of the county establishment but also of such organisations as the National Farmers Union and the Country Landowners Association. Much was made of a pledge embodied in the 1941 Act of Parliament that enabled the State to buy land for wartime purposes, but only on the understanding that, within five years of the war ending, the original owner or his or her successor should be given an opportunity to buy it back. Frustrated in his endeavours, Commander Marten pressed for a public inquiry that was eventually held in the old Corn Exchange at Blandford Forum in April 1954. This was followed by a report in which certain civil servants from the Ministry of Agriculture were convicted of high-handed behaviour and given their resounding come-uppance. In July of that year, and after considerable howling from his own back-benches, Sir Thomas Dugdale, the Conservative Minister of Agriculture who had commissioned the inquiry, accepted responsibility for the behaviour of his civil servants and resigned. Commander Marten was finally able to buy back his land and the traditional order of things was restored.

The Crichel Down inquiry is sometimes still remembered for establishing the precedent of ministerial responsibility for the conduct of civil servants. Tam Dalyell cited it a few years ago in an unsuccessful attempt to embarrass Michael Heseltine into resigning over the Westlands affair. But I bring it up here for different reasons. While the Battle of Crichel Down started out as nothing more than a local skirmish, it gave rise to a great polemical drama that put the writing on the wall for the idea of enlightened public administration, which was so central to the reforming vision of the post-war Welfare State.

The public inquiry into Crichel Down was little better than a travesty: a mixture between a backroom kangaroo court and a stage-managed show trial with stooges and prejudged victims who were mocked and abused as they tried to testify, by the Queen's counsel in charge. The appointed QC was Sir Andrew Clark, a Monte Carlo gambler, and erstwhile picaresque novelist who had stood unsuccessfully as Conservative candidate for Barnet in the 1945 General Election. Clark was, and I quote from the scrupulous and balanced assessment of I. F. Nicolson, 'a man without qualifications or experience in civil service, or government, or civil administration of any kind, or agriculture' but he had 'a known hatred of anything even faintly resembling "socialism", "nationalization", or "bureaucracy" '.[2] While in Blandford, he revealed himself to be a true 'card', attending point-to-points at Badbury Rings and sporting fancy silk waistcoats that would not, by all accounts, look out of place in Mr Economou's shop on Dalston Lane. His collection was said to include one especially choice example made of silver-blue satin and embroidered with pink rosebuds in a pattern he had designed himself.[3] At a dinner held by the High Sheriff of Dorset, Lieutenant-Colonel Sir Thomas Salt, Clark entertained his host and the other shire guests by shooting out the dining-table candles with an eighteenth-century flintlock and then, from the same distance of fifteen paces, blasting a hole in a mahogany door with a sixteenth-century long-barrelled pistol loaded with a section of candle.

In the more sober hours of the day, Clark stirred up what I. F. Nicolson has called 'diabolical confusion': pillorying civil servants and magnifying errors they may have made, allowing generations of dissipated absentee landowners to be presented as if they had been diligent farmers, and creating an atmosphere that encouraged the Press to finish off the job. The civil servant became the 'Man from the Ministry' as the stereotype of the hated wartime 'snoop' was adjusted to post-war circumstances: he was now a 'petty dictator' (*News Chronicle*) or 'tinpot Napoleon' (*Daily Mirror*), an insolent and jumped-up functionary, riding roughshod over traditional rights and probably taking back-handers as well. Some of the 'guilty' civil servants tried to defend themselves by explaining the genuinely complex administrative background to their decisions, but Sir Andrew Clark cut them short, saying that the inquiry wasn't inclined to listen to their 'lectures'. His report was riddled with basic errors of fact, but it was true to the ideological fable that he and the Press had created in the name of Crichel Down. The final meaning of those emblematic Dorset acres was simple enough and commentators of diverse outlook continue to recite it. Tory MPs talked of 'A deliberate breaking of a pledge', warning of 'the bacillus of bureaucratic control' and the 'dread contagion' it would spread all over the land unless 'the greatest vigilance' was exercised.[4] Crichel Down was the 'new Runnymede' where the 'arbitrary power' of the State was finally disciplined, and where the champions of the individual triumphed over the 'new despots' of 'an arrogant and unscrupulous bureaucracy'. As one journalist put it at the time, 'the name that was to have been associated with progress, became for ever a synonym for muddle'.[5]

Commander Marten may not recognise it from close up at Crichel House, but if he came and looked back from Dalston Lane I fancy that he would be able to glimpse the huge and spectral mill that now stands on those once-contested downland acres. It has been there ever since the Fifties, churning out rhetorical devices that have served to discredit a much broader range of 'bureaucratic' activities than those Commander Marten and his wife described as 'veiled nationalization of agricultural land'. At Crichel Down it was the Ministry of Agriculture that took the rap for an act of expropriation initially made in the name of the military, but since then the onslaught has been directed against the whole conception of planning and State intervention that lay at the heart of the post-war settlement. The rhetoric of Crichel Down now includes such ideas as Britain's 'perestroika' and the 'Berlin wall', which the bureaucratically conceived new county of Humberside has brought to Lincolnshire. All the professions associated with the Welfare State – teachers, doctors, social workers, public architects – have been exposed to it. As I will show, even the National Trust has come under attack as an expropriating agency of the modern State. In recent years, however, the easiest targets of all have been found in the inner cities, where Labour councils have drawn far more obloquy than was invited even by the 'looney left' antics of Liverpool, Brent, Lambeth, and sometimes Hackney itself. The extent to which the inner-city areas have been damaged by this onslaught has been recognised by the Audit Commission, which in 1989 suggested the government's unceasing rhetorical assaults on Labour local authorities were preventing the realisation of the government's own plans for urban regeneration.[6]

Crichel Down has lent its spirit not just to an expanding tradition of rhetoric but also to a pervasive repertoire of images. Those 725 downland acres had already disappeared into an industrialised prairie by the time Commander Marten bought them into the Crichel Estate, but something of old Crichel Down is abroad every time an idea of the traditional nation is lined up in opposition to the administrative and bureaucratic measures of the modernising State. Up there on the chalk of Crichel Down, the nation could be conjured up in traditional English guise as a superior place of husbandry, craft, human-scale (if not always classical), architecture and time-sanctioned tradition. The cult has changed a bit since then: the unspoiled landscape is now a television image and much used, over recent years, in commercials designed to promote privatisation; the old and emblematic country house has been joined by the new architecture of classical revivalists like Quinlan Terry; the pure, running spring water has been bottled at source and is available, even on Dalston Lane, as a replenishing alternative to tap water.

There's a great tradition of rural excursions in east London, from hopping in Kent to Epping Forest and the Green Line coaches; but nowadays one doesn't really have to leave the inner city to go for a walk in the English countryside. Like other East London boroughs, Hackney has been going green in recent years. This is not just a matter of the 'general leafiness' Pevsner saw as a legacy of the days when Hackney consisted of twelve hamlets, nor of the many gardens and parks to be found in the borough. The buddleia of the old bomb-sites has recently been joined by the newer green of the city farm, and of the pacifist pastorale so evident in the leafy background of the marching mural on Dalston Lane. There is the green of the 'tree nursery' that some brave community project, not actually the Freeform Arts Trust, has tried to establish in the ruins of St Bartholomew's church at Lebon's Corner; and of the saplings the council has planted along many pavements in the borough in an attempt to lift the passing heart. But another, very different, hue of green has also been creeping through Hackney in recent years – one that seems to harmonise far better with the bunkered Victorian vision of the Revd Donald Pateman up at St Mark's, with his constant struggle against urban degeneracy and his celebrations of the villages, cottages, and churches of the poetic nation he calls, for the benefit of his predominantly West Indian congregation, 'Merlin's Isle'. This is the green of the chalky downland track Revd Pateman showed alongside excerpts from W. H. Hudson's book, *Nature in Downland* (1900), in his church magazine of July–August 1990. It is also the green of the famous overgrown stretch of urban wasteland in Middlesborough over which Margaret Thatcher walked for the television cameras in order to demonstrate her government's determination to 'tackle' the problems of the inner city, and of the garden festival with which Michael Heseltine offered symbolic hope to Liverpool during the dark age that belonged to Derek Hatton. This is a visionary green to be sure, though what it envisions is not the benign de-industrialisation William Morris once imagined for the Thames or that another Victorian commentator, Richard Jefferies, thought might come 'After London', but rather the burgeoning that would surely follow once the corrupting machinery of the overweening State was rolled back. Crichel Down has come to Dalston Lane, just as, in *Macbeth*, Birnam Wood eventually came to Dunsinane.

Part Two

Brideshead and the Tower Blocks

6
Brideshead Relocated

I was struck by a huge advertisement on Dalston Lane the other day. Pasted on to a large hoarding next to the New Four Aces Club, it showed an ornate wrought-iron gate and behind it a gravel drive winding through lush sheep-dotted parkland towards a great country house that peeped out suggestively from behind ancient trees. Beneath this seigneurial prospect was printed the slogan 'Permanence in an Age of Change'. The gate, which had the word 'Araldite' figured in its metal, was ajar, but despite this teasing hint of access, the image still seemed like an affront, an indication of everything that the people of this street will never attain. Yet instinctive objectors should take heart. Dalston Lane is no longer a leafy avenue of country delights but it still serves, in its own dishevelled way, as the road to one of England's most revealing country houses.

Sutton House is the only National Trust property in the East End of London: a starred, grade-II listed building that stands a mile or so up the road on a busy corner of Homerton High Street. Built in the early 1500s, the house has since accumulated four-and-a-half centuries' worth of additions, from Georgian through to English free style. Old London guidebooks spell out its significant features: sixteenth-century linenfold panelling, Jacobean stairs and fireplaces, ancient armorial wall-painting, a mullioned window rumoured to have been cut from a Spanish Armada galleon. Writing for the National Trust in 1945, John Summerson cited Sutton House as a building that, though it may be of 'no great artistic merit' as a whole, was nevertheless of 'significant antiquity' and should be preserved as a valuable 'composition of fragmentary beauties welded together in the course of time'.[1] Local reputation relishes the mystery of the house as well as its significant history. There's talk of a ghost and a secret underground tunnel running out into the wilds of Hackney marshes.

By the time I first visited it early in 1987, this surviving fragment of the ancient hamlet of Hackney seemed to be at the end of its days. The makeshift sheds of a troublesome-looking car mechanic were built right up against its west wall; the Georgian front was boarded up, and a passing vandal with a spraycan had added humiliation to the injury of the peeling notice announcing that the building had come to the National Trust through the benevolence of one W. A. Robertson, who had made his gift in the memory of two brothers killed in the Great War. Recent 'repairs' to upstairs windows and brickwork only added to the sense of dereliction: although carried out by the National Trust, they made much Hackney DIY look positively refined. Inside, the story was far worse. The enclosed courtyard was full of junk. Damp and rot were creeping through the structure. Ancient fireplaces had been stolen or shattered and left lying around in pieces. The linenfold panelling had also disappeared. Thieves had ripped it out of the empty building a year or so earlier and sold it for £1 per foot to the Architectural Salvage and Supply Company in Shoreditch, the proprietors of which recognised its exceptional rarity and saw that it was returned to the National Trust.

Sutton House has a remarkable collection of rooms: the recently stripped sixteenth-century linenfold room, the panelled seventeenth-century Great Chamber, and an undamaged early Georgian room being among its obvious attractions. But though a mixture of styles was to be expected, it was still surprising to find stretches of Jacobean strap-work wall painting disappearing abruptly under the coats of post-war emulsion that covered them, or, for that matter, to see these remaining touches of institutional, Welfare State decor covered over in turn with punk-baroque embellishments added during the squat that had occupied the empty building in 1985. The upstairs rooms were full of fall-out from those distraught days. There was debris everywhere: tattered old clothes, fragments of bedding, broken chairs, and a shattered Gestetner machine that lay on the floor among the printed blanks for a petition demanding that the National Trust continue negotiations with members of the squat who wanted to turn Hackney's country house into a properly established commune and cultural centre under the name of 'The Blue House'. Some of the door frames had been recarved and the walls were scribbled over with mutant insignia, stoned musings, and ornately illustrated calls for 'Anarchy in the UK'. After forty-nine years in the care of the National Trust, Sutton House was certainly a sight to see.

I made this visit in the company of Martin Village, who introduced himself as a developer of the 'post-hippy' variety, and Mike Gray, a former member of Hackney Communist Party who had since turned his attention to Hackney's endangered historical buildings. As a trio we were scarcely on amicable terms. Mike Gray was there as one of the local residents who at that time were organising to prevent the National Trust going through with plans it had already drawn up to sell the lease of Sutton House to Martin Village, who was ready to convert the semi-derelict building into five private flats. Village himself seemed adamant that the last thing Sutton House needed was ignorant sentimentalists coming along and stirring up public hostility to his scheme. In his view, Sutton House was lucky to have found a developer of taste (and Village did have some credentials in that area) who was prepared at least to consider building some limited form of community access into his plans for private residential conversion. Since this was, in all likelihood, the building's last chance, it would surely be irresponsible or deluded to stand in his way. But Mike Gray was not going to be squeezed into that corner. From where he stood it seemed that the National Trust had simply decided, without consulting local people (or even its own members in the borough), that Hackney was the wrong place for a country house, and it was now eager to seize the opportunity presented by rising property prices to get rid of its awkward charge once and for all. Gray had already written to the *Hackney Gazette* urging the borough council to take the initiative over this 'unique vestige of the medieval village of Hackney' and ensure that it was saved 'for all the people of Hackney and beyond – not just for a few rich enough to purchase the no doubt very expensive flats'.[2] As another member of the emerging 'Save Sutton House Campaign' added a couple of weeks later: 'It is iniquitous that this unique link with Hackney's past should be reserved solely for the enjoyment of the few with money enough to purchase the wildly expensive flats to which it will almost certainly be converted. . . . The borough council should be opposing this "privatisation" of the heritage of the people of Hackney'.[3] These calls to action had soon goaded Mr Sandy Craig, Head of Arts and Entertainments for Hackney Council, to write in with the purpose of shifting the blame back to the National Trust. Stepping nimbly past the repeated suggestion that the council should have taken the house over as the obvious base for its proposed new museum, he remarked that he too would 'dearly love' to see Sutton House restored: 'And I am sure if it had been located somewhere like Hampstead, the National Trust would have found the funds to restore it'.

How had Sutton House fallen into this dismal state? Embarrassed by the attention their obscure property in east London was beginning to receive, the National Trust were quick to offer an apologetic account of the building's recent history. Hackney Council had leased it as an office for its social services department in 1971, and then from 1975 the house had served as the head office of the white-collar trade union ASTMS. The location was certainly inconvenient, but the property developer and union boss, Clive Jenkins, was never short of self-esteem, and he doesn't appear to have been averse to the idea of having baronial panelling in his office. ASTMS had departed with controversial suddenness, in the early Eighties, leaving the National Trust with an empty building and an unresolved stretch of lease outstanding. The trust claimed that it had tried to find an appropriate tenant to replace ASTMS. Indeed, the concerned officer obligingly rattled off a long list of potential users, all of whom had eventually dropped out or been found inappropriate: the University of New Hampshire had been interested, as had a meditation society, two education foundations, a language school, a housing coop, an inner-city enterprise agency, a Caribbean community centre, and the Sainsbury Charitable Trust. There had also been discussions with Hackney Council about possible 'community use' or turning the house into the new borough museum, and it was only when these talks came to nothing that the trust advertised in the *Estates Gazette* for a developer willing to spend an estimated £300,000 on the building. A mental health foundation expressed interest but soon backed off, and that left Martin Village as the most suitable applicant. As I was told repeatedly, the National Trust really had tried.

But though the officers of the National Trust were quick to provide this account of their present difficulties, one only had to ask them about the older history of the house to come up against a complete blank. In fact, as the trust's librarian told me with engaging honesty over the phone, the file had long since been 'lost' and the conditions under which the building had been acquired just before World War Two were wholly obscure. Local memory could fill in some of the picture. Older people, like Mr Piesse, the keyholder, remembered how the house had been home to a number of voluntary organisations during and immediately after the war. They also recalled how, before the war, it had been known as 'The Old House at the Corner' and taken for granted as part of the local scene. It was owned by the local church and was used as a boys' club – St John's Institute (or the 'tute', for short) – and there were still women in the area who remembered, with varying degrees of irritation, being allowed in as girls only to help with the washing-up and other domestic chores.

After rummaging around in the Hackney archives, Mike Gray discovered that the building had come to the National Trust after a public appeal made through the conventional medium of a letter to *The Times* in December 1936. St John's Church lacked the funds to carry out vital repairs on the building, and the rector was offering the freehold for sale at £2,500, a sum with which he intended to build new and 'more suitable' club premises. It was estimated that the repairs would demand an additional £500. The house was declared 'the most interesting secular building in the East End of London'. Though its history was 'uncertain', it was certainly, as the Royal Commission of Historical Monuments was said to have agreed, 'a monument well worthy of preservation'. The letter of appeal boasted three influential signatories: Lord Crawford and Balcarres, President of the London Survey Committee and the London Society; Lord Esher, the Chairman of the Society for the Protection of Ancient Buildings; and George Lansbury, who was here described as a Vice-President of the National Trust.

George Lansbury's involvement was something of an eye-opener. To the extent that this great East End figure is remembered at all, he is known as a radical Christian socialist – a pacifist and unilateral disarmer, an unwavering supporter of women's rights, and, at the time of the Sutton House campaign, a vociferous opponent of the anti-semitic thugs following the fascist Oswald Mosley through east London. Lansbury held numerous positions in his long life (he was leader of the Labour Party, long-standing MP for Bow and Bromley, Mayor of Poplar, and a founding editor of Labour's first newspaper the *Daily Herald*), but he is not remembered for his involvement with the National Trust. Indeed, fifty years after his death, we may be a little surprised, as the National Trust itself certainly was, to discover that this vehement advocate of social progress and slum clearance was also a conservationist. But Lansbury, who was famous in his time as the 'John Bull of Poplar', was a man who liked, in his own words, looking backwards as well as forwards.[4] As a young man he had found his socialism in the company of figures such as William Morris, the conservationist revolutionary who had welcomed him into the Social Democratic Federation in 1890. Later on, as First Commissioner for Works in the second Labour government (1929–31), Lansbury was responsible for preserving ancient monuments and managing the royal parks, and he had impressed his civil servants – who were apprehensive about the arrival of a minister determined to popularise the parks – with his enthusiasm for this apparently marginal job. As his biographer wrote: 'No previous First Commissioner had delighted more in preserving ancient monuments or been more willing to visit them'.[5]

Lansbury's committment to both conservation and social reform carried over into the appeal for Sutton House. The house would be saved for its historical interest (the leaflet cited the 'fine staircase and splendid Tudor, Jacobean and Georgian panelling', which showed it to have been 'the residence of some substantial citizen of Hackney'), but the appeal saw no contradiction between this and the continued public and institutional use it also foresaw for the building. The boys' club would move on as soon as the church had built new premises with the proceeds of the sale, but it was promised that even after that date, the institute would itself 'continue to be used for the public and social services'. Visiting Sutton House nearly fifty years later, and finding it vandalised and about to be sold on for private residential development, one could only wonder what had happened to the combination of preservation and social reform that had been the ideal not just of Lansbury but also, thanks partly to the influence of William Morris himself, of the original founders of the National Trust.

Conservation against Reform

George Lansbury died in 1940, and by the time Labour came to power in 1945 his vision of conservation and social progress combined was already beginning to look like an implausible relic. Formed after the election victory of 26 July, the Attlee government promised a new idea of the nation, confident that enlightened social reform could be achieved through the State. Tradition was a hindrance to be overcome, and history was a matter of progress, of looking forward rather than back. Intractable social problems would be tackled by the new institutions of the Welfare State. The economy would not just be mixed, it would be pushed, prodded, and squeezed until it delivered prosperity. The very soil of the nation would be revitalised as public policy reformed the wasteful traditions of the private farm. As for the remaining fragments of the old world, if these merited conservation the new government would gladly hand them over to the National Trust.

But Attlee's was not the only Utopia on offer in 1945. Evelyn Waugh's *Brideshead Revisited* had been published at the beginning of that year, and it treated the country house not as a dead relic but as a potent symbol of everything that was threatened by modernisation and reform. While Attlee's vision was full of future promise, Waugh's (which was seen as an irrelevant joke by many readers at the time) faced the other way and paid its tribute to a superior and traditional England, idealised and saluted 'at the moment of extinction.'[6] Waugh's country house was certainly no obscure boys' club in Hackney. Instead, it was a grand and fondly remembered place of classical fountains and white raspberries, of mahogany-framed bathtubs, and rounds of halma played with Nanny Hawkins; and it could hardly expect to survive in a modern world where, even before the Army came along and turned its landscaped valley (planted in the eighteenth century 'so that, at about this date, it might be seen in its maturity') into an assault course, one traditional building after another was being razed to make way for 'blocks of flats'.

There had been concern about the fate of the great country houses before the war. By 20 August 1923 the *Daily Mail* had seen trouble on the horizon: 'Rural England has still the air of a land of ancestral peace and happiness, though there are, as we know only too well, skeletons hidden away in the rural cupboards. The old family houses, for example, are changing hands; many of them are being put to use as hotels or institutions'. In 1925 C. E. Montague diagnosed the great country house as dying from wounds sustained during the Great War and described the 'chilly fear' that had crept into 'the old squirearchical life'.[7] Introducing a book on *The English Country House* in 1935, Sir Osbert Sitwell had sounded a similarly gloomy note from Renishaw Hall near Sheffield:

> Alas! How curious it is that these works of art only begin to obtain a wide appreciation when they are on the verge of being destroyed. . . . What country houses of any size, one wonders, can hope to survive the next fifty years? . . . And, indeed, as I sit writing these lines in an old house, I recall that two great houses in the neighbourhood have been dismantled and gutted within the last few years.[8]

World War Two promised only to hasten the decline. In a story called 'The Martyrdom of the House', the anarchist novelist, Alex Comfort, described the destruction of an old house by passing troops in France ('it was as if a piece of the old world . . . had come back to them, without purpose'), remarking that the violation of a historic building could seem more shocking than any human casualty: 'The deaths of people, even of people that one knows, seem somehow to involve less'.[9] The damage was less catastrophic at home, but the militarised country house still emerged as a poignant neo-romantic symbol. In 1941 Alan Sorrell painted Nissen huts and barbed wire in the grounds of Bradwell Lodge in Essex, a house that had been requisitioned from Tom Driberg, entitling the finished piece 'The Officer's Mess at an RAF Station'.[10] John Piper showed numerous country houses (including Osbert Sitwell's Renishaw Hall) under dark and menacing skies, their overgrown wrought-iron gates and tumbling classical columns emblematic of the nation's danger.[11] Michael Ayrton and John Arlott found their symbolic house in Bitterne Manor at Clausentum near Southampton.[12] The site had apparently been 'in human occupation for over two thousand years', but it now stood empty ('probably for the first time in over a thousand years'), and much 'damaged by fire and bomb-blast during the past seven years'. The pair visited it repeatedly, attracted by its 'air of peace and isolation': the grounds had been made into allotments, 'the front of the house has been used as a rifle range and hooligans have defaced the walls and torn away the woodwork.' Arlott composed a sequence of sonnets about the house while Ayrton made drawings, and they published their book 'without expectation' but nevertheless in 'the hope that some steps may be taken to preserve this parcel of land, its trees, its buildings'.

Few of these mournful visions of the English country house at war could look forward without anticipating worse to come. Indeed, the threat of post-war institutional use could, even then, seem more worrying than Hitler's bombs. In late 1939 Sir Kenneth Clark prepared instructions for artists employed through the Pilgrim Trust's 'Recording Britain Scheme', describing country houses and their parks as being especially worthy of record since 'these will be largely abandoned after the war and will either fall into disrepair or be converted into lunatic sanataria'.[13] In his novel, *Peal of Ordnance* (1947), John Lodwick shows just how wartime requisitioning gave way, for many such houses, to the institutional regimes of the Welfare State. Part of his story is set at 'Stevenham Hall' near Uxbridge, a 'low-built Georgian mansion' that stands in 'pleasant, undulating parkland, the green monotony of which is broken here and there by clumps of elms enclosed within iron railings'.[14] Despite its 'gleaming windows and a graceful portico', the house is actually in service as a home for disabled ex-servicemen, a use seen to have both positive and negative aspects. As the resident doctor remarks, 'This is a govern-

ment institution, as you know, but we only rent the house and
grounds. The coverts and all the game in them are still controlled by
the original owners'. Since the wandering hero to whom these words
are addressed has just been injured by a large and mutilating gin-trap
set in those same coverts by the game-keepers of the old regime, it is,
at least at this point, clear where the brutality lies. When it comes to
architectural and aesthetic considerations, however, the story is
different. As Lodwick writes of the huge refectory: 'Once it must have
been a very fine room indeed, but the symmetry of the oak panelling
was armed now by hideous and singularly inappropriate official fly-
bills . . . "V.D. . . . a shadow on Your health" . . . "There's Danger on
the Roads", and so forth.' Under the new regime the life of the house
is governed not by ideas of taste or ancestral continuity but by a
bureaucratic kind of regulation epitomised by the morning bell, at
which everyone jumps for the bed-pan, and the buxom, muscular
nurses who bustle about, enforcing routines, noting bowel movements, and leading the men into their regular recitations of Grace.
Enlisting the help of a Cockney called Bert, a character who may well
have passed through the boys' club at St John's Institute before
becoming a soldier, Lodwick offers his reader a spoof guided tour of a
country house in which aesthetics have been replaced by a taxonomy
of mutilation. He shows a 'recreation room' in which patients play
ping-pong, weave portraits of the royal family, or make baskets and
model ships to be sold through charity, and then a large ward in
which beds are positioned according to types of disability: 'all those
who were legless (and they were half the total number) had been
placed on one side, while on the other lay cases not less tragic but
more miscellaneous: two locomotor ataxias, then the unipeds and
single leg and arm men, and so on' right down to the unfortunate
Harry who 'don't shave no more'. Further along this gruesomely
hierarchical 'skittle-alley' of a corridor, we are promised the sight of
eleven 'geezers without no kisser', but Lodwick doesn't take us that
far, settling instead for a smaller four-bed ward in which he allows this
new martydom of the house to be entirely upstaged by the mutilated
condition of the armless and legless Cockney who lies there talking
about his pension of four pounds a week.

   Lodwick allowed the requisitioned country house to drift between
positive and negative interpretations, but it was an altogether more
reactionary evaluation that was gathered up into the emerging cult of
Brideshead. The extremes of this position were to be found in a novel
published by Dornford Yates in January 1945. *The House that Berry
Built* told of 'White Ladies', a country house in Hampshire that, for
predictable reasons, had been signed over to the nation in 1937.[15]
With their ancestral home now in use as 'an official retreat for the
Secretary of State for Foreign Affairs', the Pleydell family move to the
Pyrenees where they discover a 'little, English meadow, locked in the
arms of France' and, using their own cultural instinct rather than the

superficial expertise of professional architects, set about rebuilding the house, which could no longer be sustained in the deteriorated nation that had once been home. The war was one problem, but even before this a general election – described as 'probably the finest argument for dictatorship the world had ever seen' – had brought people into the cabinet who 'would not have qualified for the reference traditionally accorded to the incompetent charwoman'. For Dornford Yates, who was rarely short of an explanation where a convenient Jew or communist could be found, the truth had been 'swamped' and the country rendered uninhabitable by political manipulation, betrayal, and the parliamentary rise of the Labour Party.

Yet despite these dire warnings, the total levelling of the old ancestral nation never quite took place. There were many sad losses, but the securing of the country house against the taxing drift of post-war times stands, without doubt, as a major cultural achievement of the last fifty years. In the pre-war world of *Brideshead Revisited*, the 'Georgian Society' can only protest hopelessly as fine old houses all round the country are razed to make way for luxurious new 'blocks of flats'. But by the late Forties a considerably more effective lobby was stating its case against a reforming government that had already started to stumble. By 1948, for example, *Country Life* was describing its own more confident project on the back of the guidebooks it published for the National Trust:

> In a famous phrase Canning spoke of 'recalling the New World . . . to redress the balance of the old.' It is not a mere play on words to claim that one of the constant endeavours of *Country Life*, in these restless and changeable times, is to recall the Old World to redress the balance of the New. . . . *Country Life* believes that the present cannot dispense with the cumulative wisdom of the past; that unless progress and tradition go hand in hand, and good taste is preserved, there is a grave danger of destroying the good with the bad in our efforts to rebuild Britain.[16]

Cultivated as a quotation from a supposedly grander age, the country house came to sparkle with new and distinctly contemporary significance as it was played off against the grey prose of the post-war settlement. Just as the medieval heaven needed the horrors of hell to keep its celestial features clear, the preserved country house came to depend on a pervasive sense of threat for its own clarity of definition. This was hardly the combination of conservation and reform, tradition, and progress that George Lansbury had imagined at Hackney's country house. Moreover, this polarised view of the country house was not just confined to paintings and novels. By 1945, it had found effective institutional support in the Country Houses Scheme of the National Trust.

The Man of the Moment

Sutton House fell into its ruinous state in an anniversary year. The trust's Country Houses Scheme was fifty years old in April 1987, and the *Spectator*, at least, had been punctual in its celebration of an organisation that, as it claimed, had been 'holding the bridge' for half a century.[17] Founded in the 1890s, the National Trust has a long familiarity with the polar opposition between 'heritage' and 'danger'. But while 'heritage' has been among its keywords since the early days (Hardwicke Rawnsley, a founder of the trust, published a book called *A Nation's Heritage* in 1920), its meaning has been far from constant. The trust spent its early decades promoting a public and national interest in land and small buildings threatened by destructive private ownership. The large country house didn't become an issue until 1934, when Lord Lothian addressed the Annual General Meeting on this emerging theme. At this time, the trust only owned two such buildings – Montacute and Barrington Court. By 1945 the number had risen to seventeen. By 1990 the figure stood at eighty-seven. In 1942 the trust's membership stood at 6,000 and its paid staff at just six people. By now it has considerably more than two million people in membership and the staff (excluding volunteers and people working on government-funded job-creation schemes run by the trust) stands at about 2,000. The growth and re-orientation of the the National Trust as it rose to the new challenge of the country house stands among the more telling developments of the Welfare State era.

In March 1936, and at the suggestion of Vita Sackville-West, James Lees-Milne was employed by the National Trust as its first historic buildings secretary. Lees-Milne has always been a man of pronounced views on cultural matters, but his task at the National Trust was partly pragmatic. As John Gaze writes in his history of the National Trust, the country house was the 'citadel and treasury' of old England's power base and 'the campaign to remove it from its exposed position on the battlefield, obliged its would-be rescuers to penetrate and dismantle all the defences which had been erected to protect it'.[18]

While the Country House Committee, chaired by Lord Esher, worked to secure the legal and administrative changes that were necessary before the scheme could really take off, Lees-Milne was out on the road as England's most unlikely public servant. His job was to reconnoitre the great houses of England and assess their importance in a quick and decisive manner. Bunkered and suspicious owners then had to be persuaded that the National Trust could offer a genuinely acceptable solution to their escalating financial problems: not just the polite cover under which a National or Labour government was about to expropriate their land and property. The offer was accommodating enough. In fact, as Lord Lothian had suggested in his 1934 speech, aristocratic families were to be preserved along with their houses, their ancestral aura becoming a vital part of the display. Houses would have to open their doors to the public, but in the early days of the Country Houses Scheme, this inconvenience could be confined to thirty or so days in the year. Negotiations between owners and the trust were often difficult and protracted – at Knole they extended over more than ten years – but James Lees-Milne saw them through. A man of passionate right-wing outlook, he was able to bridge the gap between the statutory interest, which he represented but also held at long arm's length, and the defensive attitudes of the aristocratic owners he found lurking in the disintegrating piles of wartime England.

Lees-Milne's published diaries, covering the period from 1942 to 1947, offer a unique account of this period. As he travels around the country on his bicycle or, as petrol rationing allowed, at the wheel of the National Trust's faltering old Austin, Lees-Milne turns gossip into an art-form and, almost incidentally, creates a remarkable picture of England that could only expect to survive the war – to say nothing of Attlee's progressive peace – in scattered fragments saved and preserved by the National Trust. The house is run down, the servants have gone, and the maddened family battles on heroically in the few rooms that have not been invaded and turned into a billet by the RAF or, more exotically, as Lees-Milne found at Faringdon House in 1944, become 'stiff with' black American GIs.[19]

Some of the aristocrats who turned their ancestral homes over pleaded a socialist motivation. Sir Charles Trevelyan gave the huge Wallington Estate in Northumberland because, as he said in 1941, he was a socialist and believed it would be better in the future if 'the community' owned the great estates; Lord Astor wanted Cliveden (a house the National Trust now leases out as a luxury hotel) to be used either by the trade-union movement or by an American university.[20] But though Lees-Milne was certainly involved in the promotion of schemes that would preserve historic houses by adapting them for a variety of institutional uses, he thought about his activities in altogether more idealistic terms. Indeed, his autobiographical writings portray the early Country Houses Scheme as a kind of English neo-romanticism in action. The young Lees-Milne shared in that characteristically neo-romantic structure of feeling that combines reverence for the heritage with an equally vivid sense of the dangers threatening it. Like Charles Ryder in *Brideshead Revisited*, he idealised the country house at its apparent moment of extinction. In *Another Self*, an autobiography written in the late Sixties, he traces this polarised sense of heritage and danger back to the very foundation of his outlook as a young man.[21] After growing up in a manor house in Worcestershire, a county of traditional delights that he saw as being threatened by all the ruinous and expropriating forces that would later mass on Crichel Down, Lees-Milne arrived in Oxford in time for his worst fears to be confirmed.

One summer evening, and here the autobiography reads like a fable, Lees-Milne was taken to Rousham, a Jacobean house on the Cherwell then leased to a 'capricious alcoholic' who liked to entertain undergraduates. As he got into his stride this fellow started whipping the family portraits (Knellers and Reynoldses) with a riding crop so that the paint flaked off. He then took a gun out onto the terrace and began blasting away at the private parts of statues, which had been set in the garden by William Kent in the 1740s. James Lees-Milne describes the evening as a turning point in his life:

> It brought home to me how passionately I cared for architecture and the continuity of history, of which it was the mouthpiece. I felt sick as many people would feel sick if they watched from a train window an adult torturing a child, while they were powerless to intervene. Those Rococo rooms at Rousham, with their delicate furniture, and portraits of bewigged, beribboned ancestors, were living, palpable children to me. They and the man-fashioned landscape outside were the England that mattered. I suddenly saw them as infinitely fragile and precious. They meant to me then, and have meant ever since, far more than human lives. They represent the things of the spirit. And the ghastly truth is that like humans, they are not perdurable.[22]

This was the blinding moment of revelation on Lees-Milne's road to Damascus. Suddenly the true priorities of his life were revealed and, as his brighter but unknowing fellows caroused, he made a secret vow: 'I vowed that I would devote my energies and abilities, such as they were, to preserving the country houses of England'.

Considering Lees-Milne's influence in the years to come, it may not be entirely fanciful to see that debauched evening at Rousham as the symbolic moment from which the post-war cult of the country house has grown. It was certainly savoured as just such an inaugural moment in the tributes that were paid to Lees-Milne on the recent occasion of his eightieth birthday.[23]

While Oxford gave lasting definition to Lees-Milne's idea of the endangered cultural heritage, it is a less generally acknowledged fact that it also shaped his sense of the dangers menacing it. Indeed, if there is love in one paragraph, there must – according to the romantic structure of feeling governing this remarkable autobiography – be hatred in the next. Hatred, as Lees-Milne writes in *Another Self*, 'is deemed to be a great sin; but it can be a salutary emotion, a cleanser of the spirit. . . . One cannot love without hating, and without love one is not alive. So it is often one's bounden duty to hate'. And what Lees-Milne adopted as the primary object of his hatred was not just the wealthy vandal like the man at Rousham who wrecks irreplaceable works of art, but communism, the evil ideology that, as Lees-Milne recognised, does the same thing for the entire human spirit.

The young Lees-Milne was not a man after George Lansbury's heart. He was a right-wing maverick: a romantic anarchist, a pacifist who sympathised with the appeasers and canvassed briefly for Oswald Mosley's New Party, backing off some years before Mosley arrived at Dalston Junction to rally his blackshirted thugs to a more local vision of heritage and danger in the old Maberly Chapel. He was a passionate convert to Catholicism who saw communism as the devil's creed and wished he had fought for Franco in the Spanish Civil War. He hated Churchill for siding with Stalin in the war against Hitler, thus allowing a war of true ideals to degenerate into a war between nations, and as the war proceeded he found himself attaching far greater value to old buildings than to people. On seeing the bombed Regency terraces along the seafront at Dover, he remembers being 'far more worried by the loss of the old buildings . . . than the lives'.[24] Similarly, when he mentions Belsen after the war, it is to describe the fate of Lansdowne House in Berkeley Square – a house by Robert Adam that, as he wrote, had been mutilated and butchered by philistines in the Thirties and then forced into humiliating service as a 'luxury club'.[25]

To begin with, Lees-Milne associated his sense of danger with communism and the shameful iconoclasm of middle-class intellectuals, but after the war he tailored it to new circumstances. The communist menace was certainly still abroad, but its domestic equivalent emerged shortly after Churchill gave way to Attlee in 1945. The problem now was progressive and apparently penal taxation, the greyness of State-led social reform, and the modern 'materialism' that encouraged such disregard for traditional values. When Lees-Milne published his diaries of the immediate post-war period he called them, after Coleridge, *Caves of Ice*: they depict a shabby time, with glacial winters exacerbating the 'hideous muddle' and gloom created by Attlee's Labour government. The electricity supply comes and goes, and the Historic Buildings Committee sits shivering in its furs. The London Library was lit with candles in beer bottles and Lees-Milne remembers spending hours in the National Gallery just to keep warm. This was the unwashed age of the democratic crowd, smelly and offputting as Lees-Milne declared it to be: of public services that were filthy, irregular, and infested with crab lice. Lees-Milne gave his response to the new dawn in the Preface to *The Age of Adam*, a book he published in 1947:

> But today, since Great Britain has won the war, we exist (for human beings have long ceased to live) in a more progressive vacuum – one of political ineptitude, social decadence, spiritual deadlock and artistic gelidity. We are, for the time being, tired of destroying. There is of course so much less of merit left to destroy, and while we are still allowed by those little subfusc men at Westminster to retain a semblance of our native sanity, we may yet

soothe our minds – starved like our bellies – in nostalgic reflections upon that earlier, less progressive age, when politics was a game, society an art and art religion. And so our last solace is to let our minds drift, as often as they may, upon delicious tides of retrogression, away from the present quagmire of existence, towards the quickened elegance of eighteenth-century living.

And on those delicious tides James Lees-Milne did indeed find ample solace. He wrote about Robert Adam and Inigo Jones, who brought the classical orders into English architecture. He researched eighteenth-century England's Palladian earls and defended the Italian Baroque as a 'religious manifestation' ('Catholic and primarily Roman') against the condescension of Victorians like Ruskin, that influential 'Dictator of Taste' who had written it off with such arrogant contempt. He compiled guidebooks on the National Trust's growing collection of country houses, recovering the impressions of writers who had described these buildings in earlier, less blighted times. In one such book, he approaches Stourhead (which came to the National Trust in 1947) guided by the words of Hazlitt: 'a rural Herculaneum, a subterranean retreat. . . . Everything has an air of elegance, and yet tells a tale of other times'. On parole from the dingy secular world in which rationing was giving way to the redistributed austerities of the Welfare State, Lees-Milne lingered over the Doric portico of the 'exquisite' Temple of Flora, and hailed Henry Hoare, the maker of Stourhead, as the 'first artist to translate upon English soil the idyllic, picturesque scenery of Italian landscape painters like Salvator Rosa, and Zuccarelli'.

Lees-Milne was not alone in sensing the special poignancy of the decaying country house during the penurious early years of the Welfare State. It was at this time that Georgina Battiscombe chose to celebrate that curious 'by-product of the Romantic Movement' known as the 'English picnic' – 'A picnic is the Englishman's grand gesture, his final defiance flung in the face of fate', and we may be sure that in the post-war years there was no better place to perform this patriotic gesture than in the bewildered grounds of some hard-pressed aristocratic estate.[26] It was at this time, too, that Barbara Jones toured the great estates of Britain in search of the intriguing follies and grottoes that, as she found at Hawkstone in Shropshire, were achieving an entirely new meaning thanks to the fallen condition of their surroundings: 'Today, seeing, as I say, only abandoned or municipal melancholy in almost every park we visit, it is easy to accept melancholy as the intended mood; many of the great estates have now become so sombre that the effect of the follies is reversed, and an Awful Ruin, discovered suddenly, gives no delicious thrill of fear but a moment's cheerful release in curiosity from the heavy sadness of the rides and woods'.[27] Meanwhile, the Press was full of doleful stories on the same theme: as the *Christian Science Monitor* reported for its American readers in 1949, 'socialist Britain's latest private enterprise is opening stately homes' and, as the saying went, 'putting the peer back into the peerage'.[28] Over in Huntingdonshire, the idiosyncratic Tory Lord Hinchinbrooke was already having to add priceless Cromwellian relics to the contents of the ancestral home that he had recently been forced to open to the public, in a desperate attempt to attract more visitors. As the *News Chronicle* reported, 'Mrs Felicia Hemans, who wrote the verse we all know about the stately homes of England – "how beautiful they stand" – would have been petrified at the thought of dukes having to keep up their castles by dint of a bob or two admission fee to hoi polloi. Some future Tory–Socialist Government may indeed schedule our dukes as ancient monuments to be kept up by the state'.[29] The lions had not yet arrived at Longleat, but the Marchioness of Bath was already engaged in the distinctly novel practice of interviewing her servants in order to capture 'the backstairs life of a large country house' for publication in a booklet that would 'recall the days of elegance at Longleat, before the sunset fades, before the moths of war and depression make shreds of a domestic tapestry which can never be replaced'.[30]

As war gave way to peace, the polemical opposition between heritage and danger continued to proliferate luxuriously in Lees-Milne's diary. The instinctive aristocratic culture and naturalised social hierarchy embodied by the country house was quickly lined up against the false enlightenment of 1945. Lees-Milne viewed the democracy of the 'little people' with undisguised contempt, and he scorned attempts to harness the country house to the cause of social-democratic reform. In March 1948, for example, he visited Attingham Park in Shropshire, where George Trevelyan was setting up an adult education college, and his comments are typical: 'A little folk-dancing, some social economy and Fabianism for the miners and their wives. We felt quite sick from the nonsense of it all. At a time when this country is supposed to be bankrupt they spend (our) money on semi-education of the lower classes who will merely learn from it to be dissatisfied. The house looked very forlorn and down at heel which worried me a good deal'.[31]

This polarity between traditional nation and modern society set the private values of the aristocratic house off against the public egalitarian tendencies of the reforming present. It set the ancestral continuities of the aristocratic family off against social-democratic ideas of citizenship. It set high national culture off against the procedural and bureaucratic realities of the modern State. Quickly enough, it also developed a territorial dimension. Some areas of the nation had been lost forever and in these no one should expect to find the traditional nation at all. The East End of London was clearly one such place. In April 1946, after ten years as Historic Buildings Secretary, Lees-Milne made his first visit to what has remained the trust's only property in the East End of London. After looking over

Sutton House, the man who had done so much to bring the large country houses (real treasure houses like Knole) into the protective arms of the trust, declared this poor cousin to be a 'wretched' property and 'no more important than hundreds of other Georgian houses still left in slum areas. Very derelict after the bombing all around it. Tenanted by a number of charitable bodies. It does have one downstair room of linenfold panelling. I found it terribly depressing and longed to hurry away'.[32] Bombs may not have been so absolutely good for these slums as they were for John Betjeman's unrelievedly modern Slough, but with the true nation beleaguered and needing urgent assistance in the shires, Hackney's relic could be abandoned to the municipal oblivion that was already engulfing it. When Lees-Milne prepared the National Trust's guide to its buildings in 1948, Sutton House was not among the properties he chose to mention.[33]

Redeeming the Rubbish

None of this polarised rhetoric would suggest it, but Attlee's post-war government actually did a great deal to support the work of the National Trust. As Chancellor of the Exchequer, Hugh Dalton supported the trust's 1945 Jubilee Appeal, promising to match every pound given by members of the public with a pound from the State. Funds were available from the newly established National Land Fund, and more generally, Aneurin Bevan provided special subsidies to ensure that, at least in environmentally sensitive areas, new building was carried out in traditional stone.[34] But though the National Trust's own most recent historian acknowledges Attlee's as the first national government that was 'not only prepared but anxious to advance the Trust's interests', the symbolism that attached to the country house pointed in a different direction.[35]

From the beginning, the National Trust's entirely laudable concern that grand ancestral homes and their collections should be preserved in the public interest was shadowed by a frankly reactionary assessment of post-war social and political developments. Since the early Forties, when so many feared that the game was finally up, the country house has been preserved, developed as a countervailing image, and hammered back into the culture that nearly presided over its destruction. Saved not just from the war but from the peace that, in a phrase of Angela Thirkell's, 'broke out' in 1945, it has gone on to inspire a vast and ever more diversified cult. Disaster may certainly still loom for individual buildings, but the overall picture has improved beyond measure. By 1959, as John Cornforth has pointed out, Evelyn Waugh expressed surprise at the survival of these apparently doomed buildings, admitting in a new Preface that he had 'piled it on rather' when writing *Brideshead Revisited*. Ralph Dutton's book on *The English Country House* was reprinted in 1962, and a similar, although unacknowledged, adjustment ensured that Osbert Sitwell's 1935 'Foreword' had quietly lost the gloomy concluding paragraph quoted earlier.

Nothing in the post-war cult better illustrates how far the trust has drifted from Lansbury's imagined combination of conservation and social reform than the interior aesthetic that has been built up around the preserved country house since the war. Country houses have come to the trust through an arrangement that guarantees continued rights of residence to the family. As Lord Lothian had remarked in the 1934 address that put the large country house on the trust's agenda, it was esssential to recognise that 'preserve includes use as a dwelling house. Nothing is more melancholy than to visit these ancient houses after they have been turned into public museums'.[36] The same point was made repeatedly through the war: as Anne Scott-James wrote in *Picture Post* in 1944,

> The breaking-up of the great family may be a necessity of the times; but you would have to be peculiarly indifferent to history and tradition to see Blenheim without a Marlborough, Arundel without a Norfolk, without regret. When the prosperous electricity has eaten up the poor, but lovely valley, when all the great houses are hospitals, when the loyalty and good fellowship of the age of patronage have gone (for it was not all exploitation) – which of us will not feel a little empty and bleak?[37]

In 1934, both the large country houses owned by the trust were empty shells, but by 1945, of the seventeen houses in ownership, nine were still inhabited by the families of their donors.

It has been suggested that it was only in the Sixties, by which time so many country houses had been restored, sorted out by 'experts', and opened to the public as museums, that the 'mystery' and 'pleasing decay' of houses that remained private ancestral homes – especially in Ireland – began to achieve a 'particular appeal'.[38] In reality, however, the interior aesthetic adopted by the National Trust for its country houses has made a special feature of ancestral continuity from the very start. The family itself is incorporated into the exhibition: its possessions displayed in a vital associational context, which ensures that the whole is always more than the sum of its parts. The basic features of this interior aesthetic were outlined early in World War Two by Vita Sackville-West, a vigorous pioneer of the preserved country house who, having grown up at Knole, was busy establishing her own ancestral home at nearby Sissinghurst (recently acquired in ruinous state as the place where her ancient forebears had lived) – at the same time as writers like Evelyn Waugh, Osbert Sitwell and Dornford Yates were fearing the worst. The Battle of Britain raged overhead, but Vita Sackville-West held her ground, reinstating the garden (which is now one of the most evocative in the National Trust's care), and retreating to her writing room in the Elizabethan tower to hymn the unique qualities of the threatened English Country House.[39]

Above all, Sackville-West insisted that the authentic country house was 'a home of men and women', a 'living thing' that would lose its very soul if it were put to institutional use as a school, asylum, hotel, or a 'dead' museum. The true country-house interior was an organic domain, which had 'grown' over the centuries. There could be no serious question of 'period' rooms like those that were 'so beloved of professional decorators'. Instead, 'Everything is muddled up' in a gloriously untidy clutter: 'You may find Jacobean panelling, Chippendale tables, Chinoiserie wall-papers, Carolean love seats, Genoa velvets, Georgian brocades, Burgundian tapestries, Queen Anne embroideries, William and Mary Tallboys, Elizabethan bread cupboards, and even Victorian sideboards', all in such a mixture as to 'make the purist shudder'. Where, as Sackville-West asked with precise wartime resonance, is the 'Dictator of taste to say who is right and who wrong, what is "good" and what is "bad"? All we know is that our ancestors piled up their possessions generation by generation, and somehow managed to create a whole which is far more of a whole than any whole deliberately composed.'

In this beleaguered appreciation, the country-house interior is grasped as a place of undesigned enchantment where objects achieve an incremental and associational significance. In Stephen Bann's terms this interior is a place of 'synecdoche', where the whole is always greater than the sum of its parts and where value is emphatically not just of the tradeable kind.[40] If the continuities of ancestral residence were to be broken, then the associational magic would die. If an object were to be removed – to auction house or public museum – both that object and the setting from which it had been taken would be debased. Just as John Fowler, the advocate of 'humble elegance' and 'pleasing decay' who would become the trust's favoured 'decorator' in the late Fifties, scorned the idea of 'design', James Lees-Milne distinguished the true country-house interior from the 'contrived "old world" flavour' of an architect like Lutyens. Thus, for example, in June 1944 Lees-Milne visited Lord and Lady Braybrooke at Audley End, and his description seems to echo Sackville-West: 'The great hall and the Fish Saloon are very impressive. There is an early nineteenth-century flavour in the paintwork of the rooms. The portrait copies in the Saloon are atrocious. Some Adam suites of furniture are good of their kind, but there is a great deal of indifferent stuff in the rooms, which makes Audley End a true English country house, and not a museum'.[41] When I talked to him, in 1988, he stressed the attraction of 'a little patrician decay', remarking that in his time the trust had relished 'the old boot jack, the dog basket, the pipe and tobacco pouch, the sticks and hats in the hall'. The ancestral magic haunting the interior of the English country house was so potent it could even make ordinary household junk ('irrelevant trash', as Lees-Milne called it) glow with special significance. Indeed, since the Reynolds and Gainsboroughs could stand up anywhere, the lustrous clobber was, in some respects, more important to the atmosphere.

Since the Forties, this defensive idea of the country-house interior has emerged as one of the more influential creations of post-war British culture. Behind the door, which only the trust can open with proper discretion, lies an esoteric chamber of private association where the centuries are still in place. Preserved against a modern world where history has degenerated into false 'progress', the National Trust interior is one of the few places where the past has been allowed to accumulate undisturbed. This interior has continued to turn up regularly throughout the Eighties: at threatened country houses like Calke Abbey (where the National Trust has worked hard to retain and restore much of the ancestral 'junk' that achieved such notoriety in 1983, when the house was saved for the nation) or at Brodsworth Hall, another cluttered and time-warped pile that came to the nation's attention during a similar emergency a few years later.[42] It appeared in Bohemian, if not frankly psychotic, guise in 1987 when the contents of Stephen Tennant's Wilsford Manor – a motley collection that had been left to moulder through the many years which the untalented Tennant himself spent declining in bed – were exhibited to crowds of enthusiastic visitors who had parked their Volvos and Porsches in a stubble field and flocked into the usual striped marquee to pay culturally enhanced prices for every bit of charismatic junk that passed under Sotheby's hammer.

The National Trust interior was also there, coming back triumphantly after years of taxing reform, when Brideshead became a television spectacular in 1981 ('You see, it's like this', said Sebastian Flyte throwing open the drawing-room shutters after thirty-five years of the Welfare State), and its influence can also be detected in the obsessively detailed sets of any number of lesser television history productions: nineteenth-century dramatists like August Strindberg tried to get the clutter out of the theatre in order to create an 'intimate' dramatic atmosphere, but thanks to the influence of the country-house interior even the actors in television history dramas seem now to be chosen by the prop department. Designers have boomed on the National Trust interior, from Colefax and Fowler in the Sixties to Laura Ashley and Next in the Eighties, the latter being designed initially by David Davies, a leading advocate of 'undesign' who has gone on to greater things under his own name. The public museum, which for years has served as a metaphor for the 'institutional' inhumanity of the reforming State, has admitted defeat and started, under the directorship of figures like Timothy Clifford and Sir Roy Strong, to imitate the National Trust interior, developing styles of display that try to create a sense of interior intimacy where previously there were only objects suspended in statutory space.

This idea of the charismatic country-house interior has also become one of Britain's most successful cultural exports. In 1985, the National Trust took the real thing to Washington with its 'Treasure Houses of Britain' exhibition, mounted at the National Gallery of Art and arranged, appropriately enough, as a series of country-house interiors. Here the spectacular yields of the Country Houses Scheme were amply augmented by objects borrowed from country houses still in private ownership. Designed to promote tourism in Britain, the occasion was efficiently exploited by all sorts of interested parties. Among the shadier beneficiaries was Fine Art Investment and Display Ltd, a company registered only the previous year in the Cayman Islands, which was apparently using the exhibition to advertise a recent acquisition. The object in question was Canova's sculpture of the 'Three Graces', a statue that, three years later, would be removed from its proper associational context in the sculpture temple at Woburn Abbey and sold to the Getty Museum which, having had a chance to examine it at the Washington exhibition, came up with an offer of £7.6 million.[43] Connoisseurs of inner-city blight would find nothing in this grandiose exhibition from the squatted interior of Sutton House.

A number of the National Trust's country-house advisers published books that coincided with the exhibition. John Cornforth's *The Inspiration of the Past* offered eager Americans an education on the subject of 'Country house taste in the twentieth century', and Gervase Jackson-Stops moved into the same market with *The English Country House; a Grand Tour*, a luxuriously presented tome that included photographs by the well-chosen American, James Pipkin.[44] Mrs Alvilde Lees-Milne joined in a few months later with *The Englishman's Room*, a book that combined the customary perspectives of a 'watch the rich' magazine with a sense of the bizarre that might normally be reserved for the reptile house.[45] Among the exotic English gentlemen photographed in their dens were four champions of the National Trust interior, all of whom, as the book revealed, have somehow managed to move in to the chamber of their dreams. Professor Bernard Nevill, designer of many of Liberty's most successful fabrics, is pictured among massive furnishings bought during the sad years when so many of London's traditional clubs fell under the auctioneer's hammer. Gavin Stamp stands in waistcoat and fobwatch in 'the essential profusion of accumulated clutter' he had built up in his 'Standard Late Georgian Fourth Rate London terraced house' near King's Cross. Gervase Jackson-Stops, the National Trust's architectural adviser and organiser of the Washington exhibition, looks considerably better off in his delicately restored mid-eighteenth-century menagerie in Northamptonshire. James Lees-Milne sits at his desk in William Beckford's Grecian Library, sold to him intact, he explains, as part of a 'maisonette' in Bath.

The 'Treasure Houses of Britain' cavalcade appears to have arrived in the States at just the right time. As an American commentator remarked of east-coast fashion in the mid-Eighties: 'We are in a tasteful phase. Call it classic, call it urbane, call it "Laurentian" '.[46] As the mogul of 'lifestyle marketing', Ralph Lauren had picked up some ideas from Liberty and Laura Ashley before the exhibition opened. Since 1984, the Ralph Lauren Collection had been offering well-off Americans everything they need to create a 'total home environment', from furnishings right through to slippers and soap. The collection was available in different lines, and the one named 'Thoroughbred' offered a cleaned-up version of Calke Abbey to affluent Americans who had finally given up on modernism. Under the slogan 'How a Tradition Becomes', the brochures showed mahogany panelling, leather-bound books, ancestral portraits, and sporting accoutrements: as one commentator wrote, the overall effect was 'a bit overwhelming, like being caught inside Rex Harrison's closet'.[47] In 1986, Lauren spent $14 million retheming his 'Limited' store on Madison Avenue. Intent on recreating the interior atmosphere of a turn-of-the-century mansion, he filled it with old mahogany armoires, antique (and ever so slightly frayed) carpets, and grandfather clocks. In no time at all, people were queuing on the street to get in.

By this time the *New York Times* was also leading from its new 'Home' section. It was featuring stories about antique importers like 'Kentshire Galleries' who had used their loft building to set up a series of 'residential vignettes' that added up to 'an instant English country house interior',[48] and about the new kind of 'Establishment Decorator' who was busy fitting the English country-house look into fashion-conscious American homes: the air conditioning was squeezed behind 'matched antique wall-mouldings', the television secreted away in an antique linen press, and all that modernist space replaced by cluttered rooms full of objects that 'talk to each other'.[49] In the words of one such decorator, 'we are not only selling an object but selling the feeling that the object is part of'. As another remarked, 'There's a tremendous affluence in the air and a return to the formal and the conservative'. The *New York Times* even tried to import 'Young Fogeyism', the English cult that had first developed around the young men at the *Spectator*: staying in was announced to be fashionable, and the most stylish clubs were suddenly semi-private and designed to look like sofa-filled living rooms.[50] East-coast 'Young Fogeys' were said to admire the 'young Windsors of Britain' and to 'see home as a haven in which they can be themselves, surrounded by the broken-in comfort of proved classic quality'. Appropriately it was Tom Wolfe, that connoisseur of the cliché, who registered the arrival of this latest English contribution in New York. His compendious novel, *The Bonfire of the Vanities*, includes a hypocritical left-wing English journalist (modelled, it would appear, on Alexander Cockburn) who prospers by turning out fawning articles for magazines like *House and Garden*. It also showed the English country-house interior settling into its final resting place on Wall Street's fiftieth floor: imported, cut down to size, and squeezed into place by an enthusiastic banker ('it was as if you were in an English mansion that had been squashed').

The 'Treasure Houses of Britain' exhibition was criticised at the time for placing the private aristocratic past at the centre of its definition of the British nation and for celebrating the aristocrat as a figure of profound culture and humanity.[51] Certainly, the catalogue (a sumptuous volume of almost unprecedented tonnage) makes interesting reading. It includes an essay by Marcus Binney and Gervase Jackson-Stops reviewing 'the last hundred years' of British history from the viewpoint of the country house. This contribution makes it abundantly clear that when the country house is taken as the yardstick of civilisation, every attempt at redistribution and reform looks like high treason: death duties introduced by a liberal government in 1894, Lloyd George's 'People's Budget' of 1909, Ramsay MacDonald's 'socialist party' that caused the idea of domestic service to be considered 'demeaning'. . . .[52]

The argument about ancestral continuity and the superior aura achieved by objects in their proper associational context was also prominently displayed. While the implied criticism of the public museum fits well into an age of cuts, privatisation, and admission charges back home, it found different connections in the United States where it was used to persuade Americans that their own well-stocked museums cannot hope to rival the authenticity of a visit to the old country. This ingenious application of aesthetics to the promotion of tourism was good patriotic stuff, but there is more to the catalogue than this. In his discussion of 'The British as Collectors', Francis Haskell, Professor of Art History at Oxford University, quotes from what in the years of the country-house aesthetic has indeed become something of an inaugural moment for the National Trust. Haskell presses back through the Thirties and Forties when the unique ancestral atmosphere of the country-house interior was so influentially defined by the champions of the new Country Houses Scheme. He presses back beyond the 1890s, when the National Trust was actually formed. Haskell raised the voice of Quatremère de Quincy, the French archaeologist and theorist of museums, from the 1790s. It was then that the Museum of French Monuments was established in Paris: a public institution set up by the revolutionary authorities to save valued artefacts from the blows of overzealous republicans, and to incorporate them into programmes of political re-education. As Haskell has described elsewhere, Chateaubriand and other figures of the right condemned this disenchanting (and short-lived) museum as a wretched attempt to separate art from its proper identity with Church, Aristocracy, and Monarchy.[53] It was, so Haskell claims, in his attack on this museum that Quatremère de Quincy launched the modern arguments about the vitality of associational context and the humiliation suffered by works of art when they are exhibited in statutory public space. There could scarcely be clearer illustration of the cultural drift that has beset the National Trust since the Country Houses Scheme was set in train in the Thirties. Established in the 1890s to assert a public interest in landscapes and buildings over the delinquency and neglect of private owners, the post-war country-house aesthetic now offers to refound the organisation in the French 1790s, aligning it with a reactionary assertion of private meaning, and identifying the public interest with the rampaging egalitarianism of a murderous mob. In recent years, the National Trust has been criticised from a variety of viewpoints. Some are content to sneer at the lavender bags and mutter about 'theme-park Britain'. Others, like David Cannadine, disregard the genuine necessity of conservation and condemn the trust for propping up an exhausted aristocracy.[54] From Sutton House, however, the view is different again. From Hackney, we see George Lansbury's vision of conservation and social reform combined being replaced by a polarised opposition between 'heritage' and 'danger', which has gone on to assert the country house against every reforming impulse the century has known. The rising cult of the country house may indeed have kept the odd duke off the dole, but this is scarcely a serious objection. The more significant point, as the briefest visit to Hackney's derelict mansion would reveal, is that the restoration of the country house as a post-war national symbol has been predicated on the failure of the 'institutional' endeavour not just of the public museum but of the entire Welfare State.

7

Abysmal Heights

It is possible to gauge the residents' reactions to a housing
development to some extent by a variety of small signs such as
facial expressions . . .

The Architects' Journal, 21 July 1965.

A few hundred yards from Dalston Lane, due south of the hoarding on
which the Araldite poster appeared, stands a sawn-off Victorian pub.
The Grange Tavern bears Charrington's name, along with the
meaningless inaugural date of 1757, and a sign that struggles to lend a
Palladian air to the neighbourhood: it shows a large and classical-
looking 'grange' with horses, carriages, and the predictable collection
of gentlefolk gathered in the open space before it. Designed like so
many pubs of its time, to command the corner at the end of a terraced
street, the Grange Tavern is now an amputated stump, a relic
stranded in the midst of the famously awful Holly Street Estate, built
by Hackney Council in the early Seventies. The old street runs back
beside this sad hostelry for a few yards, but is then cancelled out by a
monolithic block of flats. To the east there are four huge tower blocks,
plonked down on a dingy stretch of 'open space', which can hardly
compare with the leafy vistas to which the pub sign alludes. Hackney
was among the last councils to recognise the limitations of 'comprehensive redevelopment' as it was practised in the Fifties and Sixties,
but the Grange Tavern stands as a monument to the fitful premon-
itions that came as the final day of awakening approached: a residue
of 'community' transferred from one slum to the next; a tiny
concession to the old map in the Town Guide Cabinet at Dalston
Junction.

I've been looking at the Holly Street Estate for years. Its four,
nineteen-storey tower blocks are widely deplored on this side of
Queensbridge Road as monstrous eyesores that should be blown up.
We survey the burned-out flats with their shattered windows and we
shudder. We read of the drug-dealing, the murders, and the sporadic
defenestrations, maintaining our own informal body count with the
help of the *Hackney Gazette*. When we get burgled we have a way of
glancing up accusingly through long-suffering sash windows.

In Dalston, as elsewhere, the council tower block serves as a
generator of infernal meanings for people who only look at it from
outside. Those who live inside have a different experience, and I

recently decided to walk along the length of this banal and heavily mythologised view so that I could turn and consider what it looked like from the other end. One Sunday I set off to meet Reece Auguiste of the Black Audio Film Collective on the twelfth floor of Rowan Court, the last of the four tower blocks to be built. I walked past Grace Jones Close – a small and generally excellent council estate dating from the early Eighties, that short period when the borough showed unmistakable signs of having finally got it right, just as the whole council housing programme was being brought to a shuddering halt. I walked through Mapledene, an attractive area of mid-Victorian terraces, where residents can sit at their kitchen tables (only a mile or so north of the City) and look out into a richly differentiated green world of gardens and wooded 'backlands'. Suddenly this closely textured realm of Victorian detail gives way to the looming cliff-like austerity of the system-built monolith and the dismal uniformity of planned grass and statutory trees. In the early Fifties Nikolaus Pevsner praised Queensbridge Road for its gracious semi-detached villas, but now it is just a wasted strip of no man's land between visually opposed worlds.[1]

The approach to Rowan Court leads past a stretch of fenced oblivion where the multi-storey car park once stood (tenants quickly learnt better than to leave their cars there, and it was demolished not long after being built). The litter drifts in the air, and one or two dispirited-looking residents prop themselves up on benches in dishevelled simulation of those tiny model citizens who still tend to grace the open spaces around architectural maquettes. Rowan Court sits on its stretch of green void, with a stinking puddle of brown liquid oozing out of the 'textured' (ie marked by the coarse imprint of shuttering boards) concrete lattice-work at its base. The external doors are missing, and there's a cavity where the intercom was ripped out within a few days of being installed. As for the foyer, it is certainly no fashionable 'atrium'. The ceiling is in ruins, with pipes and wire left exposed ever since the council came along to strip the asbestos. The walls, which have been tiled over in a forlorn attempt to improve the environment, are covered with posters: there's more of the unreconstructed Turkish Leninism that ornaments the derelict shop fronts of Dalston Lane, and the paper of the Socialist Workers Party has been pasted up page by page so that tenants can hardly avoid reading it as they wait for the lifts. The lift, which actually arrives quickly enough, is a foul metal box covered over with racist graffiti and, as I quickly find out, the atmosphere inside it is tense. Perhaps it is only on account of my presence as a stranger that everyone seems to be reciting a version of 'Tinker, Tailor, Soldier, Sailor', in their minds: a paranoid inner-city variation that goes 'Racist, Mugger, Rapist, Victim'. Nevertheless, it is already evident that things have slipped since the early Eighties, when Paul Harrison came to the Holly Street Estate in order to draw up a detailed inventory of 'the ecology of the inferno', and found that the real problems were confined to the low-rise buildings beyond the four towers.[2]

Reece Auguiste welcomes me to his mother's flat and shows me a sweeping panorama over the towers of east London. Had the experiment not gone so shockingly wrong, a new kind of connoisseurship would by now have sprung up around views like this: enthusiasts would stand here differentiating point blocks from scissor blocks and cluster blocks with the same eagerness that classical revivalists now show as they identify the figures, both overt and subtle, of analogy, alignment, aposiopesis, abruptio, and epistrophe in the facade of a church by Palladio. There are enough tower blocks in view to revive an entire forgotten taxonomy of system-building: Laing's Jesperson system, Taylor Woodrow's Larson-Nielson system (rarer than it was since all the trouble at Ronan Point over there in Newham), Concrete Ltd's Bison Wall Frame, Crudens Ltd's 'Skarn' system. Devotees of post-war planning could also stand here and trace the fading outline of the ideal geometry that post-war public authorities dreamt of imposing on London: the zoning, the distant green belt, the clearances and huge new estates, the roads – from the GLC's frustrated plan for an Inner London Motorway Box, through to the new, or dramatically widened, roads suggested in the East London Assessment Study, which only faded away in 1989. One line goes out immediately to the closely clustered towers of the Nightingale Estate, another reaches out to Clapton Park where five 'Camus' system blocks line up with the Trowbridge Estate to form a triangle around Sutton House, which is hidden among trees between the tower of St John's and a high-rise school building. I turn to see the still respectable towers of the Barbican (originally designed as low-cost public housing, and now home to millionaires like the financial analyst Bob Beckman, who has a three-storey penthouse suite in Lauderdale Tower), but they are out of sight, and I settle for the thrusting blue tower of Canary Wharf a couple of miles away on the Isle of Dogs. Looking down, I see the reverse of the view from my own window – the Victorian terraced houses, the street plan, the trees, the secluded gardens. Those, as Reece remarks with gentle irony, are surely the houses to live in; indeed, at the time of our meeting he was about to make his own descent into the more desirable world of the human scale.

During the property boom of the late Eighties, the anarchist squatters of Class War tried to reduce this view to a perspective of pure resentment and envy: 'we', the real people of Hackney, look down from our pokey flats while 'they' (or 'you' as it was by the time the threatening notices went through the letter-boxes), the yuppie gentrifiers and 'rich scum', move into the leafy terraces down there and make a packet as the value of these former 'slums' soars. But resentment is by no means the predominant feeling up here. Auguiste's neighbour on the twelfth floor is Mrs Jan Cooper, a retired

West End draper who moved into Rowan Court with her husband when the block opened in 1971. She looks down on the Victorian terraced streets of Mapledene and says, in a voice that still holds a hint of pity, that she could never go back to living in houses like that: cramped, dark, damp, insecure, and claustrophobic. Up here at least the vistas are airy and clear. She looks over to Chingford and the open country of Essex. Her eye then sweeps down over uncounted London boroughs to settle on the rising land of Blackheath to the south. These two allegorical stretches of high ground are the rims of her world, and she takes her pick of the city that lies between them: ignoring the 118 tower blocks of Newham and singling out instead the green dome of the Hackney Empire; a large gasometer that, as she's heard but can hardly believe, has a preservation order on it; the street on which a policeman had recently been murdered. She appreciates the green stretches, too, regretting the school extension that has diminished her view of London Fields, and pointing with unprompted satisfaction to the trees in the gardens and 'backlands' behind the terraced houses across the Queensbridge Road. Even Victorian slums have their attractions from a height.

Mrs Cooper remembers how fortunate she and her husband felt to be joining Hackney's fabled 'skyscraper families' when they first moved in. At that time, as she recalls, 'Everyone wanted to get in here'. People settled down behind that commanding new view with a great sense of confidence. Indeed, Mrs Cooper is adamant that even the tenants who, like herself and her husband, had lost their earlier homes to a council 'clearance' scheme were happy to bid farewell to the years they had spent cowering in the slums. As Mrs Cooper points out, her flat, which she keeps in pristine condition, is well designed and generously proportioned. The rooms are a generous size, and the ceilings, which stand at a good height, also offer unrecognised tribute to the minimum standards recommended by the Parker-Morris report in 1961 and abandoned more recently. It is, without doubt, a good enough machine for living in. The balcony even allows her to grow plants, including some myrtle-like shrubs she has raised from cuttings brought back from her childhood home in Co. Mayo. As Mrs Cooper says, 'I have no fault with the flats'. In fact, she's compared her home with the pokey little boxes, real 'rabbit hutches', the council has built since high rise went so abruptly out of fashion, and she's happy to have the one she's got. She only has to look out of Rowan Court in the other direction to see the later phases of the Holly Street Estate: those squalid, fire-scorched low-rise blocks built around 'courts' that would, as the Housing Committee promised in 1966, be 'landscaped to produce pleasant tranquil areas'. In Mrs Cooper's considered judgement it is the architects who designed those far-inferior blocks who should be shot.

There comes a point, however, at which Mrs Cooper's account joins that of Reece Auguiste, who talks of administrative collapse in the council's management of the estate and the characteristically alienated culture of Rowan Court. As Auguiste describes it, the tower block is a machine for inducing paranoia. The building imposes an 'atomist philosophy' on its tenants, and all its supposedly communal spaces are filled with anxiety, suspicion, and fear. The lift, he confirms, can be dead edgy: keep your eyes down and don't say a word. It has become almost routine for people to die alone in their flats, and to lie undiscovered for days and even weeks. As for the vandalism, Auguiste wonders whether the external doors and entry-phone system, recently fitted by the council in an endeavour to improve conditions in the block, weren't destroyed so quickly because they seemed to reinforce the isolation of the residents. Conceding that he had found the quiet of his mother's flat conducive to work during his student days, he cites sociological classics by the likes of Willmot and Young and Hannah Gavron to describe how the culture of the tower block cuts across any sense of community and confines women all the more viciously to the domestic sphere.

Auguiste suggests that the residents of Rowan Court are in-creasingly susceptible to a myth of the Golden Age and Mrs Cooper, for all her attachment to those bright modernist days at the outset, certainly shares his view that something has gone terribly wrong in the Eighties. The early years were fine and, as she stresses, they included the first black families. But then a terrifying degeneration set in, and its humiliations are inescapable. Asked to give an example, Mrs Cooper takes a deep breath and starts by pointing to the brown staining that disfigures the ceilings of her immaculate flat. Some-where upstairs a person turned on the bath and then went out, leaving the water to trickle down through all the flats below. And since, as Mrs Cooper adds in an attempt to illustrate the accumulator effect that tends to take over whenever the smallest thing goes wrong on this estate, the offending person was a squatter, neither the council nor any of the affected tenants' private insurance companies would accept liability for the damage.

Mrs Cooper does her bit on the tenants' association – she's the representative for the top half of the block – but at the same time she takes every opportunity she can to be away from Rowan Court. As she says, 'I'd go mad if I was in'. 'Hail, rain, or snow', she's packed her picnic and her newspaper by eleven o'clock, and she tries not to be back before nine: 'You name any park within reach of London Transport and I've been there'. Many tenants tell of the embarrass-ment of inviting visitors or bringing friends home to Rowan Court, and Mrs Cooper has a story that seems to speak for them all. She was recently visited by her brother, who had left Co. Mayo for California rather than Hackney, and now lives in far superior conditions near San Francisco. He and his wife came over to visit and since Hackney has no real hotels to speak of, there was no choice but to put him up in Rowan Court. Mrs Cooper will not forget the humiliation of getting up before dawn in order to sneak out and clean the lifts (people have been known to do 'everything' in there) before taking her visitors out in the morning.

She leads me on a tour of the upper floors to prove her point about the degradation of the block. The evidence is everywhere: the graffiti, the filth around the rubbish chutes, the stairways littered with the debris of adolescent drug abuse, the open access to the roof where the pirate radio stations bring their transmitters. On one particularly squalid floor, she indicates the elaborate, solid metal barricades tenants have erected in their doorways and suggests that we might just as well be in the Bronx, Beirut, or Alcatraz. The generally accepted communal decencies of the Seventies have gone, and in their place comes an endless succession of horror stories: there's the woman who has given up on civilised waste disposal, and simply heaves all her rubbish out of the kitchen window; there's the psychotic tenant who recently took against his neighbours' children and poured a lake of scarlet paint on the floor outside their door – a confused and agitated trail of footprints testifies to the success of his mad ploy.

Trying to find a pattern in this picture of mounting chaos, I ask for some benchmarks, some dates, some clearly defined milestones on this road to ruin. Reece Auguiste mentions the recent hardening of the racist graffiti into a coherent and deliberately formulated fascist form. Both he and Mrs Cooper mention the time when the respectable families disappeared. There used to be 'loads of kiddies' here, as Mrs Cooper remarks before moving on to suggest the moment when the council gave up enforcing its rules forbidding pets, and the dogs started to arrive. Back issues of the *Hackney Gazette* reveal that the council was allowing, or at least turning a blind eye to, cats on its estates from as early as 1971, when Rowan Court opened: it was hoped that they would keep the warfarin-resistant mice under control. But it was later, as the break-ins, burglaries, and assaults spiralled, that the dogs started to arrive. Not just the usual inner-city mongrels, but the whole pedigree succession of inner-city survivalism: the traditional Alsatians were looking hopelessly soppy by the end of the Seventies, giving way first to Dobermanns and Rottweilers and finally, as the Eighties peaked, to that ideal high-rise beast, the pit bull terrier. These symbolic creatures pace around in their modernist flats, howling and snarling, stinking the block up, shitting in the hallways, and occasionally coming out to strut about on the stretch of green void outside.

The decline of that 'open space' is another symbolic marker of degeneration. It may have been planned as an amenity for the flat dwellers, but now it's a truly indefensible space. The drifting airborne rubbish would outsmart even the most diligent cleaner, and the land has become public in the worst possible sense. Just as the people from the Victorian houses opposite use Rowan Court as a thoroughfare, walking straight through the foyer on their way to the shops (as Mrs

Cooper asks, 'how would they like it if we started walking through their houses from front door to back?'), the 'open space' outside has become a dog patch for half the borough. The resident curs are bad enough, but over the last few years Mrs Cooper reckons she must have seen half the population of Hackney drive up in battered cars and let out their dogs so that they, too, can shit all over her doorstep.

Finally, and really only in the last couple of years, there are the squatters – a 'floating population' drifts through the towers of Holly Street like a band of outlaws camping out on the high plains. They move around within and between the blocks, getting evicted by the council and then settling into another empty flat and claiming their rights for a year. How do they get through the solid metal of the anti-squatter doors? On some occasions the council workers have simply failed to turn the key, and on others, at least so some tenants suspect, they seem to have joined the well-established black-market trade in illicitly copied keys. I was shown flats that have been systematically wrecked by squatters, and others that are just gaping burned-out voids. Some of the squatters spend all their time 'drugging' – including, as Mrs Cooper suspects, the Vietnamese student who recently died after jumping off the balcony of his blazing flat. Others are 'perfectly decent' people who 'have to live somewhere' (Mrs Cooper has a delightful man with a cello on her floor), but their arrival still causes extensive breakdown in the system (to say nothing of the council's policy of housing the homeless families on its waiting-list). For a start they enjoy free heating and hot water, provided by a central boiler for which the official tenants have to pay. And just as the squatters have the indirect effect of cancelling the tenants' insurance, their refusal to open the door even to sanitation officials means that it is nigh on impossible to rid the block of the cockroaches and other pests that infest it. In the end, however, the squatters are not at the root of the problem. Mrs Cooper reads the *Sun*, but she doesn't need that rag to tell her where the accusing finger should be pointed: 'the council are not doing their job. That's the all of it.'

There are some exceptional moments of brightness on the Holly Street Estate – a fine adventure playground, and some brave murals that manage to lift the place a bit. These flimsy attempts to stem the decline are joined by scrawled and anonymous notices urging residents to pull back from the abyss. On one floor of Rowan Court after another there are anonymous messages by the rubbish shoot. Scribbled on cardboard, they plead that 'neighbours' should not just dump their filth on the floor or bung up the chute unnecessarily. A similar plea stands by the demolished car park, part of which has recently been turned into a community play centre and garden. It points out that this modest but also unimaginably heroic attempt to counter the degeneration is actually the voluntary work of 'neighbours', and pleads that it should not be vandalised, filled with dog-shit, or otherwise ruined. On the fifth floor of Rowan Court, the floor tiles in the 'communal' hallway have been repaired on a DIY basis by the couple who accepted the government's offer and bought their flat in this hell-house (only to find themselves the owners of an unsaleable flat and lumbered with a maintenance charge that, while not necessarily being unreasonable, threatens to exceed the old rent). These brave holding measures may be hopeless, but people persist in them knowing that while it is easy to slip down the slope it is almost impossible to climb back up. There's no turning round on the road to ruin. As Mrs Cooper said repeatedly, 'you can never get it back'.

When the time came for me to leave, Mrs Cooper insisted, with old-fashioned courtesy, on seeing me to the front door. There were six people already in the lift, but this time it didn't seem to matter whether they were black or white, men or women, squatters, tenants, or owner-occupiers. Somebody made a remark about the interior condition of the lift, and everyone came together in the helpless humour of the modern chasm dweller. These people of the new abyss are the victims not just of a council that can't manage its own resources, but of a national government that has enjoyed making symbolic capital out of the disorders of Labour authorities like Hackney, while at the same time forcing through policy changes designed to reduce council housing to a residual welfare net. In 1971, when Rowan Court was opened to its first tenants, council housing was still accepted as a respectable form of housing for the skilled working class: one didn't have to be disaffiliated, marginal, incompetent, or just plain desperate to end up there. But no longer. Ten years ago, Hackney Council planned to spend £16 million redeveloping the Holly Street Estate and landscaping its green voids, but the government wasn't having any of it.[3] In the age of 'opting out', Mrs Cooper's situation has become representative in a new way. Ageing and unable to move out of the estate that is collapsing around her, she looks back over a life of respectable endeavour and feels both betrayed and abandoned. There are elderly people like this all over the inner city: decent and hard-working in their active lives, as they feel obliged to repeat over and over again, they spend their retirement sinking down as, one after another, the promises of the early Welfare State give way beneath them. The London in which they expected to be living in their old age has become as remote as any other homeland on the block – from Ireland to Vietnam or, for that matter, the Lincolnshire of the *Market Rasen Mail*. Tempted by tabloid stereotypes, and the dubious consolations offered by such figures as the Revd Donald Pateman, vicar of St Mark's, these are the people who turned out to welcome the Queen Mother when she made her nostalgic return to Victoria Park on her ninetieth birthday, and to watch the Spitfire and Lancaster Bomber fly over on the way to Buckingham Palace on the fiftieth anniversary of the Battle of Britain. In the early Seventies they might have conformed to sociologist

Ruth Glass's conception of 'the people of the public sector': feisty, aware of their rights, not easily conned, articulate, and demanding. By 1990 they had been reduced to a very different stereotype as 'zombies of the welfare state'.[4] So much for the Queen Mother's famous demand, made during the blitz, that something must be done to improve the lot of East Londoners.

A Machine for Harvesting Subsidies

How did the Holly Street Estate come to be built in its chosen form? George Lansbury was certainly keen to develop and improve the nation's council estates, but though he wanted to see 'guest houses and theatres' added to them, he remained 'dead against skyscrapers'. This man of the people knew the advantages of a proper house with a garden, and he refused to accept that it was 'impossible to find room on the ground-floor for all who need homes'.[5] The threat may not have seemed too pressing, for even at the time of his death in 1940, council housing in Britain was not generally associated with high-rise architecture. Some modernist architects like Maxwell Fry had built flats for public authorities in London. Indeed, Alexander Korda showed some such new developments in his wartime propaganda film, *The Lion has Wings*, admiring them as part of Britain's pre-war endeavour to rehouse the urban population in 'well-built, well-lighted, well ventilated flats to replace the tumbledown slums of the past'. But these flats were not typical. Evelyn Waugh had long since recognised council housing as a plague but when, in *Brideshead Revisited*, he wrote about the fine Georgian buildings being demolished to make way for modern blocks of flats, even he was still talking about 'luxury developments' of an unmistakably private kind.

The famous Lansbury Estate, built near Bow as a showpiece for the 1951 Festival of Britain, consisted of accommodation George Lansbury himself would have appreciated: houses and three-storey flats. But, whether or not the Lansbury Estate can fairly be called 'the thin end of the wedge', all this had changed by 27 November 1967, when *The Guardian* printed a couple of photographs of 'New Homes for London'.[6] Along with a twenty-three-storey 'scissor block' nearing completion on Lewisham's Pepys Estate, the paper showed a model of one of the towers proposed for Holly Street. It stood there, gleaming with unquestioned modernity and tricked out in what John Betjeman once called the 'swish perspective' of the architect's office.[7] There was a little toy car parked in the place where, in the real world, a stinking overloaded skip is usually to be found; and a plastic bush stood among herbaceous borders where the green void would soon form. It was announced that four, twenty-one-storey 'blocks of flats' were to be built to provide homes for 1,520 people. The development, which was to 'include a three-deck car park for 220 cars', had been designed, so

The Guardian reported, by Mr J. L. Sharratt, the borough architect, working in association with 'the technical advisers of Fram, Higs and Hill (Camus) Ltd, Camus (Gt Britain) Ltd, and W. V. Zinn and Associates'.

Back issues of the *Hackney Gazette* provide a fuller impression of the days when councillors and their planners dreamt of high-rise towers on Holly Street. There is news of other superficial novelties, like the duly photographed arrival of 'hot pants' in the borough in 1971, but as the years flash by on microfilm, Hackney comes to look more and more like a place of stubborn constancy where, while old problems may indeed get rearranged, nothing fundamental changes at all. Tory Councillor, Joe Lobenstein, was campaigning for a tube station in 1971 and remarking that 'this matter should not be allowed to drag on until the 1980s and 90s'[8] – which, of course, both it and the indefatigable councillor have done. Crime and vandalism are abiding themes, and Revd Donald Pateman was well into his stride by the Sixties ('Dalston vicar lashes Great Britain'), condemning the permissive society and demanding a return to the birch and more liberal use of the hangman's rope: 'Britain is in the grip of a Reign of Terror, Death stalks the roads and gunmen are everywhere'.[9] The 'looney left' tirades of the mid-Eighties also slide into place at the head of long tradition. During the Sixties, the paper was full of controversy over the visits made by admiring Labour councillors and youth organisations to communist countries like East Germany and Czechoslovakia, and there was a furore in September 1966 when the council decided to give a grant out of the rates to the Marx Memorial Library in Clerkenwell – an organisation that now seems a merely amiable refuge for depressed labour historians, but was then seen to pose a sufficiently serious threat to the nation to be proscribed by the Labour Party. As for the tide of litter, this just rises from one decade to the next – always there and always, as people come forward to insist with impressive regularity, getting worse.

It was in 1966 that the Housing Committee of Hackney Council resolved to build the four tower blocks of Holly Street. The development would play a major part of the Labour council's ambitious 'Ten Year Housing Programme' and, while the later low-rise phases of the estate were to be built by the council's own notoriously expensive Direct Labour Organisation, the Housing Committee accepted the borough architect's recommendation that the tall blocks proposed for phase one 'would lend themselves to industrialised building'. A special Housing Standards Committee had carried out an investigation to establish which 'industrialised construction methods' were 'consistent with the maintenance of the high standards set by the Council and their predecessors to date'. After visiting the factory, talking to tenants, and examining blocks already built in Europe, the members of the committee concluded that Camus were 'capable of producing housing estates of a very

satisfactory standard'.[10] The borough commissioned Camus blocks
to be built at Clapton Park, Kings Crescent, and Holly Street, where
it was estimated that four blocks would provide 456 flats at a total cost
of £2.2 million.

Councillors were really something in those days, but even so there
were problems from the start. The building was still under way in
May 1968 when that fatal gas explosion ripped through Ronan Point.
After receiving a letter of warning from the Ministry of Housing, the
Housing Committee decided to replace the planned gas heating
system in its half-built Camus blocks with the oil-fired system about
which tenants still bitterly complain. That same year, the tower
blocks on the GLC's nearby Trowbridge Estate were also in the news.
The tenants had only moved in a few months before, but the flats were
already breaking up. Water was streaming in through the walls and
window frames, and the 'skyscraper families', whose stories were now
taking the place of those about 'prefabbers' in the *Hackney Gazette*, had
suffered a nasty bout of instant disenchantment. One tenant, Mrs
Alice Jameson, showed reporters the patched-up wall of her brand-
new nineteenth-floor flat and likened it to another of the GLC's
innovative proposals: 'It looks like a map of the inner London
motorway box'.[11]

But despite these problems, it remained customary (even among
the Tories who gained control of Hackney in 1968) to concede that the
new tower blocks had a certain aesthetic charm. As David Henderson, Deputy Leader of Hackney Council during the three years of
Conservative control, remarked at a meeting of his own party: 'In the
heyday of the Labour Council, many good houses were knocked down
out of spite and tower blocks were built instead. This looked pretty,
but all it meant was that four out of five people rehoused were in no
need of rehousing.'[12] But by the time Rowan Court was completed as
the last of the Holly Street towers in 1971, the national audit on this
kind of public housing was complete, and few people anywhere in the
country were inclined to make even this half-hearted aesthetic
concession. Slum clearance had been carried out at considerable
cultural cost, and it now emerged that the new housing schemes had
failed even to rehouse as many people as had been displaced. Costs
turned out vastly to have exceeded initial estimates, and the huge
disparity between the time it took to build comparable developments in
the public and private sectors suggested remarkable levels of inefficiency
and corruption in the public sector. Tales of extraordinary administrative incompetence had started to emerge from the new housing
estates, and people were also wondering about what Martin Pawley
once described as the 'shocking contrast' between the world of the
professionals with their jargon and graphs and the experience of
tenants.[13] Now that the question was asked, nobody could really justify
building high-density developments in urban areas that were actually
experiencing an overall reduction in population.

Rowan Court is a monument not just to the flawed ambitions of a Labour authority that, as its critics claimed at the time, seemed intent on turning the whole borough into a huge housing estate, but to a whole epoch of public policy and a planning framework that was shaped most influentially by the Conservative government of Harold Macmillan, who had come to power in 1951 promising to build 300,000 new homes a year. The inventory has been drawn up more than adequately elsewhere, but since the image of the council tower block is now surrounded more by myth than any clear understanding of the circumstances that gave rise to it, a brief recapitulation has its place here.[14]

High-rise flats were always an expensive form of housing, and they would not have been built without a planning protocol that demanded not just an increase in both housing and open space but also a combination of slum clearance and urban containment. In the days before the spell broke, the inner-city tower block could look especially attractive to defenders of the green belt and more distant parts of rural England. In a Parliamentary debate of 1955, Lord Hinchinbrooke, the maverick Tory MP for Dorset South who, as we have seen, had himself experienced some difficulty finding a future for his ancestral home of Hinchinbrooke, demanded that subsidies be shifted from the kind of housing development that only offered 'spoilation' of the countryside and concentrated instead on 'the creation of first class flats of 12, 15 and 20 storeys' in the cities.

First class or not, high-rise flats grew out of central-government subsidies. There were 'expensive site' subsidies in the Thirties, and in 1946 Attlee's Labour government had added a new increment per flat for blocks of at least four storeys high with lifts. But while Attlee laid the framework for 'comprehensive redevelopment', as it would be practised in the post-war decades, it was Macmillan's government that triggered the high-rise boom in 1956, when it introduced a progressive storey-height subsidy that gave large increments for four, five and six-storey flats, and a fixed increment for every additional storey above that. Devised by the large construction companies as machines for harvesting the subsidy, the system-built blocks had the additional advantages of confining architects to an increasingly 'in-house' role and also of necessitating new systems of 'selective tendering', which reduced competition.

Hackney's experiment with high-rise flats was accompanied by the usual allegations of corruption and graft, but whatever may have been going on locally, there can be no doubt at all that large dividends were being reaped elsewhere. Patrick Dunleavy investigated the links between national politicians, civil servants, and the large construction companies that thrived on the public housing programmes during the years of Conservative government, and his findings certainly add up to an interesting picture of corporate and personal involvement. A significant number of MPs had connections with the construction industry, but so too did two ministers in the Cabinet responsible for the high flat subsidy: Keith Joseph was heir to the Bovis fortune and Geoffrey Rippon was a director of Cubbitts. Among the construction companies, both McAlpine and Taylor Woodrow were major contributors to the Conservative Party and also such right-wing pressure groups as the Freedom Association. Dame Evelyn Sharp was Permanent Secretary at the Ministry of Housing and Local Government during the crucial years, 1954–64; she was also a friend of the construction boss, Neil Wates, and, after her retirement from the civil service, the holder of a directorship at Bovis. Kenneth Wood, Chairman of Concrete Ltd, was among the 'advisers' employed by the Ministry of Housing and Local Government from the construction industry; even as late as 1974, a Bovis executive was appointed to 'mastermind a more vigorous public housing drive'.[15]

Architects are still inclined to blame the worst excesses of the Sixties on every aspect of this planning framework, except their own professional culture. But there can be no doubt that a little self-referring professional world built up: one in which consultation with the 'client' meant nothing more than discussion with borough architects, planners, and other such experts who shared a pro-fessional outlook based on what Martin Pawley described as a 'curious amalgam of "modern" thought and scientific mumbo jumbo'.[16] Within this bogus cult of 'expertise', as Patrick Dunleavy has suggested, the system-built tower block appeared to offer a perfect 'technological short-cut' to the solution of all sorts of formerly intractable social problems. During the late Fifties and early Sixties, *The Architects' Journal*, published by the Royal Institute of British Architects, was busy projecting banal sub-Corbusian dreams on a grand scale. In a representative article dating from 1963, Derrick Rigby Childs imagined large areas of lowland Scotland covered with new 'Counterdrift Cities', which would strengthen the north against the south. These ideal places were to have names like 'Solway' and 'Hadrian's End' (but not, as it happens, 'Easterhouse'), and little line drawings showed how they would look with their impossibly high prefabricated tower blocks scattered about between domed areas in which the disadvantages of the Scottish climate would finally be overcome. Mr Childs seems to have been dimly aware that his megalomaniacal schemes might encounter certain misgivings among ordinary people, but the failures of the popular imagination weren't going to get in the way of his magisterial vision: 'in the coming age of industrialised building, I believe people will in time draw the greatest satisfaction from environments which combine strong man-made forms and natural landscape'.[17] In 1965 *The Architects' Journal* revisited the notorious Park Hill Estate in Sheffield, choosing not to dwell on the already evident failure of its much puffed 'street-deck' idea, and preferring instead to describe it as a 'neutral framework drawing life only from its inhabitants, an awe-inspiring exercise in architectural humility which defies criticism in formal terms'.[18]

This sort of clap-trap deserves to be pilloried, but it should also be recognised that some altogether more serious and reflective advocates of the new public housing programmes had long been aware of the wider problems that would eventually overwhelm their project. R. Furneaux Jordan of the London County Council was an enthusiastic exponent of the 'radical humanism' he hoped would finally see 'the Common Man' entering upon his inheritance. Like other modernists of his time he marvelled at the point blocks of the LCC's Alton Estate in Roehampton, remarking that they would give London 'a truly dramatic and lovely townscape . . . the real fruit, after thirty years, of *La Ville Radieuse*'. But while being a fond Corbusian of his time, he had sensed an underlying problem as early as November 1956.[19] Under the new conditions demanded by the public housing drive, 'the architect's employer is no longer his client', and the architect and his employer – 'ie the public authority' – need to think hard about how they can jointly serve the client, 'ie the community'. Such was the public architect's experience of 'the central problem of our era', which concerned 'the rights of the Person within the State, and the validity of the Official as an artist'. After suggesting that 'the dilemma of the LCC is that it deals with the lives of very ordinary men and women to whom it can never fully explain itself', he then surveyed the pit into which the whole endeavour of public housing ('to say nothing of the GLC itself) would eventually fall:

> Ten years ago the planner was a messiah leading post-war Britain into the promised land. Today, he is the bogeyman of Crichel Down. Neither view is valid since both are just sublimations of a mood, but at least the first was idealistic as well as necessary, while the second is as ignorant as it is anarchic. The first mood brought into being the Welfare State . . . in a sense, an ethical sense, Gladstone's Christian state. The 1956 mood could ruin everything.

'Houses' versus 'Housing'

Shortly after the end of World War Two, the architect and writer, Clough Williams-Ellis, suffered a terrible vision. He imagined all the lands and buildings possessed by the National Trust 'uprooted and set adrift and then, by some further sorcery, reassembled into one fabulous island'. The result would be like an early theme-park with 'the pith and pick of England close-packed into a compass smaller than that of the Isle of Wight, yet sampling all that we most prize'. Williams-Ellis considered this prospect ('an intoxicating medley of scenic and architectural high-lights with never a shadow, even of mediocrity, never a dull moment anywhere') and concluded that it would be like a 'cake made only of plums and brandy, and quite deadly as a diet'. Worse, it would be lifeless with 'everything arbitrarily torn out of its historic and geographic context by the roots, compressed into an ill-assorted bouquet, set apart and neatly labelled "Hortus Sicus Britannicus – the flowers of Britain Preserved"'. The idea appalled him, and he went on to draw a firm conclusion: 'thank God that even a monster syndicate of maniacal millionaires could not make it a reality or seduce the National Trust from its charted duty – the preserving of beauty as and where it is'.[20]

It would indeed be impossible to concentrate all its sites of historic interest and natural beauty on one island, but we know from James Lees-Milne's abrupt dismissal of Sutton House as an undeserving slum – a dismissal that was made in 1946, the year before Williams-Ellis's disturbing vision came out in print – that the National Trust did develop its own territorial emphasis in the post-war years. The rise of the country house had the effect of pulling conservation into the southern shires and concentrating its imagery around the leafy and aristocratic domains of the stately home. The city was left to that other great architectural symbol of the Welfare State age, the council tower block. For a while in the Sixties, it was possible to imagine these two symbols of the nation as complementary in their differences: bulldozers, technological progress, and social reform in the city; shire horses, craft-based tradition, and ancient hierarchy in the country. Preserved and displayed, the country house may well have offered a consoling image of past grandeur to a formerly imperial nation now sliding down into the irrecoverably minor status of a country that couldn't even, as it seemed for a time, gain entry into the European Common Market; but it was also offering other attractions: the lions, the exotic lifestyle of an aristocracy that was accustomed to having its newspapers ironed and its small change washed before it was placed in the appropriate pockets, and, once the kitchen quarters had been opened up, the sense of a proper community in which everybody had a nicely differentiated and proper place.

But though the high-rise boom of the Sixties did coincide with a rise in the number of visitors clocked up at National Trust properties, this territorialisation, which divided the imagery of conservation and reform between the country and the city, wasn't to settle into permanent form. Doubtless, in the Sixties, there were some former slum-dwelling council tenants who drove out from their bright new high-rise flats in east London to visit preserved country houses like Knole where they would meditate on the past and recognise their own kinship with an aristocrat who was himself now also a tenant, albeit of the National Trust, but this ideal reciprocity was just one more feature of the post-war settlement that didn't hold. To start with, a very different version of conservation emerged in the inner city, one that was less a cult of art-historical connoisseurship than an urban resistance movement committed to the defence of ordinary streets threatened by the council bulldozer. It was partly due to the success of this sort of local opposition all over the country that government policy shifted. The high-rise subsidy was abolished by a Labour government in 1968, and the system of subsidy with which it was replaced was designed to promote refurbishment and improvement as opposed to comprehensive redevelopment.

The Hackney Society held its inaugural meeting on 4 May 1967, as the 613th civic society in affiliation to the Civic Trust. As the newly elected President, John Betjeman spoke out about the threat facing a borough he had always held dear. It was, he said, 'most important to keep houses on a "Human scale", as people felt crushed by the enormous concrete slabs which are being built at the present time'. Fortunately, he added, over the last two years 'architects and economists were beginning to realise that the best way to house a large number of people in a limited space is NOT in a high block, but in the old idea of a Georgian Square with houses of about 5 or 6 stories high'.[21] The point, as Betjeman was stressing all over the country at this time, was to awaken the council to the difference between 'housing' and proper 'houses'. Yet despite the obvious message of *Coronation Street*, the immensely popular Granada television soap that celebrated the life of the traditional terraced street (and was much admired by John Betjeman) and had been on the air since 1960, the slum clearing members of Hackney's Housing and Planning Committees remained unimpressed.[22]

In December 1969, the Hackney Society decided to promote neighbourhood-based societies in order 'to get more people concerned about their environment' but its main battle was to establish the legitimacy of its defence of 'houses' against the bulldozing priorities of a 'housing' programme that was undeniably urgent. In 1971 it was involved in a case that demonstrated the open class conflict that could break out between conservationists and slum tenants. The Georgian houses of Sanford Terrace had been scheduled for demolition by a Labour authority in 1968, and after two-and-a-half years of Conservative dithering the tenants were furious that the decision hadn't been carried out. For them the houses were overcrowded and vermin-infested slums that, with their damp walls, leaking roofs, and outside lavatories, were only fit for the bulldozer. The tenants wanted demolition, and they were outraged that the council had delayed for so long. The objectors included the Hackney Society and a teacher who, as an owner-occupier, had already refurbished his house in the terrace, and they certainly didn't confine their argument to purely architectural matters. Indeed, they countered the tenants by claiming that grant-aided refurbishment by owner-occupiers or, perhaps, a charitable 'housing society' would bring much-needed middle-class professionals into an area that was, at that time, a 'one class community'.[23] The tenants replied by threatening a spoiling tactic. They declared that if a housing association did take them over, they would then refuse to leave the houses they hated so much. In those days there were Labour councillors in Hackney who described every conserved private house as at least one more Liberal voter in the borough.

Fortunately, there were some local campaigns at this time that managed to reconcile conservationist principles with local interests. On three sides out of four, the system-built towers of the Holly Street Estate look out over areas of nineteenth-century housing where campaigning residents have used conservationist tactics to prevent further council redevelopment. To the west is De Beauvoir Town, sometimes described as London's first planned suburb, and an area where comprehensive redevelopment was successfully fought off in the late Sixties. Fifteen years of blight had followed the publication of Hackney Borough Council's plan for wholesale redevelopment in the Fifties, and the enlarged London Borough of Hackney was finally proposing to press ahead with compulsory purchase, demolition, and rebuilding. The De Beauvoir Association was formed in 1967 to oppose these plans, and to press, under the terms of the new Civic Amenities Act, for the conservation of the whole area rather than just the individual buildings the Hackney planners intended to spare. The De Beauvoir Association was created by young professionals who had moved into this then unregarded area of early Victorian terraces at just about the same time as the sociologist, Ruth Glass, is said to have coined the term 'gentrification'. Among these incomers was Stuart Weir, later to be editor of *New Statesman and Society* but at that time a journalist working on *The Times* 'Diary'. One of his more telling stories about De Beauvoir Square was captured by Tony Aldous and written up for readers of the *Illustrated London News*:

> 'We're planning to keep the square', said the man, who repre-sented the ward but did not live there. 'Oh that's good', replied Weir, brightening. 'They're in poor repair, but they're really very attractive houses'. 'Oh no. We're knocking down the houses', rejoined the councillor. 'We'll just keep the square'.[24]

The conservation of houses was certainly one of its aims, but the De Beauvoir Association had other ambitions as well. It pressed for partial road closures and drew up plans for parks and a community centre. It produced a community newsletter, set up a welfare rights service, pressed the council to purchase tenanted houses that were neglected by their owners, and formed a housing association to keep working-class residents in the area (forty-two houses were bought and converted into flats and maisonettes before the De Beauvoir Trust was incorporated into the Circle 33 Trust). The incoming pro-fessionals who formed and led the De Beauvoir Association were able to generate considerable publicity for their cause and also to involve the GLC Historic Buildings Division, the London Society, and the Victorian Society (it was through this latter organisation that John Betjeman arrived on the scene), but the committee itself was made up of tenants and lease-holders as well as owner-occupiers. Indeed, it was precisely in order to maintain this mixed participation that it was decided not to establish a formally elected committee (people could just turn up at meetings and everyone who had been to at least one of the previous three meetings was eligible to vote). After winning its battle against 'Hackney's one-party state' at a local inquiry, the De Beauvoir Association went on (quite undeterred by those members of the Hackney Society who warned against straying into 'politics') to advocate tenants' rights, opposing landlords who were using various forms of harassment to 'winkle' tenants out of their increasingly valuable homes, and generally to resist what it called, with an eye to a more thoroughly gentrified area in Islington, the 'Barnsburyification' of De Beauvoir Town.[25]

Hostilities broke out again a few years later, this time to the east of the Holly Street Estate and down among the terraced streets that Mrs Cooper can see just across the Queensbridge Road from her balcony on Rowan Court. The battle for Mapledene opened on 9 December 1971 when, without any consultation at all, Hackney Council announced its intention of imposing a compulsory purchase order on a large tract of the area. For years, as many locals would complain, the council had been blighting the area by buying up perfectly good houses and them simply leaving them empty to rot, and now it was proposing to finish the job by demolishing whole streets and replacing them with a large, low-rise housing estate. The council undertook to rehouse only old-age pensioners and people who were tenants in unfurnished accommodation; but even the people covered by this limited offer were apparently unimpressed. As Donald Kearsley remarked in the report that followed his 1972 public inquiry into the affair, they 'assumed, rightly or wrongly, that this would mean living, perhaps in a tower block; in a development such as Holly Street which they have seen and do not like'.[26]

The Mapledene Residents Advisory Committee formed to defend a very different vision of the area. In the words of Ernie Greenwood, a local communist who was chairman of the committee, Mapledene was 'one of those invaluable areas where bricklayers and doctors, book-keepers and artists, all kinds and any kind of person, can not just co-exist but feel themselves to be part of a community',[27] and its future lay in improvement and conversion of the kind that some housing associations were already carrying out. If this was the social argument for the conservation of Mapledene, the architectural case was advanced through a different channel. Where the council's planners, hot in pursuit of 'housing gain', saw only run-down slums with excessively large gardens, the Hackney Society insisted that the Mapledene area was actually an example of Victorian town planning at its best, describing how its wide terraced streets had been built by Thomas and William Rhodes between 1840 and 1860 for the use of middle-income office clerks and townspeople. Far from being 'at or near the end of their useful life' and only fit for demolition, the houses were serviceable and well-designed homes, complete with features of special architectural interest: bay windows with fretted valances; cast-iron jardinières; gauged brick arches over windows and door-ways; a distinctive pattern of very slim glazing bars on the sash windows; and front doors with circular panels that appeared to be unique to the area.

The 1971 compulsory purchase order was rejected by the Secretary of State for the Environment in 1972, but that was not to be the end of the matter. In 1973 the Mapledene Residents Association was only pressing the council to clean up the filth on the neglected land it owned in the area, but by 1975 the council was back with another, albeit far less 'comprehensive', proposal for redevelopment. Thanks to the Housing Act 1974, the day of refurbishment had finally dawned at Hackney Town Hall and the new idea, which incorporated many ideas developed by the Residents Association, was to divide Maple-dene into a Housing Action Area, two General Improvement Areas, and two Priority Neighbourhoods. As part of this package the council insisted on winning some 'housing gain' by building new, two- and three-storey houses and some special accommodation for the aged on two strips of 'backland' space at the bottom of the gardens that had originally been intended for mews development. This would involve the demolition of a small number of houses, including a listed building at No. 73 Mapledene Road (which would have to go to provide access to the new buildings), and also the compulsory purchase of the last thirty feet of some householders' gardens.

The new plans were altogether less destructive than the earlier proposal, which had sought the demolition of 301 houses, but the locals rose up against it all the same. A Backlands Action Group was formed to work alongside the residents' association. In the words of its treasurer, the members of this group were diverse 'in terms of age, occupation, income and ethnic origin', but remarkably unanimous in their response to 'this threat to our standard of life'.[28] The action group came up with alternative plans to turn the backlands into allotments or 'organised play spaces' for small children. At its encouragement, residents wrote angry letters to the Mayor, signing off with appropriate flourishes ('PS. I never thought that I would ever have to give reasons why I don't want a large part of my garden compulsorily taken away'). They also drew up individual statements of their objections: Charles Bergonzi of No. 5 Albion Drive remarked that 'the area affected would be that which at present comprises a greenhouse, vegetable plot, several fruit trees including apple, cherry, peach and plum, and other trees including bay', and then went on to describe the objections of his eighty-eight-year-old mother, who was 'restricted to the garden for her leisure'.[29] As a pensioner and long-time resident of No. 21 Albion Drive, Mr J. Benjamin had 'five mature fruit trees and several gooseberry bushes' to defend; but as 'a life long supporter of our Labour Party', he was sufficiently incensed to write to the Leader of the Council, Alderman Ottolangui, describing how, fifty years previously when the Labour Party had no representation in Hackney, he had worked so hard to persuade people to vote for it that he came to be 'looked on as a heretic and extremist, and also risked losing his job'. He considered it frankly 'ironic', now that Labour was in power, to find the council 'harassing' him through his last years with one compulsory purchase order after another. The Leader of the Council didn't reply, except, as Mr Benjamin claimed, by depriving this octogenarian veteran left-over from the days of George Lansbury of his place on the Council's Committee of Workshops for the Elderly.[30] Such are the little disappointments of history. Farewell, Mr Benjamin.

Despite being warned by 'The Men of the Trees' that 'if it comes to the question of trees or houses, the trees will inevitably go', the residents used everything they could muster in defence of their gardens, including, as it turned out, the view from the tower blocks of the Holly Street Estate.[31] From here one could see how 'luxuriantly foliated' the backlands and gardens of Mapledene really were. Indeed, as the architect and, at that time, Mapledene resident, Julian Harrap, was to say on behalf of the Hackney Society, 'the pleasure and visual relief that these havens of seclusion give to the neighbourhood . . . should not be underestimated'.[32] The Backlands Action Group insisted that this 'pleasure and visual relief' was shared by the high-rise onlookers of the Holly Street Estate, although some drafted notes among the papers of the Backlands Action Group reveal momentary indecision as to whether these tower-block dwellers should be said to enjoy the view of trees 'as much as' or 'even more than' those whose gardens were 'directly affected'. Some residents took this defence of the trees of Mapledene to more eccentric lengths. Among the surviving papers is the unattributed text of an article written with the idea of submission to a magazine called *The Garden*. After citing Hackney's high rate of infant mortality, lung cancer, respiratory disease, and tuberculosis, the author wonders what the council thinks it is doing when it threatens to come along and wreck a third of the area's healing, oxygen-producing trees: 'the betting is high that no-one on our borough housing committee is watching the rise of carbon dioxide in the atmosphere . . .'. The article also mentions the problem of the different world 'over there' where the council had already done its work. The four tower blocks of the 'unhappy new' Holly Street Estate had imposed a new gale-ridden 'micro-climate' on the westerly gardens of Mapledene, and residents had good reason to fear victimisation and terror once the 'bad boys' from across the road could gain easy access into the backlands: 'as the voortrekkers depended on their laagers of covered wagons for survival, so does civilisation in modern inner city conditions need the closed quadrilateral for gardening, for quiet, for safe play for the children and against violence and theft'. The Boerish illustration was not well chosen, but the problems of crime were real enough. In their submission to the public inquiry that was eventually held at the end of 1977, the residents detailed the constant crime they were faced with. Almost every house in the area had been broken into in recent years, and many children had been 'seriously attacked' on the Holly Street Estate. There had been muggings and theft on the streets, and murders too – an old lady had been killed outside the newsagent and a man had met his end in the betting shop. Little wonder that 'the elderly of Mapledene rarely went out at night'.[33] The tenants and householders of Mapledene were already suffering 'collective deprivation', and insisted that they should not be exposed to further attack by a plan that would open up the backs of their houses to marauders and petty criminals.

The residents of Mapledene were also able to rally considerable professional support for their cause. The Backlands Action Group secured the services of Lord Gifford to present its case at the public inquiry, and, before that day came, a variety of conservation groups had been prevailed upon to protest against the council's plan. The Victorian Society wrote to the Borough Planning Officer, remarking that the listed building now threatened with demolition was especially remarkable for its 'wide pediment and giant pilasters'.[34] Julian Harrap made similar representations for the Hackney Society, quoting from Sir Nikolaus Pevsner's assessment of the area ('Much that is nice survives of that relatively early period') and pointing to the same 'giant Tuscan pilasters'. A formidable critique of the assumptions implicit in the council's plan was presented by another Mapledene resident. As secretary of the Mapledene Residents Association, Christine Huggins could tell the public inquiry that 'Consulting with Hackney Council is rather like talking to a person who is stone deaf'. Herself a professional town planner, she was well placed to counter the council's claims that housing density in the area was low. She pointed out that occupancy rates are normally used to calculate the population levels appropriate for new public housing developments, and it was quite inappropriate to take the normal occupancy rate of a tower block and then apply it to an area of Victorian housing that, as she knew even if the council planners did not, had actually been zoned for a much lower density shortly after the war. As for the housing waiting-list, the council was trying to use it as a stick with which to beat the residents of Mapledene, and Christine Huggins rejected the 'hint of moral wickedness', the implication that it was merely selfish for people to defend their own reasonable conditions just because others were unhoused. The proposal to build on the backlands was 'obsolete housing policy' and, as Huggins told the inquiry, the council's efforts elsewhere hardly provided an encouraging precedent. Indeed, most of the new developments consisted of 'flats in slab blocks or towers, many of which fail to provide for the aspirations of today's tenants'. In the end, the Secretary of State for the Environment, Peter Shore, consented to the demolition of No. 73 Mapledene Road, but the proposal to purchase and develop the backlands was thrown out. The gardens of Mapledene were saved, and the national Press took note. It was something of a watershed for a local authority to be defeated by a residents' association in a public inquiry.

Tombstone of the Welfare State

The report of the 1977 public inquiry describes Mapledene as 'an area which teeters on the knife edge between increasing blight, poverty and stress on the one hand, and increasing stability and prosperity on the other'. Thirteen years later, it is still mixed, with a variety of types of house tenure and its quota of empty and derelict council properties. Nevertheless, a lot of private rebuilding and refurbishment has gone on in the Eighties and Mapledene is now one of the more desirable residential areas in Hackney. Those large and undeveloped gardens are appreciated by an often rather transient succession of owner-occupiers. I've not heard of any diarists on *The Times* moving into the area, but *The Observer* journalist, Jane Lott, spent a few years here in the late Eighties. She wrote an article for the property page of her paper, comparing the generous size of her residence with what was available for twice the price in nearby Islington, and she also described the results of her exploration into its past: in Victorian times it had been the home of a proselytising vegetarian, and the words 'Vegetarian Lodge' could still be read by the front gate. So the gardens of Mapledene turn out to have just the right sort of tradition, rather than just the neighbours, on their side.

As for the 'blight, poverty and distress' mentioned in the report, the bulk of that is now concentrated over the road in the looming towers of the Holly Street Estate. People on that side of the road know what it is to have lived for twenty years in a technological short-cut that failed. By 1968, when the high-flat subsidy was abolished, everyone was pulling back in horror. The binge had been interrupted (except for a continuing export trade in the Third World), and the only sound was the clatter of knives and forks being thrown down, chairs being pushed back, and people muttering hasty excuses at the door. Flustered architects blamed the planners. Planners blamed the construction companies. The construction companies looked around and blamed national-government policy. Politicians of all electorally significant parties were quick to admit that a continued expansion of council housing was really not the answer to the accommodation problem. Even a critic like Martin Pawley couldn't resist bringing the whole story to an end with a resounding judgement. After using the abject miseries of the new housing estates to condemn the 'terrorism exercised by public housing authorities' over their tenants and to write off fifty years of public housing as an unmitigated 'failure',[35] he went off to pursue more exotic quarry elsewhere. Indeed, he re-emerged in Allende's Chile, insisting that all attempts at 'mass housing' were doomed to failure and advocating the very different kind of 'garbage housing' he thought developing countries might start building out of customised packaging materials – bottles, cans, and cardboard – from the west.

Various attempts have been made to alleviate the difficulties of people living on the council estates of the Sixties and early Seventies. The tenants' movement has evolved systems of self-management and control, and some specialists like Ann Sherman and the people at the Priority Estates Project have also concentrated on working out improved systems of security and administration. But while it was obvious that people were going to have to live in these towers for years, few architectural writers have been inclined to share the ordeal with them. Indeed, the problem of the tower block quickly became one of those 'boring' topics best left to social workers. The tenants didn't get that much sympathy from some sections of left-wing opinion either. Some academics banged on with increasingly surreal irrelevance about how council housing was altogether too *petit bourgeois* and respectable. In the early Seventies one such professor, Thomas L. Blair, even developed a pseudo-literary style at the expense of council tenants: he talked with undisguised contempt about 'welfstate' man.[36] Another strand of left-wing opinion reserved its hostility for the idea of 'community' that had so often been used to organise opposition to the redevelopments of the Sixties. Local campaigns of the sort that had prevented the demolition of De Beauvoir and Mapledene were dismissed as nothing more than 'gentrification'. Writers such as Richard Hoggart and Jeremy Seabrook came in for frequent bashings as the champions of traditional forms of community that were sexist, racist, and inclined to sap working-class militancy. Even in institutes that were pioneering a new regard for popular culture, researchers could write in the mid-Seventies that 'the move towards the break-up of traditional working class communities can only be welcomed by the left'.[37]

Stripped of its progressive aura, the council tower block has since undergone a symbolic conversion and emerged as a monstrous emblem of the futility of all State-led social reform. Post-war conservationists have certainly contributed to the development of this image. In 1951 Paul Elek could regret the sordid ugliness of the East End, and look forward to the day when 'new and better planned blocks of flats' were built to give people 'a better chance of a decent life', but this sort of naïve optimism wasn't to last.[38] Indeed, by the

Sixties John Betjeman's contempt for the 'vandalism of planners' was already reaching out far beyond the council tower block (the 'slab', as he used to call it), to embrace the entire architecture of housing reform. In *From Marble Arch to Edgware*, a BBC television film broadcast in 1968, he was shown walking into a close somewhere off the Edgware Road where there was a late Victorian 'improved' tenement, a modest terraced house of perhaps slightly earlier date, and a new tower block in the distance. Surveying this scene with his back to the camera, he spoke a few telling words:

> 'Improved Industrial Dwellings 1884.' That's where I'm standing. An improvement on what, I wonder. I think they thought it was an improvement on the little old London house. You've got the whole history of London in one view. There's the little house with its chimney pots. That's what they are replacing with these improved industrial dwellings – the beginnings of flats, the beginning of the end of street life and, over there on the horizon, a still greater inhumanity, the tall towers.

If Betjeman's post-war distinction between 'houses' and 'housing' could be used to discredit the works of Victorian philanthropy, it also offered new shape to the opposition between old buildings and people that had been expressed during the war by figures like Alex Comfort and James Lees-Milne. Post-war conservationists have not been forced to weigh the lives of people against the survival of historic buildings, but they sometimes do, nevertheless, appear remarkably unconcerned about the people for whom mass 'housing' was designed or, for that matter, about the human consequences of its failure. There's a hint of this indifference in the Hackney Society's mournful booklet, *Lost Hackney*, a pictorial tribute to the world in Dalston Junction's forgotten Town Guide Cabinet, which is made up of photographs of buildings (including the Victorian terraces that were replaced by the Holly Street Estate) demolished 'in the name of progress' and 'to make way for flats that are architecturally worthless and socially disastrous'.[39] Similarly, while in the mid-Seventies Colin Amery and Dan Cruickshank were in no doubt that London was threatened as much by the 'thrusting power of corporate commercial greed' as by bungled council development, this didn't prevent them from expressing their contempt for the architecture of high-rise council housing in words that risked adding insult to the injuries of the hapless tenants who lived in it. They glanced down the road to Broadwater Farm and stuck up a sign-post before moving on: 'already in Britain there are people who have no memory of their birthplace, no links left with the generations before them and no visual impressions of anything beyond their concrete balconies and the concrete balconies of their neighbours'. There are no myrtle shrubs or memories of Co. Mayo in that description: only brutalised zombies designed to prove Amery and Cruickshank's final point that 'Mass-produced environments create a suitable world only for the slaves of the production line'.[40]

In the early Seventies, Christopher Booker was also careful to be precise in his identification of the different forces that threatened London: whether they were speculative developers or public authorities of left or right.[41] But he has since trimmed his sails to a different wind. In 1977 he pronounced the epitaph for public housing in the *National Westminster Bank Quarterly Review*: 'The greatest public housing programme in history has lead not to a brave new world, but to a hideous wilderness of badly built, badly designed concrete boxes standing in windswept wastes, hated by their inhabitants and now in many cases falling down'.[42] A year later, he filmed a sequence that embodied exactly that conclusion for an influential BBC television documentary called *City of Towers*. The scene in question was shot from a cemetery overlooking miles of peripheral estate near Glasgow. A howling wind was turned up loud on the soundtrack and the camera panned round slowly to show gravestones and, beyond them, a monstrous world of dark, abysmal tower blocks. Never mind the speculators, the profiteering construction companies, the deluded expertise of both architect and planner; for Booker, the whole history of high rise culminated in this image: the tower block as tombstone not just of council housing but of the entire Welfare State.

Some commentators, and Gavin Stamp has been prominent among them, have persisted in describing the failure of post-war housing as a national tragedy rather than a political victory, and pointing out the true circumstances of the high-rise boom. But these sticklers for detail have been unable to prevent the tower block from re-emerging as a symbol of the evils of socialism. Other architectural pundits have happily adjusted the historical record to help ease the stricken tower block onto its new ideological plinth: thus, for example, Witold Rybczynski ignores the subsidies established by Macmillan's government in the Fifties, preferring to blame the high-rise disaster more generally on 'the socialist post-war governments' that favoured 'the left-leaning rhetoric of the Modern school'.[43] The right-wing think-tanks have not attempted to produce explicit arguments claiming the tower block as a socialist invention. Indeed, given the true history and the involvement of such leading think-tankers as Lord Keith Joseph of Portsoken, it has proved safer to maintain a tactful silence on the whole episode and allow the more maverick and loose-talking hit-men of the New Right to do the job for them. Thus Professor Stephen Haseler goes on about 'soulless socialist council estates' and the 'Fabian tower blocks of east London',[44] while other such ideologues have tried, if only in rhetoric, to establish the idea of the tower block as a machine in which 'stackaprole' Labour local authorities store their captive voters. For a time Jules Lubbock was striking back against these manipulative ascriptions, but his insistence that Labour had been wholly innocent of the high-rise fiasco was less sustainable than the equation he built up from a remark of Lord Kennet, Labour Minister of Housing in the late Sixties: 'Insinuate that socialism was to blame for decanting the cosy communities of Coronation Street into high rise flats, whether true or false; claim that the Tories believe in a house and a garden for all, and you have a highly effective and hard to dismantle political symbol'.[45]

It was in this atmosphere, in 1988, that English Heritage proposed a number of post-war buildings for listing, including the early tower blocks of the London County Council's estate in Roehampton – the very ones that R. Furneaux Jordan had celebrated back in the Fifties. The Environment Minister, Lord Caithness, was having none of it, remarking that 'buildings should not be listed if the public does not like them', leaving *The Sunday Telegraph* to conclude that the Roehampton towers were apparently 'too reminiscent of the dreary days of post-war, ration-book socialism' to deserve the protection of the state.[46] Not worth preserving in reality, the council tower block continues to figure in the mind of at least one Tory Minister as a symbol of the worst aspects of British life. This became apparent in a minor altercation that recently took place in the exclusive residential chambers known as Albany, near Piccadilly Circus. On 23 September 1990 *The Sunday Telegraph* reported on a row that had broken out over plans to restore some decaying 'perspective' trellis around the patio walls. The choice put to residents was between restoration of the original or its replacement with a simpler and much cheaper arrangement suitable for climbing plants. The trouble started after an anonymous benefactor offered to pay most of the required £30,000, thus persuading a majority of the eighty-seven residents to opt for the most expensive route. At this point Cyril Ray, the former war correspondent, veteran wine-writer and Labour party member, wrote round to his fellow residents objecting that 'a democratic system, such as I understand to obtain in Albany, is based on the principle of one man, one vote, and to allow a minority to pay to impose its wishes on a majority seems to me indefensible'. This was more than one of Ray's fellow residents could take. Alan Clark MP, Minister of State for Defence Procurement, was sufficiently provoked by this nasty and ungrateful outbreak of egalitarianism to circulate his own reply: 'Surely Albany is not a Tower Block with a "tenants association"? Do we not relish our distance from such vulgarities?'[47] This is where the council tower block now comes in: a lousy machine for living in, but an excellent one for discrediting political opponents. None of this bodes very well for the tenants of Rowan Court or for those among their number who took Margaret Thatcher's government at its word and bought into their slice of a building that now turns out to be somebody else's machine for maintaining proper social distances.

We have come a long way from the young James Lees-Milne's pre-war moment of vision at Rousham but, despite the endeavours of inner-city conservationists to merge conservation and social reform, we have not surpassed the romantic polarity between heritage and danger that James Lees-Milne discovered there. On one side stands Brideshead – a countervailing and predominantly rural world based on private values and culturally sanctioned hierarchy, where history is venerated as tradition and culture is based on ancestry and descent. On the other side, where the communist menace was for James Lees-Milne, lies the wreckage of 1945 piled up under the sign of the urban tower block: the commitment to public as opposed to private values, the anti-hierarchical egalitarianism, the hope that history could be made through the progressive works of an expert and newly enlightened State, the idea of a society based more on consent than descent. This polarised imagery is grounded in the true failures of post-war modernisation, but the polemical drama it has spawned offers no real answers to the problems it expresses.

Brideshead has won by discrediting the project of 1945, not by solving the problems the architects and engineers of that project set out, however inadequately, to address. Thus for example, Quinlan Terry's revival of classical architecture may be presented as an answer to the functional architecture of the public housing estate, but Terry builds his new country houses as homes for proper gentlemen, not council tenants. The lifestyle magazines' new emphasis on 'home', which if only in design terms also owes a lot to the interior styles of the country house, is similarly positioned. Thanks to this ongoing polarity between Brideshead and the tower blocks, the revival of 'home' has coincided with the revival of homelessness, which in recent years has been standing at the highest levels ever recorded. 'Home' spearheads the kind of modernisation that Raymond Williams described as 'mobile privatisation': 'home' as that convenient, credit-funded place where we go to enjoy, in the words of Witold Rybczynski, both 'cosiness and robots' in front of a television screen that occasionally brings us distancing views of a nation that has abandoned what were once assumed to be the public duties of the State. The late-night film is *The Towering Inferno* or Terry Gilliam's *Brazil*, where angels fly over a landscape as green as Crichel Down only to be rudely interrupted as the ground breaks up beneath them and hideous dark blocks burst up to an impossible height, threatening to knock them out of the sky. The news, meanwhile, offers spectacular sights like that provided by Greater Manchester on 14 October 1990: eight run-down council tower blocks at Kersal Vale in Salford, containing a total of 492 flats, being blown up to make way for an £18 million private development with flats and three-bedroomed houses, a landscaped communal garden, tennis courts, and a leisure centre. We pick up the Sunday magazine and read stories in which 'some pay to move in' while others 'pray to move out'. There's the multi-millionaire in his privatised penthouse at the

Barbican; the prosperous business woman who has moved into a former council tower block in Wandsworth, which has been emptied (asbestos still has its uses in this part of the world), sold to a private developer, and refurbished; and the miserable single mother in Newham whose life is already unremittingly awful and whose long-term prospects are even worse ('Living here is like a prison sentence').[48] Such are the lifestyle options to be found at the end of the Welfare State.

None of this comes as a surprise over in Hackney Town Hall. Not so long ago, I met Brynley Heaven, who was at that time Chair of the Housing Committee, to hear his views on the situation. He talked with great enthusiasm about some of the low-rise housing estates the council had been able to build in the Eighties. But while estates like Grace Jones Close or the new housing at Stonebridge, which was designed in consultation with the tenants, were certainly popular, Heaven was in no doubt that they also marked the end of the story. Indeed, the whole council housing programme was in 'headlong retreat' and the council faced escalating demand for a product that was less and less 'up to scratch'. Government control over council spending made it impossible for the London Borough of Hackney either to build new housing or improve its existing stock, while at the same time obliging it to spend fortunes accommodating homeless families in miserable West End hotels. There were indeed hideous problems of management and a horrendous backlog of repairs – the council was no longer even able to demolish unfit buildings.

On the subject of the tower block, Heaven had no doubt that it had 'become a convenient symbol for knocking British architecture and council housing all in one go'. Thanks to 'a cruel inversion of reality' that ignored the true circumstances of its construction, the tower block has become a kind of 'ideological bulldozer' for discrediting local democracy and 'the local provision of services'. For a while in the mid-Eighties Hackney Council had tried to free itself of this stigma by ceremoniously blowing up some of the worst of the tower blocks it had inherited from the GLC. Seating was arranged for onlookers, advertisements placed in the *Hackney Gazette*, and a happy tenant would be invited to detonate the charge. There was talk of dispatching the towers of the Holly Street Estate in this fashion, but though the prospect was much appreciated in the Mapledene area, it never came to pass. Such gestures were expensive and the truth is that the council made a spectacular failure even of the demolitions it did undertake: one tower on the Trowbridge Estate was exploded in front of the television cameras but, after rocking and giving off a cloud of dust, it merely settled into itself and stood there while the popular Press took a break from reciting 'looney left' stories and dubbed it 'The Leaning Tower of Hackney'. Brynley Heaven tried to turn even this story to advantage: didn't it just go to show that there was nothing intrinsically wrong with tower blocks and that some of them were remarkably well built? They may not be suitable for families with young children, but they have the potential to be highly desirable for single people, elderly people, and others who might 'choose to have that kind of environment'. Indeed, as he added with a gesture in the direction of Docklands, they were even building new ones for luxury use down there and calling them 'The Cascades'.

Brynley Heaven was much exercised on the subject of squatters. He had taken a firm line on this problem, forcing through some nationally publicised evictions on a number of estates. As he told me, 'We are improving. The number of empty flats is falling fast and the number of squatted properties is tumbling down. We are getting those bread-and-butter issues right'. But Heaven's days in Hackney were already numbered. Even at that time he was living in hiding – pursued by a mob of angry squatters who had traced him to his home address and meant him no good at all. A few months after our discussion, he jacked it all in and returned to his homeland on the west coast of Ireland with the expressed intention of setting up in the tourism business. According to the estimate of Mrs Cooper on the twelfth floor of Rowan Court, it was after his departure that the squatting of Holly Street's towers really began in earnest.

8

Rodinsky's Place

From the sad realities before us, I could disclose to you a faithful
though a faint picture of such desperate calamity and unutterable
ruin, that the heart must be stony indeed that did not sicken at the
sight. First I would lead you to the roof of a house, hardly deserving
the name of a garret . . .

Thomas Fowell Buxton, 1816

I have been spared the fatal romance of growing up in an English
country house, but England is full of ancestors and I can't visit
Spitalfields without thinking of a distant one of my own. Thomas
Fowell Buxton is remembered for his opposition to capital punishment and, above all, for his collaboration with Wilberforce in pressing
for the abolition of slavery. In his later years he came to be known as
Buxton the Liberator. However, between 1811 and 1818, and thanks
initially to the influence of his uncle, Mr Sampson Hanbury, he was a
director of Truman's brewery in Brick Lane, Spitalfields. While in
this position, he is said to have revised the whole system of
management and the success of this undertaking was reflected in the
vast personal wealth (sadly all that is left of it in my household is a
small, much distressed silver fork engraved with the initials TFB)
which soon enabled him to enter public life as Member of Parliament
for Weymouth. Buxton was a profoundly Christian businessman who
applied a strict form of moral accounting to his own conduct. His
philanthropic drive appears to have been shaped partly by the
influence of his Quaker mother, and partly by the ministry of Revd
Josiah Pratt at the Wheeler Street Chapel in Spitalfields. Buxton
busied himself on behalf of the Spitalfields Benevolent Society, a
parish-based organisation concerned to alleviate the distress that was
brought to the area partly by the marginal and vulnerable nature of
the silk trade in which the Huguenot weavers of Spitalfields were
engaged, and partly by the continuous influx into the area of 'the
poorest class of London work people' who were unable to find
lodgings elsewhere.

The Spitalfields Benevolent Society was accustomed to providing
soup and selling basic foods at the lowest possible price, but in
November 1816 the situation became unusually calamitous. A heavy
winter had set in abnormally early, and the local system of relief was
already quite overwhelmed. By this time, Buxton himself was no

longer living in the parish. Georgian Spitalfields held little attraction
for him, but though he had moved his young family out to Hampstead
for the sake of the country air, he still recognised the imperative of
doing something 'for the relief of my poor neighbours'. On 26
November 1816 he went to the Mansion House to deliver a speech
appealing to the wealthy people of the City of London, that they
should do something for 'the hungry and the naked' who were dying
little more than a stone's throw away from their own opulent world.

After visiting the adult school in Spitalfields, Buxton had once
written, 'I do not much admire meetings of ladies and gentlemen, but
the tradesmen speaking to the mechanics is a great treat for me . . . it
is so entertaining to hear them, such sublimity, such grandeur, such
superfine images; one fine fellow harvested a rich crop of corn off a
majestic oak, and the simile was received with a burst of applause'.
His own rhetorical style was of a plainer kind; but while his Mansion
House speech avoids the vanities of personal style or decorative
outward show, it is, nevertheless, made up of beautifully constructed
ethical tropes sprinkled with brief, and truly shocking, illustrations
drawn from the experience of one who, as Buxton put it, 'had been
doomed to the unhappy office of exploring the habitations of the
poor'.[1] The speech is driven by a sense of Christian duty combined
with a formidably rational analysis of the relationship between the
affluent City of London and the dreadful misery just over its eastern
border. Buxton had spent some of his time in Brick Lane studying
political economy, and he set out to convince his audience that 'the
persons for whom we plead are your own labourers, your own
mechanics, and your own poor'. Pointing to the fact that more than
half the poor in Spitalfields worked for masters who reside in the City,
he suggested a certain responsibility:

> Observe, my Lord, how unequal a division takes place between us
> – you have the man, and the labours of the man when he can work,
> and we have him and his family when he cannot; you have his
> strength, and we his infirmity; you his health, and we his sickness;
> you his youth, and we his age: in short, you have the labourer, and
> we the pauper; you have the profits of his labour, and we the
> charges of his maintenance.

The Poor Law, as Buxton explained, allowed parishes faced with
exceptional levels of distress to appeal to other parishes in the same
county; unfortunately however, the City of London formed a county in
itself, and was therefore without obligation to respond. Forced back on
to its own resources the parish could raise the rates, but since most of the
ratepayers were themselves poor, 'the only consequence of such
attempted advance is that we are obliged to strike their names out of the
list of those who pay the rates, and insert them in that of those who
receive them.' The speech hit its mark: it raised the huge sum of £43,339.

All that was a long time ago, but Buxton would surely have recognised the Spitalfields that Colin Ward described in 1975 as a classic inner-city 'zone of transition', a densely populated 'service centre for the metropolis' where wave after wave of immigrants had struggled to gain a foothold on the urban economy: Huguenot silk weavers, the Irish who were set to work undercutting them, Jewish refugees from late nineteenth-century pogroms in east Europe, and the Bengalis who had settled in the area since the Fifties.[2]

In the Eighties, however, things started to take a different turn. Indeed, Spitalfields achieved a national reputation less as a zone of transition than as a reclaimable area of beautiful houses and exotic contrasts that had survived the levelling embrace of the Welfare State. I made my first encounter with the contemporary perspectives of the place a few years ago when visiting Christ Church to attend a concert in the Spitalfields Festival. Just getting into the building proved interesting enough, not least because the approaching concert-goer can hardly avoid the attentions of a more regular group of supplicants also gathering in the evening shadows of Hawksmoor's massive church.

This is the derelict congregation of the crypt. Its members attend a hostel and soup kitchen famous from the days when the church yard was known as Itchy Park and that, for many of the post-war years through which the church above stood semi-derelict, provided the only regular service offered here. Ignoring the ancient injunction on the wall bidding them to 'Commit no nuisance', these time-honoured figures stage a vile performance of their own. They hurl insults at the concert-goers, begging money from them obscenely and urinating over their smart cars. My sleeve was taken by a man who dragged me through the hellish narrative of twenty-two years spent in gaol. Shuddering with horror at the deteriorated company into which he had been released, this fellow declared his own outlaw ethic in words that should be cut into the stone of Hawksmoor's building: 'I've never raped. I've never mugged. I've never robbed a working-class home'. As he sank away towards the underworld of the crypt, we ascended the hierarchical steps to hear music by Messaien and Hans Werner Henze. The *frisson* was undeniable.

Early in 1987 I went back to visit the disused synagogue at No. 19 Princelet Street – a dilapidated building owned since 1980 by the Spitalfields Trust and leased out into the new world as a 'heritage centre' concerned with the local history of immigration. In the old Huguenot weaving loft above the tiny synagogue is the room of David Rodinsky, a Polish Jew of increasingly mysterious reputation. Latterly described as a translator and philosopher, he is said to have lived here in some sort of caretaking capacity. One day in the early Sixties, or so the story goes, Rodinsky stepped out into Princelet Street and disappeared for ever. His room has since become fabled: a secret chamber still floating above the street just as it was left. Caught in a time warp of the kind that property developers are quick to straighten out, it has become the new Spitalfields' version of the *Marie-Celeste*. In the more imaginative versions of this myth, Rodinsky is even said to have left the table set for a meal.[3]

Rodinsky's room was certainly still there to be seen by the insistent visitor: ragged clothes still hanging in the wardrobe, a fur dangling down through the collapsing ceiling, a pile of 78s, lamps and odd bits of candle, an old gas mask, scattered and prophetic-looking books in Hebrew, Russian, Hindustani. Among junk heaped up on the table lies a Letts pocket diary designed for school children and dating from 1961 – a little memento to life as it was before the Filofax arrived in Rodinsky's street. Rescheduled in pencil according to the Julian Calendar, it has been marked in cuneiform and adjusted to commemorate such remote dates as Armenian New Year. The back pages (left to be filled in under printed headings like 'pocket money' or 'films seen during the year') are covered with scribbled commentaries on texts from the ancient Near East. They talk about Hittite Kings and the citizens of Ur. From the window one can see broad-roofed Huguenot weaving lofts outlined against Hawksmoor's church. A mile or so beyond looms a larger sight that Rodinsky was spared: the fifty-two floors of Richard Seifert's Natwest Tower, double-decker lifts, automatic window-washing facilities, and all.

Here again was the characteristic romance of the zone of transition where different worlds rub up against one another, languages intersect on every corner, and psychotics jabber in the street. The lighting may have been improved after the Ripper killings in 1888, but Spitalfields remains a place of unpredictable encounter – full of intriguing little surprises as one appearance gives way to the next. The story of Rodinsky's disappearance has become a *post-hoc* fable of the gentrifying immigrant quarter. The Huguenots have certainly vanished without trace, leaving only these remarkable houses behind. The Bengalis will need stronger magic if they are to pull off the same disappearing trick. As for Rodinsky, was he a latter-day prophet or just an old-fashioned mental defective? Did he evaporate romantically into thin air or was he struck down more prosaically in the street – a dishevelled-looking victim of attack or sudden illness, found in the vicinity of Itchy Park and dealt with by the appropriate authorities? The story would only retain its poetry for as long as such questions remained unanswered.

In recent years Spitalfields has been changing dramatically. The vegetable market has entered its last days and all sorts of curious conversions have been taking place around it. The Victorian underground public lavatory outside Christ Church has been bought by an entrepreneur who intends to re-establish it as a wine bar and brasserie. Within the church itself, the Holy Spirit sinks further and further into the evangelical crypt, retreating not just from Messaien and Anglo-Catholic conservationists, but from the dry ice and camera cranes of pop-video-makers who come here for the atmosphere. With its small synagogue downstairs and Rodinsky's garret under the roof, No. 19 Princelet Street has also become something of a location in recent years, a place rented out to faithless people in search of a charismatic setting. Secular but Bohemian couples have held their wedding receptions here, and journalists come here to launch their books: hoping, presumably, that the atmosphere will lend some of its originality to their undistinguished works. As long as they don't get trampled to death by the television crews who are increasingly following each other up and down the stairs, the more adventurous guests at such occasions, or at least those who tire of the implausible 'social surrealism' downstairs, can climb the perilous staircase to the top of the house and marvel at the way Rodinsky's collapsing domain seems to oscillate between two interpretations of the slum interior. Even the most starry-eyed visitor would find it impossible to see the kitchen as any more romantic than the garret where, in the freezing winter of 1816, Thomas Fowell Buxton found 'three human beings – each seventy years of age – each with ghastly lineaments of famine' and with only 'a few bricks' left as their furnishings. With its layers of engrained filth and its walls papered over with newsprint, this foul little hole stands in unmistakable tribute to the documentary tradition. It presents exactly the kind of image that was still being used, right up into the Seventies, to press the case for slum clearance and redevelopment. But this is only one aspect of the story. By the Eighties, and especially when the property market started to move, this blitzed- out imagery of the slum interior was being augumented and put to very different purposes: it was beginning to turn up in the brochures of the more style-conscious estate agents in nearby areas like Islington. In the spring of 1986, Holden Matthews started publishing an ostentatiously designed lifestyle magazine called *Inside Islington*, which gave their adverts an unmistakable Spitalfields touch. One picture (an appropriately black-and-white photograph) showed nothing more than a stretch of wainscotting and some Georgian bannisters, and was accompanied by a price of £320,000 and a text announcing that the house had been variously used over the last two hundred years 'as a brothel and clothes factory'. Another showed a totally derelict interior full of rubble and scattered corrugated iron, and came with a heading that certainly hadn't been deliberately borrowed from Thomas Fowell Buxton: 'Opportunity – arrange this two-floored pile of bricks to suit yourself'. One only had to glance at the debris in Rodinsky's main room to gain an intimation of what was to come next. None of the junk here was properly ancestral (although the wardrobe looked like a fine product of the late-Victorian east-London furniture trade), but this charismatic garret was already offering itself as a bizzarre inner-city equivalent to the cluttered and unexpectedly penurious mid-century country-house interior James Lees-Milne and Vita Sackville West had valued above all for its clobber.

Gin Lane Restored

> The number of opulent individuals in this district is exceedingly small.
>
> Thomas Fowell Buxton, 1816

In its early days, the Spitalfields Historic Building Trust certainly pursued a vision. Mark Girouard was the founding chairman and, in 1979, he surveyed the area for the readers of *Country Life* and outlined the trust's hopes for its future. Looking back through the needless decay and botched redevelopment of the Sixties and Seventies, he celebrated eighteenth-century Spitalfields as a place of true urban density where everything had been gloriously mixed up together. There had been no enforced separation of industrial and residential activities, and 'the houses of the rich merchants and weavers living in Spital Square, opulently equipped with marble chimney pieces and rococo plasterwork, were only a few minutes walk from the poorest weavers' cottages'[4]. The centre had since been 'blasted out' of historical Spitalfields by the expansion of both the vegetable market (which had traditionally been confined to the area of a single field in front of Christ Church) and the rag trade, which has grown since Victorian times to blight streets that had previously been residential. But though there could be no doubt that these developments had 'seriously affected the quality of life in Spitalfields', there was still enough left to be worth fighting about. The Spitalfields Trust was never in any doubt that 'the best way to save a threatened building is to buy it' but this was not to say that it was content to be in the vanguard of an ordinary gentrification process. Girouard described the arrival of the Bangladeshis as 'the most colourful happening in Spitalfields since the war' (it's not hard to imagine the smirk this choice of words is likely to have provoked in conventional *Country Life* circles), but he also welcomed these recent immigrants as intelligent, law-abiding, and hard-working people who would make acceptable neighbours even though they lived in housing conditions that were already something of a 'national scandal'. The Spitalfields Trust wanted to carry out an experiment with time. Depressed by the deteriorated state of Spitalfields in the present, the trust hoped 'for the revival of Spitalfields in something of the form it had in the 18th century, as an area where people of many types, races and classes can live and work together in a civilised environment and in buildings of human scale'.[5] As Girouard continued, 'such a revival would involve the reversal of the trend which has ruled in London since the 19th century, segregating people in one-class residential areas, far away from their work'. In the course of describing this remarkable post-reformist vision, he asked his countrified readers to imagine Fournier Street alive with song as it must have been in the eighteenth century: there would have been trilling song birds such as the weavers liked to keep, the songs they themselves sang as they toiled at their looms; and, on Sundays, passionate hymns would have issued from the churches at both ends of this short but characterful street. This was a conservationist vision, to be sure, but it bore little immediate resemblance to the community-based idea of conservation that had emerged in such places as De Beauvoir and Mapledene ten years earlier.

There was an opportunity to learn more on 16 September 1987, when some 150 people gathered at the conference hall in Truman's post-modernised Brick Lane brewery to celebrate the tenth anniversary of the Spitalfields Trust. As I arrived at the meeting, I passed Spitalfields' most famous residents, Gilbert and George, walking silently down Brick Lane in the opposite direction, a large pot of Dulux paint held between them. Other local residents were also conspicuously absent. Indeed, Girouard's mixture of types, races, and classes was certainly not much in evidence at this meeting: I couldn't see a single coloured face in the crowd.

Francis Carnwarth is the personable City banker who took over as chairman of the Spitalfields Trust from Mark Girouard, and he opened the event by welcoming everyone in the name of the organisation that, as he put it in a phrase that Thomas Fowell Buxton would never have applied to empty buildings, had 'saved eighteenth-century Spitalfields'. Most of the surviving eighteenth-century houses in the area had been secured in one way or another, and the job looked increasingly accomplished. As one might expect at meetings like this, there was room for some comfortable retrospection. Indeed, the memories of the trust's early days served as a glowing brazier at which the veterans and their supportive audience stood around warming themselves. Those were the days of art-historial activism, of squats, occupations, and sit-ins undertaken by the trust's members as they confronted 'greedy' developers, bungling municipal authorities, and housing associations like Newlon that, still unaware of the vital distinction between 'housing' and true 'houses', planned to erect new buildings where listed (but decayed) eighteenth-century houses still stood. In those days, the trust's members kept their sleeping bags ready rolled in case another emergency came up. 'Denied even a hot bath', as Douglas Blain, the secretary of the trust, has put it, they developed the unlikely look of squatting hippies, communicating with the Press through nearby telephone boxes, and applying the time-honoured local tradition of the soup kitchen to themselves. John Betjeman came down to visit – people were invited to join him for drinks 'at home' in a half-demolished and squatted house. One of the trust's most cherished photographs from this time shows the almost indistinguishable faces of Mark Girouard and Colin Amery staring out from within the padlocked wrought-iron gates of a threatened school hall in Spital Square. This was certainly a 'Top Person's Squat', even though, as David Mellor has pointed out, the picture is strangely reminiscent of Bill Brandt's photograph of Welsh miners standing in a lift poised to sink down into the bowels of the earth.

From these romantic beginnings the trust went on to bring credit facilities into an area that had been 'red-lined' by banks and building societies. It emerged as a campaigning property company with charitable status, able to buy houses, and then to repair and resell them under covenants designed to ensure that they would be refurbished with a care for the minutest period detail. The Spitalfields Trust resents the charge that it has merely reduced conservation to gentrification, claiming in its own defence that it has never evicted a tenant and that it has gone out of its way, when buying houses that were in 'unsuitable' industrial use for conversion back into private homes, to find alternative premises for displaced enterprises.[6] But despite the dissenting condition of Raphael Samuel who got up (to be quietly denounced by a man behind me as 'that blasted anarchist') and suggested that Georgian Spitalfields was actually a ghoulish recent invention and, moreover, that conservation was helping to destroy the life of the area, the focus of the conference was insistently, even obsessively, architectural. Dan Cruickshank gave an enthusiastic and extraordinarily knowledgeable account of the 'Minister's House', built to Hawksmoor's design just next to Christ Church in Fournier Street. He pointed to the monumental doorway that 'hovered' between baroque and Palladian, the unusual cornice with its bold cyma recta immediately over a corona, the raised and fielded panelling, the staircase with its remarkable pattern of balusters. He indicated some unique characteristics of the external pointing and dwelt on the tiniest details of the plasterwork saying, with a winning smile, 'Either you love them or you don't.' Brian Morton, a conservationist structural engineer, showed how bulging Georgian walls could be saved from over-zealous application of council building regulations. Ian Bristow drew on pictures by such eighteenth-century artists as William Hogarth and Theodore de Bruyn, to resolve the question of whether Georgian sash windows were painted white or coloured. Mark Girouard himself showed how the Vestry Room in Christ Church had served in the eighteenth-century as the centre of parish government, but he had also come with impressive proof that the 'saving' of Georgian Spitalfields had been a truly multinational endeavour. He showed a slide of a ghost-like Georgian room, complete with panelling and fireplace. There could be no doubt that this interior belonged to the eighteenth-century Spitalfields Girouard had dreamt of reviving; but though it had once been part of a house in Artillery Lane, history had long since forced it into emigration and Girouard had discovered it lying in storage like a folded tent in the Art Institute of Chicago. Such has been the diaspora of Georgian fixtures and fittings that some Spitalfields panelling is even said to have been lost to luxurious skyscraper apartments in Manhattan. Yet with this curiously unfixed room from Artillery

Lane, there seemed to be at least some chance that history might be brought back to serve, in the place where it really belonged, as a conservationist riposte to the 'relocatable walls' of the 'flexible interior' with which modern office designers were at that time trying to ease the situation of companies 'coping with corporate growth' in the booming City of London.[7]

Occasional television programmes in the Sixties showed the indigenous white population leaving for Essex with relief, but the altogether more profuse coverage of recent years has concentrated on the newest arrivals, telling the different story of rundown Huguenot houses being recovered from use as residential slum or sweat-shop, lovingly restored and re-established as private homes. The first of the new immigrants certainly didn't just buy into the area to make a killing. But if it takes conservationists, avant-garde artists, gays, and other Bohemian or single-minded types to put up with the years of chaotic living that are needed to re-open dishevelled areas like Spitalfields, the estate agents and financiers are never far behind. Like the first loft dwellers in Manhattan, these early settlers are the pioneers of a larger revaluation they may detest and even manage to steer for a bit, but that is soon enough sweeping over their ears. West of Commercial Street the sanitisation already looks complete. To the east in Fournier Street sensitively refurbished houses have been coming on to the market at prices approaching £500,000. In the late Seventies the Spitalfields Trust may have had to hunt for eccentric types willing to buy into a decayed immigrant area without such public amenities as parks or tolerable schools but, in reality, as hindsight would soon show, it was handing out personal fortunes to all its chosen purchasers, and it is not surprising that questions have sometimes been asked (and not just by frustrated would-be purchasers) about the trust's way of selecting buyers. In its early days, the trust thrived as any mutual-aid society would on the personal contacts (including the odd marriage) that produced buyers and ensured good working relationships with grant-giving bodies like English Heritage, the Historic Buildings Council, and the GLC. However, as the value of its covenanted houses soared this all began to look a little unregulated, perhaps even a bit dodgy. Justified or not, such are the embarrassing suspicions that rise when big money steps into the tracks of penurious conservationist campaigners.

By the end of the Eighties it was obvious that the rising property market threatened Spitalfields with an altogether more devastating uniformity than Welfare State regulation could ever have achieved. The owners of Truman's Brewery had finally exorcised the ghost of Thomas Fowell Buxton by turning the brewery into a huge property development. As for the old fruit and vegetable market (described by the trust's secretary as a 'grave nuisance' with its 'noise, dirt and litter') this was due to be moved to Hackney Wick in February 1991 and replaced by another mega-development that, for a while at least, was to have been designed by Richard MacCormac, a well-known architect who is closely associated with the trust. Indeed, by 1990 the Spitalfields Trust had itself been priced out of the area: unable to acquire even the most wiped-out Georgian shell for anything less than a mad price, it was beginning to reach out into other locations to the north and east.

In the early stages, however, the thrill of unlikely coexistence was very much a part of the attraction. As was made clear in Alexandra Artley and John Martin Robinson's diverting *New Georgian Handbook* (published by *Harpers and Queen* in 1985) the starting-point was an appreciation of disparity and contrast: the miraculously surviving eighteenth-century house played off against the municipal oblivion that had failed to engulf it. Treating the recovered house as 'an antique for living in', the New Georgian aesthetic made a special point of the interior, valuing it as a private realm of clobber, candles, and coal fires, and setting it off, often with the help of carefully restored shutters, against a public world given over to destructive modernisation.[8] Thanks to the Spartan settlers of Spitalfields, even the starkest imagery of the unimproved slum interior could be recovered. At the roughest edges of this scene it became positively virtuous not to have electricity or running water. Squalor itself was authenticated and 'saved' from the Welfare State, which had threatened to finish it off for good.

The individual cameos are familiar enough. Dan Cruickshank lives in Elder Street, where journalists have found him protecting his early eighteenth-century wall panelling from the wiring and plumbing of excessive modern convenience. Dennis Severs has gone further. Huguenot canaries hang in wicker cages outside his door in Folgate Street, while inside he has reconstructed the imaginary candlelit world – 'a collection of atmospheres' – of a declining historical family, living the fantasy himself and offering tours for visitors in which he stars as the raconteur. A few streets to the east, Jocasta Innes has been busy reviving traditional decorative techniques on her own walls, following up the wholesome concerns of her early book, *The Pauper's Cookbook*, with *Paint Magic*, an influential primer on antique methods of home improvement that she, or at least her willing assistants, first tried out on the walls of her own Spitalfields house. The sequence that emerges through the much publicised interiors of these restored and covenanted houses is peculiar but exact. Rodinsky's room is crossed with Calke Abbey, filled with junk and ghosts of a cleaned-up and re-ancestralised kind, and then projected through the designerish style of magazines like *The World Of Interiors, Traditional Historical Decoration, Tatler* and *Harpers and Queen*. Ten years ago, Mark Girouard's articles on Spitalfields may have seemed rather out of place in the pastoral English pages of *Country Life*, but pictures of the more recently restored Spitalfields interiors have coexisted perfectly with features on the country house, and not just those concerned with, say, the bone-chilling winter nights to be had in the cold rooms of the country's most authentically austere stately homes[9] or, for that matter, the barrenness of Peter Ackroyd's newly acquired Georgian retreat in Somerset ('There's not much furniture at all, but I like it sparse').[10] The panelled rooms may be smaller in Spitalfields, but the bibelots and the antiques, distressed or not, are back in place, and the resulting picture fits right in. In one house in Elder Street (the place is positively lurid with period decor) an old thunder box has even been carefully plumbed into the bathroom.

Out in the street that agreeable sense of disparity has also been going through its paces. I once stood outside the old synagogue in Princelet Street and watched: the dossers stumbled about, photographers took pictures of each other taking pictures of buildings, a Bangladeshi man unloaded leathers into a Georgian house that hadn't yet been returned to more 'suitable' use, an impeccably tailored but still rather implausible-looking English gentleman packed his two uniformed daughters into the car, ready to take them back to boarding school. As they slide alongside each other, like the panels on one of those flattened Rubik cubes by Fournier Street residents Gilbert and George, the appearances are caught in a shifting display of incongruity and juxtaposition that mocks old ideas of causality or of a unified social reality. Older waves of gentrification were sometimes justified on the grounds that they helped upgrade whole areas, but in Spitalfields the visible signs of what used to be deplored as 'inequality' are re-established as cultural exotica – a diverting performance in the retinal theatre of the incoming *flâneur*.

Spitalfields can no longer be called 'Britain's grandest slum' and, in the last few years, there have been new problems with the adopted style of 'Hogarth's London inside, Calcutta outside'. Robust decay is all very well when glimpsed from inside the New Georgian interior, but the Bangladeshis don't quite seem to have got the idea. There was a nasty clash early in the Eighties when chain-saws were taken to the old galleries in the Huguenot church on the corner of Brick Lane and Fournier Street – a building that had served as a synagogue before being converted into a mosque in 1976. Gavin Stamp's frustration at difficulties of this sort could, I think, be sensed in an article he wrote in 1985, which described the Huguenots as successful immigrants who had been 'indistinguishable from the English by colour and race' and did nothing to 'offend national sensibilities'.[11] Since then Bangladeshis have started demanding something rather more than a place in the background of New Georgian Spitalfields as aromatic restaurant-eurs and local colour. It has been suggested that Spitalfields should be re-established as 'Banglatown', and there have been marches in Brick Lane supporting Khomeini's *fatwa* against Salman Rushdie (who only a few weeks before had himself been walking down the same evocative street for the television cameras in order to publicise *The Satanic Verses*). The first wave of New Georgians knew how to rough it, but it is not clear how well equipped their successors are to cope with the less picturesque challenge of militant Islam.

In the meantime, however, critics are seen off with little ceremony. After touring the area with Business in the Community in 1987, Prince Charles appeared to come out against the new aesthetic, or at least to have reminded its more forgetful advocates of the 'national disgrace' that Mark Girouard had also once seen in their housing conditions. But the age of the bleeding heart is over and this royal whinge about the circumstances in which many Bangladeshis live and work was too much for one New Georgian resident of Princelet Street. Charles Clover, self-described 'yuppie' and environment correspondent of *The Daily Telegraph*, hit back in the *Spectator* (11 July 1987). He declared Spitalfields to be altogether more dynamic and enterprising than the sullen and uniform slums that exist where the Welfare State got better established. It was only the poverty of the area, and the fact that health and planning regulations were never properly enforced, that had enabled the Bengalis to gain their slight economic foothold in the first place. And anyway, 95 per cent of these Bengalis come from Sylhet, the most backward part of Bangladesh. Whole families may indeed share single rooms and even beds in Spitalfields, but this is exactly how they live in Sylhet as well. Rather than complaining that conditions were 'almost as bad as those on the Indian sub-continent', the prince should evidently have learnt the real lesson of Brick Lane: in the urban economy as much as in any flourishing Indian restaurant, variety is the spice of life.

The authors of the *New Georgian Handbook* have also divided on the social question as it re-emerged in the second half of the Eighties. John Martin Robinson, who was at that time working for the London Division of English Heritage, likes to style himself Fitzalan Pursuivant Extraordinary and there can be little doubt that he has an appropriately heraldic turn of mind. Writing under the auspices of the National Trust, he has published vigorous defences of every aspect of England's landed aristocracy, right down to the poaching laws that, at one point in the early eighteenth century, made the very act of blacking one's face a capital offence. As Robinson put it: 'Much has been made of the socio-economic background to poaching, that it provided a means of sustenance for impoverished and unemployed rural workers. The poor, it is claimed, were driven to poaching to avoid starvation; and this made the penalties against poaching seem so cruel. It is not clear what real evidence there is to support this sentimental theory.'[12]

As a member of the Crichel Down School of historiography, John Martin Robinson's sense of history is distinguished by polemical rather than chronological or factual precision. On 26 March 1988, for example, the chap was affronted by a letter that appeared in the *Spectator*. Written by a self-styled Thatcherite named C. A. Latimer, the offending communication dared to contest the idea, expressed in a previous issue, that the rich had been more generous before 1914. Lloyd George's budget put income tax up from 1s. to 1s.2d. in the pound and was, as Latimer continued, greeted with uproar in the House of Lords: 'Anybody would have thought that the world had come to an end'. The Fitzalan Pursuivant Extraordinary wasn't going to let this kind of twaddle pass; indeed, he picked up his quill and scratched out a withering riposte condemning the hapless C. A. Latimer for favouring governments that 'confiscate' the 'capital and income of private citizens' and fritter it away on 'worthwhile projects like the Blue Streak Rocket, Marsham Street Office Blocks, motorways and the creation of a counter-productive civil service bureaucracy in the scale of Tsarist Russia'.[13] C. A. Latimer was far from *au fait* with this new way of understanding Lloyd George's pension scheme, which, as he or she pointed out in a second letter published on 16 April, had surely been modest enough, offering '5s. a week if you lived to be 70, and 7s. 6d. for a married couple'. Perhaps this was the poor Latimer's first exposure to the bracing winds of Crichel Down.

Alexandra Artley, on the other hand, has turned against the more recent manifestations of the New Georgian spirit. In *The New Georgian Handbook*, she had celebrated the interest of places that were still 'socially crunchy' and had a 'healthy mix of young, old, crims [criminals], Bangladeshis, clergy and council estaters', but by the end of 1986 she had cut through the beady-eyed New Georgian style of observation, and rediscovered the non-architectural and, if Thomas Fowell Buxton is anything to go by, distinctly old Georgian themes of charity, social responsibility, and equality before the Lord. In his speech of 26 November 1816, Buxton had urged the prosperous gentlemen of the City to 'Come amongst us' to see for themselves: 'Come by night, and we will shew you the baskets and the sheds of our markets filled with these wretched creatures – there they find their nightly lodging, and there amongst its scraps and refuse they pick out their daily food'. He had assailed them with monstrous vignettes: the widows who had sold their clothes for bread and were now 'ashamed to appear in the streets'; or the father of a large family pulling out his stove to exchange it for food, 'the dread of future cold' being 'less violent than the cravings of immediate hunger'. He had told of 'the prostrate despair of manhood willing to work, but unable to obtain employment and compelled to see in the countenance of his dejected wife, and to hear the cries of his perishing children the consequences of his arrested toil', and then topped his frightful anecdote with another that was still worse: 'On Friday last I saw a man who was lately found amongst some willows in our district. There were some remains of life in him, but (I hardly know how to convey so loathesome an image,) the vermin of all kinds had already seized upon him as their prey. . . . I asked him if he had a wife? No, Sir, thank God, I can suffer better than many others, because I suffer alone'.

Alexandra Artley could spare readers of the *Spectator* such hideous excesses as these, but as she pushed her pram through inner London streets (her chosen method of social observation), she found unmistakable evidence that distress could still affect people rather than just buildings or antiques. She came across quarrelling dwarves in Clerkenwell, broken and desperate Asian women in King's Cross supermarkets, a middle-aged woman who was clad only in filthy sacking and walked barefoot, like some sort of throw-back to Buxton's time, down the Gray's Inn Road. She reported on the children of homeless 'bed and breakfast' families who spent their lives strapped into pushchairs wheeled back and forth between one forlorn official destination and another. Under the editorship of Charles Moore, the *Spectator* could just as easily have treated these pitiable creatures as picturesque freaks, but Alexandra Artley insisted on their humanity.[14] Not content with reviving the traditions of the Primrose League and the soup kitchen in her own descriptions of the city, she went on the assault against the fashionable ideologues of the New Right, attacking think-tankers like David Willets of the Centre for Policy Studies, who supported, and indeed helped to motivate, the government's attempt to reduce or get rid of child benefit, and attending a seminar at the St Stephen's Club on Gertrude Himmelfarb's pamphlet, *Bombay Values*, only to dismiss it with one disdainful sentence: 'I think this means stepping over families sleeping in the street as you enter an expensive restaurant'.[15] These contributions turned out to be more than some of her fellow contributors could bear. Auberon Waugh called together the old boys among his readers for a bullying snigger at Artley's expense: wasn't it time, he asked, for all these emotional women who have been going on like 'slightly drunk wives at middle-class dinner parties to gather under the single banner of a National Organisation of Madwomen?'[16]

Artley put up with some vicious attempts at character assassination as she picked her way across the filthy urban Waste Land that she found in the widening gap between architectural conservation and the Christian tradition of the helping hand. When I first met her in 1988, she was still sitting in the famously New Georgian sitting-room she shared with her husband, Gavin Stamp, in King's Cross, but her words revealed how fully she had detached herself from the conservationist cult she herself had both epitomised and helped to define only three years before. She had no argument with the true conservationists, or for that matter with the people who had moved into areas like Spitalfields before they became fashionable and spent hard years camping out in their wrecked houses while restoring them to some sort of inhabitable condition. Neither was she inclined to be too excoriating about all the eighteenth-century street parties and costume balls (powdered wigs and historical costumes rented from theatrical outfitters) that marked the next stage in the emergence of the New Georgian cult. But by 1986 or so, the cause had been lost. As she put it, 'architecture had become property' and conservation had collapsed into social climbing and estate agents' chit-chat. The New Georgian aesthetic had degenerated from an appreciation of 'the individuality of different types of neighbours' into a lurid appetite for 'Gin Lane *frisson* ('Gosh, darling, there are people lying in the gutter on cabbage leaves, actually dying, just like they did in eighteenth-century London'). In the new age of 'style without substance' (with Margaret Thatcher, it's 'Queen Anne at the front and Sally Anne at the back'), Georgian property has become especially desirable: 'if you've got a Georgian terrace house, you can fill it up with the Georgian knick-knacks and the distressed this and the distressed that, and suddenly you have that . . . aristocratic fragrance about you'. Artley closed with an old Georgian judgement: 'If you cannot feel the suffering and the need of human beings around you, well, then your connoisseurship is an empty thing and a wicked thing in my view'. Never mind the bogus mystery about David Rodinsky and his disappearance, this was the true meaning of his charismatic garret. First the crazy clutter of his slum gave way to stylish '*désordre Britannique*' and then, within a year or two, the country-house interior had landed in the middle of the city. Having returned from its triumphant visit to Washington DC, it was not content merely to settle back into its customary domain out in the shires. It had secured a beach-head in Spitalfields – its invasion of the inner-city had begun.

9

An Unexpected Reprieve

Sutton House is only a couple of miles from Spitalfields, and by the time I first came across it beleaguered among the tower blocks, there were unmistakable signs of relief all round. Country-house style decor had, filtered down through the lifestyle magazines to be within the reach of any of the more prosperous 'skyscraper families' who felt inclined to turn their flat into a proper home. As for the classical columns that such neo-romantic artists as John Piper and Michael Ayrton had shown scattered and broken at ruined country houses during the war, their replacements were turning up in new housing developments throughout east London. By 1984 some had been installed only a few yards west of Hackney's country house in Sutton Square, a private residential development built to designs by the acclaimed 'New Georgian' architects, Campbell, Zogolovitch, Wilkinson & Gough.[1] Rows of them also adorn the huge new Safeways at Stamford Hill: made of synthetic material of the 'Aristocast' variety, they have proved, nevertheless, sufficiently load-bearing to prop up the Conservative approach to inner-city regeneration.

The officers of the National Trust may have become remote from their building in Hackney, but by the late Eighties they knew that the property market was booming even there, and hoped that by converting it into private flats, which would be both 'close to the City' and full of 'original features', they might finally be rid of their irksome and anomalous charge in the East End. While the Save Sutton House Campaign formed to oppose this scheme as a shabby piece of opportunism, its members did nevertheless find their own way of rising to the challenge posed by the National Trust's triumphant cult of the country house. It took these local campaigners no time at all to dig up an appropriate ancestor for Sutton House. Sir Thomas Sutton had been the founder of Charterhouse School and he had apparently also equipped and sailed his own ship against the Spanish Armada. His association with Hackney's country house was unknown to George Lansbury and the others who appealed for the building, described only as 'St John's Institute' shortly before World War Two. As for the damaged and chaotic interior, while the fine furniture and ancestral portraits (sublime or 'atrocious', as the case may have been) had long since disappeared, there was certainly no shortage of rubbish. Lots of 'irrelevant trash', to use James Lees-Milne's phrase, was found under the floorboards, and a lost world turned up in an evocative handful of dust found behind the stolen panelling: scraps of paper with samples of seventeenth-century hand-writing, fragments of embroidery, old slippers, eighteenth-century pins, newspaper cuttings, old photographs, cigarette packets, even postcards from exotic holiday locations that were signed 'Clive'. All this was magical stuff for local enthusiasts, but in the end it just served to show how far Sutton House was from conforming to the country-house paradigm the trust has assembled since acquiring this building through public appeal in 1939. The charismatic rubbish only demonstrated that the house had been in that despised 'institutional' use (whether as boys' club or school) right back into the eighteenth century. As for the vital ancestral moment, this was simply too far gone: indeed, further researches revealed that Sir Thomas Sutton had probably lived in a long-since demolished house next door.

For a time it looked as if nothing could close the distance that has grown up between Sutton House and the National Trust during the years of the Country Houses Scheme. Sutton House is now administered from Hughenden Manor in Buckinghamshire, a poor cousin from the London slums squeezed under the leafy umbrella of the trust's Thames and Chiltern Region. As for the staff responsible for its care, they are trained as land agents – professionals who, while they may be qualified in the management of aristocratic estates, could hardly be less fitted for urban community work. Additionally, during the very decades when the National Trust has been busy in the shires of deep England, promoting its cult of ancestral continuity for all it is worth, Hackney was going in the opposite direction, becoming a multi-racial inner-city borough. The distance between Sutton House and the trust's regional office may be counted in a few dozen miles, but ordinary mileage can't measure the cultural chasm that has opened between them during the years of the Country Houses Scheme.

While the officers of the trust have been inclined to give up on Hackney, local people around Sutton House have responded with accusations of their own. Stories circulate about the first pair of green wellies to be sighted on Homerton High Street for a hundred years; about the ancient front door of Sutton House, which is still sometimes said to have been filched by a member of the National Trust's staff; or about the day a visiting team from Hughenden Manor went down to MacDonalds on Mare Street for lunch and started cracking stiff jokes about 'the banks of the Limpopo'. Meanwhile, some officials in the council planning department were apparently suspicious of the very idea of historical continuity and saw Hackney's dishevelled country house as an implicitly racist building. I have found no one in the planning department who will admit to having held such a discreditable view, but the discussions about the possibility of siting the new Hackney Museum in Sutton House seem to have been influenced by this perception. When Martin Village went along to sound out the possibility on behalf of the trust, he was told that the house was 'too English' for multi-racial use, and the museum was eventually placed in a building with a more neutral and, in the event, decidedly 'institutional' atmosphere. Sutton House had apparently missed its chance again: falling between the grand and ancestralised conception of the country house the trust had been peddling in the shires, and an anti-racist philistinism that had arisen in the inner city to meet it.

For a while it looked as if Sutton House, together with Lansbury's hope for a reconciliation of conservatism and social reform, would disappear into the void that has opened over the post-war years between the polarised clichés of Brideshead and the tower blocks. As it happens, however, an altogether more positive outcome appears to have been secured. The publicity generated by local campaigners embarrassed the trust, awakening its senior management (and particularly the Chairman of that time, Dame Jennifer Jenkins) to other possibilities. The original scheme for conversion into private flats was scrutinised and found wanting by the Save Sutton House Campaign (who benefitted from the advice of Julian Harrap, veteran of the Mapledene campaigns and, by now, a rather eminent conservationist architect who numbers the Spitalfields Trust among his clients). Martin Village bowed out gracefully enough and, after a number of sticky meetings, the National Trust agreed to take the apparently unprecedented step of going into collaboration with the local campaigners to see if their alternative scheme for community use could be made to work. A joint committee was set up and, as a concession to the new climate of cooperation, the Save Sutton House Campaign renamed itself the Sutton House Society. The scheme will ensure the restoration of the building and also include some new and unashamedly modern additions designed by Julian Harrap's practice. It will produce offices on the upper floors, a shop, function rooms that ensure the house is opened up for all sorts of cultural and educational uses, a restaurant, and a bar. At a later date, it is intended to install a permanent exhibition. The scheme, which offers to realise the trust's original commitment to both conservation and reforming good works, has been costed at £1.7 million: a legacy is being used to cover the first stages of the restoration and an appeal is to be launched early in 1991 to close the gap.

So the prospect is that, half a century after its acquisition by the National Trust, 'The Old House at the Corner' will finally come into its own as a place of citizenship as well as ancestry, of public as well as private values, and of cultural activity that extends far beyond the conventional lutes and tinkling harpsichords. The National Trust has become positively enthusiastic about the prospect, claiming that Sutton House has shown it a new way of thinking about inner-city properties. But as a critic of the National Trust, I too have found reason to think again. When I first heard about the problems at

Sutton House, I wasted no time stepping in on the side of the Save Sutton House Campaign, accusing the trust of manifold incompetence, describing Hackney's mansion as a forgotten victim of the triumphant Country Houses Scheme, and pointing an accusing finger at James Lees-Milne, who makes an interesting as well as easy target.[2] I'm glad to have contributed to the campaign that prevented the effective privatisation of Sutton House, but I can't pretend to be happy about some of the company in which I have found myself as a critic of the National Trust.

In recent years, the National Trust has been under fire from all sides. This became abundantly clear in October 1990 when Rodney Legg attacked the trust for betraying the ideals of its Victorian founders. Legg spoke as chairman of the Open Spaces Society, an organisation that, under its previous name, the Commons Preservation Society, had founded the National Trust in the 1890s (and which, incidentally, had also numbered Thomas Fowell Buxton among its own founder members). He claimed that 'From being an egalitarian access organisation promoting the public good, the trust has become an elitist club of art connoisseurs, and defensive in the protection of a prize collection of dinosaurs'. The response to this attack took a remarkable form. Thus, to quote only one example, an editorial in *The Independent* found it 'hard not to feel some sympathy for Mr. Legg's point of view', but it quickly went on to superimpose a significantly different critique of the trust over the one Legg had made. Far from being too secretive and haughty, the trust was actually failing 'to be feudal enough'.[3] As *The Independent* concluded, the time had come for a new Act of Parliament that would divide the monolithic trust up into smaller bodies, and 'permit some of its properties to revert to private ownership'. Rodney Legg had good reason to wonder exactly what he had started.

The truth is that once cracks have appeared in an organisation's legitimacy, they can be perceived from very different points of view. Throughout the Eighties, the National Trust has been attacked repeatedly from left of centre. Environmentalists have charged it with employing bad land-management practice. Others have accused it of managerial incompetence: of squandering resources and drifting from its social mission. As one internal critic has remarked under the cover of a pseudonym, 'The National Trust was never intended to provide relaxed culture for well-educated, well-off, car-owning clientele or indeed, as one cynic recently remarked, purely to provide employment for the products of our minor public schools'.[4] The Country Houses Scheme has been attacked as élitist, backward-looking, and implicitly racist, while other lobbyists have set out to impose a ban on blood sports.

But a very different strand of criticism has also developed over recent years. An old ally like *Country Life* has chided the trust for failing to list all its properties, refusing to consult on its estate-management policies, and generally behaving as a 'private fiefdom'.[5] There have been a number of nasty attacks in the right-wing Press. In June 1987, for example, the *Daily Mail* published a story about the apparently private affairs of the trust's director of finance.[6] As part of a remarkable package of 'perks', Mr Gordon Lawrence had, so the *Mail* claimed, received financial help from the trust so that he could buy the half-timbered Porch House, in Bromham, near Devizes, Wiltshire. Not content with these benefits, Mr Lawrence was now proposing to build a lucrative little cottage in the grounds of his historic house – despite the opposition of the parish council. As one of Mr Lawrence's fellow villagers was reported to have remarked, 'They preach to us about keeping the country's heritage, yet he can spoil it like this.'

Others, who have lent their voices to this swelling chorus of right-wing criticism, are inclined to contest the public interest that the National Trust has established in the large country house and would like, now that the fiscal climate (or at least the tax system) has been so thoroughly improved, to see Brideshead reprivatised. John Martin Robinson is among this number, or at least so we must conclude from his article commemorating the fiftieth anniversary of the Country Houses Scheme. Full of praise for James Lees-Milne and the organisation that, as he put it, had been 'holding the bridge for fifty years', he nevertheless signed off with an unmistakable farewell. However sympathetically it is cared for, a country house 'obviously loses its point when it ceases to be the seat of a great county family and becomes merely a museum.' Even with the best will in the world, as Robinson continues, it is difficult to continue to live in your ancestral home when you are no longer the owner:

> It can be galling to be told that your dinner guests cannot park in the courtyard or to be charged 6p by the gardener every time you pick a sprig of parsley, or to have a curator, not appointed by yourself, and his mistress, living under the same roof. As a result the younger generation, if not the donors themselves, have tended to move out . . . .[7]

We are never told exactly where that unfairly priced sprig of parsley grew, but anyone with an eye for metaphor will recognise that, like the usurping and dissolute curator, it originated somewhere in the vicinity of Crichel Down. Three years later the same apocryphal sprig sprung up again, this time in Peregrine Worsthorne's 'Comment' section of *The Sunday Telegraph*, where it ornamented an unattributed profile of Lord Chorley, who was shortly to succeed Dame Jennifer Jenkins as Chairman of the trust.[8] By now the currency had a decisively pre-decimalised quality, but the basic point was the same: 'One family had moved back into their own home, and the lady of the house went into the garden to pick some parsley. The next day she got a bill from the gardener for the parsley. The bill was only sixpence, but he wasn't joking . . . .' This profile adduced other examples to prove that the National Trust has 'grown too big for its boots'. Indeed, it revived the story of Castle Coole, a house near Enniskillen in Northern Ireland that had been in the news in June 1988. At that time the National Trust had just completed a massive restoration costing £3.6 million and the resident caretaker and son of the former owner, Lord Belmore, had protested vigorously at the way the 'mood' of his ancestral home had been violated. Objecting to the 'ghastly colours' chosen by the trust, Belmore was especially incensed by the 'Germolene Pink' in the grand entrance hall: this, as he insisted, was 'quite appalling'. The story was adopted by both *The Sunday Times* and *The Sunday Telegraph* as an appropriate occasion on which to turn the cluttered, organic, and essentially undesigned qualities of the true country-house interior against the National Trust and its artistic advisers. As Lord Belmore said in unacknowledged tribute to Vita Sackville West, 'They are interested only in historical and architectural purity and are ignoring what the family actually did with their possessions. That is what makes most great country houses so special. People don't want to feel it has been arranged by an interior decorator.'[9] *The Sunday Telegraph* had echoed this charge the following week, the officers of the trust were interfering bureaucrats, ill-mannered 'experts' whose knowledge of art history was wholly abstract: 'in the name of historical authenticity [they removed] all traces of human occupation, the idosyncratic details that the visitor (peering past the Private notice) longs to find'.[10] These upstarts turned the country house into a soulless museum, and in doing so 'destroyed delicate layers of family taste (good and bad), family acquisitions, family style in living – in short, what makes an historic house a living thing instead of a designer's exercise which could be labelled "English country house".' Sackville-West's war-time idea of the designer as a 'dictator of taste' was revived, but this time the reference was less to Hitler than to the usurping functionaries of the communist State. The National Trust had once been 'a struggling good cause supported by old ladies', but it has since 'grown into an intimidating leviathan' that imposes the same dead hand throughout its domain, making gardens over-formal, painting over irreplaceable ancestral graffiti, giving rooms an over-designed 'period' look of the *Homes and Gardens* or late Spitalfields variety, and terrorising caretaker-owners into silence: 'Family after family tell stories of slights, pointless changes, downright inaccuracies, and (most surprisingly) waste and destruction. But again and again, they say, "Please don't identify me".' From this reprivatising point of view, Rodney Legg was quite right: it was time for the trust to pull back from the country houses and their estates, and devote itself to the 'matchless English landscape and coastline', which had been its primary concern in the nineteenth century. It was to be hoped that Lord Chorley, the incoming Chairman, would be just 'the man to take the trust back to its orgins', thereby allowing those caretaker-owners to apply the well-tried principles of 'opting out' to their own humiliating situation.

All this is proof that the National Trust is not immune to the break up of the post-war settlement, or to the fragmentation of post-war consensus that Margaret Thatcher and her think-tankers have worked so hard to bring about. It has been the right-wing criticism rather than the persistent carpings of the left that has drawn the aged James Lees-Milne back into the field in defence of his own achievements. In recent years Lees-Milne has reviewed the rising cult and concluded that the country house will probably soon die of over-exposure. Teasingly, he has blamed Mark Girouard for this. It was he, after all, who adjusted the country-house paradigm, placing a new and vastly more popular emphasis on social history rather than just art and architecture.[11] What will be left after the hordes have tramped through the kitchens and servants' quarters? Brideshead will soon have been utterly consumed. Its mysteries will vanish and, as Lees-Milne fears, the whole story will collapse into indifference and mass boredom. Yet while Lees-Milne regrets the loss of patrician obscurity, and the collapse of the country house into a television cliché, he has no time for the right-wing ideologues who are now inclined to dismiss his work as the crypto-socialist destruction of exactly what he set out to save. In February 1984, he felt obliged to write to *The Times* to refute the charges of Roger Scruton, who had accused the National Trust's Country Houses Scheme of extinguishing, one after another, the 'little fires of our national inheritance in the ice-cold waters of the bureaucratic state'.[12] Scruton should have known better than to attack the organisation that had, as Lees-Milne pointed out, campaigned against 'penal taxation' of country-house owners at the time when it most mattered.[13]

Four years later Lees-Milne was using the pages of *The Sunday Telegraph* to suggest that the Dean of Hereford should be 'boiled in oil' for trying to sell off the Mappi Mundi, and to denounce Nicholas Ridley, then Secretary of State for the Environment, for attacking the National Trust in terms that David Cannadine has since approved as 'a system of outdoor relief for the aristocracy', and advising the impoverished owners of stately homes to sell up to the new rich. Having seen how a quick succession of 'improving' owners could impair the atmosphere of a country house, Lees-Milne was adamant that we should 'be under no illusion that yuppies will in the long run benefit the seats of the old aristocracy'.[14] Ridley had 'the blood of robber barons in his veins', and Lees-Milne, who claimed to be descended from 'honest yeomen', was now quite prepared to 'leap to the defence of the late Aneurin Bevan's vermin'. It is, as he told me in that same year, dangerous 'folly' to think that the clock can be put back or to talk of reprivatising the trust's country houses. 'Yuppies' should build new houses, and complaining caretaker-owners like

Lord Belmore should remember the facts before accusing the National Trust of ruining their ancestral homes. Lord Belmore is routinely cited as having 'given' Castle Coole to the National Trust, but in reality, as Lees-Milne well remembers, the house was bought by the government from the previous Lord Belmore with money from the Ulster Land Fund. This was a fact the present caretaker-owner 'might have borne in mind' before launching his protest. In short, by the end of the Eighties, Lees-Milne was a vehement defender of the concept of inalienability and of the fastidious kind of nationalisation that had been practised by the National Trust. Perhaps this is the real message of Sutton House. Anyone can sneer at the so-called 'heritage industry', but it takes a more discriminating soul to gaze out past the decaying tower blocks, and to recognise the conserved country house as a truly enduring creation of the British Welfare State. Lees-Milne surprised me when I met him in 1988. After remarking that, in those early years, Labour governments had always been better disposed towards the National Trust than Conservative ones, he went further and described both Clement Attlee and George Lansbury as 'saints' of a kind. Tories don't come like that any more.

Part Three

Scenes from the Privatised City

Even the Drinking Water Talks

In 1966, Hackney Council joined the London Boroughs Association in demanding the compulsory fluoridation of London's drinking water. It was promptly denounced by 'Hackney Against Fluoride', a local campaign which accused the council of seeking to infringe on 'a fundamental freedom of the individual'. But this was the age of state reform, and it was with unswerving confidence that a properly elected champion of the public good, Labour Alderman Lou Sherman, O.B.E., ran a bulldozer over their upstart objection: 'If we rely on voluntary methods, children's teeth will be falling out of their heads before fluoride is introduced.'

Twenty-five years later, it was less what the authorities were threatening to put into the water that seemed to matter, than what they were failing to take out. In February 1990 Brenda Collins, the late leader of the Liberal Council in Tower Hamlets, was ostentatiously refusing to drink the tap water provided in jugs in the council chamber. At home, moreover, she was accustomed to making tea with bottled water: not for her family the 'recycled effluent on tap' provided by the newly privatised Thames Water PLC.

By this time, however, it wasn't just the tap water that was in trouble. Early in 1990 Perrier discovered traces of carcinogenic benzene in some bottles of their superior product, and ordered a world-wide withdrawal until a newly purified issue had been prepared. This was a formidable operation, and though the world was duly impressed by the determination with which the company threw its global distribution system into reverse, there was one outlet in Hackney that escaped the recall. Getting Perrier Water into Broadway Market must be counted a remarkable achievement, but extracting it again was to prove more than the company could manage. So it was here, in a modest Londis store, that the old polluted issue of 'the yuppies' favourite booze-free tipple' was found still 'nestling among the fruit juices'. Notified by the Hackney Gazette *that of all the shop-keepers in the world it had been he who confounded the system, Mr Patel pointed a guileless finger at the distributor who had fobbed him off by pretending that the old was really the new, and immediately 'ordered the shelves to be stripped'.*

From articles in the *Hackney Gazette*,
4 October 1966; 2 February 1990; 16 March 1990.

10
The London Bus Queue Falls Apart

For as long as I can remember, conservatively inclined commentators have been lamenting the decline of the London bus queue. Indeed, it is said that this venerable British institution doesn't really exist any more: its ordered and generally accepted civilities having been replaced by a brutish stampede in which the pushiest get through first, while the frail and well mannered are left standing, if they are lucky, in the gutter.

For these prophets of doom, the line at the London bus stop symbolises the very spine of the nation, and the ominous blurring that can be seen at its edges is a sign of fatal degeneration. In reality, however, the London bus queue isn't always so bad. Things have certainly reached a sorry state in the West End, especially in the summer when no trick is too low for natives forced to dodge through swarms of back-packed visitors. Down on the corner of Tottenham Court Road and Oxford Street, the bus queue is a sordid scrum, but take a ride from there to a residential part of the inner city and the situation improves considerably.

Dalston Junction is not on any tourist's itinerary, and the crowd that gathers at the bus stop here is as mixed as could be found anywhere in the country. Its members come from all four corners of the earth, and they certainly don't look like a group of people who have been raised to the same set of rules.

The queue here exists in a state of constant disintegration. A few sticklers may stand resolutely in line at the point where the sign urges them to 'Form Queue This Side', but the overall impression is of people milling about: pacing up and down, shuffling from one foot to the other, wandering out into the road to stare down it in impatient anticipation, or leaning back against the wall ready to close in when a bus finally comes into view. Some who gather at this bus stop aren't going anywhere at all. There's one disorientated woman who turns up sporadically and hangs about for hours, muttering to herself as the buses come and go. While others set off on their journeys, she treats the queue as a refuge, moving into it as if it were an asylum, a card-board box, or the latest cut-rate experiment in community care.

The crowd may be densely packed, but it's also full of distance, and not just of the artificially created Sony Walkman variety. A fair amount of inter-racial examination goes on over distances far wider than the proximities of the street would suggest. People stand a few inches apart, and check each other out over the great chasms that centuries have placed between them. Tiny misrecognitions can suddenly flare.

Sometimes a speaker steps out to address the queue. The last one I heard was vehemently egalitarian and anti-Thatcherite, but beyond this it was hard to place him more precisely even on Dalston Lane's richly differentiated political spectrum. His sign read 'The government knows how the brain works. And it proves we all have equal intelligence. Mrs. Thatcher doesn't want anyone to know.' He stood there calling out 'Enough is enough', and occasionally venturing out into clipped and speedily recited elaborations: 'Languages are easy – I could teach you German in one minute' or 'This is the wealthiest planet in the universe. We should all be living like Kings.'

Conversations break out too. A wide range of topics is available to the seasoned bus-stop philosopher, most of which can be gathered under the single heading of 'Helpless Speculation'. Whatever your origins or standing in the wider world, to be waiting at a bus stop at Dalston Junction is to have joined the ranks of the underdog, and that is enough for a tentative opening. The initial exchange is likely to concern the invariably inadequate doings of 'they' who run the bus service so badly: stacking up the buses so that none come for half an hour and then five rush through all at once, or chopping the bus route into smaller and smaller sections so that nobody can be sure that the bus, when it finally does arrive, will take them more than half-way to their destination.

Some quite unique flights of fancy become possible once this theme is properly established: 'they' become the council, the government, the gentrifiers, the social workers, the police, or anybody else who gets you down, and temporary agreements of the most unlikely kind are struck. I've heard an affluent City type find common ground with a destitute pensioner on the subject of Margaret Thatcher's unpatriotic meanness. I've heard an amicable conversation about immigration between a West Indian for whom 'they' were the immigration authorities and a sullen white native who started out with something very different in mind.

People swap stories about the time when the first deregulated buses showed up, bringing a further touch of visual anarchy to the increasingly chaotic London street scene. The cream-and-purple vehicles of 'Kentish Buses' came thick and fast on the first day; they still reeked of plastic glue and the drivers didn't always know where they were going. There are hilarious stories about passengers guiding them along the route, or covertly hijacking them and leading them through dismal housing estates, right up to their own front door.

When the bus finally arrives, everything changes. Conversations break off as people prepare to board through a whole series of time-sanctioned manoeuvres. Knowing how the odds are stacked against them, elderly ladies turn themselves into missiles: heads down, elbows out, tongues sharpened to a lacerating point. Just as classic is the spiv's route to the top. This one is for the boys and young men, and it surely descends from the days of the old rear-entry tram: step smartly round the side, let a few people off, and then push in, your passage eased by the unstated excuse that you're only going upstairs for a smoke.

There is a white supremacist way of barging in and another associated with black defiance. There are liberal and feminist manoeuvres, too. I recently saw a young woman muscling in as brazenly as anyone and then, when she had made it to the front, pausing with a magnanimous display of sisterhood to allow two or three of the thirty or so people she had displaced into the bus before her. Finally, there is the slow advance of the disgruntled rump: the elderly and infirm, the mild-mannered, people who just don't feel up to it that day. They get to watch these deft performances from close up. They also board the bus last.

Nobody could mistake what happens when the bus arrives at Dalston Junction for an entirely orderly queue. But neither is it just the advance of a mob following the law of the jungle. Each time a bus pulls up the crowd negotiates a messy but still intricately structured settlement between the ideal of the orderly queue and the chaotic stampede. This result is far from perfect. It may drive the elderly and frail off the bus altogether. It may occasionally trigger a fierce trading of insults, racist outbursts, and even an exchange of blows. But it is still governed by an etiquette that dictates how far the disintegration can be allowed to go.

The biggest threat to the inner-London bus queue doesn't come from cultural degeneration at all. Instead, it's known as OPO – the abbreviation by which the people at London Regional Transport like to refer to their new One-Person Operated buses. The great thing about the old Route Master buses is that they allow a certain latitude. Some of the conductors may behave like tin-pot dictators and try to impose discipline, but the majority know that they are on the rear platform to defuse conflicts, pick up stragglers, and even to entertain. Compared with this, OPO has a brutalising effect: it scorns the artful compromises of the traditional London bus queue, insisting instead upon a sullen and slow moving line in which latent conflicts are far more likely to explode.

11

The Vandalised Telephone Box

Even the people at the *Hackney Gazette* recognised that they were only dealing with a minor story when, in October 1966, vandals destroyed a telephone box outside the railway station at Dalston Junction by setting fire to rubbish heaped up inside it.[1] The perspectives had changed by the time Gavin Stamp passed through Dalston Lane in 1986. Taking his life into his hands, the Chairman of the Thirties Society ventured out into the middle of the road and pointed his camera towards the derelict vicarage of St Bartholomew's. Buddleia sprouted from the disintegrating brickwork overhead and the tinned-up windows were plastered over with posters advertising Tom Robinson and other since forgotten bands, but there in the foreground stood the elegant historical structures that had caught this visitor's eye: a pair of old red telephone boxes designed by no less a figure than the classical architect, Sir Giles Gilbert Scott. By 1989, when he printed the photograph in a book about telephone kiosks, the decay had advanced further and Stamp was obliged to acknowledge that these 'well-sited' signs of remaining grace had since been removed.[2]

One day in July 1988, I stood on the concourse of Waterloo Station thinking of hopes once entertained by the late Anthony Crosland. As a leading Labour Party intellectual in the mid-Fifties, Crosland had dreamt of a less austere socialism where the uniformity of the State would weigh less heavily on the life of the nation. As he wrote in *The Future of Socialism*, it was time for a 'reaction against the Fabian tradition'. The mixed economy could be expected to deliver higher exports and old-age pensions, but only a 'change in cultural attitude' would make Britain 'a more colourful and civilised country to live in'. There should be more night-life and open-air cafés, pleasure gardens, repertory theatres, and statues to brighten up the new housing estates. There should better design, not just for furniture and women's clothes, but also for street-lamps and telephone kiosks.[3] It was the reference to telephone kiosks that brought Crosland to mind.

The Royal Corps of Transport Band was warming up the crowd for the launch of Mercury Communication's new 'payphone' system: a banner mounted over the head of its ceremoniously besworded conductor showed a victorious cavalry charge at the Battle of Waterloo and promised 'The Greatest Advance since 1815'. Here was British Telecom's private rival, much grown since it was first licensed in 1982, opening its latest assault on a public domain where the

franchise is certainly being extended. Waterloo Station may once
have had the grimy and uniform look of nationalised space, but in the
age of privatisation and niche marketing, it has come to resemble a
shopping mall: diversified, colourful, and superficially more civilised
too.

After the band had ripped through 'Ghostbusters' and 'In the
Mood', Gordon Owen, the Managing Director of Mercury Communications, stood up in his appointed space between Casey Jones
and the Knicker Box, and declared a 'first for Britain'. We were
standing in a newly 'competitive arena', and Owen was proud to be
cutting into British Telecom's monopoly for the first time. Unfettered
by a public-service obligation of the kind that prevents British
Telecom from confining its phone boxes to the most profitable sites,
Mercury would be concentrating its 'state-of-the-art' payphones at
airports, railway termini, and new shopping malls – while, of course,
loudly denying all charges of 'cream-skimming'. The new phones
would be especially convenient for people wanting to make international calls. They would accept the four major credit cards, but
coins were a thing of the past. A special Mercurycard had been
introduced, but Owen also looked forward to the day when Mercury's
growing list of private subscribers, most of which are businesses,
would be able to use the company's payphones with the equivalent of
a PIN number, logging the charge back onto their account.

Owen promised an élite distinguished by 'reliability, cleanliness,
and value for money'; and though it was obvious Mercury had no
intention of mounting a universal public service for the convenience of
every welfare bum in the land, he stressed that everything possible
would be done to accommodate the genuinely disabled consumer.
Wheelchair access had been built into the designs wherever possible,
and there was to be volume adjustment to help the hard of hearing.
The Mercurycard was notched on one side to help people with sight
problems, and phones would even squeak obligingly to tell blind or
partially sighted users when their Mercurycard is running out.

It was then the turn of Lord Young, Secretary of State for Trade
and Industry, to unveil the new kiosks. Diversity is an essential part of
enterprise culture, and Mercury certainly wasn't going to make the
mistake of coming up with a uniform design for all its locations. There
were three models to unveil, each one designed, as Mr Owen had
remarked, to be fitted into 'different parts of the society'. Fitch &
Company had come up with a 'totem concept' payphone booth that,
as their press release put it, took 'Mercury's key requirements' and
'embodied them in a powerful, physical form'. The result had already
been dubbed the 'Art Deco' kiosk, but to me it looked less like a totem
pole than an extruded Fifties-style petrol pump. The model provided
by Machin Designs was named the 'Ogee Pylon'; but while its
designers claimed this version of the Mercury logo-stand to be one in
which 'classical aesthetic values are executed in a sophisticated

system of structural components', I was inclined to agree with Gavin Stamp who at that moment was telling a radio reporter that it looked more like a conservatory of the kind you might expect to find in Islington than a proper public telephone box.

It was, however, the neo-classical payphone designed by John Simpson and Partners that made the greatest impact. The astonished guffaws were out before the covers had properly hit the ground, and it was in this kiosk that the next morning's papers would show Lord Young making the inaugural call to Sir Eric Sharp, the Chairman of Cable and Wireless (of which Mercury is a subsidiary). Both Mercury and the Department of Trade and Industry had already issued press releases insisting that Young spent the call congratulating Sharp on the speed with which his company had carried through their assault on British Telecom's heartland. However, hindsight now suggests that the old boys may actually have been sorting out the details of a different tactical exchange: the one that would elevate Sir Eric into the House of Lords as Lord Sharp of Grimsdyke, thus making way for Lord Young of Graffham to slide into position as the magnificently paid executive chairman of Cable and Wireless only two years thence.

John Simpson may be ambitious but he is no such smooth operator. Looking frankly disconcerted by the derisive hoots that greeted his cast-aluminium classical kiosk, he kindly found a moment to talk me through some of its many distinguishing features. He pointed to the ornate finial on top of the roof – a decorative touch that also serves to provide ventilation and that could, if need be, house an aerial. Then there were the winged sphinxes flanking and, indeed, struggling to dignify, the monstrous Mercury logo. The gap at the bottom of the side panels had been demanded by the brief, and was partly intended to discourage dossers from treating this new service as a public convenience of a different kind. The fluted Doric columns at the corners were certainly ornamental, but they also had the practical advantage of providing a curved edge that would be less easy to vandalise.

Flagship on the Rocks

How, I wondered briefly, might one explain all this to the late Anthony Crosland? It was at the end of November 1987 that John Butcher, a junior industry minister, had announced the government's decision to break up British Telecom's call-box monopoly. 'The idea', as he said at the time, 'is to see a much greater number of different types of call boxes installed and available to the public, and to provide British Telecom with competition in what has hitherto been a restricted market'.[4] Launched as the 'flagship' of Thatcher's privatisation programme in November 1984, British Telecom PLC had seemed to work fine for a while. Chairman, Sir George Jefferson, and Iain Vallance (who was then Chief Executive) made all the right noises as they sailed off into the new world. They promised to shake off the grim legacies of nationalisation and turned their overmanned, badly managed, and ill-equipped organisation into a properly tight ship that would be both profitable and better for its customers.

By 1987 British Telecom was declaring huge profits but it was also coming under fire from all sides. In three short years, the flagship of privatisation had been renamed the 'most loathed institution in Britain'. Consumer surveys declared British Telecom the worst public service in the land. There was evidence of overcharging (with some subscribers, including the Bank of England, eventually getting a refund). The long-promised technological improvements, which included the introduction of digital exchanges and a new labour-saving switching technology called 'System X,' had caused havoc, striking central London and City exchanges hardest of all.[5] As the service declined and complaints soared, British Telecom set about squandering large fortunes on advertising campaigns designed to manipulate public opinion. It was evidently considered easier to establish a new 'corporate image' than to improve the service.

British Telecom tried to counter the rising tide of criticism. It blamed its own engineers, who had been on strike earlier in 1987. It blamed the fact that it had once been a nationalised industry, and was therefore full of sullen and morose employees who couldn't all be retrained in a day. It blamed vandalism for the problems with its call-boxes – some 25 per cent of which were found to be out of action in a damning survey conducted by the regulatory body, Oftel. Indeed, it even toured an exhibition of ingeniously vandalised payphones around the nation's schools to show what it was up against.[6] In the end, however, it caved in. Chairman, Sir George Jefferson, may have distinguished himself earlier at the newly privatised British Airways, but British Telecom's shareholders wanted blood and he resigned ignominiously at the Annual General Meeting of September 1987. There was to be no place in the House of Lords for him.

Newspapers were quick to interpret the story. For the Conservative *Daily Telegraph*, the chaos in British Telecom didn't raise doubts about privatisation. Indeed, it provided yet more support for the dogmas of liberal theory: privatise a nationalised industry without breaking it up into competing units, and all you get is a private monopoly. *The Guardian* drew broadly comparable conclusions, declaring that British Telecom was displaying the 'classic symptoms of a monopoly': defending itself from competition, refusing to publish the criteria according to which it measured performance, failing to innovate, and overcharging.[7] Nobody bothered to recall how, in the old days of the Post Office, there had been a strong case for the essential uniformity of a public service like the telephone system. There wasn't a journalist who found anything to say about 1912, the year when the British telephone system was nationalised in an attempt get beyond the failure that had marked the earlier years of multiple and partly private ownership, or who pointed to the irony of the fact that, in those days, when Britain had what was widely known as 'the worst telephone service in the civilised world', it had seemed obvious that the telephone network should be run by a single statutory body.[8] This idea was unthinkable now that British Telecom had been turned into a private and manifestly incompetent monopoly.

A Matter of Style

Such is the general background to the Mercury payphones, but how, as Mr Crosland himself might have wondered, do we account for the style of the most eye-catching model? Why should the new kiosk look like a crudely engineered collision between the Tardis and a wedding cake? What could possibly motivate John Simpson's absurd design?

At the beginning of 1985 Mr Iain Vallance, who at that time was Managing Director of BT's Local Communications Service, announced that his newly privatised organisation would be taking a 'radical approach to the problems inherent in today's outdated payphone service'. Those old, coin-operated red telephone boxes would soon be a thing of the past, replaced by yellow, anodised, aluminium kiosks and cardphones. Privatisation hadn't freed BT of its public service obligation, but there was the need for more efficient and vandalproof facilities. The new designs would be more open than the old red telephone boxes. Litter and unpleasant smells would be blown away, and the homeless would feel less tempted to move in on cold winter nights. Just as Mercury was to do a few years later, BT stressed the needs of the disabled, who know the impracticalities of the old red telephone box in close detail.[9] Behind all the smooth talk, however, many suspected a hidden motivation. The newly privatised BT was concerned to be profitable, and a redesign would not just help to create that much desired new 'corporate image' but it would surely also provide the perfect cover under which a secret but thoroughgoing reorganisation of the service could be carried out. Confronted with these suspicions, BT admitted that hundreds of boxes had indeed been moved in the changeover but regretted that (conveniently enough, as critics recognised) it had no method of classifying these changes and was therefore simply unable to say whether the redesigned service had also been concentrated at more lucrative sites.

The man who launched the redesign has since replaced Sir George Jefferson as Chairman of British Telecom. Questioned by angry BT shareholders devoted to the old red phone boxes at the 1988 Annual Meeting, the fast-moving Mr Vallance insisted that 'there is no accounting for taste'. In fact, his newly privatised industry had already found a very good way of accounting for taste. If the old phone boxes had their admirers – not least in America where many are now in service as cocktail and shower cabinets – then so much the better. They could be auctioned off, and long may demand out-strip supply.

It was the Thirties Society that initiated the defence of the old red phone box. Denouncing the auctions as a squalid asset-stripping of the public sector, its members quickly extended the traditions of cultural connoisseurship to street furniture, declaring the taken-for-granted old red telephone box to be a vital part of the national heritage. Writing in the early Forties, George Orwell had cited suet puddings, misty skies, and red pillar-boxes, but by the Eighties the old red telephone box had also 'entered into' the nation's soul.[10] Where the philistine Mr Vallance saw only 'outdated' payphones, these campaigners looked at the kiosks with which Sir Giles Gilbert Scott had set out to civilise a rampant technology and recognised significant works of architecture that were 'wholly classical in spirit'.[11] The K2 was Scott's original kiosk. Dating from 1927, it had been brought into service mostly in London. The smaller and more familiar K6 was designed by Scott in the mid-Thirties, and was still being installed up until 1968. Thanks to a scheme announced in April 1935, the K6 had been set up in remote villages all around the country as 'a special concession' designed to commemorate George V's Jubilee. The organisers of the Jubilee Scheme recognised that money could have been saved by fitting phones into existing rural post offices, but free-standing kiosks were chosen for the sake of the extra privacy, visibility, and accessibility they afforded. Since the scheme was an extension of a vital public service, it was accepted that it should be paid for out of 'general funds' and not 'left dependent on the ability of some small community to contribute to the cost'.[12]

Quickly dubbed the 'Jubilee Kiosk', the K6 went on to become, as BT itself recognises, an 'established British institution'. Nevertheless, its arrival in rural areas was contested in the Thirties. From Oxfordshire to the Lake District, local branches of the Council for the Preservation of Rural England denounced the new kiosks as eyesores, complaining especially about the insidious 'intervention of red' into their villages.[13] But their arguments in favour of green or stone-grey camouflage were resisted by the Post Office, which rallied such forces as the Royal Fine Art Commission and Sir Edwin Lutyens in support of the chosen red.[14] Light grey would show up every 'ribald scrawl' and be stained by dogs and rain. Green wouldn't stand out to the eye of the traveller who might need to make an emergency call. And as was pointed out by John Gloag, a designer who at that time was also on the Central Executive Committee of the Council for the Preservation of Rural England, if the principle of camouflage is accepted for every modern amenity in rural areas, we will end up 'thatching everything, even motor coaches'.[15] It was eventually allowed that a dark 'battleship grey' could be used in areas of outstanding natural beauty (as long as the glazing bars were still picked out in red), but with this one variation, the Jubilee Kiosk went on to become a standard feature of the national landscape.[16]

The defenders of the old red telephone box could easily have extended their appreciation of this endangered national icon to include the interior fittings chosen in the Thirties by a special interdepartmental Post Office committee. The members of this committee came up with an interior fit for well-mannered ladies and gentlemen. They resolved that the backboard should be made of polished bakelite rather than plywood, and decided to include a cigarette holder, an umbrella rack, and the bevelled mirror that was provided for 'feminine users' despite the Traffic Section's concern that callers with urgent business would 'occasionally be kept waiting' while a lady adjusted her make-up. The committee wanted stiff-covered directories and was reluctant to accept that they would have to be chained. It was against all but the most limited publicity: there was to be no external advertisement and the limited space allowed for internal notices (which were to be properly framed on the backboard) was reserved for information about the operation of the phone itself. While it would be desirable, even in those days, to include a 'Monogram . . . like that used by the Public Relations Department', there was no space left after the functional notices had been accommodated, and the idea was abandoned.

Scott's Jubilee Kiosk was distinguished not just by its design but also by the uniformity of its presence. Similarly, though Mr Vallance's new 'pay phones' were of a distinctly mediocre design borrowed from the United States, they too had a broader significance: from now on there would no longer be one type of kiosk to be used in all places. Paving the way for Mercury's later and more exclusive collection, BT's new range were designed so that different models could, to repeat the well-chosen words of Gordon Owen, be 'put in different parts of the society'. The post-privatisation kiosks would stand as BT's humble contribution to growing social polarisation. Nobody could be entirely certain of getting a door anymore but, according to the new Vallance equation, the better your area the more kiosk you could expect to find. Users in respectable neighbourhoods and well-policed thoroughfares would still be offered a roof, some walling, and a choice between cash and cardphone. The new underclass, meanwhile, would have to settle for a sawn-off metal stump with an armoured cardphone bolted onto it. The last variety is commonly found in the vicinity of Dalston Lane.

By the Eighties the Scott kiosk had itself become emblematic of the traditional nation that, fifty years previously, it had been thought to despoil. In August 1986, a K2 kiosk in London Zoo's Parrot House became the first telephone box to receive listed-building status. An old public service that had become indefensible as a 'private monopoly' could at least be saved as part of the nation's architectural heritage. Meanwhile, the 'quality' newspapers – themselves torn between their old ways and frenzied modernisation – had been printing rousing letters in defence of the old red phone box, some of them coming from expatriates who were still shocked by the passing of steam engines and the threepenny bit. *The Guardian* managed a wistful article by Richard Boston who scorned the new designs ('all the vandal's work has been done already – except peeing on the floor') and eulogised the disappearing works of Sir Giles Gilbert Scott.[17] Newspapers all over the world (including, most eloquently, the *Frankfurter Rundschau*) contributed their own elegies to this icon of old England. BT's auctions went ahead, but they were quite overtaken by this embarrassing cult of the old red phone box: many newspapers printed evocative photos of Britain's heritage going under the hammer, but *The Independent* caught the most poignant episode of all. On 14 September 1988, it showed a kiosk being hoisted out of native land near Swindon in preparation for a journey to the Falkland Islands where it would be installed 'for members of the armed forces to use for phoning home'.

A Symbol of National Embarrassment

It was the Conservative Press that delivered the most forceful lamentations for the red telephone box, all of them stressing the uniformity of the old kiosk. Writing in *The Times*, Roger Scruton regretted the 'tyrannical pursuit of novelty' and the inevitable but 'horrifying advance of science'. [18] For him the Scott kiosk was one of the last creations of a 'disciplined tradition of design whose products also include the Gothic factory, the Palladian clubhouse, the Pullman railway carriage and the Bombay shirt.'[19] He didn't mind what a phone box looked like in a place like Birmingham ('where modern architects have already done their work'). But the Scott kiosk should continue to grace real England – every village green, every moor, every hillside should have one – as an emblem of stability. He liked the plinth, the classical outline, and the embossed crown that, far from just serving as a ventilator, stood over the nation's communications as a 'symbol of national identity, and promise of enduring government'. He was so impressed by the colour that he renamed it, turning what had been known as 'Post Office Red' ever since the Royal Fine Art Commission chose it in the Thirties into the more ideologically correct 'Imperial Red'. A vehement anti-modernist, Professor Scruton looked at the K6 and even managed to approve an 'interesting suggestion of Bauhaus naughtiness in its fenestration'.

Charles Moore, editor of the *Spectator*, took up the subject in *The Daily Telegraph*. For him the Scott kiosk spoke most evocatively of enduring national values at the very point where it was being broken up by BT's brutish workforce. More ambitious for the nation than

Scruton, he argued that the Scott kiosk could actually exert a civilising influence in those urban areas that had been ruined by modernism and the Welfare State. Even in the most dismal post-war housing estate the old red telephone box sent out signals of hope – its classical lines and proportions offering an image of the properly ordered condition to which society could return. If he had visited some of the more troubled estates in Dalston or Haggerston, Moore would have found incontrovertible support for his thesis: the young dope-dealers in these parts have only really felt at home with the 'pay phone system' since Mr Vallance removed the Scott kiosks (in which the police could trap suspects simply by putting a foot against the door in classic PC Plod style) and replaced them with open booths that could not have been better designed to provide the vigilant hoodlum with maximum visibility and a quick escape. But even without this supporting evidence, Moore recognised BT's decision to replace these kiosks as a classic example of the British ability to spit on our luck: 'we think that we have achieved something by smashing up the old, leaving its shards in the street and replacing it with a featureless affair of plastic and low-grade metal'.[20] Pressed by an unfriendly critic he was happy to go further: 'British Telecom had 77,000 little equivalents of Big Ben before they started their destruction, 77,000 objects which commanded the affection of their customers, and now they have squandered that affection.'[21]

As Chairman of the Thirties Society, Gavin Stamp had wandered the land photographing well-placed Scott kiosks wherever he found them, including that pair of K2s outside the derelict clergy-house on Dalston Lane. Stamp advanced his own intriguingly volatile version of the argument from his other position as architecture critic of the *Spectator*. As a man who found himself increasingly disturbed by the government's 'blinkered refusal to recognise the valuable and essential role' of the public sector, he valued the Scott kiosk not just as a work of architecture that may well have been inspired by no less a figure than Sir John Soane, but also as a 'sympathetic and serviceable' piece of street furniture.[22]

At last we were really getting somewhere. Would Gavin Stamp be the man to place the blame where it obviously belonged – on privatisation itself? Would he even come to the conclusion that the only way of defending the Scott kiosk and the standards of public service that it symbolised was to renationalise British Telecom immediately? Having suffered considerable inconvenience on his own line at King's Cross, Stamp had written to Chairman Jefferson protesting that 'British Telecom could be no worse if it were nationalised and that in fact it was better when it was'.[23] BT must have feared the direction in which his thoughts were moving, for at that moment Mr Stamp's phone seems to have gone permanently out of order, forcing him to conduct his business through 'new, squalid kiosks', which had already been 'conspicuously disfigured by a rash of prostitutes' sticky advertisements on the windows'. Frustration and justified anger at this 'monstrous private monopoly' took over and the argument never quite got followed through.[24]

More generally, the *Spectator* struggled to hold three contradictory positions on British Telecom at once. It remained unwavering in its advocacy of privatisation. It was anxious to see the old red telephone box saved. It wanted to see improvement and indeed innovation in British Telecom's service. But by May 1987, it was evident that this intriguing acrobatic performance was going to end in a painfully contorted heap on the floor. Just as the *Spectator* was celebrating the final demise of nationalisation as a reputable political concept, its phones joined the other victims of BT's new switching technology. A gleeful Des Wilson seized the moment and wrote in to point out the confusion of that week's editorial page: on the top half a leading article headed 'Nationalisation doesn't work', and at the bottom of the same page a note apologising for the inconvenience caused by the collapse of the *Spectator's* telephones ('A large part of our telephone system has been broken by British Telecom and has still not been mended after ten days. The company is unable to tell us what is wrong or when the full service will be restored'). As Wilson asked (to no avail), 'perhaps you could explain the inconsistency between the claims you make for privatisation and the reality'.[25]

With embarrassed fury, the *Spectator* pursued its complaints through the labyrinth of BT management, eventually laying them at the door of the doomed Chairman Jefferson only a week or so before his unexpected resignation. Lively discussion and correspondence filled the magazine throughout the summer of 1987. The letters page was used to foment an insurrection among the new shareholders. This was led by J. R. Lucas, an Oxford don who, having expressed his determination that the privatised industry's new shareholders should recognise their responsibilities and get British Telecom to 'pull up its socks', went on to BT's Annual Meeting where he chastised the new management for their 'blithering incompetence and invincible complacency'.[26] As a right-wing ideologue and think-tanker who had been a tireless advocate of privatisation, Digby Anderson also did the decent thing and communicated his embarrassment on the letters page: he admitted that BT had turned out an 'uninspiring adver- tisement for the cause'.[27] Another correspondent borrowed a spare conspiracy theory from the wilder reaches of *The Sunday Telegraph*. According to A. Green, who wouldn't give an address for fear of suddenly being put 'out of order', BT's socialist employees were targeting advocates of privatisation for special treatment.[28] Bernard Levin wrote in to whine pathetically about the 'thieving bastards' whose new-style pay phone had claimed his money without even so much as connecting his call.[29]

But no one could be entirely convinced. The *Spectator*'s whole outlook was founded on the conviction that nationalisation had disfigured the face of the nation but, whichever way one looked at it, the drama of the old red telephone box pointed accusing fingers in the very opposite direction: here was privatisation completing the mission of the destructive State bureaucracy it was meant to have vanquished. A 'Telecom Horror Contest' was launched in a bid to divert attention from the embarrassing implications of this story. It was announced with much trumpeting that a redundant Jubilee Kiosk would be awarded as a prize to whoever came up with the worst disaster story. But *The Sunday Times* had already counted up the bizarre uses to which people were putting old red telephone boxes and it was clear that the *Spectator*'s was just one more variation on the theme of the telephonic hen-house.[30] Bought at a BT auction early in 1987, it resounded through the summer with the scratching and clucking of fowl coming home to roost. It was fitting that the final winner of the Telecom Horror Competition came from Ohio: at least there was a chance that he would accept his prize and then the whole guilty, squawking, and by that time, rather filthy package could be bundled up and shipped conveniently over the horizon.[31]

It was a sense of guilt as well as shame that established the Scott kiosk as such an evocative symbol in the camp of the privateers, and there came a point where no amount of architectural talk about its fenestration, its plinth, and its delicately domed top, could hide the new meaning that the endangered Scott kiosk was acquiring by the day. Far from standing as an image of transcendant authority, as Roger Scruton imagined, the embossed crown on the Scott kiosk was actually the mark of the old Post Office. As the privatisation programme rolled on, the old red telephone box became the evocative symbol of endangered ideals of public service, of a social provision that should, as the emblematic kiosk now suggested, be reliable, uniform, and equally available to all. It had been on this interpretation that, as early as 1983, the British Telecom trade unions adopted the Scott kiosk to symbolise their cause against the privatising measures of their management.[32] Similarly, when Gavin Stamp tried to awaken BT to the value of this traditional shrine to public communication, he used an emphasis reminiscent of George Orwell's in 'England your England', describing the Scott kiosk as 'decent', 'solid', 'sympathetic', and 'serviceable'. Here again was the vocabulary of public service, taking refuge under a contemporary architectural gloss. Far from having been finished off, as the advocates of privatisation kept claiming, that old idea of the common good had escaped into heritage country. Hiding against rough weather in the old red telephone box was the petrified spirit of the Welfare State itself.

In the real world, meanwhile, Mercury was offering increased polarisation in the 'pay phone system' and a range of conspicuously ill-mannered phone-booths that shriek 'design' at a citizen who is now only distinguished by the credit cards in his or her wallet. The classical kiosk, however, has a special meaning of its own. John Simpson, its designer, is a young architect who has a growing reputation as classical revivalist, even though he has actually built very little. Simpson holds the orthodox revivalist belief that 'art and culture reached a pinnacle in the years around 1800, and that the architecture of this period is a better, indeed more appropriate, basis for development than the "modern" architecture of recent years'.[33] He stands in the anti-enlightment camp with architects like Quinlan Terry, and his return to classicism is accompanied by the usual polemical denunciations of modernism as the style of post-war egalitarianism.

As a self-defined 'real architect', Simpson is a great admirer of the old red telephone box. Indeed, as we stood together on Waterloo Station, he told me his classical kiosk was intended to be firmly in the tradition of Sir Giles Gilbert Scott. Mercury's gaudy logo makes a poor substitute for the embossed crown of the Scott kiosk but at least, as Simpson claimed in his publicity handout, his own model was a proper building rather than just a piece of nondescript and disposable street furniture. Unlike BT's new payphones, it had been designed to form 'part of the traditional urban townscape'. Indeed, it should be sited 'in the manner of statues or fountains to enhance the quality of public space'. Simpson would have liked to see his cast-aluminium classical kiosk issued in red or maroon, but Mercury evidently balked at erecting a memorial to its rival's better days. Ostensibly a tribute to the old red telephone box, Simpson's crude classical kiosk should not be mistaken for just another piece of trivial post-modern pastiche. Simon Jenkins may have greeted it as 'a phone box on which . . . an artist had been at work', but in my view it deserves to be remembered not for its aesthetic pretentions but as the monstrous contrivance that finally finished off the idea of universal public service by reducing it entirely to a matter of style.[34] In this respect, it was the true telephone box of its time.

What would Mr Crosland say about the change of 'cultural attitude' that has brought us these new designs? I imagine he would want his money back, and only be further dismayed to find that Button B has been abolished too. Meanwhile, Mercury has continued its heroic advance down British streets that are indeed acquiring the confused look of 'competitive arenas'. But while the Fitch and Machin designs (somewhat adjusted since their first appearance, on the advice of the Royal Fine Art Commission) are to be found all over the place, jostling to be seen over Mr Vallance's increasingly logo-ridden models, John Simpson's classical kiosk seems to have evaporated like a bad dream. The prototypes that were on display at Waterloo Station, between platforms 13 and 14 and outside near the taxi-rank, were quietly removed a week or two after the launch. Did good taste triumph after all? Mercury deny that the design has been dropped on account of any such embarrassment, insisting instead that Simpson's kiosk has turned out to be too heavy and bulky for the modern city street (which is evidently not quite the same as Simpson's 'traditional urban townscape') and that an 'appropriate location' has yet to be found. With the exception of a short period when it was on display at the Design Museum, John Simpson's folly – for that is what his florid, ill-conceived tribute to Sir Giles Gilbert Scott should be called – has remained firmly under wraps.

12
The Man with a Metal Detector

I was, and am, convinced of the moral and academic necessity of sharing scientific work to the fullest possible extent with the man in the street and in the field.

Sir Mortimer Wheeler, 1955[1]

England's rectory gardens may support fewer Easter egg hunts than they once did, but there are other ways of reviving a traditional sense of geography in the featureless territory of the modern State and the treasure hunt lives on. In the early Eighties we had the allegorical riddles of Kit William's hugely successful *Masquerade*. Those who weren't prepared to follow Williams's pictorial clues in search of the golden hare he had buried 'somewhere' in deep England could always turn on the television and follow a romping young television presenter, the well known Anneka Rice, as she chased less demanding clues round the countryside with the help of a helicopter. In 1987 the National Trust renewed its time-honoured partnership with Shell to launch a 'Great Treasure Hunt' in *The Sunday Telegraph Magazine*. The National Trust's clues may seem to point in different directions, but those who follow the logic of its riddle will know that they all converge on the ancestral land of Albion.

While polite society gives its sanction to some versions of the treasure hunt, there are others that command anything but respect. Mick Moran's 'Diary of a Thames mudlark' appeared in *Treasure Hunting*, a publication that claims to be 'Britain's best-selling metal detecting magazine'.[2] Moran spent the late Seventies digging up Victorian dump sites in search of old bottles, but by 1981 he had returned to his old haunts along the Thames foreshore. As an 'eyes only' mudlark, he would walk along combing the mud and shingle at undisclosed sites, and turning up such finds as a large and ornamented seventeenth-century thimble, a decorated siver buckle, a couple of Edward III pennies. By the mid-Eighties new opportunities were to be found at large construction sites in the rapidly developing city. The official archaeologists at the Museum of London were suddenly busy, but the metal detectorists had a field-day too. Moran joined the other members of this fraternity who were following lorries loaded with spoil as they travelled from construction sites like the one at the old Billingsgate Fish Market out to dumps in Essex or illegal fly-tips around London where they would search – sometimes with the consent of official archaeologists – the 'virgin mud' for its Roman coins, Danish and Norman silver, and the odd 'spectacular item of extreme rarity and beauty and of which I'll say no more . . .'.

The metal detector has its place in that richly patterned but much derided east London underworld where the pit bull terrier is already 'twinned in desirability' with the Sky satelite dish.[3] One only has to take a look at the Thames foreshore at low tide, at least within the boundaries of the medieval city, to catch a glimpse of these secretive fellows at work. They tend to operate in pairs, but sometimes only one of them is visible. The other is taking terrible risks with his life. Standing in the bottom of a sodden hole while the tide creeps back towards him, he hacks at the stratified ground and shovels it up onto a board where his partner stands with a detector. Some of the finds pass through the Museum of London, where they are identified, recorded, and occasionally even bought. I learnt more about the diverse world of the metal detectorists from Brian Spencer, who was then Senior Keeper of Medieval Antiquities at the Museum of London. Spencer described the museum's carefully cultivated links with the Society of Thames Mudlarks and Antiquarians – a small body of detectorists licensed by the Port of London Authority to work on the foreshore, and recognised as the élite among London detectorists even though they are reputed to have threatened violence in defence of their exclusive rights. He described a barely charted underworld where genuine enthusiasts mingle with fortune-hunting outlaws and shady specialist dealers like the 'pewter lady' who is rumoured to work out of an arcade near Piccadilly Circus. When I visited him, Spencer was marvelling over a unique and perfectly preserved early medieval jug that had been brought in by a detectorist for dating; there was also a fine pewter plate but, since the mudlark had stuck his fork through his find, it was going to need some careful repair, perhaps from a craftsman on the staff of the British Museum who did a bit of private work on the side. Here was another strange but representative story from the country that we used to call 'Thatcher's Britain'.

Skirmishing with the Nighthawks

Details are not always immediately forthcoming, but in recent years metal detectorists have made fabulous finds all over the country. They have also come into bitter dispute with the archaeologists and other museum professionals. In December 1986, Sothebys sold a medieval pendant called the Middleham Jewel to an unidentified buyer for £1.43 million. This beautifully engraved gold and sapphire object had been found by Ted Seaton, a metal detectorist who had turned it up at the edge of an old bridleway on private land near Middleham Castle. A month later the sale was frozen by the High Court. A fellow detectorist had lodged what would eventually turn

out to be an unsuccessful claim in the find, and there was speculation
– wholly unsubstantiated but vigorously displayed between the lines
of a report in *The Times* on 23 January 1987 – that the jewel may
actually have been dug up within the grounds of Middleham Castle, a
scheduled ancient monument. Unjustly accused and harried by both
the Inland Revenue and the VAT inspector, Ted Seaton left the
country for Spain: a move that is unlikely to have reassured his
outspoken detractors.

The sale of the Middleham Jewel to an unknown and, as the word
now goes, overseas buyer prompted a broader discussion. Charles
Sparrow, legal adviser to the Council for British Archaeology, wrote
to *The Times* regretting that what was obviously 'a national treasure of
the first rank' could not be treated as 'national property' because of
the idiosyncracy of treasure-trove legislation.[4] He suggested that the
law be reformed so that it applied to all finds of gold and silver rather
than just those that had been deliberately concealed.

The government had proved resistant to the CBA's previous
attempts to enact legislation designed to protect antiquities from the
metal detector, but the case of the Middleham Jewel was surely the
last straw. By the end of January the Conservatives had weighed this
apparent threat to the national heritage against their loathing of State
regulation (especially as it might bear on the rights of private
landowners) and announced an inquiry. When Lord Skelmersdale
broke the news to the House of Lords, there was emotive talk of the
Middleham Jewel, and there was also reference to Wanborough, a
Roman site on Lord Taylor of Hadfield's land in Surrey that was said
to have been stripped of £750,000 worth of priceless silver and gold
coins by nocturnal treasure hunters. I have heard it said that Lord
Taylor, a thorough-going Thatcherite, was not immediately
amenable to the idea of having any officers of the overweening state
interfering on his land and that county archaeologists could only look
on in helpless horror as the site was destroyed and the coins leaked on
to the European antiquities market. A few minor convictions were
eventually secured but the case against a man accused of dealing in
the stolen coins fell apart due to the eccentricity of treasure-trove
legislation and was thrown out of the Crown Court.

There can be little doubt either that treasure-trove law is an
anachronistic relic that needs reform or that a lot of destructive
looting has been going on, but a demonology has also been brought
into play. The transgressions of some villains using detectors have
been used to promote a generalised image of the 'treasure hunter' as a
vandal and rogue: the destructive expropriator of 'our' common past.
It is not surprising that *The Searcher* should be up in arms about this.
For this detectorist magazine, the recovery of the Middleham Jewel
stood as the triumph of a hobby that has been much despised and
belittled by the professional custodians of history, and now it was

being 'turned against the hobby by its opponents': the media had clearly been 'taken for a ride'.

For the last ten or so years the archaeological establishment has been feuding with the metal detectorists. While continuing to press for legislative reform, the Council for British Archaeology also launched an attack on irresponsible and 'lawless' detector use. In January 1979, the CBA passed a resolution condemning treasure hunting as 'a great threat to the country's archaeological heritage' and 'contrary to the national interest'. The resolution accepted that some detectorists were motivated by 'genuine interest in the past' and offered them a subordinate place in the active membership of British archaeology – conditional on their accepting 'the methods and disciplines' (and doubtless also the strict supervision) of the profession. Other conservation and museum bodies welcomed the resolution, and an 'anti-treasure-hunting campaign' was launched in March 1980 under the name of STOP ('Stop Taking Our Past').

STOP never quite got round to mining historical sites, but there was certainly wild talk of illegalising metal detectors and impaling detectorists on their own implements. The same diabolical rhetoric has been adopted by journalists like David Lovibond, who recently revived the imagery of St Elmo's fire to appal readers of *The Sunday Telegraph* with the prospect of their national landscape being ruined by what he called 'the Curse of the Nighthawks': 'On moonless autumn nights, England's ancient fields are lit by the muted glow of a thousand shaded torches. This is the season of the 'nighthawk', the vicious predator who comes safely in the dark to plunder the great and humble monuments of England'.[5] As news has come in of one despoiled site after another, it has begun to looks as if the very soil of England will soon be stripped of all mystery. Indeed, some archaeologists have even estimated that, if the present rate of destruction is maintained, it will only be twenty years before there is nothing left at all. Faced with this prospect, Lovibond relished the words of an archaeologist who described 'hard core' detectorists as 'the sort of people who wear baseball caps and have Confederate stickers on their Cortinas', and he was only marginally kinder about the more respectable hobbyists who made up the nighthawk's 'seedy band of fellow-travellers'.

Boudicca Rides Again

Ten years later there are still Luddites among the archaeologists who won't countenance the metal detector as anything other than an instrument of evil, but many of the professionals recognise that STOP was a counter-productive disaster. Dr Henry Cleere, Director of the CBA and a man who may still have an uphill job persuading some members of his Council, agrees that some statements made in the name of the campaign were 'a bit extreme' and that the idea of getting metal detectors banned was simply a non-starter. As one field archaeologist had warned, the exaggerated rhetoric of the 'totally counter-productive STOP campaign' (intended, in the words of its own leaflet, to tell the public 'how it is being deprived of its common heritage') had only reinforced that same public's tendency 'to see archaeologists as a group of killjoy bureaucrats with an unduly proprietorial attitude to the country's heritage'.[6]

The more militant detectorists would agree with that. STOP manipulated class prejudice to tar them all with the same brush as vandals, enemies of 'our' national heritage, and a counter-attack was obviously necessary. The Detector Information Group was established (with financial backing, as archaeologists like to point out, from interested dealers and detector manufacturers) to defend the hobby, and the detecting Press didn't hang about either. A collective columnist known as 'Boudicca' or, a bit later, 'The Boudicca Team' set her chariot against the massed legions of the archaeological profession and charged at full tilt. The counter-accusations have been vitriolic. Indeed, the CBA's crusade for the national heritage was hijacked and redirected by the enemy. The archaeologists thought they were fighting as champions of the national interest, but they had wandered unawares up on to Crichel Down where they were ambushed, set up as usurping bureaucrats, and cast against the traditional nation in the ongoing Battle of the Welfare State.

In this counter-attack, the whole heritage industry – and it was the metal detectorists who launched the first 'organic' assault on this since much-battered industry – is portrayed as a trick perpetrated on the long-suffering British people by 'Gestapo-like' State bureaucrats. The archaeologists may pretend to be working in everyone's interest (defending 'our' national heritage) but really they are just 'out and out crooks' whose 'sweeping power to nationalize land' even enables them to harass ordinary allotment holders who try to grow parsnips of more than eight inches in length without filling in a separate form for every parsnip in question.[7] There are ribald slurs about 'whatever it is professional archaeologists do in their trenches', and much is made of the site-archaeologists' preference for broad-brimmed Wellington boots (handy, at the very least, for dropping valuable finds into). It is claimed that thousands of valuable objects have 'disappeared' after being excavated by self-styled 'custodians of the national heritage'. As for the archaeologists' 'highly sophisticated aerial survey equipment', this is just another example of the identity of official knowledge and power:

> They are currently photographing the entire land surface of Britain, and then plan to declare vast areas of the countryside to be 'archaeologically significant' (in plain English this simply means that people lived there in the past). If your farm, garden, or

building site is declared 'archaeologically significant' you can expect a visit from an archaeologist armed with a statutory right of access and a large mechanical digger.

The heritage mafia may want to turn the country into a totalitarian theme park in which the locals are expected to play the part of loyal yokels, but the detectorists aren't having it. As I've been told by John Castle, a detectorist who is vigorous in his criticisms and who knows about the amateur origins of the profession, archaeology is just 'a hobby which has managed to con the establishment into paying its expenses'.

While denouncing official archaeology as a State-funded hobby, the detectorists have wasted no time organising themselves into a lobby that spreads out over the country, and has members in strategic positions (one detectorist apparently works for *Hansard* and is well placed to keep an eye on everything that comes into the House of Commons library). MPs have been lobbied and pestered, and journalists who write on the dispute can expect a mailbag crammed with fierce rebuttals: when Neal Ascherson devoted his column in *The Observer* to the issue one Sunday in 1985, he received numerous letters putting him right (including one suggestion that if he really wanted to find 'already-very-rich persons who also, but on a larger scale, "rob us all of our history to fill their pockets"', he should look at the arts pages of his own newspaper). Some detectorists have defended their hobby with brazenly tendentious and opportunistic arguments. They have tried to argue that the damage being done to historic sites is actually the work of moles and, when it suits, to justify their activities by claiming that artificial fertilisers are eroding buried objects so fast that there will be nothing left unless legal niceties are ignored and things are lifted quickly. Like some anti-fluoridationists, the detectorists fraternity is attracted to the paranoid simplicity of the conspiracy theory. I've heard talk of shady dealings linking apparently disparate events like the recovery of gold from the wreck of a sunken ship called the *Edinburgh* and the raising of the *Mary Rose* with Prince Charles's speech about 'carbuncular' architecture and, of course, his position as patron of the 'powerful' Council for British Archaeology. But while the detectorists are happy to speculate along these lines, they are also, as Neal Ascherson had suggested, inclined to see themselves as 'free-born Englishmen', the inheritors of time-honoured poaching traditions and common-land rights that should, so they assert, still apply to most State-owned land (local bye-laws banning detector users from public parks and beaches are considered especially contentious on this score).[8] There are some detectorists who defend their illegal actions on more recent historical grounds. It appears, for example, that at least one of the men who looted the Roman site at Wanborough claims to have been exacting a kind of revenge on Lord Taylor for the fortunes he has made as founder and Life President of

Taylor Woodrow, the construction company that put up countless shoddy system-built tower blocks including Ronan Point in the Sixties. Visiting a coin market near Charing Cross shortly after the looting of Wanborough, John Castle claims to have met a man who lived in one of those east London 'rabbit hutches' and was pleased to have given Lord Taylor a little of 'what the bastard deserved'.

The hard-line detectorists of Boudicca's army have found many ways of insulting the archaeologists, but they are happiest of all when denouncing them as communists who seek to elevate their own definition of the public interest over the traditional freedoms of the people. Late in 1981, John Castle warned readers of *Everything Has A Value* that 'the archaeologists' efforts to ban metal detecting is the thin edge of a very thick wedge and metal detectives, collectors, dealers, landowners, farmers ... should band together to prevent their unchecked encroachment on to our hobbies and livelihoods'. Banging away on the same theme in *Treasure Hunting* four years later, John Howland, then General Secretary of the National Council for Metal Detection, accused Dr Cleere of advancing 'East European politics' and the CBA's proposed Antiquities Bill of being nothing less than "diluted" hard-Marxist dogma ... a backdoor method of achieving control over landowners and farmers who fall for the "heritage" angle.'

The accusation has both puzzled and outraged Dr Henry Cleere. He sits in the CBA's strangely besieged office in Kennington Road ('Have you seen the place?' asks John Castle, his worst suspicions having been confirmed by the somewhat academic appearance of the CBA's building: 'what a grotty dump. . . . It looks like a squat') and traces the worst of it back to a mischievous and, as I have since heard from reliably disreputable sources, carefully sown article that appeared in *Farmers Weekly* on 28 September 1984. Cleere remembers trying to educate the journalist in the principles of the new archaeology, a structural rather than object-centred approach that, in its methodology alone, may owe something to the intellectual discipline of Marxism. But the interview was a set up, and he had already said enough for the man from *Farmers Weekly*. The 'new archaeology' was obviously just a euphemism for 'Marxist archaeology' or 'fitting the facts to a particular view of history'.[9] Dr Cleere was described as 'a rough, tough former industrial adviser' and 'an avowed socialist' who 'disapproves of private land ownership' and feels that, as archaeologists, 'we have a duty to show farmers what's best for them'. Dr Cleere is reported to have identified not small- or medium-sized farmers but the 'agri-industrialists' as his target: 'They are the people who have no links at all with the land, who just want to exploit it, to get as much out of it as possible at any cost. They are barbaric, motivated by nothing but unthinking greed.' But Dr Cleere 'is renowned for climbing on his soapbox', and *Farmers Weekly*, which is equally notorious for camping out on Crichel Down, knew what conclusion to draw: small and medium farmers should recognise their interest in common with that of the metal detectorists and oppose the CBA as 'the prime proponents of bureaucracy and standardisation' who are always 'supporting the bureaucrat against the individual' and calling for 'more law and less freedom'. John Castle, meanwhile, had been taking a look at the professional journals and he struck lucky when he turned up the March 1975 issue of *Current Archaeology*. As he told readers of *Treasure Hunting*, this included a letter inviting the editor to attend a Communist Party meeting on 'pre-Capitalist Societies', where he could hear a talk on 'Marxism and the New Archaeology' and urging him to 'carry the argument for the Marxist Archaeology of 1975' in the profession's journal. What further proof could be needed?

History from Below

So much for the polemic, but what is the world of the metal detector actually like? The hobby has grown dramatically since the Sixties, when American servicemen stationed at USAF bases started using portable metal detectors in Britain. The National Council for Metal Detection knows of well over a hundred federated clubs throughout the country, and the Federation of Independent Detectorists (these are the ones that resist clubbing) now has some thousand lone members. There are two monthly magazines, specialist book publishers, manufacturers, and self-taught electronic engineers who have built up considerable but entirely 'untutored' technical knowledge from practical experience. All this compares very favourably with the intermittent activity that History Workshop, another 'movement' committed to people's history, has been able to sustain. Indeed, the metal detector seems to have taken over the grass roots.

One October evening, I drove out into Essex, that land of torsoes; to visit the monthly meeting of the Thurrock Artefact Recovery Society. Some forty or so metal detectorists, nearly all men and a number of them from east London, gathered to talk about their activity and to discuss the finds of the previous month. People came with their collections, carefully labelled and displayed in portable exhibition cases. The society's library was laid out on a trestle table: a collection of publications that combined learned British Museum monographs on, say, Arretine and Samian pottery with rather different volumes with titles like *Glittering Prospects*. Detector magazines like the *Searcher* and *Treasure Hunting* were also on sale.

After tea and informal discussion, Brian Farrow called the meeting to order and formal proceedings began. The finds of the month were judged in two categories. A visiting expert from a nearby amateur numismatics club went through the coins with a magnifying glass. He commented on a Gallo-Belgic gold stater, an Edward I farthing, a

Henry III penny, a Henry VII halfpenny, before finally settling on a Henry VI quarternoble that, as he said almost incidentally, would probably sell for about £400. The object of the month was judged by a different man, who talked the meeting through an assortment of finds: buckles, harness bells, barrel locks ('to keep the servants off the brandy'), and a sword pommel. He commented at length on a magnificent owl-shaped plate brooch from the second century AD, the proud finder of which was brandishing a fistful of letters from interested museums. His final choice however, was a more ordinary object: a seventeenth-century spur that (most unusually) had been turned up in one piece. Prizes were given out with due ceremony: a set of glasses, a map of historical Kent . . . .

Brian Farrow chaired the meeting with a little hammer, but the formality of the occasion was constantly being undercut with humour. Throughout the find-of-the-month ceremonies, the judge's comments were met with good-natured heckling from the lads in the back row. The send-up was part of established procedure: a way of easing the seriousness of people's involvement in their hobby without really undermining it. From the chair, Brian Farrow tempered formal proceedings with similarly self-effacing quips. Announcing a forth-coming dance he told members to 'Bring your friends along and let them see what a complete load of nutters we are'. And while introducing the 'unknown finds' table to newcomers he explains that 'there's always a clever Dick about' who'll know something about whatever it is that you've dug out of the ground. Towards the end of the meeting he tells members that they can expect some 'real quality now the fields have been turned up again', and then tests the society's interest in an outing to Dunwich – a Saxon town that has been engulfed by the sea off Suffolk. After winter storms, there's a good chance of finding 'something decent' along the shoreline near this legendary place.

I was struck by an irony here. Over recent years, many reforming advocates of people's history have been criticising the 'élitism' of public museums that confine their displays to collected objects and the conventions of connoisseurship that attach to them. The social context is said to be excluded by this cult of authenticity and the advocates of democratisation have been vigorous in their demands for its reintroduction. Alerted to this criticism by the market as much as anything else, many underfunded public museums have been busily turning themselves into three-dimensional visual aids, incorporating recorded testimonies of an oral-historical kind and trading their glass cases for the more interactive attractions of the theme park. Mean-while, out in the despised world of the metal detectorist – self-taught and genuinely popular as it certainly is – things have been moving in precisely the contrary direction. A distinct approach to historical and archaeological knowledge has emerged in detector circles and it is anything but sociological in orientation. The whole history of human society is reviewed through discovered bits and pieces, and a great feature is made of authenticity. Elaborate skeins of almost impossibly arcane knowledge are built up around found objects. The succession of kings and queens is rehearsed in all the detail that a mapping of recovered coinage demands. Military history is reconstituted through the development of uniform buttons. The seventeenth century is likely to be viewed through the changing design of traders' tokens; the nineteenth through horseshoes, gintraps, and stone bottles. In the early days of the hobby, the detectorist press may indeed have been pathetic enough, but only a professional bigot could deny the extraordinary levels of 'knowledge' evident in some of the articles and publications of recent years.

If the detectorist grasps history through unearthed objects, he also tends to appreciate it as a collector and lay connoisseur. Out in the shadowy world of the metal detector the 'cabinet of curiosities' (so often claimed as the inaugural form of the European public museum) has been reinvented. The detectorist's glass-fronted cabinet is portable and home-made. Whether they be coins, buckles, or old fishing spinners reclaimed from a river bed, its objects are dated, named, and displayed in carefully chosen order. There is special-isation among these collections, and between them considerable trading and exchange. Some detector-based collections are already very substantial. Indeed, over at the Museum of London, Brian Spencer remarks that some already surpass the holdings of provincial museums. Others stress the likely financial value of these collections, counting it up in hundreds of thousands of pounds. But such collections are not just built up from an interest in striking it rich; indeed, the comparison that is sometimes made between metal detection and the football pools should not be pressed too far. As one Thurrock detectorist put it, these are 'delightful things to have . . . you want to keep them like others want to buy them'.

This object-centred historical imagination has unmistakably poetic dimensions. When the detectorist goes to work he or she leaves normal routines behind and starts bringing the world to life again. Featureless ploughed fields become places of unexpected and un-predictable discovery. Remarking that many detectorists work the same site over and again, Thurrock's Dave Smith says that a single field could hold the attention of a detectorist for a lifetime. The ploughing turns it up. Seasonal rains seem to bring different things to the surface. There is constant wonder at the way land that was searched extensively one day can still produce something new and unexpected the next. Brian Farrow says much the same, recalling how he has his 'silly minute' when he finds something. He holds the recovered object, focuses his mind on it, and tries to make imaginative contact with the person who lost it. Who was it? What where they doing? What was the world they lived in like? This may seem fanciful, but it is no more so than the process members of a coroner's jury may have to go through in order to decide whether or not an ancient find was deliberately hidden, thereby determining its status under treasure-trove legislation.

This is a romantic imagination, fascinated by ideas of fortune and coincidence, of powers still moving through the land. Alongside serious expositions on Roman or medieval metallurgy and vigorous polemic against the latest ruse of the archaeologists, the detecting magazines print stories about dowsing, ghosts, Romany wisdom, and the ways in which a leyline can be treated as 'a pointer to hoard location'.[10] They follow the routes of pirates and tell stories of King John's treasure and of Viking long boats laden with Danegeld. Mick Moran writes some of the most evocative articles in these magazines. He has Muriel Stuart's poem 'The Tower of Memory' in mind as he drops down into the darkness of an eighteen-foot pit during a nocturnal detecting visit to a building site in the City of London ('There dead men walk/again and dead lips ask, what of the isles of/ England and her sea . . .'). This self-styled nighthawk may not wear a baseball cap, but he is more than a match for Peter Ackroyd as he picks up some black 'anaerobic silt' and starts 'moulding Medieval history' in his fist.[11]

The detector's world is set off against the abstract uniformities of the modern state. It is a landscape of atmospheres, ancient recognitions, and places that have uniquely different qualities: it is full of old continuities resumed. A favourite detectorist strategy is to imagine a place as it might have looked in the distant past. You then think your way back into the mind of a hypothetical ancient with a hoard to hide and study the landmarks for a likely place – the foot of a memorable cliff, the source of a spring . . . . Some remarkable finds have been turned up in this way.

Enthusiasts describe the metal detector as a time machine, but it also helps to loosen the constraints of the social structure. The hobby has class dimensions intimately connected with this business of not having to stay precisely where you are put in the world, but every detectorist to whom I have suggested that the activity is largely a pastime of working-class men has disagreed. The overall predominance of men is accepted (fourteen to one, as the *Searcher* regretted a few years ago), but the point about class is strongly contested. I've been told firmly that the metal detector is a socially neutral tool that can be, and is, used by people of all sorts. I remember the look of exasperation that passed across Brian Farrow's face as I pressed him to tell me what his daytime job was. A question like this is worse than irrelevant: it goes in precisely the wrong direction, reducing a great richness of cultural activity to the insulting generality of its point of departure. In raising the question of class one merely reinforces the slight of centuries, leaving nothing but a bunch of amateur enthusiasts and the withering condescension that is usually implied when the word 'hobby' rolls from the professional tongue. Such are the hidden injuries of class. And it is true: every archaeologist to whom I have mentioned this point about the social composition of the hobby has accepted it as obvious and beyond question.

Since the STOP fiasco, the Council for British Archaeology has tried to develop a new relationship with the non-criminal mass of detectorists. Cooperation has replaced total war as the stated policy, if not always the instinct, of the CBA. A code of practice has been established by the National Council for Metal Detection, and even some of the more hard-line archaeologists are beginning to think differently. Dr David Bird, County Archaeological Officer in Surrey whose views toughened as he watched the looting of Wanborough, is happy to concede that 95 per cent of detectorists are responsible and worthy of respect. He explains the ferocity of the initial archaeological response by referring to the history of the profession itself. Archaeology spent large parts of the nineteenth and early twentieth century trying to raise its own procedures beyond destructive pillage. It then spent decades getting the amateur archaeologists incorporated into the disciplines of the profession. Just as everything seemed to be well settled down, the funding base that archaeology had only recently found in the State started to collapse and the metal detector arrived on the scene. So the whole process had to start again.[12] Dr Bird also explains (and detectorists who hear his claim are still liable to raise a disbelieving eyebrow) that the archaeologist is interested in quite different aspects of a site than the detectorist. Early archaeologists may indeed have followed the lure of hidden treasure, but the profession has become more sober over the years and is now far more interested in, say, the stain left by the sill beam of a vanished wooden building than gold or silver coins.

Boudicca has always argued against any 'appeasement' of the archaeologists, but the CBA and the National Council for Metal Detection have held a couple of jointly sponsored meetings in an attempt to arrive at a better mutual understanding. The second of these took place at Keele University on Saturday, 9 May 1987. The differences were clearly still there. Some of (the disappointingly few) archaeologists who turned up suffered visible attacks of panic whenever 'cooperation' threatened to go beyond dog-like obedience. And there were a lot of empty seats between the archaeologists at the front and the suspicious-looking detectorists massed in the back rows.

Nevertheless, the examples of cooperation were impressive. Tony Gregory, who used to work with the Norfolk Archaeological Unit and who has pioneered collaboration with local detectorists, no longer has to put up with such follies as the attempt made in the late Seventies to pass a censure motion against him at the AGM of the Society of Museum Archaeologists: his offence having been to publish an article describing details of his cooperation with detectorists in the *Museums Journal*. The yields of cooperation are spectacular. They include the

Anglo-Saxon Kingdom of Lindsey (or Lindissi), recently discovered by detectorists working with archaeologists from the Scunthorpe Museum, and many items found by the Society of Thames Mudlarks and exhibited in the Museum of London's 1987 'Capital Gains' exhibition. Over at Flag Fen near Peterborough, metal detectorists have helped archaeologists recover numerous Bronze and Iron Age objects from the site of a huge and recently discovered sacrificial site.[13] As President of the CBA, Professor Philip Rahtz even admitted at the Keele meeting that there is less and less justification for archaeology's characteristically last-ditch argument that things are better left in the ground than dug up by detectorists. The soil is full of synthetic chemicals and, just as the detectorists have been claiming for some time, they do appear to be hastening decay.

But the dialogue has since broken down. The National Council for Metal Detection pulled out when it saw that the CBA was still pressing for legal reforms that would at least make the reporting of finds mandatory. As for the government's inquiry into possible changes in the law governing the disposal of antiquities, it was announced on 13 December 1989 that this had come to nothing too. The portable metal detector has totally transformed the situation in which the law must work, but the principle of private property remains paramount and, despite the urgings of such writers as David Lovibond in *The Sunday Telegraph*, the government has not found a way of constraining the nighthawks without curtailing the freedoms of land-owners and antique dealers. I doubt that anyone in the Department of the Environment really believes Dr Henry Cleere to be an expropriating Marxist in disguise, but the government's inaction through the Eighties had put it on the side of Boudicca. Up on Crichel Down, the Cold War lives on. So far, the detectorists have won.

Part Four

Tales of Conversion

13

The Park that Lost its Name

Hackney was once a place of pastures and market gardens. Samuel
Pepys practised archery here. Even today there is a public park in the
borough known as London Fields. It is a place of modest attractions:
some fine old plane trees, a new community centre, an open-air lido
that, were it not for local objectors, the council would already have
demolished. In the early morning, before the dogs come out, it is often
full of seagulls.

Trains rattle by overhead. London Fields borders on the Cambridge line, and it's not a bad spot from which to observe passing
academics. They stare back glumly, thanking their lucky stars for
Granchester Meadows and mistaking the figures on the ground for
woebegone residents of the Victorian East End. It's easy to imagine
them adding those contemporary asides that keep turning up in
scholarly studies of Dickens, Doré, or life as it was in outcast London:
'Even today, one only has to take the train from Liverpool Street
Station . . .'.

London Fields certainly has its dismal aspect. There have been
vicious assaults. Huge and unattended dogs run free. Young children
from the nearby travellers' site invade the infants' playground in a
terrifying and unbelievably foulmouthed pack (not for them the clip
on the ear with which Richard North once hoped to improve the
area). As I walked out one Sunday afternoon I came across a Ford
Cortina parked up against the railings: it was emitting grunts and
rocking with copulation.

But despite the malevolence that sometimes drifts across it,
London Fields also clings to an understated respectability. On most
days of the year, it is an uneventful and slightly melancholy place. If it
has a message for the world it is no longer the progressive Victorian
one about the uplifting and civilising effect of open spaces – green
lungs as they used to be called – on the nation's most down-trodden
souls. These days the park promises nothing so ambitious. It merely
points out that people can be poor without always being beastly; that,
no matter what writers like Tom Wolfe may suggest, the inhabitants
of the inner city can get by without raping, mugging, and insulting
each other at every encounter.

The park remains uncelebrated, but its name is too good to be true.
'London Fields . . .'. It doesn't take a master class in poetry to reveal
the contemporary resonances of that archaic conjunction. In these

ecological days 'London Fields' has come into its own as a prime piece of nomenclature, a movable asset that is far too good to be squandered on an obscure dog-patch in Hackney.

The estate agents were the first to act. Assisted by the usual clutch of lifestyle journalists, they went out one night in the early Eighties, levered the name up from that tired stretch of municipal ground, and humped it half a mile down the road. No longer confined to the park or the dishevelled part-industrial part-Bohemian zone around the railway arches on its east-side, 'London Fields' was now the new name for Mapledene – a pleasant and, as we know, relatively unbroken area of Victorian terraced housing that, through this act of renaming, was now being pulled away from the abysmal Holly Street Estate at its western edge. 'London Fields' was still a place of leafy respite, but it had become one that could be bought and sold: a rediscovered 'village' within walking distance of the City.

John Milne was the first writer to offer us *London Fields*, the novel. He had grown up in a council flat in the area and though his story, issued by Heinemann in 1983, was shy of highbrow presumptions, his publishers were still serious enough to adorn it with somewhat patronising recommendations from David Lodge ('Mr Milne has talent') and Auberon Waugh ('Mr Milne seems to represent a new development in the English novel').

Milne is good on detail, but at heart his *London Fields* was a conventional fable of working-class male endeavour. Its hero was determined to break away from the poverty of his circumstances: the string of wretched jobs, the dismal estates, the cruelly observed pregnant wife with her nylon dressing-gown and her stifling need for security. He turns to athleticism, and then, via an exotic inter-racial affair ('She was ebony, pure shining carved ebony'), to the under-world of drugs, black clubs, and serious crime. Milne's *London Fields* is a place of confinement and stunted prospects. The escape route is enticing but it leads inevitably to gaol.

Then, in 1989, Martin Amis came along with the book that swept John Milne's effort into oblivion. By the time Amis has finished with it, London Fields isn't a place at all. Instead it's a monstrous condition, a post-modern pile-up at the end of another millennium. London Fields has become the immoral void where the time-expired allegories of British life go to mutate. There's suicide and murder. There's imminent nuclear catastrophe and a dark collapsing sky. There are gross couplings, and they're not discreetly hidden in a Ford Cortina either. At one point in the performance, an unprecedented gale bursts in to fell thirty-three million trees: all in a single stroke of the Ring Master's hormonal, mid-Atlantic prose. People round here may well wonder what Martin Amis thinks he's doing to their park.

The Nasty Young Man of English letters grows apocalyptic with age. These days he creeps into London Fields like a repentant mugger and practises being human. He's achieved some results through these exertions: an abstract devotion to the planet, for example, and a fatal softness for babies. Nevertheless, he's still doing horrible things to women and children. Amis's American narrator is less of a worry. He flew into London saying 'I want time to go to London Fields', but he died on the way through. He'll never know that, despite all his millennialist huffing and puffing, the plane trees in Hackney's park are still standing. I can't believe anyone in the area will miss him.

14

Remembering London's War

I

Theo Crosby Meets King Ludd in the Blueprint Café

> We live in a marvellously paradoxical world, where incredible technologies are invented, and put to the most banal and inadequate purposes.
>
> Theo Crosby, 1975

An ordinary secular motorist driving along Richmond Road at about 11.15 on the morning of Sunday, 11 November 1990, would have passed a small gathering by the pavement, just north-east of the Holly Street Estate. A vicar was presiding, but there was no sign of a church. Indeed, the small band was gathered in front of a modest block of six-storey council flats, ornamented with the usual mess of satellite dishes. Had our motorist slowed a little, he might have noticed that the congregation was gathered around a small and damaged war memorial. Had he stopped altogether and joined in, he would have discovered that this was Remembrance Day, and that the place at which the little band had gathered was the site of St Philip's Church. The war memorial, left over from the Great War, is all that remains, and even it is sadly reduced: once a cross, it is now little more than a stump of grey stone with some barely legible names on it. The church, which stood where those flats are now, was lost in the blitz, along with its vicar and church warden. The story told locally is that a large mine fell alongside the church, failing to explode until the church warden made a mistake of poking at it with his umbrella . . . .

The stunted war memorial left over from St Philip's Church lacks monumental presence; indeed, many people who have lived in the area for years haven't even noticed it. As for the annual services that Revd John Willard, vicar of nearby Holy Trinity, holds here, these are modest affairs too; but remembrance doesn't have to be grand to be meaningful, or it didn't until recently.

In the summer of 1987 the design company, Pentagram, mounted an exhibition at the Royal Academy. The moving spirit was Theo Crosby, a South African born architect who is interiors director with Pentagram, and his model showed a monument to the Battle of

Britain that he would like to see built in the Docklands area of London. Pentagram issued two suitably stylish black booklets in which Crosby argued his case and outlined a broader vision of the 'new Jerusalem' London might at last become.[1]

The first strand in Crosby's argument was cultural. There had, he suggested, been disastrous problems with the peace that broke out after World War Two. Modernist thinking took over and ' "useful" short term strategies' like schools and hospitals were given priority over 'long term monuments and civic ornaments'. This ' "liberal" decision' played into the hands of experts who were pleased to close ranks behind an 'ideology that gave them scope to experiment and blissful freedom from personal responsibility'. It also 'broke a thread leading back three thousand years'. Only now, after the humiliation of the reforming State, which did such damage to our cities and our national character, is 'the necessity of monuments' coming to be appreciated once again: the monument as a marker and 'urban instrument'. The Eighties are a 'miraculous' time: a time of 'Beginnings' in which the 'ideal city' can be rediscovered amidst all the mediocre confusion of post-war London. Art and skill can be built back into the fabric of the city. The rule of Style can be reasserted over a building technology that has been allowed to run rampant. Crosby's monument is a memorial, but it is also proposed as the spiritual lever with which we can prevent ourselves from sinking any further into the post-war swamp.

If this was the cultural justification for Crosby's monument, it was accompanied by a commercial one. The failure of vision that lasted throughout the post-war period of massive urban redevelopment has left us with no monuments except those that already existed in the old and historic urban centres. Meanwhile, tourism is booming and the British are squaring up to their new destiny as 'a nation of shopkeepers become hoteliers'. Fifteen million people visit London every year, and this figure – as Crosby projects – could well have doubled by the year 2000. Old attractions like the Tower of London and Westminster Abbey are stretched to capacity and there is a growing problem of 'throughput'. Along with new monuments, there should be education programmes designed to build public awareness of architecture. Unemployment 'will inevitably increase', after all, and it will not just be visiting tourists who have time to practise their interpretative skills as they wander the streets of the re-idealised city.

Crosby's Battle of Britain monument claims its place in a city that must be redeveloped if it is to thrive in a post-industrial, 'leisure'-orientated future. The Thames is deindustrialising fast and if Crosby has his way it will soon be restored to its proper pride of place as the capital's most significant thoroughfare. Busy with upgraded tourist amenities, the river will become a primary source of meaning again, and the ideal city that flows from it would extend along two 'axes'

Crosby had worked up from carefully chosen heritage imagery.
Running across a loop of the river from Westminister Abbey to St
Paul's, the 'Canaletto Axis' derives from that famous view, painted
from the terrace of Somerset House, of the City of London huddling
under Wren's dome while a hundred more modest spires indicate
further transcendence to the east. The 'Turner axis' also has a canvas
origin: it follows Turner's 'View of St Paul's' down from Greenwich,
crossing the river twice before it too culminates at Wren's noble
cathedral. According to Crosby, these alignments testify to 'the magic
rules of the past that governed the disposal of buildings and
particularly monuments. They are the cardinal points, the directions
of the equinox, the midsummer sunrise the turning of the year, the
evocation of growth, the stopping of time'. In addition, as our
necromantic surveyor continues, 'they assert an inner harmony' and
'carry a meaning loaded with the centuries'.

There is presently, as Crosby wrote in 1987, a dearth of monuments
along these axes; and there must be more if the city is to be grand once
again. Some were already under construction – the Globe Shake-
speare Centre (where Crosby himself had a commercial interest), the
Design Museum, the recycled Battersea Power Station – but
Docklands remained a desert: a 'vast space, destroyed more by peace
and changing technology than war'. Of course, development was
underway but 'the general effect is restless, temporary, smallscale.
There are no public buildings, no churches, nothing with aspirations
beyond private comfort and corporate greed'. So it was here in
Docklands (in this tormented place that cries out for 'an antidote, a
great marker, a communal beacon; a civic gesture') that the Battle of
Britain monument should stand. Once again, as Crosby promised –
with a sub-Heideggerean utterance he attributes mistakenly to
Gertrude Stein – 'there will be a there there'.

Realigning the City

In a book-length publicity brochure published by Pentagram in 1972,
Crosby had this to say about himself: 'His character is complex, being
an enthusiast for innovation and change yet also an active preserva-
tionist'.[2] In plain terms, he meant that he was a modernist in the
process of jumping ship. In the Forties and Fifties he had worked with
the modernist, Maxwell Fry, and been a member of both the MARS
Group and the more loosely defined 'Independent Group' that
revolved around Lawrence Alloway at the Institute of Contemporary
Arts: he had rubbed shoulders with modernists and 'brutalists' alike,
helping to organise exhibitions like the Whitechapel Art Gallery's
'This is Tomorrow' (1956), an interdisciplinary show that featured
such exhibits as a 'space-deck roof' made out of a prefabricated
system and a wall of rough concrete blocks intended 'to demonstrate
how an aesthetic intention can be expressed in the most humble

materials' and to hint at the glories to which architecture and sculpture might rise within a wholly 'mass produced environment'.[3] As a younger man, Crosby apparently worked on a plan to demolish the old Euston Station and put office blocks on its site; and his unrealised plan for Fulham, which would have replaced large tracts of terraced housing with seven-storey deck-access blocks, is even said to have provided the inspiration for Broadwater Farm. By the late Eighties, however, when Crosby put the case for his Battle of Britain monument, he was restating anti-modernist arguments he had been advancing for some twenty years. In 1970 he was castigating 'our miserably inept building industry' for covering large areas with 'identical blocks of identical dwellings', and then justifying its soul-destroying works on the grounds that they produced 'the maximum number of minimum homes for the least apparent cost.[4] While Los Angeles was at the height of its cult as a 'place without tradition', Crosby had already turned his head resolutely in the opposite direction, calling for a recovery of the sense of history that modernism had all but destroyed: 'In the future city we will need monuments, places to visit, to look and wonder at, for this is the purpose of our hard-won mobility'. Looking ahead, he could see that 'in the coming years of mass international transportation, when whole populations will move each summer, the pressure on the older established monuments will be unbelievable'. It was essential to preserve the 'gestures of communality' erected by our pre-modern ancestors but, in anticipation of the Battle of Britain monument, it was also vital to start making 'good things for our own time'. Crosby returned to his chosen theme in 1975, when he gave the Lethaby Lectures at London's Royal College of Art. Calling for a halt to modernism's 'insidious diffusion into our mental structures', he described historical buildings as the nation's collective memory, and insisted that we couldn't 'afford any more brain surgery with Colonel Seifert wielding the axe'.[5] He declared all old buildings (and certainly not just the few that had been granted listed status) to be valuable because they represented 'something outside the motives behind new constructions, something other', and called on people to fight for the conservation of 'any old building' for its 'poetic, irrational value'. While the Battle of Britain monument raised these concerns again twelve years later, it also adjusted them to a new climate: Crosby's earlier arguments were inclined to link modernism with industrialism or, as he puts it, with the values of our 'military, industrial society', but by the late Eighties, as those modish black pamphlets reveal, the most effective way of condemning modernism was to define it as the utilitarian ideology of the Welfare State.

Those curiously airy 'axes' along which our architect proposed to realign London may show what is left of modernist master-thinking once the bulldozers and demolition men have been withdrawn, but they also find precursors beyond the field of architectural theory.

Theo Crosby knows what it is to have a properly historical sense of place, but as a resident of New Georgian Spitalfields he must have sensed how the ground was already loosening beneath his feet. In 1986, only the year before Crosby invoked 'the magic rules of the past' in support of his monument, Gavin Stamp had risen to defend the memory of Wren's pupil Nicholas Hawksmoor from a repulsive necromantic cult that was emerging around his long-neglected churches in east London.[6] Stamp was worried about Peter Ackroyd's *Hawksmoor*, a recently published novel that was giving this hitherto relatively obscure architect a 'sensational and mendacious notoriety'. The real Hawksmoor was a modest, long-suffering man who had been 'laid to rest in a Herefordshire churchyard 250 years ago'. He was also 'one of the very greatest of British architects' and the churches he built after the Fire of London for the Commission for Building Fifty New Churches in such places as Stepney, Spitalfields, and Limehouse were both 'wonderful masterpieces of the English Baroque' and 'tangible gestures against heresy'. In treating Hawksmoor as a murderous occultist whose real aim was to blight his 'Rationall and mechanicall Age' with ancient 'Darknesse' and who used his great stone churches to sink a malevolent design – a triangle here, a 'pentacle-starre' there – into the heart of the city, Ackroyd had 'perverted' history, libelling the dead and, as Sir John Summerson had apparently remarked, 'defiling the wells of truth'.[7]

But though *Hawksmoor* outraged some eminent conservationists, it wasn't really Ackroyd who was to blame. Behind his derivative novel was the far more reprehensible work of Iain Sinclair, the obscure east London writer whose book, *Lud Heat* (1975), had provided Ackroyd with so much more than his acknowledged point of departure. Sinclair's early writings reveals that he started out in the Sixties under the influence of the American and now chronically unfashionable Black Mountain school of poetics. Here are ample signs of contamination: the spaced-out parenthesis that never closes, the borrowed cosmologies and hermetic speculations of a young writer who, as a sometime book-dealer, was in a good position to heed Jack Spicer's advice to young poets and read the weirdest stuff on which he could lay hands. There were no job offers from Chatto or Faber for this particular poet but, at least, there were casual opportunities to be found in the east: cutting municipal grass in Tower Hamlets, packing cigars in Clerkenwell, rolling barrels about in the ullage cellars of Truman's Brick Lane Brewery. So Sinclair went to ground in the manner of one of his own narrators, 'seeking failure and obscurity, as the only condition spiritually adequate to his self-esteem'.[8] It was during these years, when developers were proposing the total obliteration of historic areas like Piccadilly Circus, and GLC planners tried to compete with equally destructive proposals of their own like the inner-London motorway box or the comprehensive redevelopment of a hundred acres in

Covent Garden, that Sinclair carried out the poetic realignment of London that would eventually earn him dubious notoriety as the occultist surveyor who had recharted the city for Peter Ackroyd.[9]

As he sifted through the turgid stream of psychological and sociological prose that came with the post-war settlement, Sinclair built up his own exotic bibliography from the exceptional volumes that floated by. Among his more fertile sources was E. O. Gordon's *Prehistoric London; Its Mounds and Circles*, a book of Druidical ruminations published in 1925.[10] It was from the pages of this obscure tome that King Ludd stepped out into the post-war scene. The son of Beli II, Ludd ruled London just before the Romans came, and is said to have been a great builder: the old chroniclers describe how he erected walls of lime and stone, fortifying them with 'divers fair towers' and adding the monumental entrance known as Ludgate to the west of the city.

But beside reviving ancient kings, Gordon also did for London what Alfred Watkins was at that time doing for the countryside. In *Early British Trackways* (1922) and *The Old Straight Track* (1925), Watkins outlined his vision of England as an ancient landscape crossed by a mysterious geometry of 'leylines' that intersected at prehistoric sites. Gordon's survey of the major Druidic mounds in the London area produced a similarly atavistic triangulation that ran from the Llandin on Parliament Hill down through the Penton at the site of the New River reservoir to Bryn Gwyn or the White Mound, supposedly an Arthurian site on which the White Tower of the Tower of London now stands, and then back across the river to Tothill at Westminster. The original visionaries of the leyline were benevolent Christian enquirers, bent on redeeming and, if at all possible, re-enchanting the face of a nation that was still only emerging from the ruinous trauma of the Great War, but Sinclair saw other possibilities. Taking Robertson's triangulation as a coordinate, he started to add lines of his own, drawing on just about any aspect of the city that was archaic, monstrous, or merely surplus to present requirements: the routes of the Krays, the prophetic writings of William Blake, the sites of Jack the Ripper's killings and the Ratcliffe Highway Murders, old sheep tracks crossing east London, the seepage of cholera through underground water systems, the movement of books as they drift through the street markets, fragments of alien or prehistoric belief systems from the Tarot through to ancient Egyptian cosmology, the horrors reported weekly in the dead-pan prose of the *Hackney Gazette*. Sinclair's work is full of loathsome *fission*, with one dead symbolic system mutating into the next, and it was only thanks to Hawksmoor's largely forgotten churches that he managed to anchor his map of the seething abyss: those great stone edifices enabled him to reinforce Robinson's Druidical lines with the additional triangle that forms between Christchurch, St George's-in-the-East, and St Anne's, Limehouse, and also the 'pentacle-star' that emerges once St

George's, Bloomsbury, and St Alfege's, Greenwich, are brought into the picture. Such was the potent geometry that Sinclair was happy to suggest had been built into the city by Hawksmoor himself.

In recent years, Sinclair's renegade charting of the city has provoked a whole industry: Ackroyd's novel has made the journey from best-seller to A-level set book; graphic novelists have plagiarised *Lud Heat*, and listings magazines like *City Limits* have taken to recommending tours of Hawksmoor's newly interesting churches. As for the vicars of these High Baroque institutions, they are no longer just troubled by high-minded (and often Anglo-Catholic) conservationists for whom the historical fabric of the building is altogether more sacred that the decidedly low-church needs of the local congregation: nowadays, they also have to reckon with a steady stream of crazy-eyed believers who come round in search of an occult charge. But Sinclair's growing reputation as diviner and lightning conductor to ethereal powers is largely beside the point. His symbolic mapping of London actually follows an autobiographical logic that makes him less an abracadabra man than a poet of the Welfare State, the laureate of its morbidity and failure. The 'lines of force' in his London follow the routes Sinclair himself has taken as he wandered through those twenty years of marginal activity in the old East End, and it is through this autobiographical connection that the conjured historical and mythical ghosts come forward to find their equivalent in the present. The Fire of London merges with the fire that destroyed St Anne's in 1850, and then reappears, along the same 'grid of influence', as the blitz (which gutted St George's, leaving it to be preserved as a 'mummified shell').[11] Similarly the reconstruction that took place after the Fire of London – here exemplified by the Commission for Building Fifty New Churches – comes forward to find its contemporary equivalent in the secular reconstruction programmes of the Welfare State: the failure of that early eighteenth-century attempt to impose a new order on the city becomes strangely emblematic in this unexpected connection. Such are the volatile correspondences that emerge at the heart of Sinclair's baroque historical fantasy. Contemporary ideas of benevolent reform are ghosted by the drama of Sir Frederick Treeves, the London Hospital doctor whose philanthropic adoption of the Elephant Man is portrayed as a self-interested act of soul murder. Post-war ideas of planned redevelopment are confronted by the mocking inscription on the facade of a nineteenth-century improved dwelling – 'Labour/is life/blessed is he/who has found/his work' – a tablet commandment that doubles as the credo of Jack the Ripper. Sinclair recovers the density of the city through a scavenging poetic, which works like an inverted parody of future-orientated urban planning. If the 'geometry of opposition' at the heart of his London is occult, this is partly because it has collapsed into the very urban chaos to which it was intended to give form. As Sinclair says of these mantic outlines, they are 'slack dynamos abandoned as the culture that supported them has gone into retreat'. History is not just a matter of old relics: it also lies around as morbidly unfinished business, as ghosts and strange potencies that seep round the edges of every reforming design.

If this was London in the Seventies, the Eighties have proved to be a decade of beguiling simplification. Ackroyd resolves Sinclair's writhing city into a fable of failed enlightenment: an atmospheric pastiche that fits in perfectly with contemporary ideas about the death of history and the failure of the Welfare State. As for Theo Crosby, the space in which his cleaned-up Canaletto and Turner 'axes' would eventually appear was anticipated in the opening words of *Lud Heat*: 'The old maps present a sky-line dominated by church towers; those horizons were differently punctured, so that the subservience of the grounded eye, & the division of the city by nome-wound, was not disguised'. But by the Eighties, when revivalists like Crosby were trying to reinstate that classical 'subservience', the city itself had gone into hiding. For Sinclair, 'the scenographic view is too complex to unravel here, the information too dense; we can only touch on a fraction of the possible relations'; but by the time Crosby comes along with his monument, all that density has been emptied out and we are left with a couple of old riverside views hanging in thin air. The Canaletto and Turner axes extend not so much through historical urban space as through the vacuum that opens up as the modern city goes down in defeat. Such local cultures as still cling to the ground in increasingly detonated warrens along the route of Crosby's 'axes' are so beleaguered that they no longer offer any resistance. The whole apparatus of post-war public policy, with its many statutory insti-tutions and forms of expertise, is in retreat. The GLC has gone, and with it both the possibility of overall planning in the city and the contemporary political definition of urban life that might reveal the poverty of revivalist aesthetics. Crosby's vistas belong to the London of the Blueprint Café, a city reduced to the zero degree and deserted even by its own ghosts, a place of resounding emptiness where the last chance for history is to become a designer's dream. Crosby presents his Battle of Britain monument as a memorial, but it is actually an instrument of oblivion: this latter-day King Ludd's way of saying 'farewell' not just to modernism but also to the blighter post-war city of 'development' and the Welfare State.

One in the eye for the veterans

But what of the monument itself? Crosby insists that it will be touched with 'aboriginal innocence' of the kind that has previously drawn tourists to more primitive places. He also promises, somewhat more predictably, that it will give visitors 'a dose of the right stuff'. The base takes the form of the 'original tomb': a pyramid with an arched entrance, a 'cave' that is entered between Doric columns. The hollow interior is haunted by holograms and moving images – ghosts that 'come whisperingly to life on arrival and die away as the visitor leaves'. A vertical ghost-train carries the visitor up through the strata of London's war. Subterranean images of underground shelters, tube-stations, control rooms, and bunkers give way to a ground-level display of collapsing houses, fire wardens, and anti-aircraft guns. At the top are the fighters, bombers, and barrage balloons of the airborne drama.

Externally, the pyramid is 'rusticated, clad in granite'. A twenty-foot high frieze tells the story of the war from Dunkirk to the surrender on Luneborg Heath. Cut in stone above this are words from Winston Churchill's most celebrated wartime speech ('We shall fight them on the beaches . . .').[12] The tower soars up from the pyramid and is covered with 'symbols of regeneration and memory'. Six-metre high sculptures of the aviators are placed at the corners of the upper stage, and the lesser figures of 'women, helpers and mourners' stand between them. At this point, the tower twists to create 'diagonal lattices which light the figures and the pyramid roof'. Visitors step out of glass lifts that have brought them up the outside of the tower at vertiginous speed, and steady themselves on an upper platform some five hundred feet above ground. They gaze out over east London: 'a battlefield of the war and a casualty of the peace'. Tombs and sepulchres offer shelter from the weather, while the glass walls are engraved with stories of the blitz and descriptions of visible land-marks. Searchlights placed in the tombs illuminate the upper levels and 'orchestrate a dance, a cathedral of light in the sky'. After witnessing this bizarre tribute to both London blitz and Nuremberg Rally, visitors will reach the 'final experience, the sacred place high in the vast sky'. A sculpture by Michael Sandle, an artist well known for his interest in military and totalitarian imagery, will show 'a circular pit' with chairs and a table set with 'a simple meal, a corpse laid out'. Above this 'sombre scene', a Heinkel bomber crashes down through a disintegrating cathedral, while a 'tiny Spitfire fighter hurtles through beside it'. The visitor to this 'place of national pilgrimage' is expected to suffer vertigo and visual surprise: the rapid ascent in those externally placed glass lifts forming 'a major element in the experience of visiting'.

Crosby costs his monument at £30 million – about the same, he notes, as a single Harrier or Tornado jet – and he knows better than to be looking for a government subsidy. With visitors paying at the door, the monument would be 'a perfectly viable commercial investment'. In conversation with journalists he has also animated the project in autobiographical terms and answered the objections of some of his critics. As he told a generally appreciative Martin Pawley, 'I was in the war, I had a great time'.[13] The design is indeed influenced by Albert Speer and Wilhelm Krier, but the classical style is now emerging from its totalitarian deformation: 'I should have thought that everybody now accepts that in the war the Germans were good chaps just like us who fought like tigers. Anyway I think it's time we got back some of the inheritance we lost just because Hitler happened to like Classical architecture'. As for Docklands, this 'used to be a wonderful place, but it has no spiritual content. That's why we put the monument there . . . it's amazing how empty most people's lives are, they really have nothing but TV and video. What we need for our own safety as much as anything else is real cultural monuments so there is a public presence in the streets'.[13] We've certainly come a long way since 1953 when Barbara Jones declared, with a shamanistic kind of modesty, that 'a folly is glass and bones and a hank of weeds'.[14]

Theo Crosby's monument combines B-movie methods of memorialisation with the money-making exhilaration of the big dipper and the stern social purpose of an exercise in community policing. At present there are no plans to build it, and Crosby himself is apparently not seeking to raise the funds. But even if the story ends with Pentagram's model, Crosby's monument has already done its work. To start with, it has asserted very clearly that the idea of 'heritage' need no longer always stand in opposition to development. It has been customary since Victorian times to defend what is understood as 'heritage' against the ravages of modernisation, but in recent years the idea has been turning up in the vanguard of one urban development scheme after the next. Here then, from a company that has been in the forefront of the much vaunted 'design revolution' of the Eighties, is another version of the post-modern offer. Where previously there was only conflict and antagonism, the Battle of Britain Monument offered a new synthesis: we really can have both tradition and modernisation, memory and the new Beginning, heritage and the most extensive redevelopment imaginable. Crosby's monument appeared to corroborate the fashionable theorists of 'hyper-reality' who have argued, to the benefit of every property developer who can read, that in a world governed by 'simulation', history finally disappears into its own image and the real thing can no longer be distinguished from the abject fake.[15]

As it turned out, however, there were still some partisans of old-fashioned memory who wanted nothing to do with this jumped-up kind of memorialisation. The Association of Battle of Britain Pilots took one look at Pentagram's model and, after denouncing it as 'unsuitable' and 'an insult to those who died', insisted that a proper statue of Air Chief Marshal Lord Dowding, Commander-in-Chief of Fighter Command in 1940, would be altogether more appropriate. Dowding himself had apparently eyed an empty plinth in Trafalgar Square (joking that it was 'reserved for me, but much later!') and in April 1988 *The Sunday Telegraph* surveyed its readers and declared Lord Dowding the favourite contender for this still-vacant position of national honour. By this time, however, the long-overdue statue for which the memory of Lord Dowding had been obliged to wait nearly fifty years was announced for a different site: the Queen Mother would be unveiling it the following October at the RAF church of St Clement Danes.[16] King Ludd is said to have been buried under his monument at Ludgate, so perhaps Crosby should be relieved that his own tomb-like proposition so far remains unbuilt. By the summer of 1990 he had been appointed Professor of Architecture at the Royal College of Art. In no time at all the faculty had been purged of all its previous staff and a surprise prepared for the new intake of postgraduate students who had enrolled before the dawning of this new age. As apprentices to the revivalist vision, students would be expected to turn up at 9.00 am sharp every morning and get used to having their endeavours marked out of ten. As the new master, Crosby has brought in the man who drew his Battle of Britain Monument to teach them the forgotten art of draughtsmanship. The Battle of Britain Monument remains on the drawing board, but over at the Royal College of Art, Professor Crosby and his assistant, Pedro Guedes, have already started to hand down ancient truths on heavy tablets of stone.

II

Holding Ground on the Isle of Dogs

> What's it like, then, sitting out there in a bomb crater? I was here when this one got dropped. And now they call it the Mudchute Farm . . .
>
> Joe Brown addressing his audience
> from in front of his 'Bruvvers' at the
> 'Isle of Dogs Fun Day', September 1990.

The driverless trains of the Docklands Light Railway follow no recognisable axis as they wind along their toy-like overhead line, pausing at stations painted up to match them in red and blue – each one clicking and whirring, a fully automated designer logo dropped, injudiciously, into the void. Starting from Stratford, the train passes through the comprehensively redeveloped bomb-sites of the post-war LCC and then judders up a curved incline that leads into the new world of Docklands. Suddenly we are looking out at Dallas and Jeddah all rolled into one. Children gasp. A man with wide lapels, dark glasses, and a portable phone gazes out over the construction sites and the satellite dishes with an admiring smile and mutters in vague tribute to Clint Eastwood, 'there's a lot of glass and a lot of steel and a lot of concrete out there'. He's talking about Canary Wharf, the thrusting contrivance we glimpsed from the Mrs Cooper's twelfth-floor balcony on the land-locked Holly Street Estate. Having already dwarfed the council tower blocks to the north and south, Margaret Thatcher's reply to the Blue Streak rocket is still soaring up into the sky where it will masquerade as Britain's tallest building – apparently undeterred by gathering recession or, for that matter, by the critics who use it to cry down the whole Docklands experiment as, in the phrase of one embittered estate agent, 'a monument in a marsh'.

Docklands may be a new enterprise zone built in defiance of earlier post-war conceptions of planning, but it is also one of the last bastions of the generous State subsidy. In summer the local parks are full of free cultural activity – from puppet shows to parades of shire horses. Hawksmoor's church of St Anne's, Limehouse, has been cleaned up, and generally prepared for its inauguration as Docklands Cathedral. The light railway is as cushioned as any little train on an English branch line could ever have wished to be.

I get off opposite the London Arena, cross the famously inadequate 'red-brick road' with which the London Docklands Development Corporation opened up the area to new development, and walk through a housing estate to the community centre where the Island History Trust has its office. Eve Hofstettler has been described as the only salaried full-time community historian in the country. She is also one of the heroic figures from the early days of History Workshop who haven't spent the Eighties drifting away from direct involvement with what used to be called 'people's history' to tend their own academic careers or write distinctly literary autobiographies of their own. Her purpose at the Trust is to 'recover and preserve the history of the Isle of Dogs and its people'. As she explains, the memories that concern her project are connected to ordinary objects in the everyday texture of the place: things that are far from monumental and that don't necessarily receive any formal commemoration at all. It is this fabric of reminiscence that helps islanders to 'feel they belong' and 'have a stake' in their locality despite all the recent changes.

The *Island History Newsletter* for March 1990 contains an entry that exemplifies everything Hofstettler is talking about. Under the heading 'Daisy's Anniversary', it shows a snapshot of Mrs Daisy Woodard standing in front of some railings. Behind her a row of modest post-war council flats tapers away towards a church spire. In her hand, Mrs Woodard holds an old black-and-white photograph of young children playing in what looks, at first glance, to be an entirely unrelated street of terraced Victorian 'slums'. Printed next to this picture was Mrs Woodard's explanation:

On Sunday 3rd September 1939 at 11 o'clock, my friends and I were playing in Millwall Park. A Park Keeper wearing a brown uniform came up to us and said, 'Go home, there's going to be a war'.

We were sitting on the seat and he came and told us a second time, 'Go home now.' So we did.

The reason for the photo, is that last year, at 11 o'clock on

Sunday 3rd September 1989, I went and stood at the same place at the same time, holding a photograph of Glengarnock Avenue (previously Newcastle Street), showing myself and my friends Phyllis and Ronnie Still playing outside our street door. Lovely Christ Church is in the background of both photos.

I could not have let the moment go by on that anniversary 50 years later.

The old row of housing has gone and, this being 'Docklands', the name of the street has been changed too; but, as Mrs Woodard remarks, the church spire is still there to help her hold her ground.

Daisy Woodard lives with her husband, Dave, in Thermopylae Gate, a small street on what was known as the Chapelhouse Estate when it was built shortly after World War One in the first (and, as the Adam Smith Institute declared in 1985, 'ruinously expensive') wave of government-funded council housing.[17] The houses are terraced two-floor structures with pitched roofs, wide cottage-like eves, and a stretch of garden at the front as well as the back. Mrs Woodard has lived in her house for nearly fifty years, and she loves every brick of it. She tells me about a press cutting that has a picture of George Lansbury putting in the first symbolic shovel at an inauguration ceremony early in 1920. The estate was built on farmland, and the rural ideal was deliberately incorporated into its design: indeed, it is only recently that the last of the crab-apple trees that were planted in front of each house has gone.

The Woodards share vivid memories of the war. Daisy recalls being buffeted about by bomb blasts and machine-gunned by a passing plane during the famous 'dinner-time raid'. With a little embarrassment, she tells of scribbling bracing messages on scraps of paper and posting them on trees: 'There will always be an England' and 'Don't lose heart'. She remembers getting up on her birthday, saying to her mother, 'I wonder what Hitler is going to give me for my birthday' and then being knocked over by the bomb that duly came and demolished half their house in Newcastle Street.[18] Mrs Woodard certainly doesn't need one of Theo Crosby's externally placed high-speed lifts to relive the experience: even now, she only has to hear the sound of a wartime siren on the radio or television to feel an overwhelming rush of the old anxiety. Mr Woodard recalls the first night of the blitz on 7 September 1940, when the Isle of Dogs was completely ringed by fire: he had just taken a friend up to London Bridge Station and as he came back he saw the island blazing from one end to the other. Reaching for words all these years later, he likens it to a birthday cake and then, unsatisfied with this comparison, settles for Dante's *Inferno*: 'that's as near as I can get'. He remembers the curious sense of relief he felt when his periods of leave came to an end and he could go back to war and catch up on lost sleep.

I ask about the recent developments that have created 'Docklands'

where parts of three separate boroughs once stood. Mr Woodard
remarks that it is certainly confusing: as a local who has lived here all
his life, it is with some reluctance that he admits, 'I get lost
sometimes'. In the peculiar geography of Docklands the old inhabit-
ant can get lost far more easily than the newcomer who starts out
without any orientations at all. Things change so fast, as Mr
Woodard remarks, with buildings and streets going up 'like Lego',
but the name changes are most irritating. Daisy Woodard mentions
Farm Road and then, in what has obviously become an habitual
manner of speech, adds quickly, 'East Ferry Road to you, I suppose'.
When people stop her to ask for directions, she's accustomed to
replying with a question of her own: 'do you know what it used to be
called?' The Woodards have a story that seems to sum up this new
sense of unreality: they tell of a friend who was sitting outside a pub
when someone pulled up in a car and asked him if he knew the way to
a place he had never heard of, but which turned out to be the factory
where he had worked for thirty years.

The Woodards sometimes get confused, but they are not simply
opposed to the development. To begin with, they remind me that
before the London Docklands Development Corporation, there was
nothing going on at all. There was no work and everything seemed to
be deteriorating. The light railway – when it works – is a real boon,
and the Woodards have no sympathy for the dockers who, as they say,
were the real losers when Docklands came along. Mr Woodard
remarks that they were an arrogant and selfish bunch, who guarded
their privileges and insisted on passing down their highly paid jobs
from father to son. Having worked alongside dockers on the wharf,
Mr Woodard has no objection to the way history has helped him settle
old scores: the dockers were 'grabbers', 'mouthy people' who mostly
lived elsewhere and gave nothing back to the Island. As for the people
who have come in since, Daisy groups them all together under the
general rubric of 'the new people': she prefers this to calling them
'yuppies, blacks, or Pakis'. She's thankful that her job as a school
helper has brought her into contact with all sorts – 'I know people in
all the cultures' – but she has some sympathy for those old Islanders
who have had no such opportunity and have only got these insulting
epithets with which to defend themselves against change. It is
unlikely that the 'yuppies' think of themselves either as another ethnic
minority or a replacement for the old working class, but the
Woodards mean no offense: 'We like to see people walking by in suits
rather than overalls'. They also admire the exuberance of the new
buildings. Canary Wharf is fantastic, especially considering that it's
built over water: 'You've got to admire the people who can do that'.

Remembering Crosby's declaration that east London was more 'a
casualty of the peace' than a victim of the war, I ask the Woodards
about 1945. Daisy remembers the peace as 'beautiful, so quiet . . . you
could turn the lights on again and go to the pictures'. When I ask

about the Attlee government and its promise of social reconstruction, they remark that they have never cared less about politics and have no recollections to speak of. Nevertheless, they do make a start in Crosby's direction. The tower blocks put up by the council in the Sixties are obviously degenerate. Dave remarks that he would far prefer to live in one of the post-war prefabs to them, but there's no doubt about what is better still. The Woodards sit in their house on this remaining stretch of garden city – itself an unrecognised monument to a strain of English socialism, which came down through William Morris to George Lansbury and was finally buried under the derision of technocratic and Marxist professors in the Sixties – and they wonder why the council ever tried anything different. The post-war rehousing programmes broke up the local community and since then, as they concede, the island may indeed have become a 'victim of greed' with private gain running rampant over local need: why, for example, hasn't a new school been built on the island? Trying hard to view the war in a positive light, Mr Woodard supposes that it was responsible for getting rid of some slums, but he seems dissatisfied by the idea. Indeed, this is as far they'll come in Crosby's direction: Daisy turns round abruptly, breaking off the discussion by recalling how shocked she had been when she read the Island History Trust's book of reminiscences, and found George Pye, a former stevedore, describing the Nazi bombing of the island as 'good bombing'. Daisy felt affronted by the idea that the bombing that killed so many people on the island might have been 'good' in any sense at all.[19]

Unlike Theo Crosby's, Daisy Woodard's drive against forgetfulness covers the war and then extends far into the subsequent peace. She has been trying to find out what has happened to a brass memorial plaque for some of the men, including her own Uncle Frank, who were killed on the island: it recently disappeared from the outside of the Cubitt Town Library, and officials within the building are already telling her that it never existed. But she has also found a human face to commemorate within what Crosby derides as 'the "useful" short term strategies' of the Welfare State. After writing numerous letters to local papers and authorities like Tower Hamlets Council and the LDDC, she has succeeded in getting a riverside street on a new development named after Dr Maurice Blasker, a much loved general practitioner who came to the Isle of Dogs in the late Thirties and spent his life working there. Blasker was a doctor who, in Mr Woodard's words, 'took the side of the working classes', and he never spared himself if one of his patients was in need. The campaign for 'Blasker Walk' was Daisy Woodard's version of Theo Crosby's 'civic gesture': as she said of her eventual success, 'I really felt that was one of the things I'd done in my life'.[20]

When it comes to her own recollections of the war, however, Mrs Woodard is not inclined to press for formal commemoration even of this modest kind. She certainly has her remembrancers: the few old bomb-sites that have so far escaped redevelopment, the patches of newer brick where the bombs struck the railway arches on Millwall Park, and the iron pins that still protrude from the brickwork under every other arch, testimony to the bunks installed there when the arches were brought into use as air-raid shelters. Her husband mentions the tunnel that runs under the river from Island Gardens to Greenwich and that is now used mostly by tourists. Passing 'travel writers' like Jonathan Raban (who wandered through the Isle of Dogs in the mid-Seventies, condemning the 'hideous' flats but not pausing to talk to their inhabitants) may appreciate the polished teak of its lifts, but they have no access to what makes the tunnel so meaningful to Mr Woodard.[21] He remembers it as it was in the Forties, packed with people coming over to work on the island, their bicycles stacked high in the lifts. Taken together with Mr Woodard's remark that there should have been a special medal for Londoners who went through the blitz, these examples demonstrate that, for the Woodards at least, a good remembrancer is not at all the same as a fully elucidated monument that exists for all to see: indeed, it seems to work all the better if it is invisible to all but those who, if I may retrieve a word from Theo Crosby's vocabulary, were 'there'.

The Woodards are wary of the injury that can occur when personal remembrancers like theirs are dragged out of their obscurity and placed, by whatever act of interpretation, in the public domain. This reluctance to expose their memories to the glare of general appreciation is founded partly on the apprehension that they may be slighted by people who don't understand or a younger generation who apparently couldn't care less: the Woodards are quite familiar with the dramatised yawn, the 'here they go again' look that is so often adopted by the young whenever they start 'going on' about the war. But this way of cloaking one's memory in other people's obscurity is surely also connected to the wider dissociation of the locality: indeed, it offers traditional islanders another way of holding their ground against all the changes and the 'new people' they've brought into the area. Daisy Woodard recently found some initials written in concrete and dated 1940: a meaningless detail to everyone else, but she was pleased to have been able to photograph the inscription and send the picture to the man – long since moved away, but traceable through his sister – who had made it as a youth fifty years ago. By chance, as she had heard, it even arrived on his birthday. News came back via the same circuitous route that the man was delighted, but this whole ceremony of old East End remembrance took place without reference to the public domain.

Unlikely as it may seem, we are closer here to Iain Sinclair than to Theo Crosby; for while the Woodards's have no interest whatsoever in daemons or leylines, their remembrancers still add up to another collection of sites charged with meaning that is occult to all but a few initiates. Moreover, if Daisy Woodard was to chart her sites on a map, there can be little doubt where the emerging 'lines of force' would converge. As she says quite simply, 'I love the Mudchute'. This thirty-two-acre area directly north of Millwall Park started out as the place where mud dredged from the docks was dumped in the nineteenth century, and like the rest of the area it's seen some changes over recent years. Dave Woodard was among the four hundred or so local men who had an allotment up here in the Fifties, but these were closed down when the Port of London Authority saw other opportunities. The fertile top-soil was scraped off and sold to Holland, where it was apparently used to grow tulips, and there was a plan to turn the site into a new dock. When the container revolution scuppered that idea, there was talk of a lorry park and then a scheme was cooked up with the GLC that would turn the whole area into a housing estate. In the new age of Docklands the proposals have been different. There has been talk of a heliport, a car park, a chalet-based holiday village, and, predictably, a historical theme park, – but the local residents, who have campaigned long and hard against all this, have finally won out and the Mudchute is now settling into its new role as a 'people's park' and city farm.

This scruffy stretch of high ground has many associations for the Woodards; there are the rope walks along the southern edge, which Daisy knows from the Forties when she worked for a long-since defunct rope manufacturer. There's the 'newty pond' where children would go for bucolic adventures involving jam jars. Most of all, however, there are the old anti-aircraft gun emplacements that still survive on the Mudchute. Daisy remembers the guns as Big Nellie, Big Ada, and Big Bertha, and she sometimes goes up to look at the octagonal concrete structures that remain, and to think of her uncle who was killed on the Mudchute during the war. There has been some question about the future of these unspectacular relics: should they be demolished or restored and turned into public monuments? Mrs Woodard has found it hard to decide what she thinks. 'I'd like to see them preserved', she says, but then she remembers the indifference of the younger generation and concedes that it may be 'better if they were allowed to deteriorate'. And then again there is the problem of vandalism ('We didn't know that word when we were little'), so perhaps they should be demolished and removed after all.

I visited the Mudchute early one evening in August. The silver birches planted around the edge of the city farm are thickening out, and I watched some elderly people slowly putting away their tools on the remaining allotments. The dogs were out too: pit bull terriers and Dobermanns eying up collies and poodles, and generally upstaging the 'lacklustre Alsatians with bad teeth' recorded by the light-footed Jonathan Raban. The gun emplacements are rough structures made of stained modernist concrete, but they are finding new purposes on the city farm. A couple of long-horned and typically ethnic-looking inner-city sheep were scratching themselves up against one; another was in service as a goat shed and smelt to high heaven; a third had been painted over with designs for imaginary flags but was still only host to a framework of rusted scaffolding designed to support some kind of awning, long since disappeared. As Daisy Woodard concludes, the city farm seems to offer the best solution yet. The animals are big enough to deter vandals, and yet the vital balance between commemoration and obscurity is maintained: for most visitors the emplacements can disappear entirely into the modesty of their new function as pig pens and goat sheds, but others can still come here for secret and entirely untravestied communication with the remembered events of the war.

Curious to know what the Woodards made of Theo Crosby's proposed Battle of Britain Monument, I showed them Pedro Guedes's sketch. They respond with the controlled amazement of people who, as residents of this place called Docklands, have long since been bombed out of their traditional sense of proportion. 'Good Lord', says Mr Woodard, leaning back into his chair in a vain attempt to get the thing into some kind of perspective. It doesn't take Daisy a second to recognise the searchlight fantasia on the top of Crosby's urban instrument, but then she's starts to back off too. 'What on earth's that?' she asks. 'Do they want to stick that thing up around here?' I step in with a quick reassurance, but there's doubt at the back of mind. Indeed, I'm already hoping that the architecture students at the Royal College of Art are sufficiently rebellious, or that the recession hits hard enough over at Pentagram, to keep the professor from finding time to relaunch his proposal from his new position of eminence. In those black booklets, Crosby had declared that the Battle of Britain Monument 'should be placed in London's East End; it should be highly visible; it should be near the river'. Constrained by his over-formal axes, he eventually opted for Surrey Docks on the south bank of the river, the site of the creek from which Sir Francis Drake had sailed out in the Golden Hind. Had he known about the Mudchute, however, he would surely have been prepared to put a little post-modern kink into his Turner axis so that he could justify landing his monument on top of those lamentably functional concrete emplacements, thus settling the score with his own brutalist past. For a moment, I can see it putting its 'there' up there on the Mudchute, 'spawning activity and energy' all around it, as Crosby promised, 'creating value' and 'stabilising the social structure' of the locality as it did so. But I spare the Woodards this thought. For them there's always been a 'there' up on the Mudchute and, despite their misgivings about those old GLC tower blocks and the new men of greed, they would never go so far as to describe their stretch of east London as a 'wasteland' stripped of 'spiritual content'.

So the usurping image recedes, and the Mudchute reverts to its hardwon reality as a 'people's park'. A fertile but unkempt stretch of land edged with dereliction, it is a good place for meditating on the

difference between a truly historical city and the London Professor
Crosby imagined: an urban desert that needs to be themed up, for the
benefit of tourists, around a 'carefully fabricated' past. The
Mudchute Association is raising funds to build a café, a new stable
block, and a nature study centre with a teacher who can work
alongside local schools, but its members have already fought off one
proposal for a theme park, and they have no plans to replace the
ghosts that still haunt their park with 'laser-generated holograms'.
The Mudchute remains an informal garden of remembrance:
dedicated not just to the war but, thanks to the untidy blurring at its
edges and the stubborn persistence of those local campaigners who
now seem to have everyone on their side, to the public-spirited ideals
of the peace as well.

15
The Bow Quarter:
Six Hundred and Seventy Luxury
Flats in an Old Victorian Hell-house

'The achievement of marketing excellence has always featured prominently in the Group's aims. The marketing strategy is considered at the earliest stages of a development programme.'
                    Kentish Property Group PLC, Annual Report 1987

1988 was absurdly crowded with historical anniversaries. No sooner had the beacons been lit for the Spanish Armada than William and Mary landed at Torbay and started marching towards London for the Glorious Revolution. Somewhere on the road they passed a raggle-taggle encampment of hippies, poets, and radicals gathered in sad commemoration of their youth.

But while 1588, 1688, and 1968 jostled on the national stage, the centenary year of 1888 was left to muster whatever local interest it could find in east London. There were some predictable attempts to cash in on Jack the Ripper's lurid passage through Whitechapel, but in these parts 1888 was best remembered as the year when Annie Besant provoked the famous match-girls' strike at the Bryant & May factory in Bow. In October 1988 Hackney Archives mounted an exhibition that enlisted those ghostly and almost entirely anonymous faces in order to restage a time-honoured drama of triumphant class struggle. The story may not have broken any box-office records when it was turned into a musical called *Strike a Light!* in the Sixties, but it remains the rousing stuff of which socialist and feminist dreams are made.[1] Annie Besant starred as the Fabian hero, and we were offered a vivid glimpse of her riding through the East End in a dog cart with a red ribbon in her hair, denouncing the bosses and calling out for full-blooded socialism as she went. Bryant & May's shareholders put in a predictable appearance as uncaring villains who enjoyed fat dividends while their poor and unorganised victims – the half-starved match-girls – only got 'phossy jaw', the phosphorous necrosis that would eat away their faces with such damaging effects on their productivity that their eventual dismissal was as good as guaranteed.

Thanks to Hackney Archives, we could see Dr Besant researching and writing a denunciation of conditions at the factory – 'White

Slavery in London', as she called it – and then going down with her companion Herbert Burrows to leaflet the match-girls at the factory gate on 26 June. We could watch as over a thousand girls came out in an unprecedented act of mass solidarity after Bryant & May sacked some of Besant's suspected informers and demanded that every worker sign a statement refuting Besant's charges. We could cheer along as the infernal capitalist, Mr Frederick Bryant, caved in, agreeing to make the demanded improvements in working conditions, and to reinstate the strikers, 'ring-leaders' and all. Thanks to Hackney Archives, we could step back a century and observe from the sidelines as Besant formed the Union of Women Matchmakers in the wake of the strike. Unlike Besant, who would later join Madam Blavatsky's Theosophists in search of true clairvoyance, we could stand there secure in the knowledge that a new wave of unionisation among women and unskilled workers would follow from her historic intervention.

It must be admitted that this improving tale didn't exactly fit the facts. Some of Annie Besant's accusations were exaggerated while others turned out simply to be false. As the London Trades Council accepted after an inquiry, wages at the factory were comparatively high and there was no truth in Besant's claim that Frederick Bryant had compelled every worker at the factory to contribute towards the cost of the statue of the great Liberal, Mr Gladstone, that still stands by the islanded church in the middle of Bow Road, gesturing bravely at the traffic that thunders by on both sides. But whether or not the Bryant & May factory was really an exemplary and, indeed, partly cooperative institution that was informed for the better by the Quaker outlook of its founding partners, Annie Besant portrayed it with Fabian certainty as a terrible hell-house, and her account has triumphed over the modifications that more thorough-going east London socialists – from Tom Mann to George Lansbury – have tried to impose on it.[2]

While Hackney Archives exhibited this uplifting narrative relic from the days before the idea of social progress died, one only had to wander through the dishevelled council estates and gentrified Georgian squares of Bow to find that very different fables of improvement were being spun around the Bryant & May factory one hundred years later. Known for years as Fairfield Works, the old hell-house is now a listed building just up the road from '1789', a restaurant specialising in 'traditional French cuisine'. Set off against the Gothic works' cottages that stand between it and the road, the Victorian factory has an attractive detailed front with a large clock (a fine monument to Victorian work discipline) mounted prominently over the entrance. Behind this once-formidable but now dwarfed building is the massive Edwardian addition that went into operation in 1911 as the largest factory in London: a colossal red-brick structure with a huge chimney and two fantastic water towers, it stretches out along the north side of the main railway line running into Liverpool Street Station, and comes to an abrupt halt where a north-bound tangle of road spews up from the Blackwall Tunnel.

The Vision of an Architect

The original conception was unquestionably grand. The leading architect was Oliver Richards of the new practice, ORMS, and he was delighted, when the job came up in 1987, to get a brief that was truly 'European' in scale. Kentish Homes wanted to make some money, of course, but they also started out with the declared intention of building a development with the quality and imagination to win awards. ORMS and Kentish Homes travelled to Baltimore and Manhattan to look at American warehouse conversions, and then the work began. As they spelt out in their earliest presentations, ORMS wanted to retain the historical buildings, to create 'special places' within the development, to foster 'liveliness,' and to make a 'place of pride' in Tower Hamlets. They were all for 'pleasurable extras', but they were also concerned to ensure that the new development had a proper 'sense of arrival'. Oliver Richards had studied at both Cambridge and Yale and, though a proper quadrangle was obviously out of the question, he saw no reason why the classically donnish pleasures of a 'collegiate' entrance should not be available to the residents of this speculative development in London's East End. Just as, say, Yale's Davenport College is entered through a Gothic exterior that suddenly opens into an enchanting close with buildings in the very different Georgian colonial style, the denizens of the Bow Quarter would surely appreciate walking past a porter's lodge in the narrow entrance provided by the Victorian clockhouse and finding themselves suddenly in another world. The Bow Quarter would not be open to the general public, but fleeting glimpses of the verdant and unexpected wonderland within would certainly be available to uplift the spirits of those whose fate was only to trudge by on the tired pavements of Fairfield Road.

ORMS imagined the Bow Quarter looming over its forlorn area of east London like a great 'citadel', and for this to happen it was essential that the project be governed by a bold overall conception. When Oliver Richards describes the huge Edwardian factory as 'prison-like', he is not thinking along Annie Besant's lines. Though it is beautifully made with exceptionally fine brickwork, the factory is huge and austere, its elevations capable of dwarfing anything that might be built up against it. ORMS set out to create a context that would overcome this problem, putting a couple of atriums into the monolith, and organising the new buildings to the north around a series of strongly defined courtyards. They planned an ambitious lake or two, conceiving water to be sufficiently strong as a medium to stand up to a building of this scale, and they wanted to plant large trees for the same reason. They stressed the importance of detailed and carefully textured 'building edges' without which the new buildings would look like so many stunted boxes. The Bow Quarter would move north through a scaled and deliberately varied sequence of architectural types: this would start with the industrial monolith (already renamed 'Meridian View') at the southern edge, and then proceed through warehouse-style blocks ('Hayes Walk' and 'Moreland Court') with flats organised along corridors, and then large houses with staircases ('Bryant Mews' and 'Chapell Mews'), before terminating in the row of three-floor terraced houses to be built at the northern perimeter of the development ('Blondin Terrace'). It was largely thanks to ORMS's ambitious conception that Kentish Homes got such favourable planning consent from the council.

The plan was quite constrained from the start. ORMS had wanted to build a tower in the north-east corner, but as work went ahead, it wasn't just flourishes like this that had to be abandoned. Indeed, by September 1988, ORMS had resigned from the project. Oliver Richards is reluctant to give detailed examples of cheese-paring, remarking only that the developers made a number of pragmatic decisions that, he felt, put the overall quality of the development at risk. This was the tail-end of the bull market and Keith Preston, the founder and Chairman of Kentish Homes who had certainly started out with a grand vision, seemed increasingly busy elsewhere. Richards did not feel he could trust the new project manager to recognise that in a project of this size there must be 'a certain proportion of things that are memorable and special'. The Bow Quarter was by far their biggest project, but ORMS decided that to stay in would have been heart-breaking; indeed, they feared it would have torn the office apart. As they worked out their notice – getting all but some £60,000 of their money out before they handed the brief over to Forum Architects – they were driven to make savings on Blondin Terrace. Richards had tried to defend his conception of a 'triumphal' north entrance into the Bow Quarter from Blondin Terrace, but the cost-cutting was already threatening to reduce this access to a featureless gap, a hole sawn in a row of low-cost houses. He hasn't been back to see the final outcome, but he shudders like a man who fears the worst and I, having looked the site over, can do little to reassure him.

Sales Talk

The refurbishment of the Bryant & May factory involved architects, builders, and engineers, but some of the heaviest work was to be carried out by words and images alone. From the start, the development was awash with uplifting rhetoric, and here at least

ORMS's grand overall vision was allowed to luxuriate long after the disappointed firm's departure. Estate agents are adept at using language as a kind of laundry house in which even the most sordid realities can be cleaned up at hardly any cost at all. If the God-forsaken Isle of Dogs can emerge as 'Docklands', then who is to say that a nearby redundant factory built right up against one of London's busiest railway lines shouldn't benefit in the same way from being renamed 'The Bow Quarter'? However, the coinage that was dreamed up to turn the Bryant & May factory into the Bow Quarter gave an altogether new turn to the rhetoric of an east London trade that George Lansbury once dismissed as 'room farming'. As the sales line went: 'Parisians have the Latin Quarter, New Yorkers have Greenwich Village. Now in East London, a stone's throw from the City, there's a new Quarter . . .' Never mind that the charms of the famous 'quarters' here invoked as models – the Latin Quarter and the left bank, Greenwich Village, and Tribeca – follow precisely from the fact that these unsystematised stretches of Paris and New York have escaped overall planning and design. East London has always done things differently, and 'The Bow Quarter' would be generated by a single speculative stroke. Just as that unprepossessing stretch of ground squeezed between a motorway, council tower blocks, and a thunderingly busy railway line was reborn as 'a triangle between the City and the riverside life of Docklands', the redundant factory standing on it would emerge fully formed into a new life as 'the ultimate in Metropolitan Lifestyles'.

This, as *The Independent* declared, was going to be an 'imaginative' development, and a huge, ostentatiously designed booklet had been issued to outline the new dream that was to be realised on George Lansbury's weary old patch. Fashionably black with a vivid multi-coloured Q as its logo, it left no doubt what the elements of the synthetically contrived quarter were to be. To begin with, the developers were determined to make a feature of what they called 'elements of history'. But while they were concerned to show their appreciation of the site's historical attractions (describing the clock house as 'a definitive example of Victorian architecture' but also claiming that it dated from the mid-eighteenth century), their brochures had no truck with the cowering Seventies kind of con-servationism that cherished its adopted piece of the heritage against all forms of modernisation and development. Down at the Bow Quarter conservation and redevelopment were going to walk hand in hand: 'mature housing stock' would 'mingle with newer architectural elements to form one unified whole'; Jacuzzis would vie with spouting Victorian gargoyles in an 'elegant restatement of a number of timeless themes'.

The Press greeted the Bow Quarter as the first development of anything like its size to be targeted entirely at young people. The brochure addressed itself to independent but like-minded 'individuals', and the pictures left no doubt that as well as being young and prosperous, the ideal residents of the Bow Quarter would also be athletic sensualists. They would use their individually unique 'loft-style' apartments not just as homes or places for living but as the 'ideal launchpad' for their forays out into the city. These 'young and energetic' people would appreciate the nearness of Canary Wharf and the promised pasta shop ('the largest selection of pasta this side of Pisa'). They would make the most of the 'extras' that would be sprinkled through the seven-acre development to help 'enhance their lifestyle': the bar and café where 'like-minded people could sip café filtre and share the latest gossip', the ice rink and outdoor swimming pool, the library ('for times of study or insomnia') where people whose taste was more 'cerebral' could relax, the 'trim track' with its exercise stations, the fully glazed 'leisure pavilion' with its swimming pool, sauna, and gym, and the 'trained instructor' who would be there to help residents keep fit and, of course, 'have fun' while they did so. There would be lots of cycling and splashing about in the Bow Quarter, but these were the leisure activities of contracepted young adults who still knew how to play: there was not a child to be seen. The Bow Quarter offered 'a vibrant community . . . with literally something for everybody'. But in case the message still hadn't quite got across, people who were quick to buy into the Bow Quarter wouldn't just get their legal fees and stamp duty paid: the incentive package would also bring the purchaser £250 worth of Next vouchers absolutely free.

As marketing director of Kentish Property Group PLC, George Kozlowski was responsible for defining 'the conceptual route' of the Bow Quarter: and by the time he and his brochure designers had finished with it, the development had been relaunched as a seven-acre photomontage in which carefully selected television clichés were laid over clips from well-known films and resonant phrases culled from the lifestyle magazines. While the project was targeted very precisely at young adults, he insists it was never intended simply as a 'yuppie' development. The Bow Quarter was aimed at east Londoners rather than Porsche-driving city types: its target market was made up of 'locals' who had been thoroughly exposed to what Kozlowski calls 'aspirational lifestyle' imagery, and were frankly bored by the prospect of a two- or three-bedroom box somewhere out towards Dagenham. The Bow Quarter offered them a split-level warehouse apartment near the hub of things for considerably less than £100,000. The whole point of the Bow Quarter was that you didn't have to be a true 'yuppie' to move into the metropolitan dream.

I missed the press launch, for which Clement Freud was brought in to praise the development and crack a few jokes of the after-dinner variety, but I did visit the site on the Saturday in October 1988, when the first flats in the Victorian 'Clockhouse' went on sale. Designed and furnished by Next, the show flats – even in their pristine state –

had the look of used dreams; they were like momentarily deserted sets from a television soap-opera, just waiting for the actors to reappear. There were framed prints and photographs on the wall and a portentous bowl of lemons graced the kitchen table. The flats certainly didn't have the generous dimensions of a Manhattan loft, but they weren't just ordinary boxes either: I registered them as *tall* boxes, *extruded* boxes with modest floor areas but ceilings hoicked up high, and the windows stretched upwards to match. As I remember, the people from Next had tried to stabilise and domesticate these towering walls by adding dado-like strips of decorative wallpaper some six feet up from the floor.

East London has a special relationship to books: old hard-backs have become an established part of the decor in revamped pubs, and in recent years a surprising number of junk shops in the area have allowed themselves to be lumbered with large supplies of superficially attractive stock from Faber & Faber. Nevertheless, I think I was the only person to show any interest in the library on that briskly paced Saturday morning. At a time when municipal libraries all over east London were being closed or turned into video stalls, here was the Bow Quarter promising its residents a new library of their very own . I asked one of the sharp-suited men from Alan Selby and Partners what books would be stocked. He looked at me with amazement, which quickly turned into undisguised contempt, remarking that the library was going to be in the old panelled Board-room: beyond that he neither knew nor cared. Meanwhile, the red 'Sold' stickers were going up at a cracking pace, and there were more serious customers to contend with. Some of them had been queuing since the early morning in order to get a chance at the best-positioned flats. People were running around with their cheque books open, and their eyes alight at the prospect of getting in on some of the 'funny money' that tended to be around wherever the alchemy of 'Docklands' was in play. Alan Selby and Partner's staff were issuing all sorts of optimistic reassurances about probable future values. Never mind that the bull market was already over; one could still dream of putting down a 10 per cent deposit and then selling on at a nice profit before the rest of the purchase price fell due on completion. This is said to have worked a treat at Kentish Homes' Docklands tower block, 'The Cascades', and there were certainly some speculative characters who came out of the clock house that Saturday with more than one unbuilt 'unit' to their name. The whole event was marvellous to see.

This story ran for a while. With the sixty-eight apartments in the Clockhouse sold in a flash, Kentish Homes was confident enough to bring forward their first release of larger galleried apartments in the part of the Edwardian factory now described as 'Meridian View'. By the time this second weekend 'preview' came up on 12 November, a huge leaflet-cum-magazine called *The Quarterly* had been issued. This told of the success of the development, stressing the care that had been taken over fittings such as the taps, and described both the agreeable night out that could be had round the corner at the '1789' restaurant and the 'ethnic culture and social comment' that was available at the nearby (and soon to be defunct, due to cuts in funding) Half Moon Theatre. Attentive readers of *The Quarterly* would notice that the library had already started to vanish: it was announced that the developers hadn't quite decided what to do with the old board room –'elegantly panelled and all that stuff' – and were offering a £50 prize for the best suggestion.

The Quarterly was also used to define the market a little more closely. The press launch had won the Bow Quarter a lot of editorial coverage in publications like *Harpers and Queen* and *Docklands Magazine*, but though the developers had no complaints about this they were not, as *The Quarterly* insisted, really aiming at that crowd. They were offering 'metropolitan living' all right, but those galleried apartments in the Bow Quarter were also available at an 'affordable price'. Tom Mulligan from Alan Selby and Partners ('He doesn't immediately strike you as an estate agent. In fact, he looks more likely to be buying one of the Bow Quarter properties than selling them') was happy to answer the 'crunch questions' in an interview. 'Generally', as he put it with appropriate vagueness, anyone who was earning £20,000 – either individually or jointly as a couple – should qualify for a mortgage of about £80,000. And since building-society finance was offered as part of the package, that should be enough to lift you into the more modest reaches of the new development.

As for the overall concept, this too was given a new turn. *The Quarterly* borrowed American sociologist, Sharon Zukin's, coinage to describe the Bow Quarter as a British experiment in 'loft-living'.[3] The development was now said to have its roots in the American warehouse revival: 'the loft-living concept says you take a space of character and enhance it'. Where the ordinary house-builders talk of Laura Ashley wallpaper and fitted carpets, 'the loft-livers talk of sandblasted brickwork, timber floors, skylights and galleries . . .' In its new guise, the Bow Quarter was thoroughly opposed to merely decorative embellishment. Indeed, here it was coming out against the distinctly 'neo' look of the decor provided by Next in the first Clockhouse flats:

> The major direction in British residential development has veered in the past decade from the *neo-Georgian* to the mock Tudor presumably in response to the market's demand for a more 'aesthetic' style. People tend to equate *character* with desirability and it often seems that the right cosmetic features mean more than a decent sized plot of land, intelligent interior design and even quality of construction and finish. In its adaptation of traditional structures and its denial of contrivance, loft living is a complete contrast to the commercial trend.

Here was the Bow Quarter going beyond mere style to claim a full-blown philosophy for itself. Loft-living was American; its roots lay in squatting (the 'illegal occupation' of rundown industrial buildings in neglected parts of the inner city) and, as *The Quarterly* explained, it had been artists and craft workers who started the movement off, 'merging home and work' in low-rent scenarios in or near the old urban core. By the mid-Seventies, the American 'loft-living community' had attracted the middle-class people who made the whole experience legal and, of course, altogether more urbane. So this was the revised offer: by buying into the Bow Quarter you could have the 'aura' of loft-living without the hassle of squatting and doing up your own warehouse. Here was Bohemia with the rough edges smoothed off and its price slashed; loft-living is for true individuals who want a chance to 'design their own style of living within an intrinsically appealing space'.

With Sharon Zukin's marxist analysis of the 'loft-living' phenomenon serving only as more grist to their publicists' mill, it was unlikely that the developers would be too troubled when they eventually came up against the leftist-feminist memory of Annie Besant and the match-girls' strike of 1888. The coming of the Bow Quarter felt like an affront to some people. While no one could exactly object to the idea of Frederick Bryant's satanic mill being refurbished, there were still those who tormented themselves with the image of oblivious yuppies enjoying a massage and slurping champagne where slave-driven women once ached with phossy jaw: even if one can't put a preservation order on ancient misery, surely there were still some historical dues to be paid. A letter appeared in *The Independent* suggesting that the match-girls' strike should be commemorated within the new development, and Kentish Homes were quick to oblige: they announced their intention of commissioning an East End sculptor to mark the momentous event with a statue. Other 'elements of history' had already been incorporated as desirable features, and a monument dedicated to the memory of Annie Besant's intervention would only bring further 'enhancement' to the loft-living lifestyle of the Bow Quarter.

The Dream Fails

But then, a year or so later, everything ground to a halt. As founder and Chairman of Kentish, Keith Preston had proved as agile as any of the developers who were riding the wave as it surged through east London and Docklands. The turnover of Kentish Homes had soared from £3.38 million in 1985 to £25.85 million in 1988, but by the summer of 1989 the shrunken wave was receding and the only sound in Docklands was the oily rattle of coins being sucked back into an anonymous fiscal sea. At that disenchanting moment it was Andrew

Langton, Managing Director of Aylesford's, the West London estate agents, who came forward to speak for everyone in his trade: glancing around just before closing up his company's new Docklands office and beating a retreat to the firmer ground of the King's Road, he told the *Evening Standard*: 'You look at it now and it's quite easy to see why it's called the Isle of Dogs'.[4]

Kentish was the first quoted house-builder to go down in the 1989 housing slump. It had borrowed hugely to finance its expansion into the Docklands residential market, and its directors were apparently quite caught out by the downturn. Interest rates soared, demand dried up, and, by August, the Halifax Building Society had called in its loan on Burrell's Wharf, effectively putting the company into receivership. Interestingly, it wasn't just the righteous indignati of the left who found some satisfaction in the thought of Kentish's shareholders and customers getting burned. Ever since early 1987 when Peregrine Worsthorne began to complain about the braying and ill-mannered behaviour of the upwardly-mobile 'yuppies' who had started lowering the tone of his favourite London restaurants, the right had also been enjoying an open season on these partly mythical creatures, the strutting centaurs of Margaret Thatcher's bull market. As Tom Nairn has remarked, the idea of the 'yuppie' may have worked as an 'exhilarating caricature' in the United States, but it only had to be imported into Britain's stratified and class-ridden atmosphere to turn into a 'stilted sneer': 'in no time a whole Dickensian universe of animated, yet minute, contempt has arisen: all are placed and labelled, and can revenge themselves only by labelling others'.[5]

As it went down Kentish was widely portrayed as the ultimate 'yuppie builder', and no quarter was given to the victims of its collapse. The *Daily Express* spoke gleefully of 'hundreds of yuppies' losing their deposits on Burrell's Wharf and the Bow Quarter, and normally more reserved papers like *The Times* and *The Daily Telegraph* also closed in for the kill, ordering their photographers to sever the heads of specimen couples and mount them for all to see above generic names like 'Jason and Angela'. Even *The Financial Times* succumbed to the convulsion, writing of 'Docklands Yuppies' who, having got their comeuppance, were now 'beached for the duration'. The poor, derided people who had bought into the Bow Quarter found themselves stuck with a useless receipt on their deposits, *and* obliged to complete on a dream that was suddenly dissolving before their eyes. The receiver was quick to reassure them that the project would be going ahead, but it was with equal alacrity that he cut through the glossy promise of George Kozlowski's brochures to insist that his only contractual obligations was 'to provide flats' – not pasta shops, fitness instructors, skating rinks, swimming pools, or libraries. Indeed, he entered the fray sounding more like a council housing officer than a man committed to bringing off 'the ultimate in metropolitan lifestyles'.

From One 'Inward-looking Development' to the Next

Perhaps it was the ocean-blue walls and the shiny silver ceiling, but no sooner had I entered Alan Selby and Partner's office on the corner of Hackney's Clapton Square, than I felt I had sunk to the bottom of an exotic sea. I watched as Mr Selby's young 'negotiators' glided about between the burbling phones, eventually converging with unctuous olfactory attentiveness on a young woman who had drifted in to ask after a two-bedroom 'garden flat' in one of Hackney's less salubrious areas. A modest prospect, to be sure. There was a watery thud behind me and another unexpected presence slid into view. It hung there for a moment, pulsating gently at the receptionist, before floating off – a grey diaphanous outline cut through with twisted streaks of colour – and vanishing up the stairs. Shortly afterwards, I pulled myself together and followed.

Alan Selby is not the picture of thrusting dynamism I had expected. Indeed, he seems remarkably loose; he wears a double-breasted suit, a shirt with prominent and wide-set stripes, and his tie is a thick hank of silk of the kind that Peter York has suggested might be the answer to all Neil Kinnock's problems. His hair is long and back-combed, and no one could mistake his casual non-assertiveness for that of a new man. He sits upstairs in his office, shuffling some papers around, sending his assistant out for more cigarettes, and sizing me up with an eye that manages to be both soft and sharp at the same time. Selby had agreed to talk on the phone, but now that I'm there he's really too busy. I've got to understand that he's involved in a receivership. There's a lot of that about at the moment, and the way the system works is that he's paid to be on call. In most cases the call never comes, but today has turned out differently. As he puts it with finely structured vagueness, 'I'm not cancelling you specifically, but I must prepare for my next meeting'. I'm left with a few snippets. The Bow Quarter is a truly 'superb' development, and Selby is happy to have been retained by the receiver to sell the next releases in the ongoing project. It would definitely not be a good idea for me to link it with Burrell's Wharf or in any way to describe it as a 'Docklands' development. There is also a bit of passing innuendo: what makes me so sure that ORMS really 'resigned' from the project? Suzanne will fix another time for me, but I'm already guessing that when the appointed day comes she'll be phoning back to say that Alan is tied up: he's had to go abroad suddenly and, now that you ask, he won't really be in the office for weeks.

Keith Preston of Kentish doesn't want to talk either, remarking on the phone that the buildings are there to be seen, and the figures are in the public domain too. As for the rest, it's just history now and he doesn't want to keep picking it over: 'it's in the past' and 'it's time to get on with the future'. And that future is already shaping up rather nicely; it is based in the Esher area, where Preston is associated with a new property consultancy going under the superior name of Bentley & Montague.

I had gone to both Selby and Preston hoping to get a different account of the Kentish Homes/Alan Selby partnership than the one that is so readily provided by local mythology. The gossip around these parts turns Selby and Preston into the heroes of a mock-heroic Odyssey that also features a Ford Cortina and an early carphone. The story opens at an indeterminate but clearly prehistoric time before the Eighties boom, and our pair are cruising the more obscure corners of Hackney and Tower Hamlets, looking for prospects in those dismal parts of the city where the improving ideas of post-war public policy only went to die. Selby is at the wheel and, as he drives through a selection of areas where prices are low and hardly any sense of 'place' survives, Preston keeps a look-out for derelict commercial or industrial sites (a factory, timber-yard, or redundant cinema would do nicely) that hint, however modestly, at a brighter future: a previously unregarded view over a park, marsh, or church was all that it took. Having bought cheap, Preston would hire a young and ambitious architect to come up with a set of outline plans, which could be put to the council planning department. Knowing the heavily ideological nature of planning decisions in Labour-controlled boroughs like Hackney and Tower Hamlets, he learned to expect a lengthy period of procrastination and delay: he would use the time to clear the site of derelict industrial remains, taking his time so that as much material as possible could be salvaged and sold on. As Kentish's 1987 Annual Report stated, 'Our policy is to acquire apparently unattractive land without planning permission and enhance its value.' When the planners had finally been won over by the architectural quality of his scheme, he would go on to build an 'inward-looking development' that would establish its own sense of place and use its architectural presence – Kentish Homes ran to classical pillars and simulated tollbooths at the entrance – to press back at the surrounding inner city.[6]

This kind of 'inward-looking' residential development was being built all over London in the Eighties. At the upper end of the market, it was typified by 'Dulwich Gate' in South London, a walled development by Barratt's that combined lily ponds, saunas, and sub-classical (but distinctly anti-modernist) detailing with Belfast-style electronic surveillance and became nationally famous when Margaret Thatcher bought into it for an undisclosed sum in 1985. In East London the new-built private 'close' was necessarily more modest, but it was still concerned with security and with creating exceptional zones in which property values could rise above the going market rate in areas that, despite rampant gentrification, remained unreliable. Even Dalston Lane has its examples: one is called 'The Haven'; the other is 'Independent Place'.

Kentish's first examples were developed in collaboration with the rising architectural practice of Campbell Zogolovitch Wilkinson & Gough – a firm that would later dub its work with Kentish as 'B-movie' or 'pop-song' architecture. In an arrangement that was welcomed by Gavin Stamp as a return to Georgian methods, these architects would be contracted on a 'fee per unit' basis to design a house type, and to come up with standard drawings that gave a limited set of details, a layout, and an outline of the elevations for the whole site. As combined developer and builder, Kentish would then take over, supervising the construction themselves, cutting corners as they chose, and otherwise adjusting the plans as they went along. As if to emphasis their determination to freshen up the inner city after those grey post-war decades, Kentish gave the new developments leafy designations, which also had the ring of proper place-names – there was Orchard Mews, Sutton Square, and Watermint Quay – while Alan Selby and Partners cobbled together an attractive incentive package. There was the usual stage-managed razzmatazz at the openings; at Watermint Quay, the developers even brought in stars from another ideal east London square – 'Lofty' was hired for the occasion from Albert Square, that equally 'inward-looking development' at the centre of the BBC soap, 'EastEnders'.

Kentish's Hackney developments were quickly adopted as targets by Class War, the anarchist group that spent the late Eighties trying to redirect east London's indigenous racism into the more refined solidarity of its 'Mug a Yuppie' campaign.[7] In reality, of couse, the people who bought into these developments were more varied than this catch-all epithet implies. Whether or not they were designed to be yuppie Alamos, there can be little doubt that their walls were quickly breached. A few years after opening, 'Watermint Quay' in Clapton turns out to be fairly mixed: it has its classic 'young professionals' – management consultants, accountants, photographers – but it is all the more interesting for having been infiltrated by prosperous young blacks (at least one of whom is suspected of being a 'Yardie' by his white neighbours) and a number of Hassidic families who have moved in from the surrounding, heavily Jewish, area. A visit to Sutton Square, which stands one hundred or so yards up the road from Sutton House where the Metal Box factory used to be, suggests a similar diversity: plenty of east London voices, women residents (with or without young children) who appreciate the security of the development, even the odd sticker demanding 'No Vietnam in Latin America'.

There were interruptions in Kentish's sequence of 'inward-looking developments'. If we follow the route taken by that mythical Cortina as it ventured into the Isle of Dogs in the mid-Eighties, we will go past 'The Cascades', a flash new residential tower that stands in dramatic contrast to the rundown council tower blocks nearby, and that has achieved a considerable reputation since completion in 1988. Praised for its 'architecture of complexity and power' (to say nothing of its

'Sphinx-like' and 'Pagan' qualities) in the *RIBA Journal*, and hailed by
Blueprint as 'an early example of the rediscovery of the tower block as
an organ of private fantasy rather than public utility'; 'The Cascades'
is perceived more locally as a hideous monument to corruption and
graft: the guide who holds forth from one of the riverboats operating
between Greenwich and the Tower of London describes it, falsely I'm
sure, as a money-laundering machine run for the benefit of East End
crooks now domiciled on the Costa del Sol.[8] Further down into the
Isle of Dogs there is also the stripped-out shell of Burrell's Wharf, a
conversion where Kentish are rumoured to have been pioneering
such 'metropolitan' innovations as the triangular bedroom.

But these deviations notwithstanding, it was at the Bow Quarter
that the 'inward-looking development' was set finally to triumph over
its forlorn and hostile surroundings, becoming the inspiring citadel at
the heart of a city now emerging from the dull uniformity of municipal
socialism. Decentralisation gave the Liberal Council an opportunity
to sidestep the intractable problems of those old Morrisonian
departments like Housing or Social Services, with their bureaucratic
and self-defined expertise, and to concentrate on the more visible but
altogether less ambitious project of relabelling their area; the council
was failing even to provide school-places for all its Bengali children
but, by filling otherwise unimproved streets with pseudo-Victorian
lamp-posts, bollards, and fake cast-iron litter-bins dated 1989, it
could at least create conservationist 'neighbourhoods' where councillors could strut their stuff and appeal to local patriotism in a manner
that was certainly not innocent of implicit racism (Bow is recognised
as the 'heart of white man's country' by the thugs of the British
National Party as well as the Bangladeshis of Whitechapel).[9] The
'Bow Neighbourhood' was happy to incorporate the Bow Quarter
into its new 'Heritage Trail'. The Liberal councillors in Bow –
'enlightened' and 'particularly progressive' as Bow Quarter
brochures kept describing them – were using historical imagery to
turn their whole neighbourhood into an 'inward-looking development', and the Bow Quarter would be one of the main landmarks in
their administrative domain. For a while there had been other
encouraging signs too: just prior to liquidation, Kentish had
apparently even acquired the old Poplar Town Hall a few hundred
yards away on the Bow Road – a building that George Lansbury had
known well before the war, as a councillor and, by 1936, as Mayor.

'Yuppies' in Search of Common Ground

The liquidation of Kentish hasn't brought down George Kozlowski;
he's traded seats to become Director of Marketing with Alan Selby
and Partners and, since the receiver has retained that company's

services, he remains responsible for conceptualising and promoting the Bow Quarter. I ask him what kind of person was buying into the project, and he assures me that the purchasers were 'clones' of the imagery projected in the brochures: young, childless, and 'aspirational' first- or second-time buyers. Certainly, some of the people who have bought in are easily reconciled with this description: the Bow Quarter has its marketing consultants and young entrepreneurs, its accountants and tax consultants who work for City firms like Coopers and Lybrand, Lloyds Bank, and Price Waterhouse. But there are other depositors who conform far less to this used idea of the 'yuppie': first-time divorcees trying to move down in the world with some style, the odd teacher, a sub-editor on *The Independent*, people with clerical jobs in nearby offices.

There is also Mr Nolan, a middle-aged Irishman who runs a corner shop just up Fairfield Road from the Bow Quarter. He and his wife look very much at home with the micro-economics of the Mars Bar, the *Evening Standard*, and a packet of Silk Cut; but a shrewdly managed glimmer in the eye hints at larger transactions in the background. Mr Nolan has built up a nice portfolio of property in the area over the last thirty or so years, and he kept a sharp eye on the Bow Quarter as the development proceeded. He was down there on the Saturday in November 1988 when those 'lofty' apartments in 'Meridian View' went on sale, and he was happy to pick up two for himself and another for his son. Since then he's learnt to style himself a bit of a people's hero among the depositors: as a man of means he is pleased to be taking the stand that other depositors can hardly afford. He's refused to complete on his three purchases, preferring to cut his losses on the deposits, and challenging the receiver to take him to court where he will fight on the grounds that the development is no longer the one he bought into. Mr Nolan insists that he can't talk – because legal action might be pending – but he then goes on to talk and talk. He mentions other small-time speculators like himself (the people who ran the pub across the road apparently also bought three of Mr Selby's luxuriously packaged investments) but he knows better than to dwell on such unsympathetic cases as these. It's altogether more effective to stress the plight of the desperate young couple who came into his shop a few weeks ago: they were weeping (*both* of them were in floods, as Mrs Nolan insisted) because they could neither afford to lose their hard-earned deposit of £6,500 nor to complete and pay the mortgage now that interest rates had gone through the roof. And if that doesn't move you, what about the girl who works in the local council office? Having stretched herself to the very limit in order to carry off the great leap upwards to the bottom rung of the property ladder, she too was just lying in a crumpled heap on the floor: wiped out by interest rates, she had lost her deposit on a one-bedroom 'studio' flat.

When Kentish went into receivership it didn't take the people who had bought into the Bow Quarter a minute to cut through the sales talk about their individualistic lifestyle and to recognise that they now held a very different interest in common. To put it bluntly, each and every one of them stood to lose a packet. They were left gazing at the childish crayon drawings in the brochures – the bright-coloured ones that showed an ice rink and people exercising in all the windows. This was the dream that was now evaporating before their eyes, and it certainly lacked the hard definition one would expect of a contractually binding specification (as the small print on the back cover said: 'None of the statements contained in these particulars are to be relied upon as statements or representations of fact . . .). They started writing letters to one another, addressing each other as 'Dear Depositor' and spelling out the uncertainties of their position. A Depositor's Action Group was formed and special meetings were held in central locations like the Cross Keys pub in Covent Garden or the Coopers and Lybrand training centre in Bloomsbury Square. Thames Television were refused admission and when the receiver turned up unexpectedly with a couple of assistants he, too, was told to 'Bugger off' in helpless but unambiguous terms. In the midst of all the sound and fury, there was sufficient desperate talk of valium and nervous breakdowns to draw a magnanimous gesture from Mr Nolan: he remembers offering to pay one distraught young lady's legal fees and to throw in a free holiday with some friends of his in Florida. At least one person at the meeting thought he must be drunk.

With the scheme apparently disintegrating around their sadly contracted ears, the depositors embarked on a dramatic rehearsal of all their worst fears. It is one thing for old industrial buildings to make the journey from squatting to the respectable romance of 'loft-living', but it's quite another when this fable of improvement is ambushed by recession and sent spiralling off in reverse. Would the Bow Quarter start sliding back down the line from the aspirational lifestyle, to the low-life rental scene, and, God knows, even squatting artists? Would the depositors be forced to move into the supposedly exclusive Bow Quarter only to watch helplessly as the other three quarters of Bow poured in behind them? They wondered why Selby wasn't listed among the creditors of Kentish Homes. They wondered about the post-liquidation valuation carried out by Donaldson's, an estate agent based in an office on Dalston Lane and suspected, quite without foundation, by some depositors of being in Selby's pocket.

As for the receiver over at KPMG Peat Marwick McLintock, his primary aim would be to minimise the losses of Security Pacific, the American merchant bank that was the main creditor, and while he had declared that the project would continue, it was obvious that the Bow Quarter would not be completed as first envisaged: the new 'mews-style' houses would not be built and, far worse, the land on which they were planned would probably be sold on for separate development. Suddenly all the social chaos that the Bow Quarter was intended to keep out threatened to materialise at the very centre of this 'inward-looking' development. One depositor circulated a list of monstrous prospects: a prison, a hospital, a home for the elderly, council housing, a secure home for mental patients . . . As for the leisure centre with its pools and its fitness instructor, if this was ever completed it would probably become an ordinary leisure club that anyone from the nearby council estates would be allowed to join for the sake of a few pounds. Since Kentish went down, the horror stories have been piling up all over the development: within a few months it was being said (quite falsely) that the council tenants have already moved into Blondin Terrace, and the one about paper-thin walls and the preternaturally active black man with his bongo drums was featuring in corner-shop discussions of the Clockhouse. The prospect of total degeneration loomed.

Oliver Richards' 'Citadel' suddenly had the desperate look of Fort Apache on a bad day, and it was obvious that a concerted defence had to be mounted; but although the Depositors Action Group secured some minor concessions from the receiver (including a reduction of 2.5 per cent on the completion price) its members couldn't maintain a united front. The people who had bought with a view to living in the development, however briefly, quickly became irritated with the speculators who, as it seemed, couldn't give a damn about the project and only wanted to get out without being burned, and further polarisation quickly developed among the would-be residents themselves. While some of the more sentimental depositors were still dreaming out loud about holding communal barbecues on the building site, and if the worst came to the worst, forming a purchaser's collective to negotiate favourable terms with developers elsewhere, others took one look at their fellow depositors and recoiled in horror.

Considering how the Press had reported on the liquidation, it is scarcely surprising that an 'anti-yuppie' faction should have formed almost immediately within the Depositors' Action Group. Its members, who were mostly women in their late twenties and early thirties, were appalled by the idea that they themselves might be mistaken for 'yuppies', and wasted no time in passing on the insulting epithet to their marginally younger fellows – the 'barrow boys' and the 'Sebastians' in striped shirts who talked of their flats as 'units' and 'investments', and never missed a chance to stress the importance of 'getting a foot on the property ladder'. Here, as I was told, was 'Thatcher's generation' – a bunch of brats, all of them 'under 26', who had grown up without any experience beyond the dream of personal accumulation, and who could only yelp in helpless outrage now that they had been derailed. It is only fair to say that these twice-dubbed 'yuppies' among the depositors looked back with comparable reservations of their own: they saw a collection of 'media people' who seemed more interested in using the situation to publicise themselves than in safeguarding their own investment. It wasn't long before the depositors fell out in bickering disagreement between those who wanted to court publicity in an attempt to embarrass the receiver into further concessions and others who considered publicity to be the very last thing they needed: not only would it produce more taunting stuff along the lines of 'yuppies lose their shirts' but it would also damage the development, thereby jeopardising every depositor's investments still further. So the action group disintegrated, and the depositors slinked off one by one, as so many individuals with a personal interest, to see what private accommodation they could arrive at with the receiver. The communal barbecues went the way of the ice rink, the trim track, the pasta shop, and, as I suspect, the library.

In the Receiver's House

I met Roger Oldfield of KPMG Peat Marwick McClintock for lunch in his office in Farringdon Street. We sat there struggling to release vacuum-sealed sandwiches from their plastic wrapping and picking over the details of a story that continues to unfold, despite all the talk of a 'yuppie' doomsday. Oldfield was appointed receiver to the Bow Quarter in late July 1989 and, having retained Forum Architects (who originally took over from ORMS in 1988), he has since gone on to complete the Clockhouse and the new houses in Blondin Terrace. He has also pleased the Bow Neighbourhood planning officials by replacing the aluminium roof proposed for the Edwardian factory with better-looking and, as he points out, slightly more expensive, slate tiles. Oldfield has resold, albeit at a reduced rate, the flats of the twenty-two depositors who have pulled out, and he is not going to say whether he will actually be taking the troublesome Mr Nolan to court. The remaining leisure facilities have been concentrated in 'The Powerhouse', the leisure centre going up on the site of the old factory boilerhouse. The part of the Edwardian factory known as 'Meridian View' will be completed, but the second half will only be weather-sealed and left. Oldfield feels himself to be under 'no commitment' to complete the new buildings originally proposed for the centre of the development, and he may indeed sell on the land for later development along the lines laid down in the planning consent. Oldfield is adamant that the ongoing development is, in all important respects, still the one that the first depositors bought into, but there have been enough changes in the plan to justify a nervousness that seems to come to the fore most strongly over the trivial business of the library. When I put this largely symbolic question to Peter Jolly of Forum Architects, he suddenly looked alarmed and asked, 'What Library?' He then reached for his plans and quickly confirmed that the 'old board-room' – for that was surely what I meant – was indeed completed and would be available for the use of residents. Oldfield was also out of his chair in a second, turning the intercom up so that I could hear his assistant confirming that the room was indeed finished. By this time I had given up on my question about the books.

Oldfield has no time for the speculators who bought into the Bow Quarter hoping to make a quick killing: they wouldn't have offered Kentish a share of their profits had the development gone the way they expected, and he saw no reason why anyone should now offer to take a share in their losses. He has more sympathy for the depositors who had planned to move in but have since been wiped out, although he suspects they were victims of rising interest rates rather than Kentish's collapse. He has given some of them the benefit of his own experience, drawing a lesson about the long-term nature of property investments from the story of the first property he himself acquired. Some of the depositors may have hoped for quick gains, but the moral of the receiver's story is different: the modest house in South Croydon, for which he had paid £11,200 in August 1973, dropped in value when the market slumped almost as soon as Oldfield had moved in, but seventeen years later it would probably be a reasonable buy at £100,000.

The promised statue to Annie Besant and the match-girls' strike has also undergone some modification. In February 1990 the Public Art Development Trust organised a sculptural competition on behalf of the Bow Quarter. The aim was to find a local sculptor whose work would 'in some way reflect and celebrate the history of the site', and the brief mentioned the dispute of 1888, describing this 'important historical landmark' as a 'complex' event that was 'very much linked to the argument around social and political reform then current'. The winner was Maurice Agis, a sculptor who works round the corner at Chisenhale Studios, a refurbished old leather factory that would itself have been eminently suited for further conversion to 'loft-living' were it not owned by the Artplace Trust. Back in the Sixties, Agis made a certain reputation with some works that Anton Ehrenzweig used to illustrate his 'syncretistic' and gestalt-psychological theory of art. At that time Agis and his collaborator, Peter Jones, had abandoned painting and sculpture to spend a year rebuilding a 'slum basement', dividing it with plastic panels and coloured protruding rods as part of their study of 'colour in space'. Ehrenzweig hailed this work as a reaction against 'the claustrophobia and fragmentation of modern architecture'. Indeed, he claimed that 'the dynamic interior space as articulated by Maurice Agis and Peter Jones grapples explicitly, perhaps for the first time, with the problem of enclosing and opening up architectural space mainly by making use of colour'. As he continued, ' "Basic" design exercises like these are badly needed in our over-professionalized schools of architecture and could make the students sensitive to the potentially life-enhancing qualities of interior space'.[10] Agis seems to have slipped a bit since those experimental days. Indeed, he won the competition for the Bow Quarter by submitting a small piece made of smoothed Provencal stone inter-woven with a wandering band of darkened lead, an unambitious work that, as a touching concession to the brief, he had labelled 'Lest we forget'. His final sculpture will be along the same bland lines: an abstract work made of large masses of darkened steel and smooth, rounded chunk of the same Provencal stone. This polite submission may not have 'grappled explicitly' with any of the peculiar problems of enclosure that have beset the architectural space of the Bow Quarter, but it suited the landscape contractor just fine and Agis also pleased the Public Art Development Trust by proposing to work on site over a period in which he would encourage visits from schools and attempt to involve residents in his activities. When I remark that I can't see much sign of Annie Besant or the strike in his proposal, he replies, with all the abruptness of an offended artist, that he's not a 'literary' sculptor and, moreover, that the developers should have chosen somebody else if that was what they really wanted. Though Agis is no keener than Keith Preston to have awkward historical references cluttering up his creative works, he did concede that it might be appropriate for the match-girls' strike to be mentioned – since it had, apparently, taken place at the site – on a little notice stuck into the ground next to his sculpture (or 'statue', as the man from Kyle Stewart, the building contractor, insists on calling it).

For George Kozlowski the project runs on smoothly enough. 'Net realisations' may be down a bit on the new releases, but the units are selling and the original marketing strategy is still delivering the goods. The latest publicity follows the 'loft-living' scenario through to the point of calling the Bow Quarter 'The Little Apple' and locating it in 'East 3'. Adverts were plastered all over London (tubes, buses and newspapers were all suitably adorned), and they were all the more striking for appearing in such wanton profusion at a time when everyone knew the property market to be in headlong retreat. There was a sales day at the end of June 1990 that featured the usual razzmatazz. The Stars and Stripes were flying from saplings planted a year or so ago outside the Clockhouse (the trees are still so slender that with each gust of wind, the flags dragged them down until they were lying almost flat on the ground), and a motley bunch of performers were playing brass music in pretended Yankee style and haranguing passers-by with the message that they could afford it. Inside 'Meridian View' an assortment of those hyped-up and 'lofty' apartments were on show: white walls this time, fitted out with US-style black-and-white photos that tried to capture the *frisson* of the Lower East Side or the 'aspirational' movement of an American rocket blasting off for the stars. There was also 'art' of a more British kind – framed posters from the Tate Gallery announcing exhibitions of Hockney and even Cedric Morris – and books by the magazine rack, with *The Bedside Guardian* to the fore. This phrase of the Bow

Quarter had been themed to look like a university hall of residence with unexpected luxuries thrown in.

Alan Selby himself was there. He was sitting at a desk next to an architect's model of 'The Powerhouse' as it would be when completed in a few months, and a much enlarged copy of Maurice Agis's colourful drawing of 'Moreland Square' as it would look when his completed work of art was in place among the fountains and greenery. The doors had only just opened, but Mr Selby was already coming to terms with a young man who had placed a wad of £50 notes on the table. Behind this jaunty depositor stretched a line of George Kozlowski's 'clones': a racially mixed cluster of young east Londoners, some of them appropriately kitted out in US-style baseball caps and Bermuda shorts, and none of them betraying the least knowledge of, or concern about, the development's troubled past. Security Pacific were offering an incentive package designed to get people off the hook of high interest rates for the first two years, and, within minutes of opening, the whole event looked like a sell-out. Regrettably some less than desirable 'elements of history' showed up to cause trouble on the stairs just outside the show flats – one of Selby's young men was telling an irate middle-aged woman that he *was* being reasonable if only she'd listen, and that it really would all come right in the end. The truth was that a handful of last year's frustrated customers had come along with a set of awkward questions and minds set on spoiling the show. Unable to leave the past behind in the manner that Keith Preston advocates, these depositors had already waited eighteen months since exchanging contracts and, thanks to a recent 'rephasing' of the construction, their lofty apartments still weren't ready for them either to move into or sell on. They were incensed to find this new release of flats selling at significantly lower prices than they themselves had paid. Selby's men were doing their best to ease the protesters out of earshot of the new punters, finessing them further and further out towards the car park. By the time it had been shifted a hundred yards back, the protest was running out of steam: indeed, the irate lady was now going all pathetic and trying to explain her anger rather than simply vent it: 'We're sorry to get cross, but obviously we are very, very angry'. Selby's man saw his chance and started to handle her with consoling words that would help her all the way back into her driving seat: 'I'll try to get you a definite answer by the end of the next week.' Despite these interruptions – to say nothing of the embittered former porter at the Clockhouse who turned up later in the day to organise a spoiling 'bad taste barbecue' – Selby took deposits on seventeen out of twenty of the available units, and there was every reason to anticipate that the remaining three would be bought by people on the waiting-list.

Walking to the Wine Bar

I caught up with a couple of the Bow Quarter's most long-serving veterans in Blondin Terrace. Fredelinda Telfer and Lindsay Brown were in the news when the liquidation happened. Featured variously as a 'software specialist' and a 'marketing consultant', Telfer is actually the 30-year-old Marketing Manager for Bill Kenright Productions, a theatre-producing agency that, at the time of our meeting, was just staging Glenda Jackson in Brecht's *Mother Courage* at the Mermaid Theatre (outdated 'Communist propaganda', as Milton Shulman ranted in the *Evening Standard*). Lindsay Brown is an Associate Director with an advertising and PR agency: she's the one who told *The Daily Telegraph*: 'When you buy from a reputable builder, the last thing you think about is that the builder is going to disappear'. Telfer and Brown were second and third in the queue on that first Saturday morning viewing at the Clockhouse in October 1988: they had got to know one another as residents at 'City View', another Alan Selby development in Bethnal Green, and they had come down to the Bow Quarter with a bit of a hangover, and, as Telfer puts it, bought almost on whim. A month or so later Telfer was back for the first release of flats in 'Meridian View' and, finding these galleried apartments to be far superior to the one she had just bought in the Clockhouse, she promptly put down a second deposit. Her intention (the feasibility of which she had checked with Alan Selby and Partners) was to sell the first one before completion and move into the second, but when Kentish went down she was stuck with both. As publicists, Telfer and Brown knew how to court the Press and it was they who went out to draw media attention to their plight. Anticipating that no yuppie-hunting journalist with a few inches to write would see her double purchase as anything other than proof that she was a thwarted speculator, Telfer told them she had had plans to move her mother into the development.

Two years later, when I knock at the door in Blondin Terrace early one Sunday afternoon, I find Telfer 'drifting', as she puts it, after a late night. Remembering Kozlowksi's brochures, I ask how far the disillusioned resident of the Bow Quarter really has to go to find an amenable brasserie or a bar of the kind that serves 'café filtre'. Rising to the challenge, Telfer describes the twenty-five minute hike she had taken the night before through a warren of derelict factories and rundown high-rise council estates recently ornamented with 'Bow Neighbourhood' logos and the additional signs of the 'Bow Heritage Trail' with which the council is trying to theme up its stretch of the abyss. She goes up to Tredegar Road and then cuts through some Victorian streets with terraced houses of the kind that George Lansbury used to say were only built in rows to prevent them falling down. This brings her to the Roman Road, with its street market and its confusion of lamp-posts – the new Victorian ones competing with the still-unremoved concrete models left over from the Sixties. She then turns into Grove Road, with its older blue plaque commemorating the spot where the first flying bomb fell on 13 June 1944, thus (if some of Prince Charles's advisers are to be believed) inaugurating the post-war council housing programme that has subsequently done so much more damage to the area. After crossing the noxious-smelling canal she comes to a roundabout and the entrance to Victoria Park, recently smartened up with gilded crowns adorning the new 'Crown Gates'. The road cuts through the park that, if it once rang out with political argument and discussion in which figures like Besant and William Morris featured prominently, is now only noisy with conservationist activity funded by Bow Neighbourhood with help from English Heritage and budgeted to run at £1 million per year for ten years. 'Original-style' Victorian benches and traditional copper lights are going in; the iron railings are being renewed and painted up in 'Bow Blue with Gold Trim', and horsedrawn carriages are to be introducing in an attempt to give visitors what the *East London Advertiser* calls 'a taste of the good old days'.[11]

As Ms Telfer follows the road through the park she passes the old and, in its time, notoriously polluted bathing lake on the left and, further on to the right, the site of Victoria Park Lido, the grand 200-foot open-air swimming pool that was built to replace it in 1935–6. This pool was demolished and removed a few months ago as part of the re-Victorianization of Victoria Park, and it is hardly surprising that the organisers of the Bow Heritage Trail have decided against erecting another of their numerous blue signs to mark the place where it once stood. There can be little doubt, however, that this was a site of unique historical significance. Designed by the architects, H.A. Rowbotham and T.L. Smithson, as a walled and, indeed, 'inward-looking' enclosure, the pool was made of glazed brickwork with a surrounding floor of 'white Portland cement'. It included foot and shower baths, diving boards, spectator stands, an ostentatiously hygienic filtering plant, and – a 'pleasurable extra' that would surely be appreciated in the Bow Quarter – special stretches of shingle 'beach' on which east Londoners could enjoy sunbathing. The surrounding wall was built high enough to ensure that, at least before the tower blocks went up in the Sixties, the poor slum-dweller could lie there and see only trees, sky, sun, and a couple of church spires. The pool quickly became known as 'East End on Sea' or the 'East End Seaside', but the *Daily Herald* went further, sampling the view from within and exclaiming that, on a sunny day, one could easily be beside the Lido in Venice.[12]

The recently demolished pool was built by the Labour-controlled London County Council, and opened in the summer of 1936 by Herbert Morrison, Leader of the LCC, who announced that 'This is more than a swimming bath. It is East London's Lido'.[13] The LCC knew that the long-suffering people of the East End wanted not 'abstract sympathy' but 'positive action for social betterment', and Morrison promised that the new pool was a sign of far greater things to come. Dick Coppock of the National Federation of Building Trade Operatives also attended the opening. As Chairman of the LCC's Parks Committee, he had promised the LCC that 'The East End is to have the best bath in London', and now he was there to point out that the pool was 'as good as anything around London owned privately and let out to bathers at twice the price'. This summer, as he continued, 'we shall bring the seaside to East London. Why this is as good as Margate'. The pool was at once a slap in the eye for the Tories, who had recently wanted to build housing over parts of Victoria Park, and proof that, thanks to Labour, 'all the slums of the East End will go'.

The Victoria Park Lido certainly had its moment in history. It looked back a few years to George Lansbury's spell as First Commissioner of Works in the Labour government of Ramsay MacDonald and his controversial drive to make the over-regulated Royal Parks of London fit for popular use. Lansbury only held this office for two years but he still found time to introduce dramatic changes. He scattered all sorts of sports and games equipment throughout the city's parks. He declared his own war on the iron railings that kept up 'the old fiction that a park is a sort of preserve which must be protected from the immoral and those imaginary monsters who are waiting to create every kind of disorder and damage to all the flowers and trees'.[14] He came out against every 'Keep off the Grass' sign in the metropolis, insisting that 'Grass was made for man, not man for grass' and condemning the head gardeners who seemed to imagine that 'huge tracts of our parks should be preserved in order to enable them to grow the sort of lawns we see in the quadrangles of colleges at Oxford and Cambridge'.[15] Some people objected to Lansbury's activities: *The Times* described his plans as 'grotesque and horrible', dismissing him as 'The Caliban of the Parks', and there was vociferous objection from upper-class residents on the west side of Regents Park when Lansbury arranged for the provision of children's boating on the lake.[16] However, the reforms were immensely popular with the ordinary people of London and, throughout the summer of 1930, Lansbury was hailed as 'London's Fairy Godfather' and 'His Majesty's First Commissioner of Good Works'. At the centre of his campaign for personal liberty in the parks stood what came to be known as 'Lansbury's Lidos' – swimming areas Lansbury opened for everyone's use. The first of these was the 'All British Lido', which came into being in Hyde Park when Lansbury insisted, as a self-styled 'good Suffragist' who was not afraid of offending either the 'London Public Morality Council' that formed to oppose his plans or the respectable press that accused him of turning Hyde Park into Coney Island, that women and children should be allowed to join the men already permitted to swim in the Serpentine. The minority Labour government in which Lansbury pursued these policies was short lived, but the parks programme had been taken on by the Labour LCC (of which Lansbury himself was a member), which adopted the slogan 'Every East End Child to be a Swimmer' and set out to give London borough councils extensive powers to make more popular use of the open spaces under their management. Besides running swimming pools, councils would be encouraged and enabled to provide dancing, golf, lawn tennis, gymnastics, bowling, rifle ranges, boats, subsidised musical and dramatic events, cinematograph exhibitions, and pageants; they would even have the power to flood stretches of park in winter in order to provide skating and curling.[17] The pool in Victoria Park stood squarely in the tradition of 'Lansbury's Lido's', but it is now a barely distinguishable void on the winding trail from the Bow Quarter to 'Frocks', the wine-bar at which Fredelinda Telfer only arrives after she had come out of the park and crossed the borough line into Hackney.

Last Words

Telfer and Brown are good friends, but they want me to understand that they are not the lesbians some people maliciously deduced them to be from the photograph that the *Evening Standard* displayed – deliberately or not – alongside Andrew Langton's dismissive remark about the 'Isle of Dogs'. Telfer has traded her way through the whole development: she explains that she had managed to sell her first flat in the Clockhouse, and then come to an accommodation with the receiver that enabled her to buy her three-bedroomed house in Blondin Terrace for only £10,000 above what she was already contracted to pay on the still-uncompleted second flat in Meridian View. She judges her house in Blondin Terrace to be fine, but the blinds are down permanently to hide the building site that begins just outside her window. Telfer says she never thinks about the development, but she keeps casting fierce sideways glances in its direction, and these give dramatic weight to her insistence that she doesn't want to be there and, indeed, wishes that she had cut her losses on both deposits and moved on a year ago.

As somebody who works in marketing, Lindsay Brown hates to admit that she was 'sucked in by the hype'. Telfer agrees that they should have known better: she mentions the match-girls' strike, wondering how they could ever have expected a place that has seen so much misery and strife ever to come right. There's nothing in her background to encourage the view that history can simply be thrown over like that. I ask them about the new post-liquidation publicity describing the Bow Quarter as the 'Little Apple', and they are quick to exceed the criticisms I had heard from another woman who, as an otherwise content resident of the Clockhouse, had declared the imagery embarrassing ('no one likes to be set up as a "yuppie"') and beside the real point, which is that the Bow Quarter is comparatively cheap, central and – not least for a single woman whose job involves late comings and goings – secure. Telfer brandishes a full page advertisement that has just appeared in the *Evening Standard*. It shows a naked man – 'he looks like an estate agent' – lying in his galleried bed gripping his calisthenic sex-aid of a partner while last night's bottles and lifestyle magazines litter the floor below. Beneath the picture (this 'sickening, appalling, squirm-inducing garbage') there are few paragraphs of sub-American copy ('And hey, I just love my new apartment in the Bow Quarter' . . .) about the 'morning squeeze' that isn't to do with standing in the queue at Liverpool Street Station and that also 'comes with orange juice'. Looking down from the heights of her own professional authority, Lindsay Brown dismisses the advert as a pitiful performance of the kind that gives advertising a bad name.

Having dealt with the most recent publicity, the pair then pick up the original brochure, and start singling out choice passages for richly deserved laughter and derision. I look up, taking in a stretch of wall-to-wall carpeting and the relieved smiles of the sun-tanned friends who have just dropped in (a couple who, thanks to the precautionary vigilance of their solicitors, managed to get out of the Bow Quarter without losing their deposits), before being surprised by a picture on the wall that shows another person staring into a book. In the very place where Mr Kozlowski's photographers would put the hub caps, Fredelinda Telfer has hung 'The Self-Taught Man', a thoroughly workerist lithograph by Glaswegian artist, Ken Currie. Currie's subject sits at a table in a tight and barely furnished little room, a brutally rendered figure with an ungentrified industrial inferno burning into the night outside his window. His knuckles are tattooed with 'Love' and 'Hate', his face is razored over with lines in which exploitation and resistance meet, and he is staring with desperate concentration into a book that bears the emblem – certainly not a logo – of the Workers Educational Association on its cover. Here, at last, is the vanishing library. Here too is the Victorian hell-house and, in the scarred figure of the subject, a rhetorical reminder – 'literary' as Maurice Agis would probably declare it – that transformation doesn't always come easily. Seeing her Glaswegian grandfather's life in it, Telfer bought Currie's image in instalments too, but in this case she had no regrets. The picture cuts hard against the grain of the Bow Quarter, and it is not surprising that some of Telfer's visitors have been appalled by its portrayal of man as a mutilated striver rather than a toned-up 'yuppie' or drifting depositor. Perhaps the picture is only a mannerist affectation, a hopeless attempt to evoke a real historical world in which a lido could still count as a progressive step towards greater things, but it prompts me to ask Fredelinda Telfer a distinctly old-fashioned question. I ask if she has learned anything useful from her own trials in the Bow Quarter. She replies quickly enough that she's decided to study for a law degree and that it is probably only because of what the Bow Quarter has taught her about rhetoric, reality, and the disreputable nature of the contract between them, that she has been offered a place as a student next year. So she, too, can look forward to moving on.

Part Five

Visions of the New Dawn

'We'll live six miles up a muddy track, and I'll break my neck on a moped coming home from the train with an overloaded Greek satchel full of books and empty bottles.'

Richard North, *The Independent*, 16 February 1990

16
Excellence: From Fifth Avenue to Hackney Town Hall

King of the Bullshitters

In 1989, the actor Bob Hoskins visited the Dalston Rio to publicise the London launch of his film *Who Framed Roger Rabbit*. In the course of this visit to the cinema he used to attend as a boy, Hoskins explained for the benefit of an interested enquirer that 'New York is like Dalston, only bigger'. A similar proposition had formed in my mind a couple of years previously when I took a walk up Fifth Avenue one Sunday just before Christmas. The street was packed with shoppers and the Salvation Army were well dug in on the corners, tinkling handbells against the noise of blaring car horns and foraying out into the crowd to appeal on behalf of the unfortunates for whom Christmas promised only another freezing night in a doorway. The shop windows were alight with seasonal tableaux. Transworld Airlines had perched a half-hearted crib on top of a mountain of cotton wool. Alitalia had gone folkloric, flying in an ornate tree-bark creche from rural Italy and displaying it as a piece of authentic piedmontese culture.

The larger Department Stores had roped off special viewing areas on the street, put their doormen out as ushers and filled their windows with animated dream sequences in which Christmas merged with peak moments in the history of the American spirit. In one window I saw the founding fathers dressed up as prosperous nineteenth century gentlemen and greeting each other on the snow-covered steps of a gaslit Carnegie Hall. But the real crowd-puller was set in a nursery interior of the most wishful old-fashioned kind. A model steam train circled a laden Christmas tree and then wound through to the next window where the cuttings and tunnels of a snow-covered landscape awaited it. Around the train model children went through mechanical motions of their own: fixing a broken carriage, working the controls or just following things with an enchanted doe-like eye. Even the family cat twitched its tail appreciatively as the train rattled by. Saks and Co may deal in the latest styles, but the sentimentally contrived clockwork romance in their window greeted every passing shopper as Citizen Kane.

Further along Fifth Avenue I came upon a building which is a stranger to such coy discretion. Identified by large bronze letters over its prominent doorway, Trump Tower is an uncompromisingly modern glass edifice that rises in stepped and tree-covered terraces up to the height of the Tiffany building next door and then soars on up for fifty-eight saw-toothed floors.

Huge doors revolve under the watchful eye of doormen whose uniforms – made in London, of course – have been likened to those of South American generals on parade, and then deliver the visitor into an 'atrium' of bursting flamboyance. The place is an explosion of polished brass and brilliant pink marble raised to a high shine on both floor and walls, and I'm confident that Mrs Jan Cooper, of the Holly Street Estate, would have loved it. Reflective glass fills the area with a speculative sense of space and escalators rise up one side of the atrium, doubling people with their own reflections and moving the whole preoccupied assemblage up and down between five floors of exclusive shops: Asprey, Buccellati, Cartier, Charles Jourdan, Bonwit Teller . . . The atrium converges on an impressive monument to liquidity, throughput and flow: an amber-lit waterfall tumbles down eighty feet of soapy pink marble and then sits bubbling in the bistro where things slow down for a while. Above the atrium rises the tower with its floors of exclusive office space and its 263 luxurious apartments. Behind it is an enclosed 'public park'. Built under glass and planted with exotic trees and fake Victorian lamp-posts which would not look out of place in the new Bow, this unlikely amenity joins the 'retail atrium' to the IBM Gallery of Science and Art. As one visiting critic recently managed to stutter before words failed him altogether, Trump Tower is certainly 'an interesting new piece of urbanism'. For myself, I thought of Hackney's tower blocks with their dingy foyers and marvelled too: New York was like Dalston, only better.

How can the seasonal touch be brought to a place like this? A few tons of scarlet poinsettias might add to the general blaze, but the slick lines of the atrium could scarcely be expected to tolerate any pokey-looking cribs with their plaster-cast messiahs, unkempt shepherds and stinking straw. As for the window-dressing, this was equally undisturbed by sentimental clutter of the kind that might involve toytrains and simulated childhood romance. Instead, as I discovered, the Trump Tower was offering something truly unique: an encounter with the man who had already redeveloped Christmas and was now coming forward to stake his claim on Heaven itself.

Just inside those revolving doors, a monstrous neo-Baroque table had been isolated behind burgundy velvet ropes. It stood there motionless, while its legs crawled with buxom guilt figurines. Behind the table sat a blow-dried Donald Trump, looking impassive in pink silk tie and a long dark blue coat. Next to him a woman was selling copies of a book, taking them from a big pile behind her and cranking away with an American Express machine as she went. Three tall and immaculately tonsured black dudes were in attendance: dressed in charcoal suits, they were supervising the queuing crowd and keeping an eye out for assassins. Trump was settled into his chosen version of seasonal routine: leaning forward to ask the name of each approaching supplicant, and then falling back to write a dedication in felt-tip scrawl. There was Donald Trump as image on the cover of his just-published book: sixty floors up with Central Park behind him and his name overhead in the largest gold letters that Random House could find. Here was Donald Trump incarnate: selling the word to his disciples while a brassy version of 'Oh Come All Ye Faithful' filled the thronging atrium behind him.

A couple of years later, Donald Trump would be on the floor in a very different sense: a smudged deadbeat left over from the Reagan era, abandoned by his immortal consort Ivana, and propped up in a temporary kind of way by ailing US and Japanese banks that couldn't afford to let him expire completely. But none of this could be detected on the boundless horizon that Donald sketched for himself in *Trump: the Art of the Deal*. As they opened their personalised first editions on the way home, Donald Trump's admirers must have been interested to discover that the man who had recently been fêted as 'America's masterbuilder' was not driven by lust for money alone: 'I don't do it for the money. I've got enough, much more than I'll ever need'.[1] The animating impulse was of a grander kind. Where others 'paint beautifully on canvas or write wonderful poetry', Trump liked 'making deals, preferably big deals. That's how I get my kicks.'

As an artist of the deal, Trump took a distinctive approach to his work. He liked each day to resemble his retail atrium: an unpredicted 'happening', as he once described it, which declares its own unique prospects as it goes along. Not a man to weigh himself down with a brief-case, he was equally careful to avoid stifling the creative play of his imagination with 'structure' of a bureaucratic kind. Confident in his own sense of what it was to be a developer, Trump liked 'to come to work each day and just see what develops'. He styled himself somewhere between a zen master and Jackson Pollock, the process painter who talked famously of the things that happen 'When I am in my painting'. Like other artists Trump had his chosen medium: his day starts to move at about nine in the morning when 'I get on the phone'.

With Trump Tower, Donald set out to create a building with 'aura' – one that was 'larger than life' and would appeal to the 'wealthy Italian with the beautiful wife and the red Ferrari'. Whether or not he was really targetting the mafia, Trump's idea was to make people feel 'comfortable, but also pumped up to spend money'. False economies were out from the start. If customers would enjoy being taken for a ride on escalators of solid bronze, then he wasn't going to scrimp on the million dollar cost of this extra touch. If they would be more turned on by two million dollar's worth of purling waterfall than by the conventional 'art' suggested by various unimaginative advisers, then this too would be part of the deal. As for all that soapy pink marble, the name is Breccia Pernice and Trump recalls the day when he and his wife first saw a sample of this rare stone – an 'exquisite blend of rose, peach, and pink that literally took our breath away'. The transport turned out to be mutual. Indeed with Trump rejecting 60 per cent of the stone that was cut because of white streaks that were 'jarring to me', the top of an Italian mountain had been removed before the floors and walls of the atrium were clad to their creator's satisfaction.

It would be a churlish visitor who stepped into Donald Trump's atrium and refused to wonder at the sight. In stark contrast with British endeavours like the Trocadero near Picadilly Circus, Trump Tower demonstrates that a building can be glitzy without also being tacky. Ike Turner should take heart. Cruelly lampooned as the man whose front room proved that it really was possible to spend a million dollars in Woolworths, he can now visit Trump Tower and feel assured that the problem was never just a matter of taste. Quantity really can be transmuted into quality. Towering and significant structures can be built up entirely from clichés. Hailed and deplored as the building which brought the vulgarity of Las Vegas and Atlantic City to Manhattan, Trump Tower is also dedicated to the televisual opulence of Dallas and Dynasty. The tribute was recognised quickly enough, and the retail atrium became a favourite location in the next generation of soaps. The CBS mini-series 'I'll Take Manhattan' didn't just take its cameras into Donald's bistro; it also took the man himself and gave him a part as fairy godfather to Joan Collins.

Trump: the Art of the Deal was a high-rise autobiography of the kind that became increasingly familiar through the Eighties, and it didn't take Donald long to bring his readers up the fifty-eight floors of his symbolic tower. He whisked them past the offices of people like Calvin Klein and invited them to peer into what he described as the most luxurious and expensive apartments in the world. He let them rub shoulders with Trump Tower's exclusive residents: the wealthy French who came here to sit out the Mitterand years; the Asians and Arabs who couldn't get through the discriminatory vetting procedures of the co-operatives that control so many of New York's most exclusive apartment buildings; stars like Stephen Spielberg, Johnny Carson, Paul Anka and the late Liberace. He helped them over their disappointment at not meeting Prince Charles, whose falsely (and, for Donald, profitably) rumoured purchase of an apartment in Trump Tower was splashed across the front pages just after the Royal Wedding that made Charles and Diana 'the most celebrated couple in the world'. Having raised his gasping readers up this high, Donald Trump offered them the ultimate Christmas tableaux: a fleeting glimpse into the enchanted world of America's loudest billionaire. Introducing his own $12 million triplex at the very top of the Tower,

Donald was typically unrestrained in his modesty: 'In truth, I've gone a little overboard'. He gestured toward the twenty-seven solid marble columns that had been carved specially for his eighty-foot living room by 'Italy's finest craftsmen', adding that 'they arrived yesterday, and they're beautiful'. Lest any of his slower admirers should have missed the point, he went on to rub it in a bit: 'What I'm doing is about as close as you're going to get, in the twentieth century, to the quality of Versailles'.

As we took our privileged glimpse into this flagrantly celestial place a curious kind of morality play rolled into action. The first scenes were of unchecked extravagance, hedonism and luxury, but it wasn't long before an alarming giddiness set in. The pleasures of megalomania should not be underestimated, but it can still be hard to live so far beyond the limits of the normal human condition: everything about oneself – every utterance, every passing whim, every memory – starts to burn with intense significance and it is hard to stay rooted in the blaze that follows. Even such a distinguished artist of the deal as Donald Trump is susceptible to vertigo so, like Harold with his Purple Crayon in that much-loved American children's story from the Fifties, he no sooner found himself in thin air that he quickly sketched some firm ground under his feet.

If Trump was in the White House which, as we was rash enough to hint in those undiminished days, he might well be before too long, he could follow the example of Presidents Reagan and Harding, and look for astrological anchorage in the stars. But his Christmas tableaux was actually more like an old-fashioned western than a story of special people with occult powers. Trump styled himself and his friends as real men who have carved their initials into the world's most famous skyline. Their Manhattan penthouses became tents on the high plains of America's last frontier. They sit at the fireside, counting their marble columns, remembering Mother and distinguishing themselves from the lesser types who continually got in their way. As real men of action, these artists of the deal know that you've 'got to take a stand or people will walk all over you'. They have as little regard for 'suckers' as they do for 'employees'. In their book, 'an employee' is either a woman or a sub-human eunuch who 'thinks small' and is 'afraid of success': an example of 'institutional man, the type who has virtually no emotion' and just wants to 'go home at five and forget about it'.

As followers of 'gut-feeling' and 'instinct', these companions of the deal defend a simple outlook in a world full of spurious specialisation, red tape and obstruction. As men of unlimited wealth and power, they continue to think of themselves as underdogs oppressed by an unaccountable establishment and state bureaucracy. They see con-men everywhere, but between themselves they maintain a code of honour. Like true mafiosi, they know that 'you can trust family in a way that you can never trust anyone else'. They also know that sometimes it is more important to 'pay your respects' than to make money so they will pass up a promising looking deal in order to get to the funeral of an important 'patriarch'. The members of this squalid fraternity may not understand all the technicalities, but they know that a handshake is the sign of a man's word, and profess nothing but contempt for the 'lowlifes, the horror-shows' for whom only the signed contract counts. This is how Trump finally styles himself – as a man who has broken all the limits and, in the very process, reinvented morality for the whole of humankind. He has everything the world can offer but, as he liked to point out in his glory days, he has never touched a drop of alcohol or smoked a cigarette in his life. A man who got married in the church of his childhood and has gone on to stand tall as a true patriarch in his own family, Trump is also a man of charity who has done his bit for the Vietnam Veterans and other chosen causes. Indeed, he is even moral in his egotism. Some people may have jeered as he tried to write his name in large bronze letters over the world but, swaggering Donald had an answer for them: as he liked to point out, he at least had a reputation to uphold – unlike the sharks and hoods who hide their real identity under anonymous company titles. What was the message of this clockwork nativity? That morality is like money: the rich have far more than anyone else.

It was six months later, in May 1988, that I next set eyes on Donald Trump who, this time, was accompanied by Ivana, his prize wife. I was back in Dalston and though the Trumps were soon to be divorced on the grounds of Donald's cruelty, they were together in London to publicize the British release of *Trump: the Art of the Deal*. They appeared on BBC1's *Wogan*, where Donald hymned the praises of Mohammed Al Fayed, the suspect owner of Harrods ('He's a fabulous man and his wife's really a wonderful lady'), and admitted that he was maybe 'looking at different things' he might try to get off the ground in the 'world class' city, that is London. Ivana looked wonderful, but Donald was visibly rattled – indeed, his eyes kept narrowing like a rat's – by the presence of Dame Edna Everidge who was also sitting next to him on the sofa, smirking as Trump suggested that the art of the deal was really an inborn quality, praising both the sheer plastic beauty and the 'brains' of his cosmetically reconstructed former athlete and 'top model' of a wife, and then sneaking in the barbed reminder that 'Greed is a very disfiguring thing'. By this time the British scene was already familiar with the American wave on which Trump, the 'real estate beachboy', had performed his star turns.[2] Indeed, through the Eighties, the much vaunted special relationship between Britain and the United States was dramatised as an exchange of clichés: Britain provided the US with the hyped up imagery of the country house and the instant traditions that could be derived from it; while the US reciprocated by exporting the hormonal cult of the thrusting entrepreneur. We have already set out from Sutton House and found ourselves in Manhattan, but we can come home via a different, if equally scenic, route which starts in Donald Trump's retail atrium and eventually delivers us onto the steps of Hackney Town Hall.

Beyond the Man in the Grey Flannel Suit

The British magazine *Management Today* adopted a distinctive style of portrait photography in the Eighties. Here was a constant stream of successful business figures, but here also was a problematic re-dundancy of appearance: how could one promote the entrepreneurial spirit as a revivifying force by running endless mugshots of the man in a grey flannel suit? The photographers were set to work, decentring the figure, absorbing it into its own reflection, dismembering and scattering it about the place. Unlikely angles proliferated as the background was picked over for relieving features which could be drawn into the newly vacant centre of the image: anything from the fluted pillars and wrought-iron gates of some nearby classical architecture to the futuristic technology and flexible interior of the working environment. So Oftel's Bryan Carsberg, who we have already encountered as the friend of Mercury Communications and scourge of British Telecom, found himself smiling up in soft brown light as he dangled in the mirror on a green office wall. Michael Meyer of Emess Lighting was dissected by the blinds that cut across him and then reassembled from outside – his shirt-sleeved figure looming like a target in the formulaic eye of some Hollywood assassin. As for Chris Greentree, of London and Scottish Marine Oil, all that remained of him was a severed head shining above the water as the sun went down over drilling rigs beached by the receding North Sea tide.

Keen to escape the predictable routines of business appearance, these photographs certainly don't withdraw into a romantic focus on personal character. It was no part of their intention to seek out the distinguishing signs of wisdom, skill or experience in the unique lines of any individual's face. Altogether lighter in approach, they treat their subjects as provisional appearances which can be animated and defined from outside – reassembled as part of the situation in which their significance is to be found. This is a portraiture of prospect and position rather than of inborn qualities like those that Donald Trump tried to claim for himself, and it accepts the loss of deeper, more romantic ideas of subjectivity without regret.

Meanwhile management theorists have also become more con-fident in kind. Gone are the studious attempts to constitute manage-ment as a properly boring academic subject, or to justify recom-mendations and prescriptions in terms borrowed from more respect-able disciplines. The leading 'management thinkers', and this is precisely what these writers like to call one another, are no longer trying to bring the movement of enterprise under a rational description which might identify professional management with stable administrative functions of planning, resource allocation and control. Far from trying to take the unpredicatability and guesswork out of the corporate game, the more recent tendency has been to celebrate it. Unlike the welfare capitalists who tried to gentrify the jungle, the new theorists have urged us to face it as it is, recognising that losers as well as winners are swinging through the trees and chosing our role models with appropriate care.

The leading management thinkers of the 1980s were American, and 'excellence' was their creed. Thomas Peters and Robert Waterman Junior's *In Search of Excellence* appeared in 1982 and it quickly established itself as the best-selling management book ever.[2] Here was an unambiguous riposte to the Japanese economic miracle, that Pearl Harbour of the Carter era. Excellence didn't need to be imported from over the Pacific. Drawing on their experience as consultants with McKinsey and Company, Peters and Waterman Junior insisted that it was a native quality of American enterprise.

Peters and Waterman Junior certainly displayed the trappings of their own worldly success, but they also allowed a positively old-fashioned kind of sweat to grace their temples. Delivered in a style that combines hucksterism with the forceful sincerity of the big tent, their book put across a Message of the large evangelical kind. Beyond the spirit-crushing rules of the administered corporation, there were people trying to fight their way through to greater glories. Indeed, if US corporations were failing, this was probably because they had smothered the creativity of their own people. *In Search of Excellence* was not just another semi-therapeutic attempt to manage the unconscious impulses of Organisation Man, that routinized and time-serving drone who – even when discovered by William Whyte in the 1950s – came fully fitted with the miserable wife, brattish children and off-the-peg infidelities of a Joseph Heller novel that was yet to be written.[4] The new creed had a sun-bleached Californian feel to it, but it was also tuned into the spiritual tradition of 'Let my people go'. Excellence replaced the measured outputs of the coerced and managed workforce with the unpredictable creativity of small risk-taking teams to which 'rulism' and corporate planning mean only death. The advocate of Excellence sighed with relief as the regulated workplace – factory, cotton-field or centralised office – was consigned to the scrapheap of history (ie to the Third World). In place of this brutal and dehumanised scenario came an open-collared cult of diversification, limited decentralisation and self management or 'Management by Walking About'. The drone used to be managed into reluctant productivity with the sticks and carrots of behaviourism. Excellence turned away from this, starting with the reborn figure of the 'turned on' American worker – self-motivated and fired by the 'high' of his own situation as he rides Toffler's third wave towards the post-industrial shore.

The Excellent company knew that the pace of 'change' – one of management thinking's catch-all reifications – was escalating and also that constant innovation was therefore the prerequisite of success. Recognising that the people most likely to break new ground were precisely those who would be coded weird and delinquent under the rational model, it gave oddballs their head and accepted false starts as essential to development. Careful to look after its potential 'champions', it had no more time for the imported welfare bureaucracy of the Personnel Department (which turned the American citizen into Organisation Man in the first place) than it did for the laborious machinery of trade unionism. If Excellence was all about modernisation it was also about getting back to the real essence of the capitalist process. With the defeat of welfarist ideologies the distance between success and failure had been restored: once more, there was a wide open range – a grand American answer to Crichel Down – for the cowboys, campfires and makeshift settlements of the entrepreneurial revival. Thanks to new technology,the spirit of enterprise was also being freed from the worst imbecilities of the factory system. As a New Age utopia, Excellence promised a recovery of history. When the twenty-first century breaks there will still be cowboys everywhere, but we will also find the market restored to the purity of Adam Smith's description: excavated and cleansed of encrustation after 150 years in the industrial bureaucratic swamp.

The success of *In Search of Excellence* prompted a flurry of like-minded books by writers who were entirely immodest about their own contribution to knowledge. Every one of them was a pathbreaker, and some even quoted Thomas Kuhn to show how revolutionary they really were. *In Search of Excellence* announced itself as nothing less than a paradigm shift and its successors repeated the boast. In this parody of scientific progress each succeeding management thinker who got a book out became a Galileo or Einstein. The claims made for Excellence as a new paradigm are certainly open to question, but there can be little doubt that its advocates were hell-bent on the destruction of an older, more familiar one. As Tom Peters and Nancy Austin put it in *A Passion for Excellence*: 'if we were allowed to be business czars our first act would be to remove the word "commodity" from the language of commerce. We despise it more than any other word in the business vocabulary . . .'[5] This comment was made against the lamentable tendency of banks to calculate the moving and irreducible spirit of enterprise only in the general economic terms of its existence. With the banks being treated as if they were marxists, it is not surprising that the new management thinking should also have used an ingenious disappearing trick to deal with the claims of the Keynesian state with its attempted planning of economic activity. This scenario – built on an idea of social totality which confronts private economic activity with its broader social responsibilities – is simply vapourized. History vanishes, with its implied causes and effects, as the more exuberant notion of 'Change' steps in to replace it. The new entrepreneur is surrounded by 'change' which comes at him with all the irresistible power of the Megatrend. Innocent of history and bravely resistant to Future Shock, he proves to be a magnificent surfer as he rides the waves of New Age time. The third wave (Kondratiev rather than Toffler) is already receding. The fourth one is based on electronics and cresting at this very moment. The fifth, gathering on the horizon, has already found its shape around new developments in bio-technology and computer science . . . . As Tom Peters eventually revealed in his third book – nothing less than the 'Handbook for a Management Revolution' – excellence is really all about 'thriving on chaos'.[6] The discovery was convenient since, as Tom Peters admitted, many of the companies that he had been citing as examples of Excellence in practice a few years earlier were by this time crawling about on the floor nearly as abjectly as the unquoted Donald Trump.

While the cramped old world of historical cause and effect is replaced by the unpredictable and wholly externalised play of 'change' at one end of Excellence's conceptual field, a bizarrely innocent rendering of the human individual stands at the other. Known variously as 'the winner', 'risk-taker' or 'champion', this numinous figure has been designated 'the peak performer' in a recent study by Charles Garfield, a former world-class weight-lifter who has since gained a doctorate in clinical psychology.[7] Leaving the rats to his behaviourist colleagues, Dr Garfield went out to take a close look at people who have cultivated 'what the German writer Goethe called "the genius, power and magic" in ourselves'. These are the 'everyday heroes', the people who 'translate missions into results' and who form 'the basic unit of excellence in every organisation'. Peak performers are realists, but they are fired by the unwavering belief that 'in the final analysis, I will make it'.

Where traditional management thinking tries to help corporations get better productivity out of Organisation Man by 'tacking on skills to the same old person', the peak performer is interested in complete personal transformation. For him there is no question of merely going through the motions or of surrendering personal identity for a corporate one. The peak performer glows in his or her achievement. Fully engaged and finding realisation through action, peak per-formers are the stars of the routinised world that they re-enchant. Like the exceptional cancer patients who survive against all the odds (and the weight-lifting doctor has written a book about these peak-performing individuals too), these achievers prove that 'the primary locus of control for a peak performance is not external but internal'. Peak performance can't be reduced to its social circumstance: it's about liberating resources that are 'locked up within'. The external world serves as a fortuitous trigger mechanism. Some of Garfield's peak performers tell of being 'jump started' by watching people they admire. Others have been to a place where Wordsworth is sung to a country and western tune, speaking of 'sweet spots in time', which have offered them 'a glimpse of themselves as capable of "a great deal more than I previously thought possible" '.

Like other advocates of Excellence, Garfield declares his allegiance to 'people' rather than abstract principles, but his humanism is essentially light. The peak performer goes with the flow; he doesn't pretend to be a rock in anybody's idea of a stream. He incorporates 'change', flexibility and opportunity into the essence of his character. This is what Garfield calls 'self-management': an interesting variation on a long-standing political idea, to be sure. If it once involved the members of a political body making their own decisions, self-management was now about handling yourself to your own best advantage. According to Dr Garfield, it was also 'an idea whose time, in the 1980s in the United States, has come'.

Dr Garfield saw the peak performer as both the exemplar of American democracy and the helmsman of human evolution – a process which, while it may seem mortally exhausted in Dalston, was apparently limbering up for another great leap forward on the West Coast. But there is another side to this superhuman figure. Refusing all social definition of his personality and character, the peak performer is at least as likely to be a psychotic megalomaniac as an exemplar of the civic ideal. Since the mid-Eighties many American entrepreneurs have contributed their own books on the theme of 'I did it my way'. Most of these autobiographies, and Donald Trump's is no exception, are co-written by named individuals who are taken on as narrative engineers rather than mere ghost-writers; their job is to design and maintain the textual machinery that will keep the monstrous 'I' of the autobiography intact. The trick is to bring off some kind of reconciliation between the superhuman status and position of the successful entrepreneur and his 'only human' attributes as a regular Joe. To find a sustainable individuality in that reconciliation would be an achievement indeed,[8] and Warren Avis is only one of the business heroes who have come unstuck in print. His *Take a Chance to be First* tried to make a case for the special nature of this regular Joe.[9] Avis styles himself as a real gunslinger (nothing less than 'the fastest gun in the west') and sprinkles his autobiography with tips on 'the basic secrets of hitting the bullseye'. As befits a man who uses his Acknowledgements page to announce how much his co-writer has learned from working with him, Avis finds everything fitting into place as he looks back over the years. Indeed, there is no part of his remembered life that doesn't glow in the light of his subsequent glory. Cock-ups are redeemed by success (there's a lesson to be drawn here: 'Learn from your mistakes!'), and the most trivial of experiences show special powers at work: 'even when walking through the park, I try to be observant about the things around me. I might be figuring how to make the park more beautiful. Or in strolling down Fifth Avenue in New York City, I may be musing about how to improve the congested traffic. Even while relaxing out on a farm, I may be considering a different way to arrange the fences or shrubs to get more productivity or beauty out of the land'. 'Be yourself!' is the message, and the risk of autism is plain to see. If the remembered self of these autobiographies tends to be undifferentiated – a great big baby-like thing – it is also forever young. The new man of success has little patience with the old humanist idea that age confers wisdom; for him age is far more likely to be a humiliating and meaningless biological fact. As Avis says in a candid aside, 'I often have trouble acknowledging my age because I feel younger than I really am . . . it took me nearly ten years to face up to the fact that I had passed the fifty-year milestone'.

Excellence comes to Hackney Town Hall

In Hackney we have 'fifty year milestones' of a rather different sort but, if the *Hackney Gazette* is to be believed, the council at least struggles bravely to keep up with Donald Trump and his flamboyant atrium. Provoked by an article reporting the council's plans to give the Town Hall a 'facelift', an anonymous pensioner recently wrote in to protest: 'As I sit shivering in the draughts whistling through my half-century-old corroded windows in this decaying ex-GLC estate, I feel greatly comforted to learn that the council plans to turn the Town Hall foyer into a "million pound marble paradise"'.[10] There was a time, so this correspondent insisted, when 'a vote for Labour would ensure the election of true representatives of the poor, the elderly and the sick. Regrettably, this is no longer the case . . .'. Another outraged correspondent denounced these plans to turn the Town Hall into a 'marble mecca', declaring that 'the people's party has forgotten its people', and predicting that unless something is done to remind councillors of their true responsibilities, 'the whole borough will die, but the Town Hall will shine'.

It should be said in mitigation that the plans which provoked this controversy were only drawn up after the rude demise of a much grander vision dreamed up by the council at a time when, with the property market still soaring, it was possible to imagine making huge fortunes from planning gain and the sale of disused public buildings along the edge of the City in Shoreditch. The idea had been to transform the whole area around the Town Hall into a new Civic Centre which would put new muscle on the wasted heart of the borough and, as was hoped, even possess the magical power to attract a tube line, a combined artery and vein, into the area. By comparison with this otherworldly scheme, the later proposals which had been approved 'in principle' by the Corporate Services Committee were modesty itself. They included a ramp that would be fitted to provide wheel chair and push-chair access into the town hall, new facilities for parents visiting the building with babies, and improved security. Inside the foyer visitors would find a proper seating area, an information kiosk, and the new decor that had prompted the *Hackney Gazette* to announce the coming of a new 'civic pleasure palace'. There would be 'curved glass walls' and soft lighting, but what really incensed people was the proposed marbling of the foyer: a new marble floor, marble plant pots and even a marble fountain. A Tory councillor had initiated the reaction by declaring that to propose such a scheme 'at a time when the council is failing to carry out repairs because it is strapped for cash' was 'an insult to council tenants'.[11] When Councillor Tommy Sheppard, Chair of the Corporate Services Committee, replied to the criticisms, he did so in tones that anyone but the most ideologically impaired think-tanker would recognize were no longer those of a bulldozing local government Commissar. Starting out in the old-fashioned style, he declared that 'the Town Hall belongs to the people of Hackney and we take our responsibilities seriously. We are not prepared to let the building go to rack and ruin'.[12] But he quickly went into retreat, insisting that 'some money will have to be spent to provide a Town Hall which Hackney people can be proud of and which meets modern standards of accessibility and security', and then backing off altogether on the marble which, as he reassured readers of the *Hackney Gazette*, would only be fitted if 'outside sponsors' could be found.

This fleeting vision of the foyer turned into a down market version of Donald Trump's retail atrium, was not the only indication that, by 1990, Excellence had finally arrived at Hackney Town Hall. Response had been sluggish in April 1984 when *In Search of Excellence* was first published in Britain: indeed, on their promotional visit, the authors cited the initial reception of their book as further proof of the complacency and incompetence of British management. It wasn't long, however, before Excellence became a popular creed even in this backward country. Martin Wiener had already put Raymond Williams's expanded definition of culture onto the business school agenda with his book on English culture and its responsibility for the decline of the Industrial Spirit, but the coming of Excellence changed the emphasis again.[13] Far from just being the problem, culture was now the solution: indeed, for a while, management consultants couldn't stop talking about it as the force that inspired and sustained the 'turned on' workforce. Many of the leading American books found an eager readership here and a native series of copycat publications was quick to emerge under titles like *The Winning Streak* or *The Roots of Excellence*. Indeed, as we watched John Harvey Jones go through his motions as the BBC's first management consultant hero ('The Troubleshooter'), and studied once again the gleaming post-fluoridation smile of Richard Branson, we may well have wondered to what extent the British businessman really still has to struggle against the vast condescension of posterity in order to make his way in from the margins of cultured society. Excellence gave its name to a conventional lifestyle magazine *(Excel)*, but it was also adopted by *Marxism Today*, albeit under the quaintly customized name of 'post-fordism'. In those formerly Communist circles as elsewhere, the cult of 'change' was replacing older conceptions of history and Tom Peters's 'Management Revolution', which came complete with 'Prescriptions for a World Turned Upside Down', is easily fitted into the accommodating mould of what that magazine now calls 'New Times'.

Throughout the British public sector the idea of Excellence was soon standing in for the customary but increasingly unsustainable view that common standards should be maintained across a whole range of institutional provision: as the generalised standard disintegrated, the exceptionalist 'Centre of Excellence' was borne. In the universities and polytechnics the message was clear: if you want to escape the knife, get designated 'excellent' by any means possible. And since, under the new criteria, 'excellence' often came down to nothing more than financial expediency, it is not surprising that new rites of self-designation and cargo-cult behaviour should have emerged within the anthropology of academic life. Rather than waiting to be encouraged by external assessors, the smart department was quick to develop courses with some connection to 'management' and the prosperct of 'self-financing' students and research. It would then issue a glossy brochure with the word 'excellence' printed in large letters all over it and hope for the best. All this was more grist to the mill of Malcolm Bradbury, the prospering campus novelist who, having laid the universities open to attack with *The History Man*, now tried vainly to redeem himself with a series of ostentatiously clever puns on the word 'cuts'; but there were other defenders of public education who saw the universities being gutted and attempted to work out a more adequate line of defence. The late Raymond Williams pointed to 'the irony of a rhetoric of "centres of excellence" ' – which he mistook for 'an evidently "traditionalist" concept' – being 'deployed in the "modernizing" interest of new forms of external assessment and contract', remarking that 'if there are indeed "centres of excellence" it might be supposed that those in such centres, who have presumably excelled, would be better judges of what is needed than the ministers, officials and laymen who are, by their own kind of definition, outside them. Yet that difficulty, which might make serious people hesitate, is at once bypassed in grotesque images of the academic "ivory tower" (the other face of a centre of excellence) which requires immediate reconstruction by those who live (with or without excellence) in "the real world".'[14] Raymond Williams was not widely read in what management thinkers call 'the literature', but he knew that the 'real world' had become 'code for short-term money' and it seems unlikely that he would have been much cheered to discover either that the managerial definition of 'excellence' was founded on an idea of culture not entirely dissimilar to his own, or that both Tom Peters and Dr Charles Garfield have indicated that an education in the Humanities or Liberal Arts may form a more appropriate background for the leading managers of the future (who will, it is said, need to be flexible and creative thinkers able to operate over and above immense technological resources) than the business schools with their rigid and over-valued MBAs.

However, it is in local government that Excellence has found its most unexpected application. In November 1984, the Local Government Training Board held a seminar for an invited group of chief executives and chief officers to consider the possible applications of *In Search of Excellence* to British local authorities. The event was opened by Royston Greenwood and John Stewart of the University of Birmingham's Institute of Local Government Studies, who presented a paper predicting that *In Search of Excellence*, despite its focus on '*private* corporations, and *American* ones at that', would soon be the most talked about management book in the world of local government.[15] Greenwood and Stewart chided the Audit Commission which, in keen pursuit of its adopted three E's (Economy, Efficiency and Effectiveness), was already seeking to apply the idea of Excellence to British local government without any adjustment beyond the substitution of the word 'Vision' where Peters and Waterman stressed 'Shared Values'.[16] If Excellence was to be useful, it would need to be properly converted into 'the local government context', and it was with this in mind that the meeting focused on each of the 'eight basic attributes' of Excellence in turn. There were some linguistic differences – nobody in the conventional world of local government was immediately likely to embrace words like 'niche-manship' or 'chunking' (the process of creating temporary and inter-disciplinary task forces to solve problems). While it was conceded that existing local government structures did not generally reveal a 'Bias for Action', people felt that any attempt to move in that direction 'would involve a major challenge to established patterns of thinking'. 'Autonomy and Entrepreneurship' demanded flexibility of a kind that didn't come naturally in a divisionalised and unionised environment. 'Productivity through People' sounded all very well in principle, but it would be hard to achieve in the prevailing atmosphere of demoralisation and retrenchment. As for being 'Hands-On Value-Driven', it was in the nature of local government to define values in political and adversarial terms, and this would surely militate against any attempt to build shared values which could genuinely be held in common. It was also pointed out that the committee structure in local authorities had a decidedly centralising effect on their entire organisation and seemed to leave little hope for either 'Simple Form, Lean Staff' or 'Simultaneous Loose-Tight Properties'.

Such were the reservations but, as the report of the meeting records, 'we all finished the discussion recognising that there was more in the book for UK local government than might seem at first glance'. The work of translation was duly begun. While some brave voices on the left had started to argue that the local government system 'taken as a whole *is* chronically inefficient',[17] John Stewart went on from that seminar to draw the basic attributes of Excellence into the package that he would soon be offering as a 'new' management of local government tailored not to the old world of ever-expanding services (1952–75: RIP) but to a new climate of 'resource constraint'.[18] By the time he had finished with it, the maxim 'Close to the Customer', had nothing at all to do with hucksterism and sales magic. Instead it meant ensuring the quality of services and revaluing not just the user of those services but also the staff – stuck at the bottom of bureaucratic pyramids – who work at the point of contact with the public. 'Bias for action' also lost its swagger, functioning instead as a critique of the organisational culture which has made so many local authorities chronically unresponsive to the changing patterns of local politics and need. Flexibility and entrepreneurialism came to include the idea that 'disorganisation' might be positively useful, breaking through those ossified functional divisions and fostering productive kinds of 'unlearning' between them. Far from being poisoned at the American well of Excellence Stewart came back with a conception of management as the galvanising and critical process which sets out to overcome what he called, with a lugubriousness that everyone in Hackney knows to be fully justified, 'the countervailing tendencies of the bureaucratic mode'.

In the course of itemising the problems local authorities have with being 'Close to the Customer', John Stewart remarks that more often than not 'the entrance to a town hall, built to celebrate the pride of the Victorian entrepreneur, is not inviting at all.'[19] Hackney Town Hall dates from the 1930s, but it still finds ways of being uninviting. The citizen-customer must ascend two gaunt flights of steps, without the assistance of so much as a hand-rail, and then, after teetering like a nervous actor on the exposed stage above, proceed through a doorway flanked by numerous notices announcing committee meetings and identifying the services which both are and are not available at this entrance. On busy days there can be quite a crush up there – with some people hawking the *Socialist Worker* or *Militant*, and others trying to organise a family photograph to mark the occasion of a birth or wedding. The principles of mutual aid apply at all times: able bodied climbers embarking on the ascent must expect to assist others who are frail or encumbered with pushchairs and young children. For Sir Alfred Sherman the entrance to Hackney Town Hall is the Marxist Hell-mouth through while the entire borough of his childhood has disappeared. In reality, however, the building doesn't live up to this lurid vision. The foyer is drab rather than infernal. There is serious pressure on the space, and the old marble floor is worn and cracked. There is no need for marble fountains, sponsored or not, but the Corporate Services Committee is right to insist that it could do with both reorganisation and a facelift.

No one who lives locally could step into Hackney Town Hall, without already knowing that the council is in a shocking state of crisis. There is a profusion of conventional indicators – the constant flood of complaints received by the local government ombudsman, the unfillable posts, the rate of staff absenteeism which stands at three times the national average – but residents are also familiar with a whole range of more baroque manifestations which only need the briefest reprise. Not content with periodically misplacing large sums of money in the internal accounts, the Finance Department has recently proved itself incapable even of issuing pay cheques to the council's own employees. As for the Housing Department, this has been in unbelievable disarray. Its offices are jammed with furious, desperate and not infrequently violent customers and demoralised staff, who can offer no relief but have learned all sorts of ways of hiding behind bureaucratic imcompetence. Chronically underfunded, the department still manages to lose large amounts of its inadequate government allocation because it can't manage to spend it, even on chronically necessary repairs, in the stipulated period. The problems of homelessness are so acute that ordinary transfers have almost entirely ceased, and tenants on the disintegrating housing estates are learning to pursue their grievances against the council through the courts. In a recent case, Phyllis Lowbridge of the Holly Street Estate, was awarded £4,000 compensation under the Public Health Act. She had complained repeatedly about the cockroaches infesting her flat (the place was 'running alive' with them) but nothing had been done: the county court ordered the council to embark on a programme designed to rid the entire Holly Street estate of infestation, and it was with some glee that the *Hackney Gazette* pointed out that the Director of Housing, Bernard Crofton, could face imprisonment if he broke the injunction binding him to this action.[20]

Meanwhile, the consultants who have looked into various aspects of the council's internal management pile up one unbelieving report on top of another. The lawyer, Andrew Arden, was brought in to investigate freemasonry and its possible corruption of the council organisation, but he didn't need proof of exotic conspiracies to come up with a detailed inventory of extraordinary organisational follies. As for the London Business School students who visited the council over a week in March 1988, they were quite swept off their feet by what they found. Their reports comment on the lack of financial indicators, the pervasive indifference to 'customers' and the evident need for a total 'culture change', but they were most appalled by the apparently total disregard shown by individual Directors for 'the

process of corporate management'. They attended a senior management meeting and could hardly believe the masquerade that was
played out before their innocent eyes:

> At the meeting we attended, out of seventeen or so members of the
> team present, only three remained for the duration of the meeting.
> We viewed the coming and going of team members, plus their lack
> of response to issues, as contempt for the whole process of
> management top down. Individual members of the team were seen
> to be reading their own correspondence, drafting reports and
> memoranda, checking reports, missing documentation for agenda
> items, while decisions were attempting to be made. The whole
> meeting can be summed up by the attitude to previous minutes
> (two meetings behind) and the start of the meeting (at the
> appointed time no executive member had arrived and the meeting
> started fifteen minutes late with several Directors missing.[21]

I met John McCafferty, leader of the council, to ask him what he
was doing to get a grip on this chaotic situation. We sat in his panelled
office and he took me back to the mid-Eighties when Hackney and
other Labour councils had confronted the government over rate-
capping and, as McCafferty remembers well, been roundly defeated.
At this point some left-wing members of the Labour group left, saying
that from now on local politics would be about nothing but drains and
that there was no longer any point in being a councillor; but
McCafferty counts himself among those who recognised, not just that
drains could be political, but that the time had come for a return to
basic questions of service delivery. He describes this as the watershed
that put an end to the era of gestural politics in which radical
councillors had been content to plaster right-on slogans and un-
achievable resolutions all over the failing council machine. During
McCafferty's period as leader the red banners bearing the (often
inaccurate) unemployment figures have been taken off the municipal
buildings, and although no one has yet uprooted the nuclear free zone
signs, they too have come to be seen as a bit of an embarrassment.
New Times have broken out in the Town Hall, and questions of
management are to the fore.
    While McCafferty has no respect for the Conservative government
that was prepared to use money gathered through the poll tax in
Hackney to subsidise the model Tory borough of Wandsworth so that
it could set a tiny poll tax rate for its own residents, he knows better
than to blame all the council's ills on hostile Tory legislation. As he
says on the subject of Hackney's stricken housing estates, 'capital
investment won't solve those difficulties on its own: there are
organisational and social problems too'. Meanwhile, the government
is obliging councils to introduce Compulsory Competitive Tendering
across a wide range of services according to a phased timetable

extending from 1989–92: a development which is turning out to be an intriguingly mixed curse.

I had heard from elsewhere in the council that one of the advantages of Compulsory Competitive Tendering lies in the fact that it obliges the council to 'specify the services which are of critical importance'. McCafferty agrees. Rather than passing vainglorious resolutions, the councillors now have to make real policy decisions. The drawing up of specifications for tender may demand new skills, but it is something that McCafferty takes very seriously: as he says, a bad specification would let private contractors run all over you. To begin with Compulsory Competitive Tendering may have led councillors to become involved in internal management decisions, but McCafferty hopes they will soon be able to draw back. As the new 'strategic' approach to management starts to work, politicians should be able to stop sabotaging the organisation from above by bombarding officers with endless requests for reports on all aspects of the council's activities, and get on with the job of defining policy.

Compulsory Competitive Tendering is also changing the council's relationship with its trade unions. It wasn't long ago that management consultants who had worked with Hackney Councils could only write pleading articles in *New Socialist*, suggesting that the time had surely come for socialists to 'do some serious thinking about the white-collar public service union, Nalgo' which has become a 'key contributor' to the 'dynamic conservatism' of local government.[22] But Compulsory Competitive Tendering seems to be doing the impossible. Defensive of its Direct Labour Organisations, Hackney Council made a political decision to have an internal tender wherever possible, but the tender has to be in at a certain time, and it has to be competitive. McCafferty hesitates, in time-honoured local government fashion, over the question of what is on and off the record, but there can be little doubt that Hackney has benefitted from the realism that Compulsory Competitive Tendering has introduced into the council's industrial relations. If fluoridation and tower blocks were among the council's 'technological shortcuts' to progress in the Sixties, those for the Nineties are internal management devices, and Compulsory Competitive Tendering is apparently prominent among them.

McCafferty has certainly risen to what consultants, including John Stewart who has been engaged by the council, describe as the management challenge. He describes how he took on the Trotskyist left of his party, facing them down with quotations from Lenin which proved that the great leader himself had recognized the importance of getting your aims clear, defining the processes by which you will achieve them, setting priorities and monitoring the results. McCafferty says the key phrase in Hackney Council these days is 'redirecting resources'. Internal research functions have been strengthened and set to work clarifying options in this area.

McCafferty accepts that 'You must live within your means', but he is firmly of the view that you should also 'try to maximise your means'. A new clause has been added to council reports, designed to show what additional income might follow from a recommended course of action. Under his leadership, the council is committed to trying to sell its skills to other authorities and also to local businesses. Indeed, the council is apparently coming up with a plan to retrain every manager in Hackney – a service which will even be offered to already 'Excellent' companies like Marks and Spencer.

McCafferty's ambitions for the revival of Hackney Council are shared by Jerry White, his recently appointed Chief Executive. As a self-taught social historian – he is an editor of *History Workshop Journal* and the author of two highly regarded historical studies concerned with the London poor – White draws his inspiration from a broader range of sources than is available to most people in his position.[23] He must be the only local authority chief executive who quotes from *Our Mutual Friend* to illuminate London's litter problem. In Dickens's novel London's dirtiness was a source of pride: indeed, as he points out, Paris was said to be cleaner only because the French were so poor that they couldn't afford the luxury of throwing anything away. Knowing this, Jerry White finds a certain irony in the fact that, for a while at least, it looked as if French companies would be bidding for street cleansing tenders in British cities. While he continues to study the works of earlier municipal socialists like Herbert Morrison and George Lansbury, White has also drawn on more recent ideas as he sets out to bring about a 'revival of public service' in the ailing council machine, and to inspire his managers and, through them, his 15,000 strong workforce to the achievement of 'Excellence under constrained resources'. Determined to free the council and its workers from the siege mentality that comes with fighting off endless short-term crises, he has embarked on a strategic planning exercise designed to refocus the entire organisation around a common set of priorities and a shared commitment to quality and 'customer care'. He has prepared a 'statement of values', recently adopted by the Council under the overall maxim of 'Public Service – Quality with Equality', and called for each divisional management team to draw up an action plan to ensure that this message is fully communicated throughout the organisation. In internal reports and bulletins designed to inform the workforce about the challenge of 'Strategic Management in a Cold Climate', White has expressed the hope that the 'statement of values', once accepted throughout the organisation, will prove to be 'a major contribution to the process of cultural change in Hackney', moving the organisation 'further down the path already mapped out by cash limiting, service planning and improved managerial practice and accountability over recent years'. He has countered the suggestion that strategic management is just a luxury in the seething chaos that is Hackney – 'like responding to an earthquake by designing a hospital'

– insisting, rather, that it is an absolute necessity. He has also identified a number of obstacles, remarking that 'cynicism and low morale in some (but not all parts) of the organisation contribute to a culture which is resistant to a revived public service commitment', and suggesting that there are particular dangers at the third tier of the management structure, for 'if managers at this level believe that Hackney will never change for the better then the core values message and the commitment it seeks will both be undermined'.

This attempt to revive a Lansbury-like spirit of public service by means of management and planning is ambitious, but it has also been carefully worked out. A number of 'Strategy Implementation Groups' have been set up to co-ordinate work on 'key areas of interest to the council'. Special 'Service Days' are being held to provide council workers with an opportunity to meet with senior management and recommend ways of improving the quality of council services: as the chief executive has specified, 'Invitations should make it clear that the sessions are for workers to have their say. All points raised should be recorded (preferably on a flip chart) and management should make a commitment to provide feedback to workers on points raised'. Training is recognised as 'absolutely vital' if managers at all levels are to fulfil 'their key role of making change happen in practice' – as is the fact that Hackney has previously been 'very slow to invest in management development'. Jerry White was not unduly peturbed by the scepticism of the first internal responses to his plans: what, after all, would anyone expect? The unions declared that 'some injustices in the workplace' needed to be sorted out before their members could give any commitment to the statement of values, but their demands seemed reasonable enough. Far from insisting on more money, they were content, for the time being at least, to stipulate that the council should start paying its employees on time.

Leaving the Town Hall, I walked a few hundred yards down Mare Street, past the beleagured Housing Department to the office of the Corporate Standards Unit. Housed in a dismal cave opposite a Bingo hall, this unit was set up to produce policies that would enable the council to fulfil its legal obligation to submit services to competitive tender while also, in the words of the unit's head, giving 'in-house contractors the best possible chance of success in competition'. The Corporate Standards Unit works with 'chunks of the front line', preparing bids and suchlike, but it also has a more general function within the Chief Executive's department as an internal consultant on the broader organisational developments that will need to follow from Compulsory Competitive Tendering.

It was here that I met Geoff Sheridan, a corporate standards officer who was once a prominent member of the International Marxist Group. In the Seventies, when it was still acceptable for a man to do such a thing, he wrote regularly on *The Guardian* Women's page; indeed, it was as secretary of the *Guardian* freelance group that he negotiated the first minimum terms agreement with that newspaper. He ran *Socialist Challenge* together with Tariq Ali, later becoming business manager of the Labour Party's now defunct 'theoretical journal' *New Socialist*.

Geoff Sheridan has not put every aspect of his Trotskyist past behind him. During the course of our discussions he urged me to remember that nationalisation had by no means always been an essential policy of the revolutionary left. It wasn't part of the Bolshevik programme at the time of the Russian Revolution; indeed, he went so far as to suggest that nationalisation only took the form it did under Lenin because factory owners and their senior managers kept running away. Yet despite such residues as this, Sheridan has certainly adjusted himself to new times; indeed, he has recently completed an MBA. As he remarks, 'going through that did pose a number of questions for me', but while fellow students may have found him rather impolite to those visiting speakers from the business world who he judged to be too 'carried away with Excellence', Sheridan has no regrets about having made the transition from mere 'comment to action' in this unexpected and rather less than revolutionary fashion. Indeed, he doesn't feel remotely apologetic about his new interest in financial management, business planning and organisational culture: after all, 'managing change' is what working for Hackney Council is all about.

As a corporate standards officer, Sheridan is a master of the new language that Compulsory Competitive Tendering has brought into local government. To begin with, he explains, there is the 'client' – ie the part of the organisation that puts services out to contract. Then there are the Direct Service Organisations (DSOs) which, as former Direct Labour Organisations (DLOs), must now gain contracts on an individual basis in competition with such private companies as may chose to tender. The recent changes mean that there are now two different and, as Sheridan suggests, increasingly conflicting cultures in the council: one is to be found in parts of the organisation that are subject to competition while the other is confined to those that are not. The managers of the Direct Service Organisations work under intense pressure. They have to win their contracts, and job security, for them as well as their staff, only extends to the length of the contract. Clients and councillors are constantly on their backs. The Department of the Environment has the power to terminate a contract if any irregularities are found in the way it was awarded or in the event of unsatisfactory service. As Geoff Sheridan explains, the DSOs also have to work on a different accounting basis than those parts of the council apparatus, generally described as the Support Services, that are not exposed to this competition and scrutiny: they work on a profit and loss trading account and are required to make an annual financial report which obliges them to break even. The Support Services, meanwhile, operate through traditional local authority budgeting:

they make an internal bid for a certain amount each year, and in the event of any overspend they can either press for a higher allocation or simply reduce the services they are providing. These options are not available to the DSOs which, in the case of any overspend, are likely to find themselves in dire straits as the end of the financial year approaches – broke, under investigation by the Department of the Environment, and unable to save money by cutting down on services which they are contractually bound to provide.

Having assessed these 'two cultures' carefully, Sheridan is concerned to alleviate the difficulties of the DSOs – especially in their relationship with the Support Services, such as Personnel, on which they still depend. He suggests that a new system of time recording should be introduced into the Support Services so that it becomes possible to charge the DSOs for services received on a real rather than abstractly apportioned basis, a change that would bring questions of quality to the fore for the first time. While there should be a formal procedure for complaints, it would probably be inappropriate to subject Support Services to financial penalties if they let the DSOs down. Nevertheless, the Corporate Standards Unit was investigating internal pricing mechanisms through which some Support Services could themselves be put on full operating accounts, like the trading accounts on which the DSOs are already working, so that they would only be paid for services that were 'actually demanded and delivered'.

Sheridan is all for efficiency, but when we met in the dingy corridor to which the Corporate Standards Unit banishes its smokers, he was wary of treating Compulsory Competitive Tendering as a technological short cut to organisational change: he didn't like the idea of 'using a mechanism to force through changes that should really be brought about through management'. Far better, as he put it, to work on the assumption that 'when it comes down to it, most people would prefer to do a good job than not'. We also discussed the potential dangers of introducing a system of performance appraisal for council staff: while it was important to ensure that there was 'an incentive to do better and a price for doing badly', Sheridan remained against the idea of performance-related pay. Similarly, while there was a lot to be said for increasing flexibility on promotions, it should be remembered that the present rules, which demand that all posts are filled through the formal interview and selection procedure, were designed to eliminate bias and to safeguard equal opportunities. Throughout this conversation too, the idea of Excellence kept flickering in the background. It was there when Sheridan remarked that it was far better to have some sections of the organisation feeling right about their activity than to have an equality of gloom and demoralisation across the entire organisation. It was there when he pointed out that absenteeism is lower in DSOs and, moreover, that persistent absentees are actually visited at home by their managers. It flared up again as he described the difficulties of bringing about 'Change in an era of cuts', but insisted, nevertheless, that a concern for quality assurance (already demanded under Compulsory Competitive Tendering) should be fostered throughout the organisation. As he says, 'Quality assurance – I could go into it if you want. The key question for this borough is how do you get quality without money?' Paris is clean, he suggests, not because people can't afford to throw anything away, but because expenditure on street cleansing per head of population is much greater than it is in London.

Is all this just more frantic rhetoric pasted over the boarded up shop-fronts of a dying borough? In the latter half of 1990, Dalston Lane started to look a little cleaner. I had suspected as much for a few months when some friends from Slovakia came over for a visit shortly before Christmas and confirmed my suspicions. In recent years Dalston has become fabled in Bratislava as the place to go if you want proof that there were some things that even the most corrupt Communist authorities did better than their counterparts in the west. But my last Slovak visitors came through the door crestfallen and full of disappointed questions: 'Where's the litter?' they asked. 'What is Dalston without the rubbish?'

The street cleansing contract came into operation on 1 August 1989: it was the first tender to go out under Compuslory Competitive Tendering but, as it happened, those French companies kept their distance and there were no bids other than that of the Direct Service Organisation. Meanwhile the council has declared street cleaning a 'top political priority' for the borough, and Dalston has been targeted as a notoriously bad area. A relentless war is being waged against the shop-keepers who have got used to simply dumping their rubbish out on the street on the supposition that a few more tons will hardly make any difference. The dustcarts no longer sail through the borough like pirate ships with their crews hanging off the rigging, gesturing rudely at selected passersby and offering all sorts of unofficially privatised services on the side. A new technological short-cut is also in use. The manager of the DSO may dream of an even more miraculous machine that can deal with the ultimately challenging debris of the market in Ridley Road – crushing, chewing up or vapourising those mountains of discarded boxes, but the council has already acquired eight Mark IV 'Applied Sweepers' from the manufacturers in Scotland: great green machines that can traverse the jagged pavements of Dalston Lane, spraying, sweeping and sucking as they go. There are plans to stable at least one of these monsters permanently in Dalston.

This recent improvement is only partly to the credit of Compulsory Competitive Tendering. Indeed, the council had broken the militant corruption of the worst depots before the government came up with this scheme (the battle for equal opportunities as it was fought over years in the Millfield Depot was especially heroic). The Corporate Standards Unit can also claim some of the honours. Geoff Sheridan was among the troubleshooters when, at the end of the first year, the DSO's performance was found to have fallen below the required minimum standard: the Department of the Environment was investigating and it seemed likely that the council would be forced to put the contract out to tender again, but the Corporate Standards Unit saved the day by proving that the initial specification had underestimated the length of roads in the borough by 25 per cent. A year or so previously, when the initial contract was being prepared, it had fallen to Geoff Sheridan to come up with a 'Competitive Tonnage Rate' – a figure which could not be derived unless it was established how much a loader could reasonably be expected to lift in the course of a normal working day. The variables had to be assessed carefully. They included the distance between the dustbins and the tip; whether collection is from the back or the front; whether it is from flats or door to door along a terraced street; whether the rubbish is in bags or bins . . . . After considering these factors and making the necessary allowances, the figure Geoff Sheridan recommended as appropriate for Hackney was 4.5 tons of rubbish per day. Excellent or not, that was certainly a good start.

17
Refounding the City
with Prince Charles

In our time it is a lucky city, especially in Britain, that does not have its heart torn out and thrown away. But it is *our* time. We can see reason again if we really want to . . .
Prince Charles, A Vision of Britain, October 1988.

Prince Charles may never have travelled along Dalston Lane but he became known, during the Eighties, for his fleeting visits to east London. One fabled day in March 1986, he boarded a battered orange minibus hired from a left-wing community group in Tower Hamlets, and journeyed through the city in a company that included geographer, Alice Coleman, architects, John Thompson and Richard McCormac, and Nicholas Falk, the urban planner and environmentalist who had organised the expedition. The party visited the notorious Aylesbury Estate in Southwark and then zig-zagged up through east London into Hackney, where the prince alighted, boarded a more reputable-looking official car, and drove round the corner for the opening of Lea View House in Hackney, a pre-war housing estate which had been refurbished by Hackney Council's Direct Labour Organisation, according to a model scheme of 'community architecture' devised by Hunt Thompson Associates.[1] In July 1987 Business in the Community conducted the Prince, together with a clutch of business leaders, on an equally fabled tour of Spitalfields, where he inspected the conditions under which many Bangladeshis live and work, urging big business to show that it 'has a heart', and insisting, somewhat after the manner of Thomas Fowell Buxton, that there was 'a great deal' the magnates of the City could do to help with 'the problems that actually exist on their doorstep'.

On 6th June 1990, Charles returned to Hackney to open the Mother's Square, a much praised development designed, once again, by Hunt Thompson Associates for the City and Hackney Health Authority, Newlon Housing Trust, and Access Homes Housing Association combined. As a pioneering experiment in 'balanced community housing', the Mother's Square scheme includes shared equity flats for first-time buyers, family housing, warden-assisted accommodation for the elderly, a nursing home, and a psycho-geriatric day hospital. There was some doubt as to whether Mother's

Square represents a new London square in the tradition of Nash, or whether it is actually just an ornamented cul-de-sac, built on a backland site behind a number of listed Georgian buildings and unified by a classical facade that avoids differentiating between residential and institutional accommodation.[2] The neo-Georgian style of the development certainly made its mark. The architects were reported to have no time for 'replica Georgian buildings' but they nevertheless claimed, rather grandly, to have 'gone back to Palladio's original designs'.[3] The Mother's Square features a ground floor colonnade, diminutive due to modern storey heights but complete with precast concrete pillars, and a portico with Ionic columns. On the first floor each house has the advantages of a genuine *piano nobile*, and the pitched roof is covered with natural Welsh slate. At the seminar on 'Health in the Community', which preceded the opening, Lady Wagner, author of the Wagner Report on community care, hailed the scheme as a 'shining example' that 'shows what can be done to make "Care in the Community" live up to its promise', adding that 'to find that it has been put into practice in a Georgian context is bliss indeed'. Lord Scarman described how, when he had arrived at the Mother's Square earlier that day, he had been 'overcome by the sheer beauty of the place': so impressed had he been that 'a quotation came back to me in flashback to my boyhood, the first lines of Coleridge's 'Kubla Khan': "in Xanadu did Kubla Khan a stately pleasure dome decree" '. This 'visionary poem' may indeed have been written under the influence of opium, but for Lord Scarman it embodied 'the same love of all mankind that I have found today in the Mother's Square'. Himself susceptible to visions, Prince Charles was also moved to generous praise. He had, so he announced, been following the progress of the scheme with interest over the last few years, and now that he had seen it he was 'enormously impressed, particularly by the work of the architects who have managed to create something with a strong sense of both intimacy and community'. Having talked with 'all the different types of people who actually live here', Charles was especially gratified to find that 'both the facilities and the level of care that they were looking for' had been provided in this model of 'an integrated community'. It all went to show 'how much can be achieved, even within a strict budget, when people work effectively together'. The prince closed by offering his 'warmest and heartiest congratulations' all round. As the *Hackney Gazette* reported, he even found time to commend an eleven year old resident for her 'Sod the Poll Tax' T-shirt.[4]

These forays into east London were carried out partly in a spirit of research, and they certainly helped to shape Prince Charles's increasingly pronounced views on the subject of architecture and urban planning. Nevertheless, by October 1988, Charles's concern with the inner city had been drawn up into a full-scale 'Vision of Britain' and projected far out into the green fields of England that lay at its heart. The search for 'urban villages' in the inner city would continue but, thanks to this visionary transposition, Prince Charles's own most ambitious experiment with urban form would be found not in Hackney or Whitechapel, but down in Dorchester where, at the end of that famous television programme, our future monarch had committed the Duchy of Cornwall to re-establishing the true architecture of urban life under the guidance of master planner, Leon Krier.

While this remarkable transposition took place, the country resounded with clamorous argument on the subject of Prince Charles's views on architecture. As the newspapers set out to trace the identity of Charles's architectural advisers, they lifted the curtain on a conventional court comedy full of stock devices: the jostling for preferment, the self-important silence with which favoured courtiers guarded the confidentiality of their monarch, the speed with which they dropped opinions held so passionately before their elevation, the expulsions that followed indiscretion (Farewell, Rod Hackney!). A battle of the ghost-writers raged, for neither the Prince nor the eminent modernist architects who rose up (often with courts of their own) to defend themselves against his charges, were willing to follow the example of those impeccable US business heroes who identify and acknowledge their co-authors. Some commentators raised serious questions about the consequences of Prince Charles's onslaught, pointing to the subversion of the planning process, and to the cowering, merely camouflaged architecture that threatens to be the real outcome of his interference. But in this broader discussion, too, there were stock rhetorical devices. Those in favour of the prince suffered from a terrible tendency to fawn unctuously, but few of his opponents could speak without at some point resorting to the sneering insolence of a triumphant *petit-bourgeoisie* that no longer has to bow and scrape in deference.

This 'Great Debate' was brought to its modest peak at the Victoria and Albert Museum on 2 November 1989, when an 'official' debate was held to coincide with an exhibition of the Prince's 'Vision of Britain'. On one side of the table sat the somewhat unlikely pair of Leon Krier and the television personality Lady Lucinda Lambton; on the other were their opponents, Martin Pawley and Professor Colin St John Wilson. Lucinda Lambton was in no doubt that Charles was a really splendid fellow who had 'given England a voice'. Professor Colin St John Wilson presented a most unfortunate persona. Indeed, he could hardly have done better had he deliberately set out to confirm public suspicions about the glutted arrogance of his profession. He described, rather unconvincingly, how unpleasant it was to come under attack from the prince – Wilson's new British Library had been described as more like an academy of the 'secret police' than a proper library – and then waved a yellowed press cutting in the air to prove that he himself had said it all before. If the upstart prince would only read this article, which Professor Wilson himself had written for *The Observer* in 1950, he would discover that he was not the first person to have advocated 'community consultation'. After throwing a few insults in the direction of Leon Krier, said to be smiling like 'the cat that's got the cream', Professor Wilson leaned back with a look of blustery indifference and made a big display of scrutinising a West German newspaper while Krier talked, and Wilson's supporters in the crowd sniggered in suspicious, if not openly orchestrated, unison.

A more sustained counter-attack was launched by Martin Pawley, who has certainly come a long way since we last encountered him along the edges of the Holly Street Estate in the early Seventies, blithely writing off the entire history of public housing as a 'failure' and heading for that conference in Central America where he would outrage the comrades from East Europe by suggesting that progressive regimes in the developing world should think about building low-cost houses out of recycled garbage. Indeed, while Prince Charles was preparing his assault on an architectural profession that, as he saw it, had broken with the human scale, Pawley had been turning himself into an arm-waving modernist of a distinctly old-fashioned sort. He had started to talk about building 'units' rather than 'homes', insisting that homelessness was 'a matter of production' and prophesying that 'Sooner or later an election will be won by a party that offers a massive housing programme again'.[5] Not content with the aspirations of the Sixties, when politicians triggered the high-rise boom by promising 300,000 or, if they were especially rash, half-a-million new homes a year, Pawley now wanted to see a housing programme that used 'advanced technology and modern methods' to produce one million houses a year.

In his earlier responses to Prince Charles, Pawley had been content to liken himself and the architects with whom he identifies to farmers faced with ignorant town-dwellers who have the affrontery to hold views about the countryside: architects too have their 'Constable syndrome',[6] as he wrote with undisguised contempt for non-professional public taste. By the time of the 'official debate' at the Victoria and Albert Museum, Pawley had reason to be feeling more than usually dyspeptic. Indeed, he had just been sacked as architecture correspondent of *The Guardian* for venturing the view that he was now about to express again. These circumstances had evidently exacerbated his already-pronounced weakness for pressing superficial likenesses way beyond the point of folly, and he wasted no time describing Prince Charles as another Hitler. 'In all modern history', as Pawley asserted in a remarkably stupid utterance which did not confine its abuse to the Prince of Wales, 'only one event has ever elicited a more favourable public response than the first showing of "A Vision of Britain", and that was Hitler's annexation of Austria'.[7] Prince Charles's supporters may see his 'totalitarianism' as benevolent, but to Pawley this royal interference in architectural affairs was akin to 'the brutal suppression of modern architecture' that took place in Hitler's Germany: indeed, Charles's espousal of traditional forms of architecture threatened to place him on the same level as Pol Pot, who had also tried to turn back the clock on the modern city. As for the oneliners with which Prince Charles condemned modern buildings – 'a glass stump', 'a Victorian prison', 'a hardened missile silo' – these were no different from the insults with which Hitler's hacks had set out to destroy the reputation of earlier modernists, calling their buildings 'cages for apes' and 'stalls for animals that cause physical and mental illness', or insisting that 'Flat roofs equal flat heads'. After requoting some of these fascist epithets from his own earlier books, Pawley insisted that Prince Charles's 'Ten Principles' – maxim-like prescriptions not unlike the flipchart axioms of a latter-day management thinker – were 'no different' from the 'principles for the guidance of men' that had been adopted by the professional and craft institutions under Hitler, and equated the prince's 'extolling of self-help community enterprise' with the Nazi call for 'democracy directed from the bottom up'.

Perhaps Pawley was trying to upstage Maxwell Hutchinson, then President of the Royal Institute of British Architects, who in a not-untypically fatuous moment had used Charles's professed intention of 'throwing a proverbial royal brick through the inviting plate glass of pompous professional pride' to suggest that the prince should really be numbered among the inner-city rioters of Brixton, Tottenham, and Toxteth.[8] His exaggerated outburst certainly had a dramatic effect: it was embraced by the tabloids as final proof that the architectural establishment lacked any proper sense of proportion, and also by Colin St John Wilson, who supported it vigorously and stood up in front of the television cameras the next day to warn Prince Charles about the company he would end up in if he persisted in trying to turn the clock back. Perhaps someone warned him that Pawley's stunt was backfiring, for a few hours later he was back to temporize and modify his words, and to say that Prince Charles probably wasn't another Hitler after all. Doubtless, the nation was glad to have the Professor's reassurance on this matter. Such was the 'official debate', but while it tells us a lot about the decadent state of modernist culture in Britain in the Eighties, it does nothing to explain the curious route that takes us from the shattered environs of Dalston Lane to the promised recovery of the human scale City of Man along the western boundary of Dorchester. We must conduct an investigation of our own.

The Famous Eccentricities of a Prince

Despite the insinuations of Norman Tebbit, there can be no doubt that Prince Charles is a man with a definite job of work to do. As a holder of royal office his task is to animate the symbolism of a political power that can no longer be openly exercised. The frustrations of this position are all too easily imagined and at unguarded moments, Prince Charles has himself spoken out about them. Describing his unease with royal protocol he has insisted that he must have a more serious role in the nation's life than the symbolic one of 'cutting ribbons'.

In his search for an active role the prince has at times appeared rather eccentric. The popular Press has wasted no time in setting him up as a quirky fellow who talks to his plants, but this is to trivialise a pecularity that involves far more than personal predilection. The British Constitution demands a certain kind of 'eccentricity' from the prince every time he takes a stand in the world, insisting that his public utterances – his 'interventions', as he himself calls them – be expressed at the margins of the nation's political culture.

The prince's choice of public themes suggests that he is determined to make a virtue of this necessity. Over the last decade he has explored the twilight zone at the edges of the nation's public life with unusual conviction, returning to the centre to speak for an extraordinary collection of causes. No sooner have we become accustomed to the prince of homeopathy, Mandala symbolism, and the paranormal, than he reappears as the prince of organic farming, defender of the European environment, and the hideously polluted North Sea. We've had the Prince of the disabled, of 'small is beautiful', and, if only on occasions when the Duke of Edinburgh has needed a deputy, the Prince of exploration, Outward Bound, and cliff-top *esprit de corps*. Charles has given us the prince of the inner-city, advocate of business secondment, and determined supplier of bootstraps to the nation's most disadvantaged youths, but he has also found a more contemplative roles as Prince of the nation's traditional lifeworld: its threatened grammar, plain speech, and common sense; its sense of situation and neighbourhood; the figurative conventions of its landscape; its patterns of craft and ornamentation; the human scale of its towns and villages; the intrinsic qualities of its spring water; even its traditional varieties of apple. Charles has become the prince of traditional aesthetics, of 'character' and endangered local detail; wherever he goes there is a vague sense of dappling, of light playing in leaves and shadows falling across fluted stone. It seems entirely in character that he should recently have disclosed how frequently he diverts his journeys across England, travelling off down lanes and farm tracks in search of ancient barns, the mere glimpse of which is enough to 'lift the spirits'.[9]

As he has worked on his adopted themes over the last decade or so, Charles has also been giving the nation a curious lesson on the nature of its own periphery – one that has been all the more striking given the generally pitiful performance of the Labour Party as Her Majesty's parliamentary opposition over the same years. Even the tabloids have had to recognise, if only in passing, that their society's margins are not just littered with 'eccentric' causes and feckless derelicts who have made their beds and must now lie on them. Indeed, Prince Charles has demonstrated that the relation between the politically defined centre of national life and its periphery is rather more dynamic than that. He has shown that the periphery is where the disorders of the centre are most manifest and, as he has insisted with a romanticism that could hardly be more out of kilter with prevailing political attitudes, where the future must be found. There is scarcely one of his chosen themes that does not imply a critical indictment of the centre. The environment becomes a theme in opposition to unrestrained industrial development. The marginalised inner-city population to which the prince has drawn public attention (tenants, the unemployed, ethnic minorities) is made up of what sociologists call the 'new victims' who have emerged despite, and partly because of, the consolidation of the Welfare State which was meant to solve the problems of deprivation.[10] As for the prince's notorious interest in the alternative therapies and in spiritual capacities conventionally dismissed as 'irrational', here too he has been confronting the centre with its own discarded off-cuts: dimensions of mind which are now recovered in an attempt to heal the wounds caused by the rationalistic outlook which tried to get by without them. When it comes to architecture as the prince as defined it, the periphery does not just consist of the classical and vernacular styles that were marginalised by the rise of modernism. Indeed, it is historical in a quite different sense from the one intended by critics who have condemned the Prince for his nostalgia.[11] Deliberately or not, Prince Charles has resumed the arguments that flared around comprehensive development and high rise housing in the late Sixties. As he has gone on about 'the whole sad legacy of Sixties housing', he has reopened controversies on which the architectural and planning professionals were quick to close the book long ago.

Prince Charles has stirred up considerable political discussion on his chosen themes, but he himself is careful to maintain a politics-shaped hole at the centre of his public outlook.[12] The nation to which his speeches are addressed is held together by duties of *husbandry* rather than political government: husbandry as a social as well as ecological principle. His nation may not be made up of citizens (people defined by their rights in relation to the State), but Charles himself is not happy with the idea that it is composed, as some critics have suggested it must inevitably be, of craven pre-democratic 'subjects' cowering under royal power. Instead, his speeches show us a republic of 'ordinary human beings': uncomplicated and brow-beaten 'poor mortals' among whom the prince presents himself only as first among equals.[13] Like the ordinary Briton, he is an 'amateur' struggling to be heard in a world full of 'experts'. Like the ordinary Briton, hemmed in as the Prince declares him to be by 'an enormous amount of red tape', Charles knows what it is to be 'frustrated at every turn': he, after all, has to put up with the prophylactic and spirit-killing form of bureaucracy that is Royal protocol.

Charles has set up his stall as prince of all the obstructed human 'potential' in the land. He talks repeatedly of unfulfilled 'talents', of enabling 'ordinary' individuals to rise up into their true capacities. Underneath all the standardisation and imposed uniformity of modern life, there are 'individuals' with the more intuitive kind of consciousness that Charles's mentor, Laurens van der Post, associated with the African bushman and also, although in a different way, with his admired Margaret Thatcher. For Laurens van der Post, nothing that is 'truly done' and 'matched to the living word' can ever be in vain, and the lost world of the Kalahari bushman still indicts the West for bringing about a catastrophic 'decline in the quality and range of consciousness'.[14] Charles is following in van der Post's footsteps when he speaks out for the 'irrational and mysterious' dimensions of the human soul and calls on the architectural profession to honour our still partly pagan instinct for embellishment and decoration. Indeed, Charles sometimes makes his nation sound like a land of white bushmen, overlaid by the 'forces of uniformity' and the spurious collective ideas of the modern world, but well grounded underneath and still capable of 'flights of vision' that move the earth. The 'poor mortals' of his speeches on architecture and town planning come across as aboriginal types struggling to survive in the age of the Welfare State: put-upon, badgered, ridiculed for their archaic ideas, herded through a modernisation process that has left them feeling three quarters extinct.

The prince who tired of cutting ribbons has indeed found himself a new vocation helping ordinary people to 'snip the red tape here and there'. He has traded the ceremonial scissors for the robuster machinery of the 'pilot project'. Set against a background of failed modernisation, the pilot project is an idealistic attempt at re-enchantment. It brings people together in 'partnership' so that they may 'settle their differences', 'take the lid' off, and allow all the 'initiative and enthusiasm and desire' that Charles mentioned after his tour of Spitalfields to bring a little transformation into the world. It seeks to put effective management at the service of those inspirational 'flights of the spirit' Charles wants to see taken seriously again. The prince has his own laboratories in which to practise this social alchemy; the Treasury may have tied up the purse strings with 'management acts', but the Duchy of Cornwall still includes a few places where what Charles (or at least the typist who transcribed his 1987 Spitalfields speech) used to describe as the 'Bottoms-up' approach is being tried.

The Revivalist Fable

Charles has proved adept at cutting and pasting from all sorts of sources, but his personal 'Vision of Britain' amounts to more than the collection of 'styles' – conservation, community architecture and classical revivalism – that he is said to have drawn from his changing circle of advisers.[15] In one fundamental at least, Charles's vision is not essentially stylistic at all. Instead it is organised around a highly schematic interpretation of British history since World War Two, one that draws together and, indeed, summarises many of the themes of this book. Charles has articulated his most rousing versions of this historical fable around the image of St Paul's Cathedral, the building he has adopted as the spiritual centre of his much put-upon nation. In his Mansion House speech he used the mediocre post-war office blocks in Paternoster Square, immediately to the north of St Paul's, to redeclare the memory of the war against the failures of the peace that followed it: 'You have, Ladies and Gentlemen, to give this much to the *Luftwaffe*: when it knocked down our buildings, it didn't replace them with anything more offensive than rubble. We did that . . .'. Here is the prince's fable stripped down to its basic narrative structure. First there was the war, recalled here as the last moment of national greatness, a trial by fire from which the nation emerged purified and triumphant like Wren's cathedral. Then came the peace, which quickly betrayed the promises of war and degenerated into a forty-year period of destructive modernisation. Against this background, the present rises up as an urgent moment of choice. Either the destruction continues until everything is lost or the nation rallies to its senses, and the tide of destruction is reversed. The present offers the opportunity or, in Charles's phrase, the 'second chance' we never dared hope for: the miraculous moment of reawakening when the return to true values can begin. With its broken pledge and its defence of a traditional realm usurped in its own name, this fable is like an epic rendering of the battle for Crichel Down – expanded from those few hundred acres of obscure Dorset downland to engulf the entire nation and its post-war history.

The revivalist fable is not the invention of the prince. In one form or another, it is widely dispersed through our culture – a product of the history that it purports to explain. It has been suggested that Prince Charles's references to St Paul's and the *Luftwaffe* were derived from a speech by Michael Manser, but if a single source can really be claimed for an idea that has been so much in the air of the times, it will not be found here.[16] At heart, the revivalist fable is pure John Betjeman. It was Betjeman, albeit in the playfulness of his younger days, who advocated selective Nazi bombing of such modern British towns as Slough. It was Betjeman, as we have already seen, who travelled through the nation's Victorian inner cities in the Sixties, denouncing the modern 'slabs' (a word that Prince Charles himself likes to use) being thrown up all over the place and stressing the difference between post-war conceptions of 'housing' and the proper 'houses' on which more recent polemicists have placed the prominent 'pitched roofs' which are also favoured by the prince.

Above all, it was Betjeman who enlisted the Old Masters in the struggle against post-war development, using their views of the old city to condemn the London of his time as an inferior mess. In 1942 he published a book full of pictures of the 'vintage London' that had 'disappeared altogether, swallowed long ago by the gaping gullets of private property, big business and municipal 'progress'.[17] After the war, it was the views of St Paul's that served Betjeman best of all. In the early Seventies he published a similarly minded poem called 'Meditation on a Constable Picture'. The picture in question looks down onto Wren's cathedral from the leafy distance of Parliament Hill, but in the poem it seems to merge with Canaletto's view from the terrace of Somerset House; Betjeman cherishes the wide flow of a still 'unembanked Thames' and dwells lovingly on the 'steeple surrounded' dome of St Paul's. The closing challenge is clear: 'Ere slabs are too tall and we Cockneys too few / Let us keep what is left of the London we knew'.[18] Charles is a Cockney prince in Betjeman's sense, but by the time his vision was fully articulated there were other precedents too. Those paintings by Constable and Canaletto had appeared again in 1978, when they were used to illustrate 'the rise and fall of a twentieth century dream' in Christopher Booker's crushing assault on high rise architecture, the BBC documentary *City of Towers*. Nine years later, Theo Crosby added Turner's view of St Paul's from Greenwich to this growing collection of indicting canvasses, proposing, as we have seen, that London should actually be re-idealised by means of a monument-building programme that would advance along his Turner and Canaletto 'axes'. These pictures had been cited in many condemnations of the present state of London by the time Prince Charles exhibited them again, with Christopher Booker at his side, in *A Vision of Britain*. Indeed, Jules Lubbock, in one of the last articles he wrote for the *New Statesman* before slipping into the diplomatic silence that becomes a principal architectural courtier to Prince Charles, even presented a socialist GLC version of this time-sanctioned outlook:

> A wonderful new public view of St. Pauls Cathedral from the South Bank next to Blackfriars Bridge and the Oxo Tower ... was opened after being closed to public view by wharves and warehouses for almost two centuries.
>
> To whom do we owe the reinstatement of this small and mercifully almost unencumbered view of our capital's skyline, the very symbol of the British people in the face of Nazism, which has, nonetheless, since been so shamefully mutilated by the City towers?
>
> The television news was silent; it just said that a further stretch of the Thames walkway had been opened, as if it were all part of the great programme of Metropolitan Improvements created by the government. In fact, the view is seen from a new riverside garden,

part of the first phase of the Coin Street development, achieved only after 13 years of unremitting campaigns by the Association of Waterloo Groups, first against plans for a multi-storey hotel by Gerald Ronson's Heron Corporation and then against a projected 20-storey slab of offices designed by my old friend, the Cossack of Coin Street himself, Richard Rogers, for Stuart Lipton, then of Greycoats.[19]

Lubbock ended his article by blaming me, among others, for failing to develop the 'alternative vision' that, as Lubbock remarked in terms that may well remind us of George Lansbury's hopes for Sutton House, 'could inspire people from every class and background who want both progress and conservation'. Six weeks later, however, the whole nation discovered that he had found an altogether more appropriate leader for 'the greatest political crusade of the coming century'. It was on 1 December 1987 that Prince Charles stood up at the Annual Dinner of the Corporation of London Planning and Communication Committee at the Mansion House and asked: 'What have we done, Ladies and Gentlemen, to St Paul's?' Coin Street was not mentioned, but the blitz was, along with Herbert Mason's famous photograph, printed in the *Daily Mail* on 31 December 1940, of the dome 'standing out', as Charles put it, 'against the whirling smoke and flames' – a picture that turned the cathedral into 'a symbol of faith and a monument to Britain's resolve', and that now 'reminds us of the place St. Paul's occupies at the very heart of our nation as the spiritual centre of the capital city'. Unfortunately, St Paul's was now buried in 'a jostling scrum' of mediocre office buildings. Charles invoked Canaletto, but he also cited Canaletto's nephew Belloto, whose paintings had been used as 'blueprints' in the rebuilding of Warsaw after the destruction of World War Two.

This is how St Paul's was drawn up into Prince Charles's vision of Britain, but equally familiar precedents cluster around his insistence that the peace has turned out to be more destructive than the war. Towards the end of May 1984, Prince Charles asked RIBA 'what have we done to our capital city since the bombing during the war?' But just two weeks earlier, Gavin Stamp had used the same rhetorical device in a *Spectator* article attacking Peter Palumbo's controversial plans for the No. 1 Poultry site in the City of London: he expressed his dismay at the idea that Mies Van de Rohe might be allowed to do to the City of London what the *Luftwaffe* had failed to do.[20] This idea had found an earlier incarnation in Colin Amery and Dan Cruickshank's 1975 book, *The Rape of Britain*, although here it was still more of a reasoned observation than a polemical slogan:

[Britain's] towns and cities suffered heavy damage from Nazi bombers during the Second World War, but they had survived until then as a remarkably intact built history of the nation. So there was a lot to lose. Britain has not suffered from civil strife in the streets (except in Northern Ireland) and so it is fair to say that the damage to our towns since 1945 has been done by ourselves.[21]

By the early Eighties a different version of this trope was appearing in Leon Krier's writings about the Nazi architect Albert Speer. Krier is vituperative about the ease with which an 'ignorant' post-war Germany identified the classicism of Speer's architecture with facism and converted to modernism and bulldozers. The International Style encouraged 'moral depravity' in the architectural profession and the result is plain to see: an 'industrial modernism' that has 'turned culture itself into its own most bitter enemy'. 'All that industrial zeal has not produced a single place or monument which people could long for or dream about.' Once again, it wasn't Allied bombing that had destroyed the cities of Germany, but the monstrous architecture of a reconstruction that, in Krier's view, has condemned the German people to live in buildings that, while they may fall apart with age, could never in a million years become 'home'.[22] By the time Theo Crosby tried to turn the revivalist fable into a monument, it had passed into general circulation as a trivializing cliché that could be used to discredit more or less any aspect of the nation's post-war experience (indeed, by then even Auberon Waugh had come up with the diverting proposition that Shirley Williams had been far worse than Hitler).

Prince Charles has consulted directly with many of the conservationists who have helped to shape the revivalist fable. Until recently, Gavin Stamp was listing himself at London's Architectural Association as the only architecture critic in the country who was not an adviser to the Prince of Wales, and he certainly does appear to be an exception among the conservationists we have encountered in earlier chapters. Colin Amery, Dan Cruickshank, and Theo Crosby attended a special meeting held by Prince Charles at Highgrove House on 18 September 1987 (the question under discussion was 'Is architecture too important to be left to the architects?'),[23] while Christopher Booker, Leon Krier, and, of course, Jules Lubbock – the former scourge of 'Herr Krier' and the other revivalists who, as Lubbock claimed in 1987, would never be able to cleanse classical architecture of Hitler's stain – have found much larger roles to play.[24] As for the revivalist fable itself, while it offers only the most schematic interpretation of the nation's history since 1939, it would be foolish to dismiss it as if were merely a lie. Indeed, like all myths this one owes its power precisely to its truth. Far from being concerned only with the rise of modernism within an increasingly arrogant professional taste, it testifies to deep disruptions and disappointments in the nation's post-war experience and has undeniable subjective depth as a result. But while the fable bears witness to the anxieties of the post-war period, it also draws them into a rhetorical war of the worlds –

exactly the sort of 'crusade' that Lubbock demanded – in which the difference between good and evil is always plain to see.

This is the fundamental problem at the centre of Charles's 'Vision of Britain'. The revivalist fable articulates truly vital cultural themes, but it submits them to a morbid process of simplification, which can itself come to stand in the way of proper understanding. Advocates of the revivalist fable may criticize the post-war reconstruction for failing to build monuments, or for being exclusively concerned with what Theo Crosby called 'short-term strategies', but there is something scandalous as well as trivialising about the way in which an argument about architectural style has been used to obliterate the fact that, for many people at the time, the post-war reconstruction *was* the memorial: there was to be a 'New Britain', not just a fancy obelisk in the ground. Similarly, while the revivalist fable treats St Paul's as a timeless and enduring icon of the national spirit, we only have to compare the meaning that it holds now with that which it achieved during the war, to suspect that the fable has actually reduced Wren's cathedral to a brittle polemical device.

A Spurious Polarisation and a War Redeclared

The young James Lees-Milne may have found himself attaching far greater value to damaged historic buildings than to lost lives, but for the artist and film-maker Humphrey Jennings, it was the human dimension of the blitz that seemed most important. As he wrote to his wife on 20 October, 1940:

> 'Some of the damage in London is pretty heart-breaking but what an effect it has had on the people! What warmth – what courage! What determination . . . . Maybe by the time you get this one or two more 18th century churches will be smashed up in London: some civilians killed: some personal loves and treasures wrecked – but it means nothing; a curious kind of unselfishness is developing which can stand all that and more. We have found ourselves on the right track at last!'[25]

The spirit of the East End, revealed during those continuous nights of destruction, was also praised by Prince Charles's grandmother, who visited the area in 1940, insisting famously that something must be done for the people who had gone through all this. Jennings was among the film-makers and photographers who turned the surviving dome of St Paul's into a symbol during the very height of the blitz: one that spoke less of imperial destiny than of enduring civilian courage, social idealism, reason and evolution. He even wrote a poem in which he imagined Darwin's head superimposed over the dome. The revivalist fable is inclined to treat the Welfare State as the betrayal of the spirit of the blitz, but the architects of post-war social policy saw it as the post-war embodiment of that very same spirit. In 1941, the socialist Ritchie Calder described the Blitz as 'the biggest slum-clearance scheme in British history', regretting that the indiscriminate bombing had destroyed 'the handsome modern flats which the workers had won for themselves', but insisting nevertheless that the destruction opened great 'possibilities of reconstruction'.[26] A year later Lord Beveridge wrote that a 'new spirit' capable of sustaining the British through 'Total War' would only really make its way if those in power recognised that 'we have treated our work people as if they were "economic men", unamenable even in war to any motive stronger than personal gain'. The essential thing was to assert 'the principle of service' over that of 'personal gain', and this applied as much to the post-war peace as to the war itself: indeed, Beveridge hoped that, after triumphing over 'the evils of war', the same spirit of service would be unleashed against 'the evils of peace' which he was inclined to personify as Want, Disease, Ignorance, Squalor, and Idleness.[27] While Beveridge entertained such hopes for the 'new spirit' that would win the war and then build the 'New Britain', Richard Titmuss showed how the more institutional forms of the Welfare State emerged from the provisions of war time: right down to the cod liver oil and orange juice of every post-war childhood. Throughout the war, as he wrote in the late Forties, 'pressure for a higher standard of welfare and a deeper comprehension of social justice steadily gained in strength'.[28] Titmuss praised the 'war-warmed impulse of people for a more generous society', and declared that the idea of universal social welfare (as distinct from measures directed only towards the deserving poor) was much advanced by the fact that 'the assistance provided by the government to counter the hazards of war carried little social discrimination, and was offered to all groups in the community'.

Half a century later, St Paul's has been stripped of its progressive associations and stands as a more purely architectural icon, set off against the reforming ambitions of a peace that failed. By the time Prince Charles's 'A Vision of Britain' opened at the Victoria and Albert Museum, no one was even much inclined to differentiate the planned architecture of the supposedly reforming Welfare State from that of speculative office development (for Betjeman in the late Sixties, this was already only the difference between high-rise 'slabs' and high-rise 'cliffs'). The slogan for a poster prepared for the event by Saatchi and Saatchi (and printed with Prince Charles's approval) said all that was necessary: 'In 1945, the Luftwaffe stopped bombing London. Two years later the blitz began.' The text elaborated on this highly generalized proposition:

Hundreds of splendid historical buildings were destroyed. Tens of thousands of homes were flattened. Entire communities were obliterated. But it wasn't the work of Heinkels, Junkers and Dorniers. This devastation was even more efficiently inflicted by our very own local councillors, government ministers, planners, developers and architects.

It was on east London ground that had already been cleared in this rhetorical manner, that Prince Charles asked the nation to consider the 'sad legacy of Sixties housing' in his famous television programme. Indeed, he provided an unmistakable glimpse of Crichel Down as he cruised along the Thames, telling Christopher Booker how in Liverpool 'crushed tower blocks' were being mixed with soil and used to turn derelict sites in the inner city 'back into countryside'.

The revivalist fable is inclined to merge the architecture of social reform with that of speculative greed, but it has also helped to open a damaging new schism between conservation and modernism. Here again, a complex history of inter-relatedness is reduced to the brutal simplicities of a polemical opposition. Up until the late Sixties, modernism and tradition or conservation often went hand in hand. Modernist architects like the Smithsons played a significant role in the unsuccessful campaign to save the Doric Euston arch from demolition in 1961–2. Sir Nikolaus Pevsner dedicated his life to a similar combination. The work of early and mid-century artists like Paul Nash, Eric Gill, John Piper and Kenneth Rowntree also ridicules the idea that there could be any simple polarisation of tradition against modernism. Even the few professional conservationists of the pre-war years held views that cannot be assimilated to the simple-minded polemical oppositions of recent years. A.R. Powys was the highly regarded Secretary of the Society for the Protection of Ancient Buildings. In a series of articles with titles like 'Tradition and Modernity' and 'Real England and Housing' (the very titles of which reveal a determined ambition to keep superficially opposed ideas together), he advocated combinations that seem particularly striking now: conservation and new council housing, traditional buildings and houses built of modern industrial materials. He was especially adamant that 'traditional' and 'modern' architecture should not be divided as they had been in the nineteenth century when what he called 'The Battle of Styles' was so 'vigorously and uselessly waged'.[29] Those who assumed that 'no new architecture deserves consideration unless it also deserves the title "modern"' were certainly at fault, but Powys was also critical of the 'Traditionalists'. Indeed, now that the 'Battle of Styles' has been recommenced, we can grant Powys the last word on such follies as John Simpson's classical telephone kiosk:

It is assumed by the 'Traditionalists' that tradition and conformity to tradition are good: and it is probable that building traditions are indeed a good influence on this art. But the 'Traditionalists' make one mistake that is so serious in the adherence to their theory, that it immediately shows the application of their conclusion to be false. They use the word *tradition* in a sense that it does not bear. The kind of architecture they admire and desire is not *traditional*, but one which represents an academic *revival*. What they admire in buildings is the conscious reproduction of ancient forms reshuffled into new arrangements.

This new schism between modernism and tradition, far worse than a mere 'Battle of Styles', is accepted by Prince Charles's critics: indeed, it is vigorously supported by figures like Maxwell Hutchinson and Martin Pawley who simply take up the modernist side of the divide, dismissing every appeal to tradition as 'heritage nonsense', calling for taller skyscrapers and, by implication, the demolition of a few more listed buildings.[30] But it was in the classical revival, so dear to Prince Charles, that the destructive effects of this polarisation first became apparent.

To start with, everything sounded wonderful. While the modernists were carving up the world, a few principled men clung to the shadows, guarding spurned traditions and dreaming of a re-enchantment that the real world would apparently never see. They turned their backs on the corrupted schools of architecture and worked in provincial practices, eking out a living at the point where architecture and traditional building skills met: a bit of restoration work, a few modest cottages, the odd church, and the occasional more prestigious commission in Downing Street or the Inns of Court. Raymond Erith was among these solitary figures and his most famous words, paraphrased by Prince Charles in *A Vision of Britain*, were spoken from the heart of this obscurity in 1971: 'All my life I have been waiting for the revival of architecture. I do not think that it will happen, but if the right idea could be put out at the right time, I think it could happen. The world could be beautiful again. And nothing, really, but a blind spot stops it.'

While standardised system-built blocks were going up in the cities, a revivalist like Quinlan Terry was recovering the abandoned art of draughtsmanship and making symbolic lino-cuts, which showed biblical truth betrayed and the human scale 'House of Joy' going to waste under a tangle of allegorical briars. During the building booms of the Sixties, Terry was travelling to Italy where he would measure classical buildings in Imperial inches and study their smallest detail. His answer to the functionalist tower blocks came in the resolutely minor form of a lino cut showing a beautifully elaborated croquet shed designed for Miss Watts at Aynho.

It is often said that practice makes perfect, but this maxim hasn't always applied to the classical revivalists, who like to sing songs of innocence rather than experience. Of course they speak highly of traditional apprenticeship but opportunities for this kind of training have been scarce in the modern world and, for a time at least, the truest classical revivalist appeared to be the one who had refused to build anything at all. Reluctant to compromise with the practical world of 'fallen materiality' where briefs are drawn up, he preferred to theorise, to coin gnomic and cosmological epithets that mock the alienated rationalism of the mainstream, and to draw up frankly counterfactual schemes for the world as it might be if only that 'second chance' was seized.[31] Theo Crosby's Battle of Britain Monument is in this tradition, as are John Simpson's alternative plan for Paternoster Square and his proposed new villages like Upper Donnington, both of which featured prominently in Charles' *A Vision of Britain*. But the true master of this genre, and the inspiration for others, is Leon Krier who opted for the wilderness after a disillusioning spell with James Stirling had convinced him that no individual architect who insisted on confronting the inadequacies of his brief could expect to stay in work: as he wrote, 'the challenge to our generation is to refuse to build now'.[32] In his isolation Krier came up with 'amusements' of his own: he fitted ideal buildings into the background of Seurat's painting *The Bathers*. He drew up a plan for Pliny's villa as it might once have been on the Laurentine coastline, and he sketched a marvellous 'Completion' of Washington DC which refounds the American capital on a polycentric basis, offering it the prospect of Swiss canton-style democracy and using infill development to lower the offices of state bureaucracy which have grown up to dwarf the White House.[33]

But somewhere early on in this revival of classical architecture, the crude social polemic moved in. We have seen its disfiguring effects on John Simpson's phone box and Theo Crosby's Battle of Britain Monument, but it also seems to have become a load-bearing material quite central to the structure of Quinlan Terry's buildings. Terry's belief in the divine origin of the classical orders is well known, as is his reported habit of paying tithes to his local church. But his fundamentalism is not limited to this religious belief. Indeed, he builds quite explicitly against a modernism that begins, as he has argued, with anti-traditional Victorians like Darwin, Freud and Marx, and which comes forward to embrace the whole reforming architecture of the post-war settlement and Welfare State. This polemic recoils on his buildings, using them as so many bunkers and pill-boxes in a front-line struggle against the forces of egalitarianism and false progress. It turns the new classical house into a machine for recivilising the post-war mob. The differentiation of its rooms becomes a mechanism for enforcing true morality, while its classical style works to re-establish proper hierarchy at both ends of the recently confused social scale: it makes proper and fulfilled workers (Terry is especially proud of the fact that his building sites are generally content places where workers have enough craft to find meaning in their labours), and it also makes a true 'gentleman' of the *nouveau riche* owner. The 'human scale' turns

out to involve people 'knowing their place' in more sense than one and
Terry rounds his own achievement off by quoting from the Book of
Ecclesiastes with triumphant relief and applause from above: '. . .
and there is no new thing under the sun'.

The same polemical reduction occurs in the writings of the classical
revival's undiscriminating advocates. It is to be heard in Clive Aslet's
cheer-leading applause for everything Terry has done, but it has
taken a more influential form in the writings of David Watkin who,
having assaulted Pevsner in the Seventies for identifying modernism
with the *Zeitgeist*, has more recently likened the modern movement to
a 'giant act of political nationalisation' and declared its break-up to be
a 'process curiously akin to the rhetorical emphasis on freedom of
choice and privatisation which characterise Mrs. Thatcher's
Britain'.[34] At the end of this squalid little cul-de-sac, the *Zeitgeist*
reappears, associated this time not with the International Style but
with a fundamentalist classicism, which offers newly built private
country houses in mocking 'answer' to the miseries of the failing
council tower block. It is to Gavin Stamp's enduring credit that he has
resisted this crude attempt to re-establish the *Zeitgeist* in classical
form.

At one time or another, Prince Charles seems to have subscribed to
most of the positions available within the revivalist fable. Sometimes
the polemic carries him away, as it did most obviously in April 1989
when he spoke at the launch of the Civic Trust's 'Building a Better
Britain' exhibition. After extolling the virtues of the traditional
English village, he moved on to discuss Romania and the monstrous
programme of 'systematisation' with which President Ceausescu was
at that time still destroying 'his country's cultural and human
heritage'.[35] Pausing to imagine the headlines that would follow if he
pressed ahead with the outrageous comparison that he (or perhaps
some ventriloquising 'adviser' from Crichel Down) had in mind, he
quickly stressed that 'what happened here in the 1960s is, of course,
not comparable'. But despite the disavowal, he couldn't resist making
the accusation all the same: 'We in this country are painfully aware of
the trauma caused by uprooting traditional communities at the
behest of "benevolent", know-all planners. We hope that we have
learnt something from such an experience.' Here was our future
monarch sinking, like a right wing think-tanker, into the boozy club-
land rhetoric of Britain's *perestroika*.

Yet there have been plenty of other occasions on which Charles has
tried to avoid being sucked into the stale polemical oppositions of the
revivalist fable. When he went down to Bow in *A Vision of Britain* to
lend his symbolic hand to the demolition of some dismal post-war
council buildings, he resisted the temptation to swing away at
residential tower blocks, the 'colossal fossils' that were his real target:
better for the people's prince to be seen tearing down a car park than
the lamentably inadequate homes of George Lansbury's poor. When

in 1989 he wrote a letter to publicise *The Saving of Spitalfields*, the book that the Spitalfields Trust published after its celebratory tenth anniversary conference, he singled out Raphael Samuel's dissenting contribution for showing 'a welcome wider concern' with 'the interaction between conservation, development and an existing community'. Similarly, his views on architectural style are often of a less sweeping and more liberal kind than those of the fundamentalists. He has tried to remain democratic in his recommendations, insisting that the recovered aesthetic 'code' must exist in a consultative framework and encouraging people to use the public inquiries of the planning machinery at a time when the government has taken to suspending or overriding them. Like the classical revivalists, he wants architecture to impose its order on human behaviour, but he chooses to stress the 'healing' influence that good hospital buildings can have on the 'human spirit', not the reinforced social hierarchy of Terry's brazen new country houses. Despite his evidently 'classical sympathies', Charles has also stepped back from pledging exclusive allegiance to one style, insisting that the qualities he seeks in architecture are not confined to the classical revival alone. Yet the challenge has been clear from early on: will the 'Vision of Britain' fade away like Coleridge's Xanadu, leaving only a cloud of morbid social polemic behind it, or will it lead on, as the Prince has promised, to real activity in the world – a reinstatement of the *polis* and the true human scale city of man?

Perhaps Prince Charles indicated his determination to escape the merely suburban prejudices of the revivalist fable by signing up Leon Krier, sworn enemy of all cul-de-sacs, as the Master Planner for his proposed development at Poundbury, Dorchester. Krier's is a classical vision, to be sure, but as Charles demonstrated in his television programme, the Poundbury project was not just an experiment in style. He reviewed some of the architectural endeavours of his ancestors: the ornate Brighton Pavilion proved that 'there was a time when the Prince of Wales could build on a grand scale', but other buildings in London showed that previous monarchs had experimented in social reform, in what John Betjeman would recognise as 'housing' rather than just 'houses'. As the Prince concluded, 'We have created somewhat God-forsaken cities from which nature or . . . the spiritual side of life has almost been erased, but we don't have to build towns and cities we don't want, in which we feel manipulated and threatened . . .'. The restitution of the true city, with its 'agreed way of doing things', was surely within our power: indeed, after talking his viewers through a quick tour of Siena, Charles concluded by saying, 'I'm hoping to put something like that into practice in Dorchester'.

A New Town Near Crichel Down

> The urban district is an independent small city, an ideal creation
> between the village and the metropolis. It integrates all functions
> such as dwelling, working, leisure, etc., with all the public and
> private institutions of the urban community.
>
> Leon Krier[36]

South-west Dorset is a long way from St Paul's, but one has only to
scratch at the surface to discover that the revivalist fable has found its
way down here too. A version can be heard in the public bar at
Bridport's George Hotel where an affable, and still slightly Bohemian
circle of middle-aged refugees gather to recall London as it was when
they lived there in the Sixties: their idea of the radiant city is built up
around the memory of Biba's rather than St Paul's, and they conjure a
potent imagery of black muggers and degenerate council tower blocks
like those on the Holly Street Estate to justify their own continued
exile in a small town whose main contribution to history turns out, all
these years later, to have been the hangman's rope. It has even found
a monument at Mapperton Manor, where the former Lord Hinchinbrooke, who we have already seen 'putting the peer back into the
peerage' in the Forties and hoping, in the Fifties, that high rise flats in
the inner cities would save rural England from undesirable urban
encroachment, lives on among his collected paintings as plain Mr
Victor Montague. After decades spent blasting away at the post-war
establishment – the stifling bureaucracy of the Welfare State and the
'moral deterioration of character' that came with high rates of
taxation – this Lord who wanted to see 'the removal from our history
books of the European doctrine of a proletarian democracy, state
planning and regimentation', disclaimed his peerage in 1964, intend-
ing to stand against the Common Market for the House of
Commons.[37] Failing to get a seat, this impeccable man whom
Michael Foot once described as 'the most formidable of Tory Die-
hards' withdrew to Mapperton where he tended his formal gardens
and, with his back firmly turned on the modern world that had
spurned him, employed a Dorchester architect named R. J. Stephen-
son to build him a Doric Orangery that was completed in 1967. The
building has been plagued with leaks, but it should still be listed
among the heroic precursors of the Classical Revival that has
flourished since.

But Prince Charles has more ambitious ideas down here, and so too
does Leon Krier, the master planner who, for several decades now,
has been elaborating ideas for the reurbanisation of the modern city:
ideas that would at last be put into practice in the most challenging
'pilot project' of all. It is in Dorset that Krier was to take us from
conservation, with its desperate attempts to protect the disintegrating
fragments of the human-scale city of man, to the moment of renewal,
where we discover how to build it again. Following the council's

request for land on which the development could take place, a 450 acre site had been made available on the west side of Dorchester. The land in question is green, flat, and relatively featureless, but it has nothing in common with the void-like 'open spaces' of the inner city council estate and we can also be sure that the archaeologists who have been sifting through its soil for many years, have never found any 'crushed tower block' among the bones and potshards of ancient Britain. Indeed, the Poundbury acres were traditionally of the historic English downland variety although, like the larger stretch at Crichel Down, twenty or so miles to the north east, they have in recent years succumbed to intensive farming. In addition, and this is fortunate for Krier who has pronounced his desire to 're-establish a precise dialectic between city and countryside', the site is surrounded by landmarks that offer the prospect of great vistas, even 'axes', along which the new city might be aligned. The huge green rings of Maiden Castle stand only a mile or so away – quite undiminished, at least from a distance, by the nocturnal metal detectorists who have covered them with pock-marks. A rise further to the west is capped by the single column of the Hardy Monument – built to commemorate the Admiral Hardy who kissed the expiring Lord Nelson but casually rededicated to the memory of Thomas Hardy by thousands of passing tourists each year. It would, as the Prince of Wales pointed out in his television programme, have been easier for the Duchy of Cornwall to sell these well disposed acres for private development (the Duchy has done this before in Dorchester – hence the stretches of mediocre suburb along the town's southern edge), but that is no way to found an exemplary new town.

I missed the 'Community Planning Weekend' of 15–19 June 1989, an event that had been organised along the lines of an American 'Charette' by community architects, Hunt Thompson Associates. But I got to Dorchester a few weeks later and found Krier's Italianate model (flown in for the planning weekend from Vienna, where it had been made in his brother Rob Krier's offices) still on display in the old Crown Court building, itself carefully preserved to commemorate the Tolpuddle Martyrs, who were sentenced there in 1834. The model showed a distinctly anti-suburban and polycentric area of town built up around four different quarters with large public buildings, squares, monuments, terraced houses, and gardens. The outline planning permission stipulated that 20 per cent of the development must be given over to low-cost housing, and it was clear from the model that this proportion would be distributed throughout the development, and that no impoverished estates or ghettos would be allowed to form. There was a clock tower where in a less secular age a church would certainly have stood, a clear hierarchy of streets, and all the signs of a high density, mixed use area that one would expect from an uncompronising enemy of functional zoning in towns and cities. Prince Charles had talked about the work of the Seaside Development

Corporation in Florida and also Siena (the Poundbury site was frequently described as being about the same size as the area covered by this great medieval city). At the Charette, Leon Krier had cited Georgian Weymouth as another example of the kind of urban texture he wanted to re-establish, but I think of different examples as I remember that model. I recall Mark Girouard's 1979 vision of Spitalfields restored to a Georgian density in which rich and poor lived right up against each other, with industrial and residential activities all mixed up together in the same place. The inward focus and the variation of building types in Krier's carefully modelled new quarters brings to mind Oliver Richard's 'collegiate' plan for the Bow Quarter. I also think of another paradoxically comprehensive stretch of undevelopment even closer to home: indeed Krier's model looked like Dalston with the cars, litter and council estates taken out. Its street plan was reminiscent of the time-warped map in the 'Town Guide Cabinet' at Dalston Junction, and while the clock-tower was undoubtedly superior, it still bore an unmistakeable resemblance to the crude and sadly even clockless tower – a recognisable tribute to Krier nevertheless – that stands as the crowning glory of the brand new 'Dalston Cross' shopping centre. The opening of this unlikely establishment in the heart of Dalston may have brought yet more depression to the marginal traders of Dalston Lane, but it certainly lifted the spirits of Revd Donald Pateman over at St Mark's. He felt sure that Prince Charles would have approved its 'Southwell-Minster-like tower', surmounted as it was by a 'miniature spire' that was even 'lit up of a night'. Cynics have derided this modest attempt at transcendence as another example of tacky classicism, but Revd Pateman was having none of this. The scourging vicar of Dalston knows when words of praise are due, and he included them in his church journal: 'How refreshing to see such a thing in these drab modern days'.[38]

The Poundbury planning weekend, with its 'Town Meeting' at the Country Museum and its two 'Open Days' on the site at Poundbury Farm, was intended to be a model consultation exercise and more. Prince Charles told the television cameras that he hoped it would be 'educative' a well as 'participative and consultative': the aim, after all, was to produce a development 'along more civilised lines' than had prevailed over the past forty years. The *Declaration for Dorchester* produced at the end of the weekend reads partly like a notice of the sort that the founding fathers of a second New England might nail to a gnarled oak tree – 'We support . . . We propose . . . We believe . . . We commend . . .' and partly like written up 'bullet-points' culled from the overhead projections of a slick management presentation of the sort in which Tom Peters excels. It hopes that 'innovative techniques' will be 'promoted to secure civic facilities, affordable housing and meaningful and well-paid employment in a balanced community where a high quality of life can be enjoyed by people of all circumstances'. It talks of 'compatibility', 'financial responsibilities', and being 'responsive to changing needs', as well as of acting as 'an inspiration throughout the world'. The 'masterplanning principles' were supported because they would 'allow for the organic and considered creation of urban quarters which will, by their very nature, promote human dignity and fulfillment [sic]'.

But despite the apparent unanimity of this declaration, there were problems at the weekend. The police came along in the form of Chief Superintendent David Trickey, and declared that the proposed ban on culs-de-sac and development zoning was 'flying in the face of all crime research'. There was also tension between some of the speakers. Alert viewers might have sensed this in the unseemly crush that developed behind Prince Charles when the television cameras were rolling: there was Leon Krier looking splendidly aesthetic in what seemed to be a white silk suit, and there were the streetwise and rather hungry-looking advocates of community linkage squeezing in next to him. The same competitive strain was evident in the list of speakers prepared for the planning weekend: this has the interesting characteristic of describing John Thompson of Hunt Thompson Associates first, and at rather greater length than Leon Krier, the master planner, who was firmly relegated to second place. Krier took his revenge in *The Architects' Journal*, where he was quoted as saying that Hunt Thompson were not on the list of architects being considered for involvement in the scheme, and 'I don't think they should be'.[39] But questions of corporate interest and personal pride aside, the planning weekend struggled to combine a number of barely reconcilable aims. Even in this consultative aspect, it had to address two quite different constituencies. There were the reporters from the national and professional press who came pouring down to Dorchester to see Prince Charles putting his already televised 'A Vision of Britain' into action, but there were also the local people who were faced with the prospect of a massive development on their historical doorstep. Additional tensions followed from the fact that while community architect John Thompson had been hired in to look after this side of the event, the Charette was also intended to introduce the famous 'code' promised by Charles and developed by Leon Krier, for whom democracy resides more in the aesthetic conception of a town than in populism or 'demagogic' consultation about its architectural detail.

There had been some concern on the part of the community architects designing the planning weekend that Krier would wreck the whole consultation if he introduced his proposed extension of Dorchester with full Italian references attached. But in fact Dorset and Italy are inseparable to begin with, and Krier's Italianate aesthetic had struck some people I met as considerably less exotic than the imported flip chart technology of community consultation. James Lees-Milne would certainly have agreed with Krier's expressed view that 'Most good things in England came, at one time or another, from Italy', but down in Dorset the legacy is actually more mixed than that. To begin with, and as the road signs say (obediently followed by most of the journalists who came down to cover the planning weekend), Dorchester is a Roman town. But Dorset knows the Italian connection in other ways that are easily connected to the pressing problem of 'incomers' and the squeeze they put on the local housing market. Italianate ideas of the picturesque cleared more than a few villages in the county and, since the eighteenth century, they've also contributed largely to the rise of tourism and 'seaside retirement' in the area. One only has to visit the County Museum to find the skeleton of an Ancient Briton with a fatal Roman bolt-head lodged in his spine – one of the most famous, and increasingly emblematic, finds from Sir Mortimer Wheeler's pre-war excavation of Maiden Castle.

None of this adds up to much for David Oliver, architect and planner with the West Dorset District Council. He was most enthusiastic about Krier, but when I met him he played down the Italian emphasis: 'That's just the way Leon draws'. He pointed out some German style roofs on the Viennese model, and insisted that they weren't going to be building any of those either. The project will be Dorset vernacular, he assured me: 'We will build an English town'. Oliver is a stickler for quality and justifiably proud of having saved West Dorset from such impositions as fake half-timbering in the ubiquitous Wimpey style. An admirer of good modern architecture, he is regretful that Dorchester lost its only Art Deco building some years ago. Indeed, he welcomed Krier less as a revivalist than as an advocate of good and practical ideas that will help to secure 'a better environment in a development'.

For Oliver the Poundbury development was firmly a local matter, and he describes the problems it must help to address. The centre of Dorchester is under intense pressure. The town is full of listed buildings, but it has lost its old family firms and needs to attract national shops with very different building requirements. The council had recently given the go ahead to a scheme for a shopping centre by the developers, MEPC, that would commit the obvious offense of putting a multi-storey car park up along the town's ancient walls. As Oliver puts it, 'aesthetics are always squeezed'. The town has made fortunes selling council houses, but government policy forbids it from using this money to improve or safeguard the city. The logic is relentless: it ensures that 'the best we can achieve' is rapidly reduced to 'the least we can afford'.

Meanwhile, the housing market had been going through the roof. A recent survey had suggested that a typical couple might be able to raise £32,000 for their first house, but the constant pressure of incomers means that the house in question was likely to sell for £75,000. The Association of District Councils had recently found Dorchester to be one of the worst places in the country when it came to the gap between first time buyers and the cheapest property on the

market. Moreover, the incomers who have hiked the prices are adept
at protecting their own self-interest in Green terms: they no sooner
arrive in the area than they become ardent conservationists who will
resist all proposals for new building through an influential cluster of
lobbying and amenity groups. As Oliver asked of the Duchy's
planning weekend, how do you design a consultation process that will
actually get through that circle of three hundred articulate 'society'
people – specialists in public inquiry procedures as Oliver knew all
too well – and reach the wider population? As a local man himself,
Oliver wanted an answer to that question.

Following Oliver's lead, I went down to James Road, at the south-
east edge of the Duchy's site, to meet some protestors whose
grievances weren't actually just self-interest dressed up in Green. A
quiet cul-de-sac of semi-detached houses, James Road was built in the
Fifties: some of it as Council housing and some for the use of the police
and prison service. Thirty years later, all but one or two of the houses
have been sold into private ownership and show the usual signs of
home improvement. I met a teacher, a doctor, and a physics surveyor
from the UK Atomic Energy Authority research centre at nearby
Winfrith, and they were all wondering what exactly was happening.
On examining Krier's initial plans when they first went on public
display, they found that two houses in James Road had disappeared
to provide access into the new development. They also discovered
that a row of houses would apparently be built up against their own
back gardens, obscuring their view over to Maiden Castle. Since these
were the only demolitions mooted for the whole 450-acre site, the
residents of James Road were inclined to ask just what sort of
'Community Consultation' Hunt Thompson Associates had been paid
to carry out. Suddenly the spectre of compulsory purchase and the
bulldozer loomed, threatening to turn this development into another
desperate story from the Sixties: Dorchester's version of the Holly
Street Estate. They didn't feel any better when they turned up at the
Charette to hear Krier explain why he had thought of building along
their much loved and generally well-tended gardens: he called them
'tatty backsides', which would benefit from being screened from view.

In the absence of explanation, these people had been left to take
Krier's model far more literally than was ever intended. If Leon
Krier wasn't an architect, what exactly was he? As for this idea of an
Italian Hill Town in Dorchester, to the residents of James Road this
all sounded like the children's world of Mitsumasa Anno: wasn't it a
bit too ideal and toy-like? Was Krier perhaps a bit 'wrapped up in his
own ideas'? I was asked why nobody at the 'Charette' had been
prepared to answer their detailed questions about the plans –
particularly about a large round building with pillars that appeared
dangerously close to their road. I doubt that any expert in
'community consultation' could have filled this gap. The Duchy,
which has admitted it could have handled the consultation better,

should have employed a full-blown aesthetician like Demetri Porphyrios to go down and explain that, for Krier, the architect's work is 'to enshrine the ideal in a *disegno* for reality to approximate', and moreover that 'the *disegno* never exists as an empirical reality'.[40]

But it was through their appreciation of suburban form that the residents of James Road revealed their most significant difference with Leon Krier. They are *happy* to live in a cul-de-sac which, as they say, is safe for children. They *like* the zoning that keeps anyone from running a business next door, and I hardly dared ask them what they thought of the idea of a development that was, in Krier's words, to be 'dimensioned on the basis of the comfort of the walking man' rather than the modern convenience of the motor car.[41] As I listened I was reminded of an architectural debate of fifteen years ago. It was in the early Seventies, after a decade in which modernists had repeatedly cited the Italian hill town as the paradigm that justified – and the irony is irresistible – high-rise redevelopment in the cities, that writers like Nicholas Taylor started to rediscover the virtues of the suburb, so frequently dismissed as 'urban sprawl'. English towns, so Taylor insisted, hadn't needed to be walled – the fighting had stopped earlier – and the suburb was the desirable form that followed.[42]

I met Krier in Belsize Park in July 1989. We discussed Albert Speer whose architecture had been disfigured, as Krier was quick to agree, by political polemic. Nevertheless, he thought it 'vastly exaggerated' to suggest, as I did, that a comparable deformation might now be at work in the current classical revival. The essential point, as Krier put it, was that the modernist architects of the Sixties had neither repented nor accepted responsibility for their incomparably more abysmal works, and a united front would be necessary until they did so. Quinlan Terry's work was itself in some respects very modern, but it had shown something of what was possible and opened up the way for others. Try as I did, I couldn't really draw him on the subject of John Simpson's classical telephone kiosk either; indeed, he insisted that, whatever the short-comings of this admittedly 'crude' proposition, Simpson really knew about the design of towns and villages. I questioned the increasingly conventional definition which treats Krier as the man who has applied the principles of the classical revival not just to individual buildings but also to the wider design of towns. Weren't the principles different in some respects, and wasn't the ambition not just wider but also more profound? But we left these questions in the air. We talked about Dorset – the tours he had made through the area, and his sense of Dorchester, which he had got to know well. By coincidence he dwelt at some length on the qualities of the Georgian Corn Exchange in Blandford Forum. It was here in 1954 that Sir Andrew Clark, QC, that other famously silken visitor to these parts, held his inquiry into the Crichel Down affair, but Krier was only concerned with the building as a work of architecture. It has an impressive facade of Portland stone, three high arches, three

windows, and a well-placed clock over all. While it stands as tall as a
church, it nevertheless consists only of two storeys, thus going to
show, as Krier pointed out, that there is great flexibility of scale
within classical form.

Krier's talk is peppered with stern judgements, but while he is not a
man to hold back when he thinks something is 'disgusting' (the
absurdly suburban architecture of Coin Street) or 'appallingly
stupid' (that was the 'Chelsea Harbour' development in West
London), he is far from contemptuous of untutored public taste.
Rather than deploring the vernacular vulgarities of the typical
Wimpey estate (those much derided boxes with pitched roofs and
their doors and windows more or less in what Quinlan Terry
describes as 'the right place'), he sees them as testimony to a
persistent common sense on which the responsible architect can
build. Similarly, while he is no doubt that community architecture
can degenerate into demagogy, or that certain unnamed 'operators'
have built large practices by manipulating 'the wisdom of the people'
for their own ends, he insists that, by making its return to popular
taste, it has acted as a check on modernism and helped to clear the
ground on which architectural aesthetics can now be re-established.
Community Architecture was, in other words, a necessary tran-
sitional moment. Meanwhile, traditional style builders are already
doing a lot better than they were when the new towns went up. One of
his most effective counterblasts at the Victoria and Albert Museum's
'official debate' on Prince Charles's 'Vision of Britain' was that the
schools of architecture, while under the leadership of modernists like
Professor Colin St John Wilson, had refused to engage with the
problems of ordinary speculative housing, seeing this kind of building
as beneath contempt.

Krier is sometimes described as an ex-Marxist: an incorrect
impression provoked, he suggests, by the excursions he once made
into socialist theory in order to argue against the development ideas
entertained by communist authorities in Italy. Nevertheless, there
can be no doubt either that his intellectual foundations are much
wider than those of most classical revivalists or that they bear the
unmistakable mark of having been laid in the Sixties. Krier insists on
some of those almost forgotten counter-cultural truths. He stresses,
for example, that 'Economic arguments are always ideological': in
architecture especially economic 'reality' has turned out over and
again to be based on inadequate short-term assumptions (the true bill
for the tower blocks, as Krier remarks, is still coming in and councils
all over the country are in financial chaos as a result). He is also
withering about the kind of horse-trading that enables developers to
override planners and force great shopping centres into historic towns
like Dorchester: the English talk politely about 'planning gain', but in
Italy this process of 'selling the town to hacks' would be recognised as
the corruption that it is. He describes industrialisation as a process

that has only facilitated the centralisation of capital and political power, and his view of the New Town of Milton Keynes is similarly uncompromising: as he has written, 'It can't be by accident that the name of the greatest capitalist economist should echo so conspicuously in the name given to this new town. Here the loss of the last bit of cultural authority has made the architects the ruthless executors of the interests of the building industry'.

Nothing in what Krier told me suggested that he regretted having cited Theodor Adorno's claim that the autonomy of bureaucratic procedure was like that claimed by high art: the planning regulations surrounding urban development were indeed 'no longer verified by reason'.[43] He cites Herbert Marcuse and Ernst Bloch as writers who have influenced him in the past, but his most important source is now to be found in Hannah Arendt's philosophy of the public realm. It was Arendt who insisted that the public realm must have a permanence, not just within but also over and above, the society to which it gives meaning and form. As Arendt put it in a passage that Krier himself likes to quote: 'If the world is to contain a public space, it cannot be erected for one generation and planned for the living only. It must transcend the life-span of mortal men; without this transcendence into a potential earthly immortality, no politics, strictly speaking no common world and no public realm is possible'.[44] This was the point that Krier wanted to save from the debacle of Albert Speer, insisting that the idea of architecture as a 'long-term intervention' that gave 'permanence' and 'longevity' is not in itself fascist. For Krier, the offence of modernism was to turn architecture into 'an object of consumption rather than long term use'. In doing so it refused even to engage with the primary aesthetic challenge: 'it is only through beauty that permanence becomes acceptable'. In modern industrial society, as Krier adds, the public realm has degenerated to the point of becoming almost entirely fictional. We were back at Raymond Williams's idea of 'mobile privatisation' – a notion of which Krier had never heard, but which he willingly endorsed.

The code Krier has drawn up for the Dorchester development is being defined in entirely practical terms. As Krier said, it was important that it should not be 'too tyrannical' or it would force people to seek ways of circumventing it. It must also 'encourage excellence' – a quality that has been 'outlawed' or confused with 'the creation of eccentricities' when it should be about 'the creation of masterpieces within a simple framework'. The code governs all the overall uses of the site (zoning it on a plot-by-plot basis), the size of quarters and the amount of public space. It specifies the balance of workshop and residential use. It ensures that the agreed 20 per cent low cost housing is distributed evenly through the development, and in so doing tries to prevent the place ever becoming a 'yuppie ghetto'. The Poundbury code also provides guidelines for the construction of buildings: banning such modern contrivances as cavity walls and expansion joints, and insisting that houses have cellars but not convertable basements. It specifies that each garden must have at least one tree growing in it, and limits shrubs and bushes to a list of specified 'native' varieties. Satellite dishes are also outlawed. Far from being concerned only with 'antique peddling' of the kind he is sometimes accused of, Krier describes his code as an attempt to re-establish a public realm, at least in this one corner of Dorchester. In the spirit of Arendt, it is concerned with the restoration of the kind of democracy that can only exist at the level of the quarter or town – Krier doesn't need to visit Hackney Town Hall to know that 'When democracy gets too big it becomes politics'. He is also quite clear about the religious implications of his activity; as he told me, religion is fundamentally about values held in common. There may be no 'founding fathers', no really fundamental thinkers, among the theologians any more, but since a city is certainly a place where there will be something in common, its inauguration should indeed be conducted as 'almost a religious ceremony'.

Krier was full of confidence when I met him early in 1989. He was delighted to have found 'a project' that would enable him to put into practice the ideas he had feared would always remain entirely theoretical. As he has written, in a line that is strangely reminiscent of one that use to be recited, not so long ago, by those revolutionary Trotskyists who now write satirical novels, run their own television companies, or specialise in the problems of Compulsory Competitive Tendering: 'criticism without a project is merely a higher form of surrender'.[45] In some respects, Krier would have preferred to start by redeveloping a piece of existing suburb; but while this would have been the truly paradigmatic 'pilot project' of our age, the complexities would have been tremendous, and Poundbury made a good start. At the time of our meeting, he appeared to be rather enjoying the perplexity of professional advisers faced with his disciplined but unorthodox method of work. While he cited Charlemagne and Napoleon, remarking on the cruelty that has accompanied the architectural development of the European city, he was taking a decidedly pastoral approach down in Dorset. The two demolitions originally hypothesised for James Road have been dropped: indeed, once the residents of James Road protested, the first phase of development was quickly shifted over onto less contested ground near the Bridport Road. In general, Krier said that public response had been fantastically supportive, and he was looking forward to involving local and vernacular builders in the development. Britain is 'particular', he suggested, in that many highly capable builders still exist: indeed, he had driven through Dorset and found that in 'virtually every village' there were local builders doing good work. As the dispenser of 'locations' in a town that for a long time has had none, he had found all sorts of possibilities coming into view. There had been some talk about a new Crown Court and, when it came to that

sadly secularised clock tower on his original model, there was even
some suggestion that a proper church might be built: ecumenical, as it
would have to be these days, but still equipped with a proper spire.
Back in the summer of 1989, there seemed to be every reason to feel
bouyant about the possibilities of re-enchantment. Krier was not at
all disconcerted to hear that some of the people of Dorchester had
declared their preference for ordinary suburban development: as he
said, people say they want suburbs when you ask them in private, but
the planning weekend had demonstrated that they became more
ambitious, and also more responsible, when the discussion is
conducted in a proper public forum . . . .

Eighteen months later, the ground at Poundbury remains unbroken. By August 1989, the news came that Leon Krier had
'dramatically scaled down' his plan for four quarters.[46] He was
quoted as saying: 'The basic concept has not changed, but I am much
happier now it is more modest. The original plan would have been a
big risk. If it didn't work we would have been left with fragments. The
smaller development will be a complete piece of town itself'. By
December 1990, nearly a year after the date at which it was originally
hoped work might begin, the news was beginning to leak out that both
Prince Charles and Leon Krier were 'increasingly frustrated' by the
bureaucratic obstructiveness of the Duchy of Cornwall and the
Treasury that controls it through those heavy handed and distinctly
unvisionary 'management acts'. The champions of that 'Vision of
Britain' were apparently losing the battle against 'red tape' in their
very own camp.

The problems are only partly to do with the sudden decline of the
property market. This has reduced demand and profit margins, but
serious questions have also been raised concerning the will of the
Duchy of Cornwall's staff to see Charles's vision through. Leon Krier
knows about problems of this sort; like Raymond Williams, he is
familiar with people who talk about 'the real world' when what they
actually mean is money. Long before the Poundbury project was
dreamed up, he wrote that 'It can no longer be short-term budgets
which should dictate the form of Architecture and the City, but
Architecture and the City must dictate the form of long-term
budgets'.[47] This point is hardly accepted either by the Treasury or by
the Duchy of Cornwall.

Charles's position at the Duchy is rather like that of a rich child
whose money is held in trust: in order to get anything done, he must
consult with the men in grey suits on the Duchy's Council, and they
are the advocates of the most unvisionary kind of realism. Krier has
himself had occasion to suspect that the Duchy really doesn't want to
complete the scheme: the landowning situation in this country is such
that the Duchy can make money far more easily by just dealing in
land and not bothering with development at all. Add to this what
Krier describes as 'the delusion that grew out of the Thatcher years',

namely the idea that a town can be built purely on market forces, and the prospects begin to look entirely hopeless. While Krier is in no doubt that his town will need nurturing in its early years, and that the Duchy 'should behave as if it were a public authority not a developer', he also insists that his project is financially perfectly viable: as he says, 'you build what you can afford, and leave the rest until later'. But the accountants of the short-term gain can't understand this approach, any more than their predecessors in the Sixties could begin to estimate the crippling long-term costs of the tower blocks. So more and more people have been employed to revise Krier's scheme. To begin with it was the quantity surveyors who came up with cash-flow calculations which, as Krier tried to demonstrate by working up his own figures, were based on an inappropriate itemisation of costs. Then came the marketing people who were particularly adamant that the industrial buildings should be separated out from the residential areas: they could see no advantage in designing the development in such a way that some properties would always be less valuable than others because of their unnecessarily inferior locations. I gather that a separate company was eventually brought in to work Krier's scheme up, or down as the case actually was, into what was effectively a counter-scheme that made less provision for industry and reduced Krier's public buildings to little more than a symbolic presence. For a while, it looked as if Poundbury was going to collapse into another mediocre suburb with a business park attached. I understand that a letter of resignation was despatched, but Prince Charles couldn't let his 'Vision of Britain' die such a miserable death and, as things stood at the end of 1990, the project was going forward with Krier in place as master planner, even though he was now in the paradoxical position of having to work through the company that had been brought in to cut his plans down to 'realistic' size.

Predictably, these difficulties have been greeted with much delighted crowing from the architectural establishment. Maxwell Hutchinson has rubbed his hands in glee, suggesting that Prince Charles might at last be learning something about the constraints under which architects normally work. Martin Pawley has declared that, since the project has come to nothing, it was obviously unworthy of the energy and time that so many people had put into discussing it.

Must Xanadu always just fade away into thin air? The Duchy of Cornwall will struggle on, but in Hackney we settle for more modest moments of grace. At the opening of the Mother's Square, a journalist found a resident who was prepared to declare, 'I feel that I am living in Wonderland now'.[48] Unexpected things happen at Dalston Junction too. Just before Christmas, I noticed a huddle of people gathered at the Town Guide Cabinet. Going over to investigate, I saw a light burning with manic brightness at the centre of the map – just beside the label announcing 'You are Here'.

Notes

Chapter 1

1. Nikolaus Pevsner, *The Buildings of England: London*, Penguin Books, 1952, p. 162.
2. As I discovered afterwards, Sir Alfred was merely reciting a text which he had printed under the title of 'How Hackney went to Hell' in Peregrine Worsthorne's 'Comment' section of *The Sunday Telegraph*, 22 July 1990.
3. Readers who would like a less partisan treatment of the nineteenth-century idea of 'Degeneration' and its application to the city should consult Daniel Pick, *Faces of Degeneration; A European Disorder, c. 1948– c. 1918*, Cambridge University Press, 1989.
4. Paul Harrison, *Inside the Inner City; Life under the Cutting Edge*, Pelican Books, 1983, p. 32.
5. Lord Joseph printed the finished version of his disquisition under the title 'We did not go far enough; we failed her', in *The Independent*, 23 November 1990.
6. Douglas Oliver, *The Infant and the Pearl*, Silver Hounds, 1985. This poem is also included in *Three Variations on the Theme of Harm*, Paladin, 1990.

Chapter 2

1. See *Hackney Gazette*, 23 March 1990.
2. *Hackney Gazette*, 12 January 1990.
3. Ian Nairn, *Outrage*, a special number of the *Architectural Review*, Vol. 117, no. 702, June 1955.
4. On theming see John Thackara's 'Unthemely behaviour', *The Guardian*, 8 January 1987. As Thackara concludes: ' "Lifestyle design" disenfranchises the "non-targeted", and kills off the old-style street with its volatile mixture of nationalities and classes. The marketeers claim that theming replaces outmoded class barriers; but control of space planning and the imagery therein remains in the hands of those, such as brewers, who have a close resemblance to old-style bosses'. This is an important point, well made, and I'm glad to say that the majority of the people on Dalston Lane have no reason to understand a word of it.
5. Barbara Jones, *The Unsophisticated Arts*, Architectural Press, 1951.

6. Richard M. Titmuss, *Problems of Social Policy*, HMSO, 1950, p. 263.
7. Lord Beveridge, *Voluntary Action; A Report on Methods of Social Advance*, Allen & Unwin, 1948, p. 301. As Beveridge writes, 'In a Totalitarian society all action outside the citizen's home, and it may be much that goes on there is directed or controlled by the State. By contrast, vigour and abundance of Voluntary Action outside one's home, individually and in association with other citizens, for bettering one's own life and that of one's fellows, are the distinguishing marks of a free society' (p. 10).
8. *Ibid.* p. 324.
9. As an influential report claimed, the 'Political sympathies of those who staff QUALGOs are almost invariably left-wing. The middle-class Tory lady, once so dedicated a worker for charity, has been elbowed out by ridicule, snubbing and such unacceptable demands upon her time as obligatory attendance at training class'. See Teresa Gorman *et al.*, *Qualgos Just Grow; Political Bodies in Voluntary Clothing*, Centre for Policy Studies, 1985, p. 9.
10. See, for example, Ali Mantle, *Popular Planning Not in Practice; Confessions of a Community Worker*, Greenwich Employment Resource Unit, 1985.
11 Sue Cavanagh and Vron Ware, *At Women's Convenience: A Handbook on the Design of Women's Public Toilets*, Women's Design Service, 1990.
12. Owen Kelly, *Community Art and the State: Storming the Citadels*, Comedia, 1984, p. 1.

Chapter 3

1. Roy Kerridge, 'Best place for shoes outside Lagos', *The Independent*, 2 June 1990.
2. *Hackney Gazette*, 13 April 1990.
3. The law of Dalston Lane has long been recognised in the advertising trade. Before the war when such organisations as the SCAPA Society for Prevention of Disfigurement in Town and Country were campaigning against inappropriately placed poster sites, the trade journal, *Advertising Display*, replied by stressing the service rendered by the advertisers whose works obscured the debris and dishevelment of 'eligible building sites': as the text accompanying some carefully chosen photographs asked: 'Is this "Disfiguring the Face of Britain"?' See *Advertising Display*, March 1929.
4. In November 1990, the Duke of Westminster went to the High Court to prevent Westminster City Council from selling flats on the Grosvenor Estate to anyone living or working in the area. In 1937 the duke's ancestor had assigned the estate to Westminster City Council on the condition that its flats be used as 'dwellings

for the working class . . . and for no other purpose'. Mr Justice
Harman found against Westminster City Council, which had
claimed that the term 'working class' had no meaning any more,
and was reported as having 'ruled that the working class still
exists'. See *The Independent*, 27 November 1990.

5. Jim White, 'Are you being served – or sold out?', *The Independent*,
24 May 1990.
6. Peter Fuller, *Marches Past*, Chatto & Windus, 1986, p. 125.
7. Sara Maitland, *Three Times Table*, Chatto & Windus, 1990. See
also Maitland's article 'God's own country', *Evening Standard*, 23
May 1990.
8. Paul Harrison, *Inside the Inner City*, Pelican Books, 1983, p. 32.
9. Roger Scruton, *The Philosopher on Dover Beach*, Carcanet, 1990, p.
293.
10. The best account of this literary tourism remains Benedict
Anderson's blistering article on the James Fenton/Granta style
of voyeurism. See Anderson's 'James Fenton's Slideshow', *New
Left Review*, no. 158, July/August 1986.
11. These remarks were made by Michael Fallon, and reported in
The Times, 26 December 1990.
12. See, for example, Auberon Waugh, 'Tramps and vagrants have
nothing to do with the housing problem', *Spectator*, 7 January
1989.

Chapter 4
1. Mary Douglas, *Purity and Danger, An Analysis of the Concepts of
Pollution and Taboo*, Routledge, 1966.
2. 'Lynn' describes how he was thrown out of No. 99 Balls Pond
Road for setting up this experiment in Appendix 2, Paul Keeler,
Planted, Stanhope Press, 1968, pp. 20–1. The fact that the only
rule in this house was one proscribing the use of drugs did not
prevent the tabloids from whipping up a storm over the 'Hippy
HQ' where 'Food, clothing – even girl-friends – will be shared';
nor, as was claimed in a famous court case of the time, did it stop
Detective Sergeant Rigby of Dalston Police Station from sending
an infiltrator down to plant cannabis in the house ('He wore
jeans, but they were very new') a few months later.
3. Maberly Sabbath School, *Minute Book 1836–1856*, Hackney
Archives.
4. Elizabeth Wilson, *Hallucinations*, Radius, 1988.
5. I refer to 'The Invisible City', an exhibition held at the
Photogaphers Gallery as 'London Project II' in November 1990.
6. John Farleigh, *It Never Dies: A Collection of Notes and Essays 1940–
46*, Sylvan Press, 1946.
7. Wanda Ostrowska, *London's Glory: Twenty Paintings of the City's
Ruins* (with text by Viola G. Garvin), Allen & Unwin, 1945.

8. *Hackney Gazette*, 9 February 1990.
9. *Hackney Gazette*, 2 March 1990.

Chapter 5

1. See I. F. Nicolson, *The Mystery of Crichel Down*, Clarendon Press, 1986.
2. *Ibid.*, p. 120.
3. R. Douglas Brown, *The Battle of Crichel Down*, The Bodley Head, 1955, p. 87.
4. *Ibid.*, p. 33.
5. *Ibid.*, p. 10.
6. Audit Commission, *Urban Regeneration and Economic Development: The Local Government Dimension*, HMSO, 1989.

Chapter 6

1. John Summerson, 'Town Buildings' in James Lees-Milne (ed.) *The National Trust: A Record of Fifty Years' Achievement*, Batsford, 1945, pp. 97–102.
2. *Hackney Gazette*, 13 February 1987.
3. Julie Lafferty, letter in *Hackney Gazette*, 3 March 1987.
4. See the title of Lansbury's book of reminiscences, *Looking Backwards – and Forwards*, Blackie, 1935.
5. Raymond Postgate, *The Life of George Lansbury*, Longman, 1951, p. 248.
6. Evelyn Waugh, *Brideshead Revisited*, Penguin Books, 1987. Charles Ryder is a country-house painter of little talent who owes his overblown reputation to his countrymen's tendency to 'salute their achievements at the moment of extinction'.
7. C. E. Montague, 'Country Houses', in *The Right Place*, Chatto & Windus, 1925, p. 163.
8. Osbert Sitwell, 'Foreword' to Ralph Dutton, *The English Country House*, Batsford, 1935, p. vi.
9. Alex Comfort, 'The Martyrdom of the House' collected in *Letters from an Outpost*, Routledge, 1947, pp. 1–14.
10. Sorrell's picture is reproduced in David Mellor (ed.) *A Paradise Lost; The Neo-Romantic Imagination in Britain, 1935–55*, Lund Humphries, 1987, p. 125.
11. On Piper's wartime work, see Malcome Yorke, *The Spirit of Place; Nine Neo-Romantic Artists in their Times*, Constable, 1988, pp. 70–105.
12. John Arlott and Michael Ayrton, *Clausentum*, Jonathan Cape, 1947.
13. See David Mellor, 'Recording Britain; A History and Outline', in David Mellor, Gill Saunders, and Patrick Wright, *Recording Britain; A Pictorial Domesday of Pre-War Britain*, David & Charles, 1990, p. 10.

14. John Lodwick, *Peal of Ordnance*, Methuen, 1947.
15. Dornford Yates, *The House that Berry Built*, Ward Lock, 1945.
16. Quoted from the cover of James Lees-Milne, *Stourhead: A Property of the National Trust*, Country Life, 1948.
17. John Martin Robinson, 'Holding the bridge for fifty years', *Spectator*, 18 April 1987, pp. 35–6.
18. John Gaze, *Figures in a Landscape; A History of the National Trust*, Barrie & Jenkins, 1988, p. 125.
19. James Lees-Milne, *Prophesying Peace*, Faber & Faber, 1984, p. 54.
20. See Gaze, *op. cit.*, pp. 129–30.
21. James Lees-Milne, *Another Self*, Hamish Hamilton, 1970. I have described Lees-Milne's autobiography more fully in 'James Lees-Milne: A Superannuated Man?', *Modern Painters*, Vol. 2, no. 1, Spring 1989.
22. *Another Self*, pp. 94–5. Bevis Hillier has provided further details of that visit to Rousham. The 'capricious alcoholic' turns out to have been Maurice Hastings, brother of De Cronin Hastings, the enthusiastic modernist who ran the *Architectural Review*. The consenting Oxford don among the bright undergraduate guests – all 'vastly entertained' by their sodden host's performance – was none other than Sir Maurice Bowra himself. See Bevis Hillier, *Young Betjeman*, Murray, 1988, p. 248–9.
23. See Hugh Montgomery-Massingberd, 'A veteran in the war with the Philistines', *The Daily Telegraph*, 6 August 1988. Also John Martin Robinson, 'Distinction and Class', *Spectator*, 6 August 1988.
24. *Ibid.*, p. 143.
25. James Lees-Milne describes how Lansdowne House was destroyed by 'speculative Philistines' acting in a way tolerated by the 'smug and cynical' public of the decadent inter-war period. The Americans salvaged 'a few pickings out of the holocaust'. Indeed, the drawing-room, 'with its pilaster painted in glowing arabesques, may now be viewed by shamefaced British visitors to the Philadelphia Museum of Art'. See Lees-Milne's *The Age of Adam*, Batsford, 1947, p. 113.
26. Georgina Battiscombe, *English Picnics*, Harvill, 1949, p. 1.
27. Barbara Jones, *Follies and Grottoes*, Constable, 1953, pp. 81–2.
28. *Christian Science Monitor*, 7 June 1949.
29. *News Chronicle*, 5 May 1949.
30. The Marchioness of Bath, *Before the Sunset Fades*, Longleat Estate Co., 1951.
31. James Lees-Milne, *Midway on the Waves*, Faber & Faber, 1985, p 29.
32. James Lees-Milne, *Caves of Ice*, Faber & Faber, 1984, p. 35.
33. James Lees-Milne, *The National Trust Guide – Buildings*, Batsford, 1948.
34. Bevan's subsidies enabled the Council for the Preservation of

270 — Notes

Rural England to ensure that Halifax stone was kept in use in the Sheffield area. See the feature on Mrs Haythornthwaite of the CPRE in *The Architects' Journal*, 10 July 1963.

35. Gaze, *op. cit.*, p. 145.
36. Quoted in Gaze, *op. cit.*, p. 121.
37. Anne Scott-James, 'A year's work by the National Trust', *Picture Post*, Vol. 22, no. 4, 22 January 1944, p. 15.
38. See J. Cornforth, *The Inspiration of the Past, Country House Taste in the Twentieth Century*, Viking, 1985, pp. 2–3.
39. Vita Sackville-West, *English Country Houses*, Collins, 1941, pp. 47 & 30.
40. Stephen Bann, *The Clothing of Clio; A Study of the Representation of History in Nineteenth-Century Britain and France*, Cambridge University Press, 1984.
41. James Lees Milne, *Prophesying Peace*, p. 72.
42. For Brodsworth Hall, see Paul Routledge, 'For Sale: the House that firmly shut its door on the twentieth century', *The Observer*, 10 April 1988. On Calke Abbey, see my *On Living in an Old Country; the National Past in Contemporary Britain*, Verso, 1985, pp. 38–42.
43. See Kim Fletcher and Godfrey Barker, 'Mystery behind the Three Graces', *The Sunday Telegraph*, 25 February 1990.
44. Gervase Jackson-Stops and James Pipkin, *The English Country House; A Grand Tour*, Weidenfeld & Nicolson, 1985.
45. Alvilde Lees-Milne, *The Englishman's Room*, Viking, Harmondsworth and Viking, New York, 1986.
46. This remark was made by Jack Hyde, head of the menswear design and marketing division at the New York Fashion Institute of Technology, and reported in Lisa Belkin, 'Lauren look Permeating City', *New York Times*, 8 December 1986.
47. Witold Rybczynski, *Home; A Short History of an Idea*, New York, NY, Viking, 1986, p. 7.
48. Suzanne Slesin, 'For Connoisseurs: A Floor of English Collectables', *New York Times*, 20 January 1987.
49. Suzanne Slesin, 'Establishment decorators: a new breed', *New York Times*, 11 June 1987.
50. Michael Gross, 'Staying Home in Style', *New York Times*, 1 March 1987.
51. Linda Colley, 'The cult of the country house', *The Times Literary Supplement*, 15 November 1985. David Cannadine, 'Brideshead re-Revisited', *New York Review of Books*, 19 December 1985.
52. Marcus Binney and Gervase Jackson-Stops, 'The last hundred years' in G. Jackson-Stops (ed.) *The Treasure Houses of Britain: Five Hundred Years of Private Patronage and Art Collecting*, Yale University Press New Haven, Conn., and London, 1985, pp. 70–8.
53. Francis Haskell, 'Les musées et leurs ennemis', *Actes de la Recherche en science sociales*, 49, 1983, pp. 103–6.

54. David Cannadine, *The Decline and Fall of the British Aristocracy*, Yale University Press, 1990.

Chapter 7

1. Nikolaus Pevsner, *The Buildings of England: London*, Penguin Books, 1952, pp. 168–9.
2. Paul Harrison, *Inside the Inner City; Life under the Cutting Edge*, Pelican Books, 1983, pp. 227–337.
3. See Paul Harrison, *op. cit.*, pp. 238–9.
4. Ruth Glass, *Clichés of Urban Doom and other Essays*, Blackwell, 1989.
5. George Lansbury, *My England*, Selwyn & Blount, pp. 233 & 68.
6. Alice Coleman described the Lansbury Estate in this way in *Utopia on Trial: Vision and Reality in Planned Housing*, Hilary Shipman, 1985, p.8.
7. John Betjeman, 'Foreword', *The Rape of Britain*, Elek, 1975.
8. *Hackney Gazette*, 26 March 1971.
9. *Hackney Gazette*, 2 September 1966 and 30 September 1966 respectively.
10. Housing Committee Minutes, 26 October 1966.
11. *Hackney Gazette*, 27 September 1968.
12. *Hackney Gazette*, 2 March 1971.
13. Martin Pawley, *Architecture Versus Housing*, Studio Vista, 1971, p. 105.
14. My summary is largely derived from Patrick Dunleavy's excellent book, *The Politics of Mass Housing, 1945–1975; A Study of Corporate and Professional Influence in the Welfare State*, Clarendon Press, 1981.
15. *Ibid.*, p. 21.
16. Martin Pawley, *op. cit.*, p. 93.
17. Derrick Rigby Childs, 'Counterdrift Cities', *The Architects' Journal*, 20 February 1963.
18. *The Architects' Journal*, 21 July 1965. It should also be recognized that genuinely gifted architects indulged in remarkable justification of their work. Sir Denys Lasdun made a programme of BBC's *Monitor* in the Sixties in which he invoked the idea of African village community structures to justify the design of a cluster block in Bethnal Green. Watching it now, one can't help feeling he might have done better to look at the kind of 'community' that existed in the very place his building was to occupy.
19. R. Furneaux Jordan, 'New Standards in Official Architecture', *Architectural Review*, November 1956.
20. Clough Williams-Ellis, *On Trust for the Nation*, Elek, 1947, p. 13.
21. Hackney Society Minute Book, Hackney Archives.
22. Betjeman's enthusiasm for *Coronation Street* is described in

Alexandra Artley and John Martin Robinson, *New Georgian Handbook*, Ebury Press, 1985, p. 43. He repeated his defence of 'houses' against 'housing' in his 'Foreword' to Colin Amery and Dan Cruickshank, *The Rape of Britain*, Elek, 1975.

23. *Hackney Gazette*, 8 January 1971.
24. Tony Aldous, *The Book of London's Villages*, Secker & Warburg, 1980 (this book is a collection of articles written for *Illustrated London News*).
25. *Hackney Gazette*, 26 March 1971.
26. Donald Kearsley, report on the first Mapledene inquiry, 1973.
27. Ernie Greenwood, statement to the 1977 public inquiry.
28. Gayne Wells, proof of evidence for the 1977 public inquiry.
29. Charles Bergonzi, proof of evidence for the 1977 public inquiry.
30. Mr Benjamin described his removal from the Committee of Workshops for the Elderly, of which Alderman Ottolangui was Chairman, in his proof of evidence to the 1977 public inquiry.
31. Letter from W. E. Matthews, Technical Adviser of Men of the Trees, to Gayne Wells of the Backlands Action Group, 17 February 1977.
32. Julian Harrap's statement made on behalf of the Hackney Society to the Public Inquiry into the Albion Drive, Mapledene Road (No. 3) Compulsory Purchase Orders 1976.
33. Donald Kearsley, report on the first Mapledene inquiry, 1973.
34. Letter from Julian Orbach of the Victorian Society to Hackney Borough Planning Officer, 17 June 1977.
35. Martin Pawley, *Architecture Versus Housing*, p. 105. Martin Pawley, *Garbage Housing*, Architectural Press, 1975, p. 53.
36. Thomas L. Blair, *The Poverty of Planning: Crisis in the Urban Environment*, Macdonald, 1973, pp. 85–97.
37. The Work Group, 'A Critique of "Community Studies" and its role in social thought', University of Birmingham, Centre for Contemporary Cultural Studies, 1976, p. 18. This argument, which is representative of views still held in some sociological circles, assumed with Marxist thinkers like Westergaard, that local community ties impede the development of true class consciousness, bringing about instead a 'sectionalist, parochial self-interest', which has little to offer the Marxist intellectual.
38. Paul Elek, *This Other London*, Elek, 1951, p. 52.
39. These words are from the Preface contributed by Roger White, Secretary of the Georgian Group, to Elizabeth Robinson, *Lost Hackney*, Hackney Society, 1989.
40. Colin Amery and Dan Cruikshank, *The Rape of Britain, op. cit.*
41. See, for example, Christopher Booker and Candida Lycett Green, *Goodbye London: An Illustrated Guide to Threatened Buildings*, Collins, 1973.
42. Christopher Booker, 'Physical Planning: Another Illusion Shattered', *National Westminster Bank Quarterly Review*, February 1977, p. 62.

43. Witold Rybczynski, *Home; A Short History of an Idea*, Viking, New York, NY, 1986, p. 202.

44. Quote from Stephen Haseler, letter to *The Independent*, 8 December 1988; and 'The Spectacle of Tory radicals hoist by their own petard', *The Independent*, 16 June 1988.

45. Jules Lubbock, 'Politics of the portico', *New Statesman*, 1 May 1987.

46. Mira Bar-Hillel, 'Ugly fifties monuments denied protection', *The Sunday Telegraph*, 13 March 1988.

47. Kenneth Rose, 'Albany at Large', *The Sunday Telegraph*, 23 September 1990.

48. Marina Cantacuzino, 'Some Pay to Move In; Some Pray to Move out', *The Telegraph Sunday Magazine*, 8 May 1988.

Chapter 8

1. *The Speech of Thomas Fowell Buxton Esq., at the Egyptian Hall, on the 26th November 1816, on the Subject of the Distress in Spitalfields*, published by the Association for the Relief of the Industrious Poor of Spitalfields, 1816. See also Charles Buxton (ed.) *Memoirs of Sir Thomas Fowell Buxton with Selections from his Correspondence*, Murray, 1848.

2. Colin Ward, 'Awkward Questions in Spitalfields', in *Housing; An Anarchist Approach*, Freedom Press, 1976, p. 59.

3. According to the Spitalfields Historic Buildings Trust's own account of its first ten years, Rodinsky's room stood untouched and forgotten for some twenty years before 'the Trust opened the door for the first time since his mysterious departure' to discover that 'Rodinsky's table was still laid for a meal, his bed covers turned down, pyjamas still on the pillow'. The Spitalfields Historic Buildings Trust, *The Saving of Spitalfields*, 1989, p. 24–5.

4. Mark Girouard, 'The East End's Streets of Silks', *Country Life*, 15 November 1979.

5. Mark Girouard, 'An Area to Fight For', *Country Life*, 22 November 1979.

6. See Stuart Blain's 'Foreword' in *The Saving of Spitalfields, op. cit.*, pp. 18–19.

7. Early in 1987 Facility Group Interiors were offering seminars on the 'flexible interior' at London's Business Design Centre. Delegates would be told how to overcome 'fixed walls, spaghetti-like cabling, furniture and storage systems more suited to a Victorian study' and, more generally, how to turn the office into 'a powerful instrument of management'.

8. Alexandra Artley and John Martin Robinson, *The New Georgian Handbook, a First Look at the Conservation Way of Life*, Ebury Press, 1985.

9. See Deborah Devonshire, Nicholas Coleridge and Simon von Ausberg's contributions on the theme of 'Cold houses' in *Harpers and Queen*, February 1987.
10. See Rosalind Russell's article on Peter Ackroyd's rural retreat near Barnstable, 'The squeak of the wild', *Evening Standard*, 26 September 1990.
11. Gavin Stamp, 'A culture in crisis', *Spectator*, 12 October 1985 and 'The real Hawksmoor', *Spectator*, 29 March 1986.
12. John Martin Robinson, *The English Country Estate*, Century, 1988, p. 167. This book is full of such tendentious claims. For the real story of the Black Act of 1723, see E. P. Thompson, *Whigs and Hunters; The Origins of the Black Act*, Pantheon Books, New York, N.Y., 1975.
13. *Spectator*, 2 April 1988.
14 Among the most notable of these articles by Alexandra Artley is 'The real poor', *Spectator*, 13 December 1986, p. 9–12. Here Artley sets out with her pram – 'a good way to get to know an area' – and reports back on the destitution to be found on her own doorstep in King's Cross.
15. Alexandra Artley, 'Diary', *Spectator*, 10 October 1987.
16. Auberon Waugh, 'An appeal to all the nation's madwomen . . .', *Spectator*, 31 October 1987.

Chapter 9

1. See Artley and Robinson, *New Georgian Handbook*, p. 45.
2. See my article 'Why the blight must be so stark', *The Guardian*, 1 August 1987. Also the BBC 2 documentary, *Brideshead and the Tower Blocks*, 30 October 1988.
3. 'Split up the National Trust', leading article in *The Independent*, 24 October 1990.
4. I quote this from an article that testifies to the existence of an internal debate on these issues within the National Trust. See Fors Clavigera, 'Whither the National Trust?', *Countryside Monthly*, September 1984, p. 224.
5. Michael Hanson, 'Trust the National Trust', *Country Life*, 16 July 1987.
6. Michael Seamark, 'National Trust boss upsets the villagers', *Daily Mail*, 8 June 1987.
7. John Martin Robinson, the *Spectator*, 18 April 1987.
8. 'Right man to restore faith in the Trust?' *The Sunday Telegraph*, 11 November 1990.
9. Geordie Greig, 'An earl in the pink sees red', *The Sunday Times*, 5 June 1988.
10. Anthea Hall, 'National Trust is destroying our stately homes', *The Sunday Telegraph*, 12 June 1988.

11. James Lees-Milne, review of Mark Girouard's *A Country House Companion*, in the *Spectator*, 28 November 1987, pp. 45–6.
12. Roger Scruton, 'The Stately and the State-Controlled' was published in *The Times* on 21 February 1984 and collected in Scruton's *Untimely Tracts*, Macmillan, 1987, pp. 113–15.
13. James Lees-Milne, letter in *The Times*, 24 February 1984.
14. James Lees-Milne, 'False guardians', *The Sunday Telegraph*, 27 November 1988.

Chapter 11

1. *Hackney Gazette*, 4 October 1966.
2. Gavin Stamp, *Telephone Boxes*, Chatto & Windus, 1989, p. 49.
3. C. A. R. Crosland, *The Future of Socialism*, Jonathan Cape, 1956, pp. 521–2.
4. *The Independent*, 26 November 1987.
5. System X was described as the '£5 billion blunder' by *The Sunday Times* (9 August 1987).
6. The travelling exhibition of kiosks that had been filled with flour, set in concrete, or incinerated with a butane lighter was described in 'Troubles by the boxful for BT', *Evening Standard*, 28 September 1987. British Telecom likes to treat vandalism as if it were an entirely recent problem, but there is literary evidence to suggest that telephone kiosks were suffering rough treatment even in the Forties when, according to BT's convenient theory of post-war degeneration, British manners should still have been intact. The hero of John Lodwick's novel, *Peal of Ordnance* (1947), enters a telephone box in Oxford Street to find the usual disordered scene: 'The booth smelt of urine and spittle gouts. He opened the directory; obsolete, tatty and well-thumbed . . . signatures in the bargain (Jack H. Rossback; U.S.N. Yonkers, N.Y.), and here and there addresses underlined with words of advice: "Call her up any time. She'll be there" (p. 98). By the Sixties, the problem had changed somewhat. Lionel Kearns, a Canadian poet who was accustomed to visiting London at the time, wrote a poem about a character called Roderick who enters a telephone box and then finds that the door has disappeared: trapped, he spends his time calling his friends for help and, when his money runs out, chatting up the girl at directory enquiries. In the end, the booth fills up with beard and excrement, and it becomes impossible to tell from outside whether Roderick is living or dead. See 'Telephone' in Lionel Kearns, *By the Light of the Silvery McLune*, Daylight Press, Vancouver, 1969.
7. *The Guardian*, 24 September 1987.
8. Charles R. Perry, 'The British Experience 1876–1912: the impact of the telephone during the years of delay', in Ithiel de Sola Pool (ed.) *The Social Impact of the Telephone*, MIT Press, pp. 68–96.

9. As it was put by Nick Kane, Director of Marketing for BT Local Communications Services, the old red telephone boxes 'no longer meet the requirements of our customers. Few people like to use them. They are expensive and difficult to clear and maintain and cannot be used by handicapped people'. Quoted in Gavin Stamp, 'Save the Telephone Box', *Spectator*, 9 February 1985.

10. George Orwell, 'England your England', *Inside the Whale and other Essays*, Penguin Books, 1968, pp. 63–90.

11. See Clive Aslet and Alan Powers, 'The British Telephone Box . . . take it as red', The Thirties Society, 1987.

12. Quoted from papers held at the Historical Information Centre, British Telecom Archives, London.

13. The BT Archives include a number of patiently argued letters written by the Post Office's G. E. G. Forbes to CPRE supporters who had protested against this shocking 'intervention of red' in the English scene. In the final sentence of a letter concerning the Lake District (dated 24 June 1936) he is reduced to wondering 'whether the exclusion of these minute patches of red from the District is so important as all that'.

14. The battle against red continues to rage in distant villages. Visitors to Litton Cheney in Dorset will find a Jubilee Kiosk that is green, thanks to the nocturnal and evidently rather hasty activities of local vigilantes.

15. 'Colour of "Jubilee Design" kiosks', memo 2687/36 in British Telecom Archives.

16. The decision to allow battle-ship grey to be used in 'very exceptional cases' was made on the recommendation of the Royal Fine Art Commission, but not until 1948.

17. *The Guardian*, 2 April 1985.

18. Roger Scruton, 'Putting heritage on the line', *The Times*, 29 January 1985, p. 10.

19. The 'Bombay shirt' sounds plausible enough, but it turns out to be a product of Scruton's fertile imagination. Perhaps the professor was thinking of the 'Bengal stripe' that, despite its embarrassing adoption by yuppie fashion, is still the classic pattern for the bourgeois gentleman's shirt.

20. Charles Moore, 'Better red than dead', *The Daily Telegraph*, 29 December 1986.

21. Moore came up with this resounding statement while attempting to bluster his way past accusations I had made in an article for *The Listener*. I had argued, as I do here, that privatisation was to a considerable extent responsible for the destruction of the old red telephone box, and that the *Spectator*'s response to the affair was therefore both guilt-ridden and thoroughly confused. Moore was quick to dismiss me as 'hopelessly confused' in return, but in reality he was only tying himself up in worse knots as he tried to

see me off without so much as mentioning the central issue of privatisation at all (*Spectator*, 22 August 1987). I thought of Moore again in October 1988 when a company called International Payphones Ltd started complaining about the cosy 'BT and Mercury duopoly'. IPL wanted to add to the stylistic anarchy of the late twentieth-century British street by setting up a third pay phone service with a range of kiosks that looked as if they had been bodged together out of old biscuit tins. Here was the privatisation argument being extended into a bid for 'complete deregulation of the pay phone service in Britain', and the Department of Trade and Industry's refusal to licence IPL was of a distinctly embarrassed rather than principled kind (reported in *The Sunday Times*, 23 October 1988). Here again, the *Spectator* refrained from comment.

22. The passages quoted here are from articles that Gavin Stamp contributed to the *Spectator*. Stamp's more recent account of the affair of the old red telephone box does not fight shy of identifying privatisation as a principle cause: 'If the ethos of the 1920s was that of responsible public service, then that of Mrs Thatcher's Britain is asset-stripping – the profitable disposal of anything of value in the public realm, regardless of the best and long-term interests of the British people'. See Stamp's *Telephone Boxes, op. cit.*, p. 25. Stamp also gives his own critical assessment of John Simpson's classical kiosk here, describing it as both 'painfully over-elaborate' and 'naively literal'. Classical columns are 'preposterous' on a structure as small as a telephone kiosk, 'but Simpson felt that Classicism requires complete Doric columns'. In Giles Gilbert Scott's design, by contrast, 'the Classical language is so well digested and understood that only its essence governs the appropriate form' (pp. 27–8).

23. Gavin Stamp described his communication with Jefferson in a letter to the *Spectator*, 6 June 1987.

24. Gavin Stamp, letter to the *Spectator*, 15 August 1987.

25. Des Wilson's letter was printed in the *Spectator*, 30 May 1987.

26. *Spectator*, 25 July 1987.

27. *Spectator*, 27 June 1987.

28. *Spectator*, 4 July 1987.

29. *Spectator*, 22 August 1987.

30. Tim Rayment, 'A phone box needs love when it's number is up', *The Sunday Times*, 17 May 1987.

31. Charles Moore's report on the completed competition appeared in the *Spectator*, 22 August 1987.

32. In 1983 the Telecom unions tried to broadcast a television advert that used the Jubilee Kiosk as the emblem of standards of public service endangered by privatisation. The Independent Broadcasting Authority refused to allow transmission, claiming that the intended advertisement was 'political'. British Telecom,

meanwhile, had no trouble broadcasting much repeated advertisments that, in the words of their own maker, were intended to prepare the ground for privatisation. This story was covered in *Change of Owner*, a highly revealing film made for Channel 4 by Richard Belfield and Christopher Hird of Fulcrum Productions and broadcast on 26 April 1988.

33. Quoted from Alan Powers, *Real Architecture; An Exhibition of Classical Building by the New Generation of Architects*, Building Centre Trust, 1987, p. 58.

34. Simon Jenkins, 'Philistines lose the battle of the boxes', *The Sunday Times*, 31 July 1988.

Chapter 12

1. Sir Mortimer Wheeler, *Still Digging; Leaves from an Antiquary's Notebook*, Michael Joseph, 1955, p. 104.

2. Mick Moran, 'Diary of a Thames mudlark', *Treasure Hunting*, June 1985.

3. See Iain Sinclair, 'Isle of Dogs', *London Review of Books*, 10 May 1990.

4. *The Times*, 1 January 1987.

5. David Lovibond, 'Curse of the Nighthawks', *The Sunday Telegraph*, 22 November 1987.

6. Mark Bowden, 'Heavy Metal', *Museum Professionals Group News*, Autumn, 1983. The STOP campaign pamphlet is included in *Metal Detectors and Archaeology*, a report of the Council of Europe's Committee on Culture and Education, Strasbourg, 1981.

7. The Boudicca Team, 'Boudicca or is it Cassandra?', *Treasure Hunting*, April 1983. The parsnip story derives from the case of one Ian Gray whose patch of earth lies within the grounds of Fulham Palace. See also Boudicca's, 'Let's give the people the facts!' and 'A message to our farming friends', both in *Treasure Hunting*, December 1981. The latter article warns farmers that 'If any part of your farm is declared to be "of archaeological significance" this will give professional archaeologists a statutory right to come on to your land and dig holes'. They will then find the archaeologists cashing in: 'Do not believe any "guff" you might be given about professional archaeologists not claiming Treasure Trove rewards.'

8. This point was made by Neal Ascherson, 'The means of grace, the hope of glory, *The Observer*, 20 October 1985, collected in Ascherson's *Games with Shadows*, Radius, 1988.

9. Richard Thomas, 'Should the law protect the past?', *Farmers Weekly*, 28 September 1984, pp. 30–1.

10. Mike Crow, 'The ley, a pointer to hoard location?'. *Treasure Hunting*, September 1985.

11. Mick Moran, 'In the Shadow of the Tower', *Treasure Hunting*,

May & June 1987. When questioned by readers concerned about the safety of his nocturnal trips to construction sites in the city and the tempting romanticism of his writing, Moran replied that he had no intention of changing either his 'lifestyle or form of writing to suit the nanny's of the metal detecting world': 'I am an adult male with forty years experience of this sad world. All my adult life I have gone my own way and refused to be bound by the petty restrictions that those of a more grandnanny temperament would bind me with . . . . If I chose to search a dangerous site I will do so and would sooner die at forty years of age, albeit reluctantly, clutching a newly discovered pilgrim badge, than die at seventy in the humiliating shackels of old age, or shoved from pillar to post in some grotesque old folks home' (*Treasure Hunting*, July 1987). For other detector users, this intransigence in the face of a routinised world has a 'survivalist' aspect: when the magazine, *Detector User*, folded, its editor, Greg Payne, moved on to a publication called *Survival Weaponry and Techniques*.

12. Tony Gregory's analysis of the treasure-hunting phenomenom is broadly similar, and places considerable stress on the class composition of the professional and amateur interests. See his 'Whose fault is treasure hunting?', *Archaeology and the Public; Proceedings of the 1985 Conference of Young Archaeologists*, York University, Department of Archaeology, 1986.

13. David Keys, 'Fen hides prehistoric pathway to the gods', *The Independent*, 24 June 1989.

Chapter 14

1. Theo Crosby, Pedro Guedes and Michael Sandle, *The Battle of Britain Monument*, Pentagram Design Ltd, 1987; Theo Crosby, *Let's Build a Monument*, Pentagram Design Ltd, 1987.

2. Pentagram Design Group, *Pentagram; The Work of Five Designers*, Lund Humphries, 1972

3. Lawrence Alloway *et al., This is Tomorrow*, Whitechapel Art Gallery, 1956. See also David Robbins (ed.) *The Independent Group; Postwar Britain and the Aesthetics of Plenty*, MIT Press, Cambridge, Mass. and London, 1990.

4. Theo Crosby, *The Necessary Monument*, Studio Vista, 1970, p.8.

5. The lectures were printed in Theo Crosby, *The Pessimist Utopia*, Pentagram Paper No. 2, 1975.

6. Gavin Stamp, 'The real Hawksmoor', *Spectator*, 29 March 1986, pp. 35–6.

7. Peter Ackroyd, *Hawksmoor*, Hamish Hamilton, 1985, pp. 22 & 186.

8. Ian Sinclair, *White Chappell; Scarlet Tracings*, Goldmark, 1987.

9. Christopher Booker and Candida Lycett Green provided a brisk

and useful survey of redevelopment plans in *Goodbye London: An Illustrated Guide to Threatened Buildings*, Fontana, 1973.

10. E.O. Gordon, *Prehistoric London; Its Mounds and Circles*, Covenant Publishing, 1925.

11. Iain Sinclair, *Lud Heat*, English Language Society, 2nd edition, 1986, p. 25.

12. These powerful words may not have been any more 'original' than Crosby's own monument. Writing in the Forties, George Speaight suggested that Churchill drew his rhetoric from the nineteenth-century toy-theatre plays that were a prominent feature of his childhood. See Speaight, *The History of the English Toy Theatre*, Studio Vista, 1969.

13. Martin Pawley, 'Monumental folly', *Designer*, November-December 1987, p. 36. See also Pawley's 'Reaching for the skies', *The Guardian*, 8 September 1987.

14. Barbara Jones, *Follies and Grottoes*, Constable, 1953, p. 1.

15. See, for example, Umberto Eco, *Travels in Hyper-Reality*, Picador, 1986.

16. Derwent May, 'Readers Choice for a Plinth', *The Sunday Telegraph*, 10 April, 1988, p. 26. For Dowding's own interest in the Trafalgar Square plinth, see the letter from D.B. Ogilvie in the same issue (p. 11).

17. Douglas C. Mason, *Room for Improvement – A Strategy for Housing Reform*, Adam Smith Institute, 1985, p. 24.

18. Described in Eve Hofstettler, *The Island at War: Memories of War-Time Life on the Isle of Dogs, East London*, Island History Trust, 1990, p. 32.

19. George Pye's remark goes as follows: 'But I will say this, you had walked right round the Island and every firm on the Island was bombed. I said that was good bombing. Every firm copped it, so it was good bombing, you know, you have to give and take'. See Eve Hofstettler, *The Island at War*, p. 19.

20. As Daisy Woodard wrote in the conclusion to a letter to the *Islander*, 'So come on, whoever out there has the power to name and rename places, what about a Blasker Close or a Blasker Street?'

21. Jonathan Raban, 'On the Water Margin', *For Love and Money*, Collins Harvill, 1987, p. 296.

Chapter 15

1. Written by Joyce Adcock and Gordon Caleb,*Strike a Light!* was staged at the Piccadilly Theatre in 1966.

2. Looking back in the Thirties, George Lansbury remarked that 'the agitation and the strike had much to do with' the eventual elimination of 'phossy jaw', but he also had high praise for Sir George Paton, the Bryant & May chief who, as joint Managing

Director from 1901, ran the later Edwardian 'model factory' as a place 'with every modern convenience, both for efficient working, and for the meals and leisure of the workers', and who, as Chairman and benevolent monopolist in the Twenties, insisted on conditions of work that spared Bryant & May any trouble during the General Strike of 1926. Watching 'the healthy, lively, well-dressed girls coming out of the factory gate', he remarked that they could have been 'a different race' from their Victorian precursors. See George Lansbury, *Looking Backwards – and Forwards* Blackie, 1935, p. 55. Also the official company history by Patrick Beaver (*The Matchmakers*, Henry Melland, 1985). On the background to the match-girls' strike, see William J. Fishman, *East End 1888*, Duckworth, 1988.

3. Sharon Zukin, *Loft Living; Culture and Capital in Urban Change* Radius, 1988. This British edition was published just in time for the reviews to catch the Bow Quarter publicist's eye.

4. *Evening Standard* 2 August, 1989.

5. Tom Nairn, 'Yuppies: The Fifty-first State', *New Statesman and Society*, 30 June 1989.

6. This account of Kentish Homes' working methods is drawn from Andrew Saint, 'The Hackney Classic', *Architects' Journal*, 18 May 1983.

7. The confusion of class war's politics was nowhere more evident than in their leafleting campaign against 'rich scum' in East London: one of the victims of this attempt at intimidation was Anita Dobson, the actress who played Angie Watts in *East-Enders*, and who had been enabled by recent success to buy an apparently very ordinary flat in the postal code of her own birth. See Julie Burchill's sneering riposte 'Going yup in the world', *New Society*, 12 June 1987.

8. David Hamilton Eddy, 'Castle Mythology in British Housing', *RIBA Journal*, December 1989, p. 28–33. The Cascades has also drawn some frankly mythical interpretations from professional critics. At the Chartered Society of Designers' Jubilee conference in Glasgow, 5–7 July 1990, Alice Rawsthorn, design correspondent of *The Financial Times*, showed a slide of The Cascades and described it as a refurbished council tower block. This suited her polemical purpose of setting up the building as a symbol of the yuppie invasion of Docklands, but it neglected the fact that The Cascades is actually an entirely new building, and, moreover, that there was no public housing on the site.

9. The description is quoted from Andrew Tyler. 'The New Kids on the Block', *Sunday Correspondent Magazine*, 5 August 1990.

10. Anton Ehrenzweig, *The Hidden Order of Art*, Paladin, 1970, pp. 175 & 186–7.

11. *East London Advertiser*, 5 May, 1989.

12. Hannen Swaffe, 'Way Down East on Sea', *Daily Herald*, 16 June 1936.

13. Quoted in 'East London's Lido', *Sunlight*, Autumn 1936.
14. George Lansbury, *My England*, Selwyn & Blount, n.d., p. 229
15. *Ibid.*, p. 231.
16. See Raymond Postgate, *The Life of George Lansbury*, Longman, 1951, p. 249. As Edgar Lansbury writes of the middle-class protesters at Regents Park 'Their children and nurses had had that part of London to themselves ever since those spacious terraces had been built, in fact the park itself was an amenity which they had taken into account when leasing their houses and flats. Was it fair then that "paddly pools", running tracks, swings, see-saws, and other contraptions should be provided free of charge so that ragamuffins from the slums of Camden Town and St Pancras might share the spaciousness, the cleanliness and the fresh air of the west side of the park?' (*George Lansbury, My Father*, Sampson Low, Marston & Co., 1934, p. 63).
17. The LCC programme, embodied in a General Powers Bill prepared for Parliament, was reported in the *Manchester Guardian*, 5 May 1935.

Chapter 16

1. Donald Trump with Tony Schwartz, *Trump: the Art of the Deal*, New York: Random House, 1987.
2. Bob Fitch included Trump on his roster of 'real estate beach-boys' who 'ride the waves of the business cycle until the inevitable wipeout sends them sprawling'. See his 'The Next New York', *The Village Voice*, 17 November 1987.
3. Thomas J. Peters and Robert H. Waterman, *In Search of Excellence; lessons from America's best-run companies*, Harper & Row, 1982.
4. William H. Whyte, *The Organization Man*, Simon & Schuster, 1956.
5. Tom Peters and Nancy Austin, *A Passion for Excellence; the leadership difference*, Collins, 1985.
6. Tom Peters, *Thriving on Chaos; Handbook for a Management Revolution*, A. Knopf, 1987.
7. Charles Garfield, *Peak Performers; the new heroes in business*, Hutchinson, 1986.
8. Victor Kiam, *Going For It!; how to succeed as an entrepreneur*, Collins, 1986.
9. Warren Avis, *Take a Chance to be First: the secrets of entrepreneurial success*, Macmillan, 1986.
10. *Hackney Gazette*, 28 December, 1990.
11. Reported in *Hackney Gazette*, 7 December, 1990.
12. Letter to *Hackney Gazette*, 28 December, 1990.
13. Martin Wiener, *English Culture and the Decline of the Industrial Spirit 1850–1980*, Cambridge University Press, 1981.

14. Raymond Williams, 'Crawling from the wreckage', *Times Higher Education Supplement*, 5 June 1987, p.13.

15. See *'Excellence' and Local Government*, a report from the Local Government Training Board, January 1985. By the time this report appeared, the Audit Commission had already drawn on *In Search of Excellence* in their annual Yellow Book of guidance on local authority management arrangements, *Arrangements for Securing Economy, Efficiency and Effectiveness*.

16. See also *Good Management in local government; successful practice and action*, a booklet published by the Local Government Training Board in collaboration with the Audit Commission and the Institute for Local Government Studies, 1985.

17. Paul Hoggett, 'Waste Disposal; making Municipal Socialism Work', *New Socialist*, March 1987, pp. 30–35.

18. John Stewart, *The New Management of Local Government*, Allen & Unwin, 1986.

19. *Ibid.*, p. 55.

20. *Hackney Gazette*, 30 November, 1990.

21. This passage is quoted from John McInally & David Summersgill's 'Hackney Report' which is among papers written by London Business School students after a visit to the London Borough of Hackney in March 1988.

22. Paul Hoggett, 'Waste disposal', *op. cit.*

23. Jerry White is the author of *Rothschild Buildings* (Routledge, 1980) and *The Worst Street in North London; Campbell Bunk, Islington, between the wars* (Routledge, 1986).

Chapter 17

1. Hugh Pearman and Richard Ellis, 'Charles in secret tours of inner cities', *Sunday Times*, 6 December 1987. See also A. Holden, *Charles*, Fontana, 1989.

2. See Louise Goodison, 'The Home Front', *The Architects' Journal*, August 1990. Also Martin Spring, 'Pillars of society', *Building*, 15 June 1990.

3. Margaret Coles, 'Looking after local needs', *The Daily Telegraph*, 30 November 1988.

4. *Hackney Gazette*, 8 June 1990.

5. *The Guardian*, 8 June 1988. For Pawley on 'units', see his discussion with Jules Lubbock in *Marxism Today*, March 1988.

6. Martin Pawley, 'Prince and country', *The Guardian*, 31 October 1988.

7. Martin Pawley's speech was reproduced under the title of 'What Martin Pawley really said', in *Building Design*, 10 November, 1989.

8. Maxwell Hutchinson, *The Prince of Wales: Right or Wrong?*, Faber & Faber, 1989.

9.   Prince Charles described his interest in ancient barns at a conference organised by the Historic Farm Buildings Group on 29 November, 1990. See John Young, 'Prince says destruction of barns is a disgrace', *The Times*, 30 November 1990.

10. See, for example, Zygmunt Bauman, *Memories of Class; the pre-history and after-life of class*, Routledge, 1982.

11. See, for example, Deyan Sudjic, 'A prince for the past', *The Times*, 31 October 1988.

12. It should be acknowledged that Charles is the first Prince of Wales to have scooped a book from a radical press. The story of Liverpool's Weller Street Housing Co-op was on the brink of publication with Comedia when Charles decided to contribute a Foreword and it was quickly shifted to the more respectable house of Faber. I know about this because I was the editor of Comedia's short lived 'Organisations and Democracy' series in which it was due to appear. For the final version see Alan McDonald with the Weller Streets Housing Co-operative, *The Weller Way: the story of the Weller Streets Housing Co-operative*, Faber & Faber, 1986.

13. The main sources from which Prince Charles is quoted are as follows: Speech at a Royal Gala Evening to Celebrate the 150th anniversary of the Royal Institute of British Architects at Hampton Court on 30 May 1984; Speech given at the Corporation of London Planning and Communication Committee's Annual Dinner at The Mansion House, 1 December 1987; Interview with Brian Redhead on Radio 4's *Today* programme, 4 December 1987; Speech given in Tower Hamlets, East London, 1 July, 1987. Charles's polemical television programme on British architecture was called *A Vision of Britain*, produced by Christopher Martin and first broadcast on BBC1's *Omnibus* programme, 28 October 1988.

14. For these and other examples of van der Post's theory of alienation see Laurens van der Post, *A Walk with a White Bushman; Laurens van der Post in conversation with Jean Marc Pottiez*, Chatto & Windus, 1986.

15. See Charles Jencks, *The Prince and the Architects*, Academy Editions, 1988.

16. Anthony Holden, *Charles*, Weidenfeld and Nicolson, 1988, p. 240.

17. John Betjeman, *Vintage London*, William Collins, 1942, p. 3.

18. John Betjeman, 'Meditation on a Constable Picture, *A Nip in the Air*, John Murray, 1974.

19. Jules Lubbock, 'Distant Prospects', *New Statesman*, 23 October 1987. Unfortunately, Lubbock's enthusiasm for Coin Street, is not justified by the buildings that went up on the site. Indeed, for all its 'community' involvement, the development only shows the folly of suburbanising a central site. Lubbock certainly

moved on fast: as Director of the Prince of Wales School of Civil Architecture he is no longer arguing that 'Dr. Watkin and Herr Krier can never purge classical architecture of the stain placed on it by Hitler' (see 'Distant prospects', *New Statesman*, 23 October 1987).

20. Gavin Stamp, 'A Monument to the Dead', *Spectator*, 12 May, 1984.

21. Colin Amery & Dan Cruickshank, *The Rape of Britain*, Elek, 1975, p. 10.

22. Leon Krier, 'An Architecture of Desire' in Krier (editor), *Albert Speer: Architecture 1932–42*, Archives d'Architecture Moderne, 1985.

23. Elizabeth Grice and Hugh Pearman, 'Charles' kitchen cabinet', *The Sunday Times*, 6 December 1987.

24. See Jules Lubbock, 'The Politics of the portico', *New Statesman*, May 1987.

25. See Mary-Lou Jennings, *Humphrey Jennings Film-maker/Painter/Poet*, BFI, 1982, p. 25.

26. Ritchie Calder, *Start Planning Britain Now; a Policy for Reconstruction*, Kegan Paul, 1941, pp. 7–9.

27. See W. H. Beveridge, *The Pillars of Security, and other war-time essays and addresses*, George Allen & Unwin, 1943.

28. See R. M. Titmuss, Problems of Social Policy, London: HMSO 1950, pp. 507–514.

29. A. R. Powys, 'Tradition and Modernity' in *From the Ground Up*, Dent & Sons, 1937, pp. 43–4.

30. Martin Pawley makes dismissive sneers about 'heritage nonsense' in *The Guardian*, 8 June 1988. Also throughout his *Theory and Design in the Second Machine Age*, Blackwells, 1990. In this typically overstated book, Pawley declares the modern city to be 'a war zone' between information technology and 'the accumulated infrastructure of centuries'. He then concludes that 'the most radical thing that any of us can do is to do nothing, to wait while the instantaneous forces of the Second Machine Age work out how to construct a future upon the relics of the past . . .'. It would be hard to imagine a more craven abdication of responsibility than that.

31. As the young classical revivalist Janusz Maciag puts it 'Only in the classical orders is there to be found the architectural expression which mediates and simultaneously encompasses the fallen materiality of man and the glory of Heaven'. Quoted in Alan Powers, *Real Architecture; an exhibition of Classical Buildings by the New Generation of Architects*, op. cit., p. 53.

32. Leon Krier, 'The Idea of Reconstruction', in Demetri Porphyrios (editor), *Leon Krier; Houses, Palaces, Cities*, Architectural Design, 1984, p. 38.

33. See the writings and drawings collected in *Leon Krier; Houses, Palaces, Cities*.

34. David Watkin's influential assault on Nikolaus Pevsner appeared in his *Morality and Architecture*, University of Chicago Press, 1977. Watkin is here quoted from his review of J. Mordaunt Crook, *The Dilemma of Style: Architectural Ideas from the Picturesque to the Post-Modern*, in *Landscape*, February 1988, pp. 87–9. Clive Aslet's hagiographical study of Terry was published as *Quinlan Terry; the Revival of Architecture* (Viking, 1986).

35. During the course of this speech, Charles quoted from an open letter to Ceausescu which had said, 'By striking at the peasant house, by replacing it with a pokey flat in a tower block, you strike not only at the soul of the people but also at the patrimony which belongs to all mankind'. He then concluded, with what we can now see as a certain historical irony, by remarking 'Clearly what they need in Romania is a Civic Trust!'. See *The Times*, 28 April, 1989.

36. Leon Krier, 'Architectura patriae', in Demetri Porphyrios (ed), *Leon Krier: Houses, Palaces, Cities, op. cit.*, 1984, p. 102.

37. Lord Hinchinbrooke's speech on the European contamination of British political culture is quoted from the *Liverpool Daily Post*, 11 January 1961. His fear of the moral consequences of progressive taxation which forces people to use 'savings or inherited capital or income without any thought of future generations' was expressed repeatedly in speeches given in the late Forties and early Fifties throughout South Dorset, where Hinchinbrooke was MP.

38. See Revd. D. Pateman's article 'Good old Charles', in St Mark, with St. Bartholomew, Dalston Church Journal, Christmas 1988.

39. *The Architects' Journal*, 21 June 1989.

40. Demetri Porphyrios, 'Cities of Stone' in *Leon Krier; Houses, Palaces, Cities*, p. 17.

41. Leon Krier, 'The City within the City', *Ibid.*, p. 70.

42. Nicholas Taylor, *The Village in the City*, Temple Smith, 1973.

43. Krier, *Houses, Palaces, Cities*, p. 20.

44. Quoted from Arendt's *The Human Condition* in Krier, p. 57.

45. *Ibid.*, p. 7.

46. 'Rethink for the Prince's village', *Building Design*, 4 August, 1989.

47. Krier, p. 39.

48. Quoted in Louise Goodison, 'The Home Front, *The Architects' Journal*, 8 August, 1990.

Acknowledgements

I owe special thanks to Douglas Oliver who, besides lending me his car, has also provided me with the title of this book and an unexpected line running back to Lord Beveridge; to Iain Sinclair with whom I have shared a succession of East London locations over the last few years, and who has contributed a number of choice items to my growing bibliography of Dalston Lane; and to Sharon Zukin, who has watched the arrival of the English country house in New York, and kept me supplied with clippings from *The New York Times*. My editor, Neil Belton, has made helpful suggestions throughout.

Others who have contributed more general evidence, dropped hints, opened doors or tried to find me more gainful employment elsewhere include Eve Hostettler, Reece Auguiste, Vron Ware, Martin Goodrich, Christopher Frayling, Lisa Tickner, Gayne Wells of Mapledene, Ian and Emma Beck, Angus Calder, Stephen Bann, Jerry White, Jean Field, Neal Ascherson, David Mellor, Barry Barker, Julia Unwin, Ken Worpole, Stuart Weir, Patrick Hammill of the Hackney Society, Mike Petty, David Morley and Tim Putnam. Julian Henriques directed my BBC2 documentary on Sutton House in 1988, while Jamie Muir of 'The Late Show' has accompanied me on more recent televisual excursions into the territory of this book, contributing a number of mid-century references which I have been quick to take up.

Some passages of this book, or earlier investigations of some of its themes, have appeared previously in *Modern Painters, The London Review of Books, Freibeuter, The Listener, New Society, New Statesman and Society, The Guardian* and *The Independent on Sunday*. I am also grateful to the archivists and librarians of Hackney, Tower Hamlets and British Telecom, and to the Nuffield Foundation which provided me with an award from its Small Grants Scheme, thus enabling me to look further behind the immediate surface of things than would otherwise have been possible.

My principal debt is to the people who appear in this book. They have given most generously of their time and views, as have my family, lumbered, once again, with a muttering maniac upstairs.

PATRICK WRIGHT
London
February 1991

Index

Goodrich, Martin, 18
Gordon, E.O., 163
Gray, Mike, 46–7, 48
Greater London Council (formerly
  London County Council), 11, 16,
  17, 20, 30, 70, 78, 81, 105, 162, 165,
  168, 174, 199–20
Greenwood, Ernie, 85
Greenwood, Royston, 221
Gregory, Tony, 150
Guedes, Pedro, 168, 175
Guevara, Che, 21

Hackney Co-operative Developments,
  16
Hackney Gazette, 12, 47, 69, 73, 77,
  122, 163, 218
Hackney Irish Association, 36
Hackney Society, 83, 85, 87, 91
Hackney, Rod, 234
Hare, David, 19
Harrap, Julian, 87, 88, 114, 115
Harrison, Paul, 7, 24, 69–70
Haseler, Stephen, 92
Haskell, Francis, 66–7
Hatton, Derek, 41
Hawksmoor, Nicholas, 162, 163, 164
Heaven, Brynley, 95–6
Heller, Joseph, 214
Henderson, David, 78
High flat subsidy, 79
Himmelfarb, Gertrude, 110
Hinchinbrooke, Lord, *see* Montague,
  Victor
History Workshop, 146, 149, 169, 226
Hofstettler, Eve, 169
Hoggart, Richard, 90
Hoskins, Bob, 207
Huggins, Christine, 88–9
Hunt Thompson Associates, 232,
  252, 254, 256
Hurd, Douglas, 16
Hutchinson, Maxwell, 236, 247, 262

Industrial Society, The, 26
Innes, Jocasta, 106
Island History Trust, 169, 172

Jackson, Glenda, 198
Jackson-Stops, Gervase, 64, 66
Jefferies, Richard, 41
Jefferson, Sir George, 129, 130, 135
Jenkins, Simon, 137
Jenkins, Clive, 47

Jenkins, Jennifer, 114
Jennings, Humphrey, 244
Jones, Barbara, 13, 58, 167
Jones, Inigo, 58
Jones, John Harvey, 219
Jones, Peter, 195
Jordan, R. Furneaux, 81, 93
Joseph, Lord Keith, 4–9, 25, 80, 92

Kennet, Lord, 93
Kent, William, 56
Kerridge, Roy, 19
Kinnock, Neil, 22, 187
Kipling, Rudyard, 22
Klein, Calvin, 210
Korda, Alexander, 76
Kozlowski, George, 182, 186, 190,
  196–8
Krier, Rob, 252
Krier, Leon, 234, 235, 243, 248,
  250–62
Krier, Wilhelm, 166
Kuhn, Thomas, 215

Laing, R.D., 29
Lambton, Lady Lucinda, 234
Langton, Andrew, 185–6, 201
Lansbury Estate, 76
Lansbury, George, 48–9, 53, 67, 76,
  87, 112, 114, 119, 170, 172, 178,
  181, 190, 198, 200, 227, 242, 249
Larkin, Philip, 28
Laura Ashley (fashion retailers), 63,
  65, 184
Lauren, Ralph, 65
Lawrence, Gordon, 116
Lees-Milne, Alvilde, 64
Lees-Milne, James, 54–60, 62–3, 64,
  82, 93–4, 101, 115, 116, 118–9, 244,
  254
Legg, Rodney, 115–6, 117
Leigh, Edward, 37
Leigh, Mike, 7
Lenin, V.I., 225, 228
Levin, Bernard, 135
Liberace, 210
Liberty (department store), 64–5
Lipton, Stuart, 242
Lobenstein, Cllr Joe, 77
Local Government Training Board,
  221
Lodge, David, 156
Lodwick, John, 33, 51–2
London Docklands Development
  Corporation, 168–9

Waugh, Evelyn, 50, 51, 55, 60, 61,
  63, 76
Weir, Stuart, 84
Westminster, Duke of, 20
Wheeler, Sir Mortimer, 255
White, Jerry, 226–7
Whyte, William, 214
Wiener, Martin, 219
Willard, Revd John, 158
Williams, Kit, 139
Williams, Raymond, 94, 219, 220,
  259, 261
Williams, Shirley, 243
Williams-Ellis, Sir Clough, 81–2
Wilson, Colin St John, 234, 236, 258

Wilson, Elizabeth, 35
Wilson, Des, 135
Wolfe, Tom, 24–5, 65–6, 155
Women's Design Service, 17
Wood, Kenneth, 80
Woodard, Daisy & Dave, 169–75
Worsthome, Sir Peregrine, 116, 186

Yates, Dornford, 52, 61
York, Peter, 187
Young, Lord, 127, 128
Yuppies, 24, 118, 122, 171, 182, 186,
  189, 190–4, 202

Zenith Productions, 20
Zukin, Sharon, 184, 185